American Naval Bibliography Series

by MYRON J. SMITH, JR.

THE AMERICAN NAVY, 1918-1941:

A Bibliography

by

Myron J. Smith, Jr.

American Naval Bibliography, Vol. V

The Scarecrow Press, Inc.
Metuchen, N. J.   1974

Library of Congress Cataloging in Publication Data

Smith, Myron J
   The American Navy, 1918-1941: a bibliography.

   (American naval bibliography, v. 5)
   1. United States. Navy--Bibliography. 2. United
States--History, Naval--Bibliography. I. Title.
II. Series.
Z6835.U5S63   016.3593'0973   74-11077
ISBN 0-8108-0756-4

for

JAY

that he may never know war

FOREWORD

The sea has always played a crucial role in civilization and more often than not, great fleets seemed to be involved in the momentous crises of world history. The same
has held true for the United States from the dark days of
the Revolution to the yet unresolved Middle East crisis of
1973. Our nation has always needed strength afloat in order
to enjoy the broad benefits of seapower. The demonstration
of this need and its application thus makes this series of
bibliographies on the American Navy of special value.

The thousands of titles in this massive five-volume
project by Myron J. Smith, Jr. demonstrate the far-reach-
ing influence of the sea in American history. It is un-
fortunate that this work was not available to those creating
naval policy during this 1918-1941 period. With the object
lessons of sea power clarified by World War I, one might
have expected that American leaders, many of whom made or
remembered that success, would have spared no efforts in
maintaining sea forces commensurate with the nation's newly
won place of world importance. Yet Washington followed instead the idealistic chimera of disarmament agreements and
seemed to put its head in the sand during the rapidly mount-
ing world peril of the 1930's.

We see from the citations in this volume the dis-
astrous story of naval disarmament in which the United
States failed even to build up to agreed strength. In the
1930's, the American government spent the smallest share
of its budget on its sea forces since the doldrums after the
Civil War. It failed to build the sea power required when
depression cut down the Royal Navy's domination of the
oceans. As ambitious rulers expanded conquests on three
continents, America failed--even though as the richest and
strongest nation the responsibility for freedom's preserva-
tion lay squarely upon her.

This volume ends as the bitter results of American

v

parsimony and lack of foresight collapse in disaster. Subsequent publications by Mr. Smith will undoubtedly cover the tragic payment demanded in blood and treasure for this massive mistake. Yet this payment can only be in part, for the costs still mount in a world shattered forever by the typhoon of World War II--a storm which might have been averted by sufficient United States power afloat. In the thirty years plus since the end of the period covered herein, have we learned our lesson? Will we avert the fatal mistake of weakening our fleet or shall we reap the whirlwind of our own destruction by failing to insure our way of life, dependent, as throughout our history, upon sea power.

Ernest M. Eller
Rear Admiral, U.S.N. (ret.)
Annapolis, Maryland
January 1974

CONTENTS

INTRODUCTION

When the Great War "over there" was decided in
1918, America turned her back on Europe, rejected the
Treaty of Versailles, with its accompanying League of Nations, and retreated to an idealistic isolationism. Although
keenly interested in world peace, witness her participation
in several naval limitation conferences, she rigidly held to
this position for most of the next two decades. In the process, U.S. sea services were trimmed to a point where
preparedness came doubly hard when an even larger conflict
erupted in 1939. All of this is not to say that American
naval progress was halted. It was, however, dangerously
slowed and in some cases, overly placid. Secure in the
"certain" knowledge that future wars would feature a deci-
sive Jutland-type fleet action, the proponents of the battleship reigned supreme. Training exercises were planned
around this assumption and strategic considerations--the
ORANGE plans--lent the idea the sanctity of 17th-18th
Century British "Fighting Instructions."

Although advances were nevertheless made in naval
education, naval aviation, and submarine and amphibious
warfare, to cite but a few, by the same token, lapses continued in mine and torpedo warfare as well as in logistical
planning for far-off operations. Aviation was probably the
most important and interesting naval development of the
1920's and 1930's, particularly if weighed in light of the
poundage of literature cited in this work. Various planes
and aerial techniques were tried out, many of which went
hand-in-hand with the new "airplane carriers." Despite
public enthusiasm for aviation, which defied the laws of
gravity and cost a good deal less than battleships, even
this advance met considerable opposition. Courageous
exponents such as "Buaer" Chiefs T.T. Craven and W.A.
Moffett had to do long theoretical and verbal battle with the
battleship admirals on the right and the Billy Mitchell air
enthusiasts on the left. At times the fight for an effective
and independent Naval Air Service appeared nearly to fail,

ix

but fortunately the battle was won.

       To many inside the service and out, naval aviation in
those years was as exciting as space flight is today. In
1919, the NC flying boats made history and headlines by
crossing the Atlantic. Employing aircraft, Admiral Richard
Byrd enjoyed almost a monopoly in the area of naval exploration. And no one who ever saw one in flight will for-
get the majestic beauty of the great rigid airships Shenandoah,
Akron, Macon, or Los Angeles. Meanwhile in other circles,
the Coast Guard and Marine Corps gained greater knowledge
and appreciation. The "Treasury's navy" continued its
active tradition of rescue work, expanded its participation
in such operations as the Bering Ice Patrol, and even took
time to engage the agents of organized crime in the "rum
wars" of the Prohibition era. The Marine Corps, fresh
from its experiments with aviation in the various banana
wars, also found its raison d'être. With the creation of
the Fleet Marine Force and the adoption of the Tentative
Manual for Landing Operations, it evolved from what historian Robert Sherrod called "a simple, rough-and-ready
gang" to a "specialized organization with a primary mission. "

       Regardless of these advances, the cost-consciousness
of the Great Depression, combined with the country's turn
to isolationism, held the American Navy in the inter-war
period to a shoestring operation. When the Axis nations
began their sword-rattling and aggressions in the middle-
to-late '30's, the rush for naval "preparedness" was con-
siderably less than that seen in the years preceding World
War I. Mr. Roosevelt's program for naval expansion was
gingerly advanced to the tune of great national debate. Even
when France fell in 1940, there was still much opposition
in America to building up a fleet which many felt would
only be used in an "aggressive" war--or to rescue the chest-
nuts of the United Kingdom. And then, Pearl Harbor.

About the Present Volume

       As the reader will quickly note, the amount of naval
topics available for study, new or even first interpretations,
based on these years 1918-1941 is numberless. For writing
ideas, one might consult this bibliography to learn what has
been published and then check Dean C. Allard and Betty
Bern, U.S. Naval History Sources in the Washington Area

and Suggested Research Topics (3rd ed., Washington: U.S.
Government Printing Office, 1970) to find what might be
worthy of further investigation. One should not overlook the
possibilities of interlibrary loan to obtain needed volumes,
consulting his local library to initiate the process.

While some of the more general attempts by others
to provide bibliographic coverage to the literature of the inter-
war period have been quite successful, most of these have
been of a very general nature. None are addressed solely to
material concerning U.S. sea services. The present work is
not offered strictly as an aid in correcting such deficiencies
in guides to printed sources, though as such it may serve,
but primarily as a non-subjective beacon of bibliographic control in the previously little charted waters of American naval
history, 1918-1941. In choosing references, the criteria employed in the four earlier volumes of the American Naval
Bibliography have been followed. Citations are again provided from books, scholarly papers, periodical or magazine
articles, important general works, and doctoral or masters'
theses. Due to the growth in accessibility of the great numbers of U.S. government documents, that section herein has
been largely reduced in volume from our earlier works where
the previous bibliographic control was slight. Annotations of
a non-critical nature are supplied wherever deemed needed
to clarify or amplify the contents of a work.

As the actual time period of the bibliography spans
little more than two decades--as opposed to eight in Volume
II--the over 4700 numbered entries are arranged in a single
alphabet by author or title, in the manner of Volumes I and
III. Joint-author, compiler, translator, and editor cross
references are provided within the body of the text, each
receiving an entry number. The abbreviations U.S.N.I.P.
(for United States Naval Institute Proceedings) and SciAmer
(for Scientific American) are employed throughout. Where
earlier editions have been reprinted, the symbol "Rpr." and
the year of the latest reissue follows the pagination data.
An index arranged by subject completes the book.

No tool of this nature, with its inevitable omissions,
can hope to include the efforts of writers who may have been
skipped or who might follow our 1973 cut-off date. To keep
abreast of the latest sea service research, a periodic
search of the newer issues and editions of the following is
recommended:

Air University Index to Military Periodicals. Maxwell Air
    Force Base, Ala.: Air University Library, 1949--.
    v. 1--.

Albion, Robert D. Naval and Maritime History: An Anno-
    tated Bibliography. 4th ed. Mystic, Conn.: Marine
    Historical Association, 1972. 370 p.

America: History and Life--A Guide to Periodical Litera-
    ture. Santa Barbara, Calif.: Clio Press, 1964--.
    v. 1--.
    Quarterly.

British Museum. Department of Printed Books. General
    Catalog of Printed Books: Additions. London: Clowes,
    1963--.
    A subject index is published every four years.

Dissertation Abstracts International. Ann Arbor, Mich:
    University Microfilms, 1969--.
    Begun over 30 years ago as Dissertation Abstracts.
    Refer to the "A" Schedule, "The Humanities and
    Social Sciences."

Historical Abstracts: A Quarterly, Covering the World's
    Periodical Literature, 1775-1945. Santa Barbara,
    Calif.: Clio Press, 1955--. v. 1--.
    Contains coverage of the United States to 1964 when
    America: History and Life was begun. Still useful
    for naval developments of the period in Europe.

"The Military Library." Military Affairs. Washington:
    American Military Institute, 1937--. v. 1--.
    Quarterly. Contains book reviews, periodical cita-
    tions, and now references to recent doctoral disser-
    tations on military history.

"Notable Naval Books of the Year." United States Naval
    Institute Proceedings. Annapolis: U.S. Naval Institute,
    1950--. v. 76--.
    Contained in the December issue of the USNIP.
    "The Professional Library" in each monthly issue
    contains brief reviews of significant new volumes.

Readers' Guide to Periodical Literature. New York: H.W.
    Wilson, 1916--.
    All the Wilson Indices include references from im-
    portant journals.

United States. Library of Congress. Library of Congress
  Catalog. Books: Subjects. A Cumulative List of
  Works Represented by Library of Congress Printed
  Cards. Washington: U.S. Government Printing Office,
  1950--.
    Quarterly with annual cumulation.

_____. _____. Science and Technology Division. Antarctic
  Bibliography. Washington: U.S. Government Printing
  Office, 1965--.

_____. Navy Department, Naval History Division. U.S.
  Naval History: A Bibliography. 6th ed. Washington:
  U.S. Government Printing Office, 1972.

Writings on American History: A Bibliography of Books
  and Articles on United States History Published During
  the Year--. Various publishers, 1902--.
    Not issued in 1904-1905, 1941-1947. The latest
  volume is for the year 1960.

For those interested in books which are to be published,
your attention is directed to: Forthcoming Books. New
York: R.R. Bowker, 1966--. v. 1--.

    With this volume, the American Naval Bibliography
comes to an end. As in 1941 the United States was drawn
into a war in which its Navy was involved with others'
navies, both ally and enemy, all over the globe, coverage
of those years could not be attempted as part of an "American" Naval Bibliography. The coverage herein is rather
complete for the road to Pearl Harbor; however, the events
of that infamous Sunday are not included. The bibliographic
decks are being cleared so that we may begin the compilation of a work which, for the first time, will provide comprehensive English language routing through the shoals of
World War II naval literature.

    For their aid and advice in the completion of this final
volume, the following persons and libraries are gratefully
acknowledged: Mr. Walter B. Greenwood, librarian, and
Mr. Fred Meigs, assistant librarian, Navy Department Library; Dr. Dean C. Allard, Head, Operational Archives,
U.S. Navy Department; Dr. Benjamin F. Cooling, Director
of Research, U.S. Army Military History Research

Collection; Miss Judy Greeson, librarian, Huntington College
Library; North Manchester (Ind.) College Library. Special
thanks are extended to the reference staff of the Indiana
State Library, and to Mr. Fred J. Reynolds, librarian,
Public Library of Fort Wayne and Allan County. For their
gracious help and understanding, the staff and board of the
Huntington Public Library deserves my deepest appreciation
and commendation. Lastly, Rear Admiral Ernest M. Eller,
U. S. N. (Ret.), a gallant young officer of our period who
came one day to command the Naval History Division, your
kindness in penning the Foreword, and your words of praise
and encouragement are very much appreciated.

                                          Myron J. Smith, Jr.
                                          Huntington, Indiana
                                          December 1973

We are the only nation in the world that waits till we get into a war before we start getting ready for it.

--Will Rogers
August 10, 1924

I. THE BIBLIOGRAPHY

1 Abbott, Patrick. Airship. New York: Scribners, 1973. 192p.
   As we shall see in later references, the Interwar Period was the heyday of the rigid airship in the U. S. Navy.

2 Abbott Hall, U. S. N. R.: The Record of the United States Naval Reserve Midshipmen's School, Abbott Hall, Northwestern University, September 1940- August 1945. Chicago: Abbott Hall Publications Committee, 166p.

3 Abend, Hallett. Japan Unmasked. London, 1941. 322p.
   The possibilities of a maritime war with the Japanese kept American naval planners on their toes during the Interwar Period. For that reason, many citations to Japanese activities are cited herein for the light they are able to show on the actualities and potentialities of a conflict which finally came.

4 "Aboard the Airship Los Angeles to Porto Rico and Back." Literary Digest, LXXXVI (July 4, 1925), 58-62.

5 "Activities of the Bureau of Engineering." Marine Engineering, XLII (February 1937), 97-98.

6 Acworth, Bernard. The Navies of Today and Tomorrow. London: Eyre & Spottiswoode, 1930. 277p.

7 _____. The Navy and the Next War. London, 1934. 305p.

8 Adams, Charles F. "Our Navy and Our Nation." USNIP, LVI (1930), 886-887.

9 Adams, Hancock. "Improving Uncle Sam's Navy."

National Republic, XVIII (November 1930), 5-7.

10   . "Uncle Sam's New Naval Plan." National
   Republic, XIX (March 1932), 5-7.

11   Adams, Henry H. Years of Deadly Peril: The Coming
   of the War, 1939-1941. New York: McKay, 1969.
   559p.

12   Adams, Robert B. "Typical Vessels and Boats of
   U. S. Coast Guard." USNIP, LV (1929), 401-
   405.

13   Adamson, Gordon. "Motor Torpedo Boats, a Technical
   Study." USNIP, LXVI (1940), 977-996.

14   Adamson, Hans C., jt. author. See Lockwood, Charles
   A., no. 2221.

15   "An Adequate Navy Now Being Built." Sphere, XXII
   (November 1938), 14-15.

16   "Admiral at the Front: [Thomas] Hart." Time,
   XXXVIII (November 24, 1941), 36-38.
   Commanding the U. S. fleet in Asia.

17   "[Admiral Byrd] Off for the Antarctic." Newsweek,
   XIV (November 27, 1939), 13.
   Richard Evelyn Byrd was born in Winchester,
   Va., October 25, 1888. A graduate of the Naval
   Academy, Class of 1912, he won promotion to the
   rank of Commander after his flight with Floyd Bennett
   over the North Pole in early 1926. With three com-
   panions, he flew the Atlantic the following year. His
   first expedition to the South Pole, over which he flew
   on November 29, 1929, lasted through 1928-1929.
   The second Byrd Expedition there occupied the years
   1933-1935, while the famous third adventure covered
   1939-1941. Important discoveries were recorded
   during each of these. During World War II, he
   served on the staffs of both Admirals King and Nimitz
   and in 1946 commanded yet another Antarctic expedition. Winner of many awards and author of numerous books and articles (those appropriate to this
   period being cited below), the admiral died at his
   Boston home on March 11, 1957.

18 "Admiral Byrd Receives New Honor from the Society."
    National Geographic, LVIII (August 1930), 228-238.

19 "Admiral Leahy Recommends Defense by Offense."
    Christian Century, LVI (August 16, 1939), 987-988.
    The admiral served as Chief of Naval Operations
    from 1937-1939 thereafter holding an important posi-
    tion in the deliberations of the President and others
    on national defense.

20 "Admiral Leahy Testifies." Christian Century, LV
    (February 16, 1938), 195.

21 "Admiral Stark Asks Bigger Navy in Case of Allied
    Defeat." Time, XXXV (January 22, 1940), 6.
    Harold R. Stark served as Chief of Naval Opera-
    tions from 1939-1942.

22 Admiral William S. Sims, U.S. Navy, 1858-1936.
    London, 1936. 20p.
    Reprinted from the December 1936 issue of the
    National Bulletin of the Military Order of the World
    War.

23 "Admiral [William V.] Pratt Retires as New Deal Policy
    Comes in." Newsweek, I (July 8, 1933), 8.
    The admiral served as Chief of Naval Operations
    from 1930 to 1933, thereafter becoming an important
    commentator on naval topics. Many of his writings
    are cited below.

24 "An Aerial Torpedo." SciAmer, CLV (July 1936), 32-
    33.

25 Agar, Augustus. Footprints in the Sea. London:
    Evans, 1959. 321p.

26 _____. Showing the Flag: The Role of the Royal
    Navy Between the World Wars. London: Evans,
    1962. 293p.
    With some comments on the U.S. Navy.

27 Agar, William. Food or Freedom: The Vital Blockade.
    America Faces the War Series, no. 7. New York:
    Oxford University Press, 1941. 32p.

28 Ageton, Arthur M. "Annapolis, Mother of Navy Men."

USNIP, LXI (1935), 1499-1514.

29   _____. "Healthy Minds in Healthy Bodies. " USNIP,
      LXI (1935), 1552-1554.

30   "Aircraft and the Hawaiian Maneuvers. " Aviation, XVIII
      (June 22, 1925), 690-691.

31   "Aircraft Carrier: Warships Like the Enterprise May be
      the Decisive Factor in Naval Combats. " Life, X
      (March 31, 1941), 58-60.

32   "Aircraft Carriers. " Engineer, CXLIV (July 1, 1927),
      6-8.

33   "Aircraft Carriers: British, French, and American View-
      points. " USNIP, LIV (1928), 706-710.

34   "Aircraft Carriers Give the American Navy a Long Arm."
      Popular Science, CXVIII (January 1931), 36-37.

35   "Aircraft Carriers in a Fleet Action. " USNIP, LII
      (1926), 2329-2335.

36   "Aircraft Carriers, 1908-1962. " In: U. S. Navy Depart-
      ment.   Naval History Division.   Dictionary of Ameri-
      can Naval Fighting Ships.   Washington: U. S. Govern-
      ment Printing Office, 1959--.   II 461-486.

37   "Aircraft Defense More Expensive than Battleships?"
      Aviation, XVIII (January 5, 1925), 19.
         An editorial.

38   "Aircraft Have Influenced Warships Design: Drawings. "
      SciAmer, CLVIII (March 1938), 158.

39   The Aircraft Yearbook.   New York: Aeronautical Cham-
      ber of Commerce of American, 1920--.

40   "Airplane Arresters and Catapults. " USNIP, LII (1926),
      1871-1879.

41   "The Airplane-Battleship Rumpus. " Literary Digest,
      LXXXIV (March 7, 1925), 8-9.

42   "Airplane-Carrier Langley. " SciAmer, CXXIX (July,
      1923), 42.

CV-1 was converted from the fleet collier Jupiter
and joined the fleet on March 20, 1922.

43   "Airplane Carrier Saratoga Launched at Camden. "
Marine Engineering, XXX (May 1925), 258-259.

44   "The Airplane Carrier Saratoga Prepared for Dock
Trials. " Marine Engineering, XXXI (October 1926),
611+.
CV-3 was built on the hull of an incomplete battle-
cruiser, retaining the heavy ship's original machinery.

45   "Airplane vs. Battleship. " Literary Digest, LXVIII
(February 19, 1921), 14-15.

46   _____. Review of Reviews, LXIV (October 1921),
429-430.

47   "The Airship Los Angeles Again Takes to the Air. "
Aviation, XX (April 26, 1926), 628.

48   Akers, George W.   "The Groundwork for Today's Naval
Reserve. " USNIP, LXV (1939), 494-500.

49   _____. "National Policies and Defense. " USNIP, LX
(1934), 897-902.

50   _____. "The Promotion of Goodwill for the Navy. "
USNIP, LX (1934), 1390-1392.

51   _____. "Tender Memories. " USNIP, LXIX (1943),
1567-1571.

52   "Akron: Court Finds McCord Erred. " Newsweek, I,
(May 27, 19, 1933), 28.

53   "The Akron Disaster. " SciAmer, CXLVIII (June 1933),
313.

54   "The Akron Flies with a Record Load in Test Flights. "
Airway Age, XIII (October 3, 1931), 291-292.

55   "The Akron, Greatest of Airships. " Electrical Journal,
XXIX (January 1932), 24.

56   "The Akron Horror. " Literary Digest, CXV (April 15,
1933), 3-4.

57 "Akron Inquiry Report Raps Shifting of Airship Officers."
    Newsweek, I (June 24, 1933), 27.

58 "The Akron Proves Her Mettle as a Storm-fighter. "
    Literary Digest, CXIII (May 28, 1932) 28-30.

59 "Akron, World's Greatest Airship. " Popular Science,
    CXVIII (May 1931), 52.

60 "Alaska Flights. " Newsweek, IV (July 21, 1934), 23.
    By American naval aviators.

61 Albion, Robert G. "The Administration of the Navy,
    1798-1945. " Public Administration Review, V (May-
    June 1945), 293-302.

62 _____. "Distant Stations. " USNIP, LXXX (1954),
    265-273.
    The dispersion of American squadrons to dis-
    tant seas.

63 _____. "Problems of Sea Power. " Princeton Univer-
    sity Faculty-Alumni Forum (June 14, 1935), 17-31.

64 _____ and Jennie B. Pope. Sea Lanes in Wartime:
    The American Experience, 1775-1945. 2nd ed. , enl.
    Hamden, Conn. : Archon Books, 1968. 396p.

65 Alden, Carroll S. "A Brief History of the Naval Trans-
    portation Service Since June 1937. " Unpublished
    Paper, Individual Personnel File, Operational
    Archives, U. S. Navy Department, Naval History Di-
    vision, 1943. 10p.

66 _____. "The Changing Naval Academy: A Retrospect
    of Twenty-five Years. " USNIP, LV (1929), 495-501.

67 _____. "Officers and Gentlemen in the Making. "
    USNIP, LXI (1935), 1494-1498.
    Life at the Naval Academy in the mid-30s.

68 _____ and Allan Westcott. The United States Navy:
    A History. Philadelphia: Lippincott, 1943. 452p.

69 _____., jt. author. See Stevens, William, O. , no.
    3790.

70 Alden, John D. "ARD-1, the Pioneer." USNIP, XCI
    (1965), 70-79.
    The first mobile floating drydock launched in 1935.

71 Alexander, J. T. "Trial Trip Data of the Saratoga."
    Marine Engineering, XXXIV (December 1929), 685.

72 Alexander, Jack. "Secretary [Frank] Knox, the Navy's
    New Boss." Life, X (March 10, 1941), 56-60.

73 _____. _____. Reader's Digest, XXXVIII (May
    1941), 121-124.

74 Alexander, Joseph E. "Introducing Mobile Artillery."
    Walla Walla, IX (October 24, 1936), 13-17, 19.
    As employed by the Marines.

75 Alexander, Robert J. "The Disarmament Policy of the
    United States, 1933-1934." Unpublished PhD Disser-
    tation, Georgetown University, 1953.

76 Alexander, W. A. Elementary Instruction in Square Knot-
    ting. Brooklyn, N. Y.: F. A. Toombs, 1920. 16p.

77 Allen, A. H. "Making Cylinder Barrels for Packard V-
    12 Torpedo Boat Engines." Steel, CVIII (January 20,
    1941), 74-76, 78, 80-81.

78 Allen, Archer M. R. "Standardizing Terms, Procedures,
    and Records in Navigation." USNIP, LIV (1928),
    562-568.

79 Allen, Ezra G. "Tactical Ramblings." USNIP, L (1924),
    389-399.

80 _____. "The Organization of the U. S. Fleet." USNIP,
    LVI (1930), 829-830.

81 Allen, Gardner W. "Naval Convoys." Massachusetts
    Historical Society Proceedings, LVII (1924), 392-414.

82 Allen, Gwenfread E. Hawaii's War Years, 1941-45.
    Honolulu: University of Hawaii Press, 1950. 418p.
    Rpr. 1971.
    Before and after Pearl Harbor Sunday.

83 Allen, Harry C. Great Britain and the United States: A

History of Anglo-American Relations. New York: St.
Martin's, 1955. 1024p. Rpr. 1969.

84 Allen, Hugh. The Story of the Airship. Akron, O.:
Goodyear, 1932. 96p.

85 Allen, Jerome L. "Leaves from a Greenland Diary."
USNIP, LXVIII (1942), 201-208.
By a Navy commander stationed there at the start
of U. S. World War II participation.

86 Allen, R. G. D. "Mutual Aid Between the U. S. and the
British Empire, 1941-1945." Royal Statistical So-
ciety Journal, CIX (1946), 243-277.
Lend-Lease, etc.

87 Allen, Walter H. "The Twelfth Regiment (Public Works)
at Great Lakes." USNIP, XLVII (1921), 367-376.

88 "Alone: Excerpts from Admiral Byrd's Diary with Commentary by C. J. V. Murphy." American Magazine,
CXX (September 1935), 16-17+.

89 "Alphabet-Number Soup for Army and Navy Planes."
Science News Letter, XXXV (June 3, 1939), 342.

90 Altham, Edward. "The Next Naval Conference."
Quarterly Review, CCXLV (July 1925), 41-51.
That to be held in Geneva in 1927.

91 "Aluminum Destroyers." Time, XXXVIII (December 8,
1941), 72.

92 "Always Ready: Coast Guard Planes Warn Shipping to
Safety." Literary Digest, CXXII (September 26,
1936), 9-10.

93 "America and Japan Engage in Naval Race as Disarmament Preliminary." China Weekly Review, LXVI
(September 16, 1933), 94-95.

94 "America and the National Defense Problem." Congressional Digest, XIII (April 1934), 97-122.

95 "America Asks the World to End the Submarine." Literary Digest, XCVI (February 18, 1928), 5-7.

96 "America Bares Its Weapons of Attack as the Time for Action Draws Nearer." Life, XI (August 4, 1941), 11-15.

97 "American and Japanese Naval Building." Christian Century, LI (February 7, 1934), 173.

98 "American, British, and Japanese Naval Strength Under the Washington and London Treaties." Congressional Digest, XIII (April 1934), 122. A tabulation.

99 "American, British, and Japanese Proposals at the Geneva Conference and Their Bearing on Competitive Navy Building." Iron Age, CXX (September 15, 1927), 691-692.

100 No Entry

101 "The American Expeditionary Force: The Military and Naval Mission to London." New Republic, CIII (August 26, 1940), 275.

102 "American Foreign Policy and the Big Navy Question." Food for Forums, (May 1938), 1-36. A publication of the New York State Department of Education.

103 American Heritage, Editors of. The American Heritage History of Flight. New York: American Heritage, 1962. 155p.

104 _____. Naval Battles and Heroes. Junior Library. New York: American Heritage 1960. 153p. Useful for adults seeking a quick survey.

105 "The American High Speed Cruiser and Its Prototype." Engineer, CXXIV (July 21, 1922), 55-57, 66.

106 "American Marines in Haiti Exonerated." Current History, XVI (August 1922), 836-841.

107 "American Naval Airships." USNIP, LXXXII (1956), 452-455. Reprinted from the January 6, 1956 issue of Engineering. In general throughout this compilation, the word "airship" refers to lighter-than-air craft.

108   "American Naval Policy. " Engineering, CXXIII (January
      14, 1927), 33-35.

109   "The American Naval Programme. " Edinburgh Review,
      CCXLVII (April 1928), 209-227.
      A British view.

110   "The American Navy. " Saturday Evening Post, CCVII
      (October 20, 1934), 22.

111   "American Navy Building Program Lags. " SciAmer,
      CXLV (November 1931), 333.

112   "The American Occupation of Iceland. " American-
      Scandinavian Review, XXIX (September 1941), 255-
      259.

113   "The American Paper Fleet Becomes a Reality by Con-
      struction Plans. " Trans-Pacific, XXIV (June 13,
      1940), 4-5.

114   "American Shipyards Meet the Axis Challenge. "
      Machinery, XLVIII (November 1941), 125-173, 180-
      188.

115   Americana Annual.   New York: Americana Division,
      Grolier Corp.   1923-1942.

116   "America's Naval Temptation. " Literary Digest, XCVII
      (April 7, 1928), 18-19.

117   "America's Navy and Japan's. " Living Age, CCXLIII
      (October 1932), 185-186.

118   "America's New Crescent of Defense: Map and Photo-
      graphs. " National Geographic, LXXVIII (November
      1940), 621-628.

119   "America's Strategic Position in the Pacific: U. S. A.
      Air and Naval Bases in Relation to Japan and Singa-
      pore. " Illustrated London News, CXCIX (July 26,
      1941), 118-119.

120   "The Americas United: The success of Secretary [Cor-
      dell] Hull's Mission at the Havana Conference. "
      New Republic, CIII (August 5, 1940), 175-176.

121 Ammon, William B. "Fijian Adventure. " USNIP,
     LXIII (1937), 224-230.

122 _____. "Radio in Naval Tactics. " SciAmer, CLIII
     (November 1935), 245.

123 _____. " 'The Way of You American Navy Officers.' "
     USNIP, LXI (1935), 1800-1803.

124 Anderson, George E. "Ambassador Dawes and the
     Possibility of Settlement of the Naval Armaments
     Controversy. " Commonweal, X (May 8, 1929), 8-10.

125 Anderson, James B. "Sailing the Uncharted Seas of the
     Sky in the Shendandoah. " American Magazine, CII
     (September 1926), 64-65.

126 Anderson, Joseph B. "The Rigid Airship and the
     Weather. " USNIP, L (1924), 1629-1645

127 Anderson, R. Wayne. "U. S. S. Kearsarge--Fifty-Six
     Years and Three Careers. " USNIP, LXXXVI (1960),
     102+.
          BB-5, the only U. S. battlewagon not named for a
     state, was commissioned in 1900. After World War
     I, she was converted to a floating crane and served
     in that capacity until sold out in August 1955.

128 Anderson, Walter S. "Guns Allowed Aircraft Carriers
     --A Paradox. " USNIP, LIII (1927), 539-543.
          As a result of the Washington Treaty.

129 _____. "Limitation of Naval Armament. " USNIP,
     LII (1926), 427-443.

130 _____. "Submarines and the Disarmament Confer-
     ence." USNIP, LIII (1927), 50-69.

131 Anderson, William H. Philippine Problem: Our Prob-
     lem for Forty Years. New York: G. P. Putnam's,
     1939. 338p.

132 Andrade, Ernest, Jr. "Submarine Policy in the United
     States Navy, 1919-1941. " Military Affairs, XXXV
     (April 1971), 50-56.

133 _____. "United States Naval Power in the Disarma-

ment Era, 1921-1937. " Unpublished PhD Dissertation, Michigan State University, 1966.

134 _____ . "The U. S. Navy and the Washington Conference. " Historian, XXXI (1969), 345-363.

135 Andrews, Adolphus J. "Admiral with Wings: The
Career of Joseph Mason Reeves. " Unpublished B. A.
Senior Paper, Princeton University, 1943.

136 _____ . "Naval Personnel of Today. " USNIP, LXII
(1936), 1402-1407.

137 _____ . "Our New Navy. " Vital Speeches, VII
(August 1, 1941), 618-620.

138 Andrews, Hal. "Fifty Years of Naval Aircraft. "
11 parts. Naval Aviation News, (February-Decem-
ber 1961).

139 Andrews, Lewis M. , Jr. "On Watch, 2 a. m. " New
York Times Magazine, (November 16, 1941), 3.

140 Andrews, Philip. "Battleships Are Vital to the Command of the Seas. " Current History, XXIII (December 1925), 394-396.

141 Andrews, R. B. "Aboard a Super-Electric Dreadnought."
Popular Mechanics, LV (May 1931), 786-789.

142 Angell, Norman. "Parity or Reduction. " Nation,
CXXX (March 5, 1930), 266-268.

143 "Anglo-American Cooperation and Demands That Japan
Reveal Naval Plans. " Literary Digest, CXXV (February 19, 1938), 2.

144 "The Anglo-American Naval Problem. " New Republic,
LIV (April 4, 1928), 204-206.

145 Annual Register: World Events. London and New York,
1919-1941.

146 Annunzio, Gabriele d'. International Naval Disarmament Conferences at Washington and Genoa, November 1921-April 1922. New York: Vanni, 1950. 107p.

A series of articles which appeared in the Gazetta del Popolo (Turin) Nov. 24, 1921-Apr. 26, 1922 and, translated in the New York American, Nov. 28, 1921-Apr. 30, 1922.

147 "Another Eagle's Nest to Confute the Navy's Critics." Literary Digest, LXXXVII (October 17, 1925), 17. The carrier Lexington, CV-2, also converted like the Saratoga, from an unfinished battle-cruiser.

148 Ansel, Walter C. "The Arrangement of Main and Secondary Batteries in Capital Ships." USNIP, LXIII (1937), 749-753.

149 _____. "Naval Gunfire in Support of a Landing." Marine Corps Gazette, XVII (May 1932), 23-26.

150 "Antarctica Prize: Byrd's Report Stresses the Value of Palmerland as a Naval Base." Newsweek, XVII (May 19, 1941), 21.

150a Appler, William. "History of the Navy Supply Corps." The Review [Defense Supply Administration] XLVII (May-June 1968), 46-48, 123, 125, 127, 129-130.

151 "ARD-3, Floating Drydock." Time, XXVIII (November 30, 1936), 15.

152 Ardman, Harvey. "U S. Code-Breakers vs. Japanese Code-Breakers in World War II." American Legion Magazine, XCIV (May 1972), 18-23, 38-42. Beginning before Pearl Harbor.

153 Arima, Seiho. "The Anglo-American Naval Programme." Contemporary Japan, VII (1938), 58-67. An English language article written from the Japanese viewpoint.

154 Armagnac, Alden P. "America Starts Work on the World's Biggest Navy." Popular Science, CXXXVIII (January 1941), 122-125.

155 _____. "Bombers or Battleships?" Popular Science, CXXXVII (October 1940), 52-56.

156 _____. "Can Mines Conquer Sea Power?" Popular Science, CXXXVI (March 1940), 78-83.

157 _____. "The Navy's Triple Threat: Fire Power,
     Speed, and Armor." Popular Science, CXXXIX
     (August 1941), 86-91.

158 _____. "New Fighting Ships Change Naval Warfare."
     Popular Science, CXXX (January 1937), 11-13+.

159 _____. "Planting the Stars and Stripes in the Ant-
     arctic." Popular Science, CXXXV (November 1939),
     63-66.
     By the Byrd explorers.

160 _____. "Uncle Sam's New Ocean Empire." Popular
     Science, CXXXII (June 1938), 22-25.

161 "Armaments: Should the United States Spend $800,000,000
     to Build a Navy Second to None?" Literary Digest,
     CXXV (February 12, 1938), 4.

162 Armes, Edward. "Amateur Dramatics in the United
     States Navy." Playground, XVI (April 1922), 28-29.

163 Armitage, Merle. The United States Navy. New York:
     Longmans, Green, 1940. 282p.

164 "Armor Versus Budgets, Limitations on Docking Facil-
     ities Affect Greater-Tonnage Drives." Literary
     Digest, CXXI (February 22, 1936), 9.

165 "Army and Navy Nurse Corps Insignia." American
     Journal of Nursing, XLI (April 1941), 440.

166 "Army, Navy, and the Airplane." Literary Digest,
     LXXIV (March 14, 1925), 71-72.

167 Arnheiter, Marcus A. "The Navy in San Francisco
     Bay: A Current History of Yerba Buena and Trea-
     sure Islands." Unpublished Paper, Individual Per-
     sonnel File, Operational Archives, U.S. Navy De-
     partment, Naval History Division, 1968. 169p.
     Contains some historical data relative to our
     period.

168 Arnold, Joseph C. "An Elementary Description of the
     'Water Recovery' Method of Obtaining Ballast for an
     Airship." USNIP, LVI (1930), 731-733.

169 Arnold, Thurman. Defense Inventory. Round Table
     Pamphlets, no. 191. Chicago: University of Chicago
     Press, 1941. 29p.

170 Arnstein, Karl. "Developments in Lighter-than-Air
     Craft. " Society of Automotive Engineers Journal,
     XXIV (May 1929), 465-473.

171 _____. "Some Design Aspects of the Rigid Airship."
     American Society of Mechanical Engineers Trans-
     actions. LVI (1934), 385-392.

172 _____. "Why Airships?" U. S. Air Services, XVII
     (December 1932), 25-31.

173 Arpee, Edward. From Frigates to Flat-Tops: The
     Story of the Life and Achievements of Rear Admiral
     William Adger Moffett, U. S. N. Lake Forest, Ill.,
     1953. 276p.
         After a distinguished earlier career, the admiral
     became Chief of the Bureau of Aeronautics ("Buaer")
     in September 1921. He served as a technical ad-
     visor at the Washington Conference and as an out-
     standing spokesman for naval aviation. A firm be-
     liever in the value of rigid airships, he was killed
     on April 4, 1933 in the Akron disaster.

174 Arroyo, Edward B. "Naval Reserve Educational Cen-
     ters. " USNIP, LXII (1936), 832-835.

175 Arthur, Reginald W. Contact: Careers of U. S. Naval
     Aviators. New York: Timely Publications, 1972.
     612p.

176 Artz, Frederick B. 1917 and 1941. America Faces
     the War Series, no 9. New York: Oxford Univer-
     sity Press, 1941. 24p.

177 "As the Antipodes Saw Our Sailors. " Literary Digest,
     LXXXVII (October 10, 1925), 21.

178 "As the British View Our Big-Navy Program. " Literary
     Digest, XCVI (January 14, 1928), 16-17.

179 Ashbrook, Allan W. "Naval Mines. " USNIP, XLIX
     (1923), 303-312.

180 Ashbrook, Lincoln. "The United States Navy and Air
     Power: A History of Naval Aviation, 1920-1934. "
     Unpublished PhD Dissertation, University of Califor-
     nia at Berkeley, 1946.

181 _____. "The United States Navy and the Rise of the
     Doctrine of Air Power. " Military Affairs, XV (Fall
     1951), 145-156.

182 Ashley, William J. "Great Guns. " USNIP, LXI (1935),
     627-631.
        Refers to heavy naval ordnance.

183 Asmold, Walter. "Naval Academy Athletics--1845-
     1945. " USNIP, LXXI (1945), 1155-1167; LXXII
     (1946), 105-117.

184 _____. "Naval Posture. " USNIP, LII (1926), 684-
     690.

185 Asprey, Robert B. "The Court-Martial of Smedly But-
     ler. " Marine Corps Gazette, XLIII (December 1959),
     28-34.
        An abortive effort caused by the general's re-
     marks concerning Italian dictator Mussolini.

186 _____. "John A. Lejeune: True Soldier. " Marine
     Corps Gazette, XLVI (April 1962), 34-41.
        1920s and 1930s.

187 Aston, George. "Sea-Diplomacy and Sea-Law. " Quart-
     erly Review, CCL (April 1928), 215-237.

188 Atkins, John B. "Between Geneva and the Deep Blue
     Sea. " Independent, CXX (February 4, 1928), 104-
     106.
        Agreement and disagreement coming out of the
     1927 Geneva Naval Conference.

189 Atkinson, James D. "The London Naval Conference of
     1930. " Unpublished PhD Dissertation, Georgetown
     University, 1949.

190 "Atlantic Convoy: The System That Turned Aside Defeat
     in the Last War is Put to a Still Severer Test. "
     Fortune, XXIII (April 1941), 98-101, 124+.

191   "The Atlantic Fleet and the Panama Canal." SciAmer,
      CXXI (August 30, 1919), 209.

192   "The Atlantic War Makes Portland, Me., a City of
      Rumors and Waiting Wives. " Life, XI (November
      24, 1941), 31-35.

193   "Attack Likely via Dakar: Geography and the Defense cf
      the Caribbean and the Panama Canal. " Science,
      News Letter, XXIX (January 11, 1941), 30.

194   Atwater, Jon. "Deep Sea Collegians: A Month Aboard
      a U. S. Battleship Helps in Turning Students into
      Naval Officers. " Current History, LII (April 1941),
      29-30.

195   Aubuchon, Norbert. "Wildcat: The Lethal Loser. " Fly-
      ing, XCII (January 1973), 36-43.
           Born as a biplane and nurtured on misfortune, the
      F4F was an important development of naval aviation
      in the 1930s.

196   Austin, Bernard L. "Our Navy Now and in Prospect. "
      China Weekly Review, XCI (December 16, 1939),
      101-103.

197   _____ . _____ . Far Eastern Review, XXXVI (Jan-
      uary 1940), 17-18+.
           This second version includes a list of new Ameri-
      can naval vessels under construction.

198   AuWerter, Jay P. "The New Navy 'Ranger' Engine. "
      Aviation, (June 1940), 48-49, 116.
           Refers to the motor employed aboard certain air-
      craft.

199   "Aviation and the Navy. " Outlook, CXXVIII (June 8,
      1921), 246-247.

200   "Aviation in the Coast Guard. " U. S. Coast Guard Mag-
      azine, XI (June 1938), 1+.

201   Baarslag, Karl. Coast Guard to the Rescue. New
      York: Farrar & Rinehart, 1937. 328p.

202   Babcock and Wilson Company. Babcock and Wilson's

Production for War, 1898, 1917, 1941. New York,
1942. 44p.

203 _____. Fifty Years of Steam. New York: Bartlett-
Orr Press, 1931. 67p.
During which time this major manufacturer of
boilers and power plants placed many units aboard
vessels of the American Navy.

204 _____. Marine Steam. New York, 1928. 281p.

205 Bachman, Richard A. "The American Navy and the
Turks. " Outlook, CXXXII (October 18, 1922), 288-
289.

206 "Back to the Naval Building Race. " New Republic,
LXXXVI (February 12, 1936), 5-6.

207 "The Backbone of the Fleet. " SciAmer, CXXV (September 3, 1921), 158.
The battleship.

208 Bacon, Reginald H. S. and Francis E. McMurtrie.
Modern Naval Strategy. Brooklyn, N. Y. : Chemical
Publishing Company, 1941. 208p.

209 Badger, Charles J. "A Larger American Navy. " Century Magazine, XCVII (April 1919), 787-796.

210 Bagby, Oliver W. "Naval Mining and Naval Mines. "
USNIP, LI (1925), 2244-2257.

211 Bakenhus, R. E. "Public Works of the Navy: Some of
the Accomplishments and Responsibilities of the Civil
Engineer Corps. " Civil Engineer, VI (June 1936),
359-363.

212 _____. "Shore Establishment for the Navy. " Civil
Engineering, III (August 1933), 443-446.

213 Baker, Leonard. Roosevelt and Pearl Harbor. New
York: Macmillan, 1970. 352p.
Events leading to the disaster.

214 Baker, Wilder D. "Submarine Capabilities and Limitations. " USNIP, LI (1925), 1398-1407.

215 Balchen, Bernt. Come North With Me: An Autobiog-
     raphy. New York: E. P. Dutton, 1958. 318p.

216 _____. et al. War Below Zero: The Battle for
     Greenland. Boston: Houghton, Mifflin, 1944. 127p.
     Contains data on the parts taken by the American
     navy and coast guard in the period after April 9,
     1941 when the Danish minister to Washington asked
     the U. S. to take over protection of that area.

217 Baldridge, Harry A. "Aviation at the Naval Academy."
     USNIP, LI (1925), 1632-1645.

218 _____. "The Naval Academy Museum--the First
     Hundred Years. " USNIP, LXXI (1945), 1007-1022.
     Contains examples of exhibits dating from this
     period.

219 _____. "The Second Year of Aviation at the Naval
     Academy. " USNIP, LII (1926), 2003-2010.

220 Baldwin, Elbert F. "Cruisers. " Outlook, CXLVI (Aug-
     ust 10, 1927), 471.
     One of the major issues of the Geneva Naval Con-
     ference.

221 Baldwin, Hanson W. "Air Power Again Battles Sea
     Power. " New York Times Magazine, (January 26,
     1941), 4-5.

222 _____. "America Rearms. " Foreign Affairs, XVI
     (April 1938), 430-444.

223 _____. The American Navy. London: N. p. , 1941.
     214p.

224 _____. Defense of the Western World. London: N.
     p. , 1941. 304p.

225 _____. "Military Lessons of the War. " Yale Re-
     view, New Series XXX (June 1941), 649-668.
     Includes naval lessons as well.

226 _____. "The Naval Defense of America: Sea Power
     Today and the U. S. Navy. " Harper's Magazine,
     CLXXXII (April 1941), 449-463.

227 _____ . "The Navy and the Merchant Service in Behalf of Amity. " USNIP, LVI (1930), 737-740.

228 _____ . "The Navy Clears for Action. " New York Times Magazine, (September 21, 1941), 3-5.

229 _____ . "Notes on Naval Reserve Training Cruises. " USNIP, LVII (1931), 513-514.

230 _____ . "Our Eyes Turn Intently to Sea Power. " New York Times Magazine, (February 19, 1939), 1-2+.

231 _____ . "Our Good Gray Ships. " New York Times Magazine, (April 23, 1939), 4-5+.

232 _____ . "Our New Long Shadow. " Foreign Affairs, XVII (1939), 465-476.
An analysis of the American naval expansion program and the U. S. strategic position in the Pacific with emphasis on Guam.

233 _____ . "The Spy Flourishes in an Era of Rearmament. " New York Times Magazine, (June 26, 1938), 4-5+.

234 _____ . "Terriers of the Fleet: Destroyers. " New York Times Magazine, (August 18, 1940), 4-8.

235 _____ . "The Tradition That is Our Navy. " New York Times Magazine (October 27, 1940), 9-10.

236 _____ . "Wanted: A Naval Policy. " Current History, XLIII (November 1935), 125-130.

237 _____ . "Wanted: A Plan for Defense. " Harper's, CLXXXI (August 1940), 225-238.

238 _____ . "What of the British Fleet if Britain Falls?" Readers' Digest, XXXIX (August 1941), 1-5.

239 _____ . What the Citizen Should Know About the Navy. New York: Norton, 1941. 219p.

240 _____ , jt. author. See Palmer, Wayne F. , no. 2964.

241 "Balking Poachers in the Frozen Arctic. " Popular
     Mechanics, XLI (April 1924), 571-573.
     The work of the Coast Guard.

242 Ballantine, Joseph W.   "Mukden to Pearl Harbor. "
     Foreign Affairs, XXVII (July 1949), 651-664.

243 Ballou, Sidney.   "The Condition of the American Navy. "
     USNIP, L (1924), 1509-1517.

244 _____. "Limitations of Aircraft in Naval Warfare. "
     USNIP, LI (1925), 746-760, 1745-1750.

245 _____. "Navy Day--1924. " USNIP, L (1924), 1977-
     1981.

246 _____. "Seagoing Aircraft. " USNIP, L (1924), 1795-
     1801.
     Those employed on the Langley.

247 Banning, Kendall.   The Fleet Today. Rev. ed. New
     York: Funk & Wagnalls, 1941.   348p.

248 Barde, Robert E.   The History of Marine Corps Com-
     petitive Marksmanship. Washington: Marksmanship
     Branch, U. S. Marine Corps, 1961.   467p.
     Covers the years 1901-1959.

249 Barkman, Floyd T.   "Men of the U. S. Navy at San
     Diego. " Missionary Review, XLVIII (March 1925).
     196-200.

250 Barley, Frederick R.   "Parity Up or Down. " Nation,
     CXXIX (November 20, 1929), 581-582.

251 "The Barlow Flying Torpedo. " SciAmer, CXXXIV
     (April 1926), 270.
     A unique torpedoplane.

252 Barlson, John S.   "The Naval Academy, a Suggested
     Mission. " USNIP, LX (1934), 1268-1239.

253 Barnes, Charles A.   "Salvaging Hulls of Battleships. "
     Marine Review, LIV (August 1924), 330-332.
     Those scrapped under the terms of the Washington
     Conference.

254 Barnes, S. M. , et al. "The United States Naval War
     College: A Staff Study. " Unpublished paper, Files
     of the U. S. Naval War College Library, 1954.
     Particularly useful for the 1920s and 1930s.

255 Barnett, George. "Report on the Affairs in the Repub-
     lic of Haiti, June 1915-June 30, 1920. " Unpublished
     Paper, Subject File 1911-1927, ZWA-7, Box 850,
     RG 45, National Archives, 1920. 109p.
     A report dealing with Marine activities during and
     after the command of Admiral W. B. Caperton. The
     histories which we will cite from the "Z" file of RG
     45 are, in most cases, suitable for publication and
     fall more into the category of unpublished papers
     than manuscripts. For that reason, they are in-
     cluded herein.

256 Barrett, George. "The Hurry Up School of the Navy. "
     New York Times Magazine, (May 11, 1941), 31.

257 Barringer, Bernard. "Our Navy, as Built and Building,
     the Most Powerful in the World. " SciAmer, CXXII
     (April 17, 1920), 421.

258 Barron, Gloria J. Leadership in Crisis: F. D. R. and
     the Path to Intervention. Series in American Studies.
     Port Washington, N. Y. : Kennikat Press, 1973. 145p.

259 Barrows, Nathaniel A. Blow All Ballest: The Story of
     the Squalus. New York: Dodd, Mead, 1940. 298p.

260 _____. "Forty Fathoms Down with the Diving Navy."
     Popular Mechanics, LXXII (October-November 1939),
     481-485, 674-677.

261 Barry, Robert. "What of the Auxiliaries?" USNIP,
     LXII (1936), 983-990.
     They were not covered under the London Naval
     Treaty of 1935, but were considered by the U. S.
     Congress late in the decade.

262 Bartlett, Arthur. "The Coast Guard Go-Getter and
     Ideaman: Motor Boat Owners, Organized by Admiral
     [Russell R.] Waesche, Prepared to Assume Diverse
     Duties. " Readers' Digest, XXXIX (July 1941), 43-
     45.

263 Bartlett, Ernest H. "Canada's Navy." Canadian Geo-
    graphical Journal, XXIII (November 1941), 214-253.

264 Bartlett, Harold T. "Mission of Aircraft with the
    Fleet." USNIP, XLV (1919), 729-741.

265 _____. _____. Air Power, V (May 1919), 15-17.

266 _____. "Rigid Airships--United States Ship Shenan-
    doah." USNIP, L (1924), 161-172, 762-795.
    Professional discussion of the citation included.

267 "Bases Chosen: New U. S. Bases." Time, XXXVI (De-
    cember 2 1940), 19-20.
    Those obtained from Great Britain in exchange for
    those 50 overage destroyers.

268 "Bases Keep the Fleet Afloat." Life, IX (October 28,
    1940), 92-93.

269 "Bases: Naval Back-Stop, Second Element of the Sea
    Power Factor at the London Parley." Literary Di-
    gest, CXX (December 7, 1935), 36-37.

270 Bassler, Robert E. "Education and Training of the
    Officer Personnel in the Army and Navy." USNIP,
    XLIX (1923), 1818-1838.

271 Bates, Cecil R. "The Fita-Fita Guard." Leatherneck,
    XXIII (October 1940), 6-9.

272 Bates, J. Leonard. "Fifty Knot Destroyers?" Marine
    Engineering XXXV (May 1930), 241-242.

273 _____. "The Future of the Capital Ship." Marine
    Engineer, XXXIV (May 1929), 251-252.

274 _____. "Problems Involved in the Design of Air-
    plane Carriers." Marine Engineering. XL (Septem-
    ber 1935), 334-337.

275 _____. "The United States Battleship Tennessee."
    Marine Engineering, XXV (August 1920), 642-643+.
    BB-43, launched in 1919 and scrapped 40 years
    later.

276 Bates, James L. The Origins of Teapot Dome: Pro-

gressives, Parties, and Petroleum, 1909-1921.
Urbana: University of Illinois Press, 1963.   278p.

277   Bathe, B. W. , jt. author.   See Macintyre, Donald, no.
2340.

278   Batson, Alfred.   A Vagabond's Paradise.   Boston: Little,
Brown, 1931.
Nicaragua.

279   "Battle of the Cruisers. "   Literary Digest, XCIV (July
9, 1927), 5-6.
At the 1927 Geneva Naval Conference.

280   "Battle of the Navy Yards. "   Independent, CXIX (November 26, 1927), 517.

281   "Battleship Guns on Submarines. "   SciAmer, CXXIII
(December 4, 1920), 575.

282   "Battleship Maryland to be Most Powerful Fighting Craft
in the World. "   Marine Engineering, XXVI (August
1921), 595-596.
BB-46, launched in 1920 and sold out in 1959.

283   "The Battleship of the Future. "   Popular Mechanics,
LXXIV (September 1940), 366-367.

284   "Battleship Washington launched at Camden. "   Marine
Engineering, XXVI (October 1921), 752-754.
BB-47, cancelled in 1922.

285   "Battleships: America to Spend $100, 000, 000 Building
Two, 85 per cent Going to Labor. "   Literary Digest,
CXXII (December 13, 1936), 15.

286   "Battleships, 1886-1948. "   In: U. S. Navy Department,
Naval History Division.   Dictionary of American
Naval Fighting Ships.   Washington: U. S. Government
Printing Office, 1959--.   I, 189-199.

287   "Battleships to be Bombed. "   Aviation, X (March 14,
1921), 328-330.

288   Bauer, K. Jack.   "List of United States Warships on
the Great Lakes, 1796-1941. "   Ontario History, LVI
(March 1964), 58-64.

289 _____. Ships of the Navy, 1775-1969: Combat Vessels. Troy, N. Y.: Rensselaer Polytechnic Institute, 1970. 359p.

290 Baughman, Corland C. "Pilot Chart of the Upper Air." USNIP, LIV (1928), 130-134.

291 _____. "The United States Occupation of the Santo Dominican Republic." USNIP, LI (1925), 2306-2327. From the naval and marine point of view.

292 Baumer, William H., jt. author. See Dupuy, R. Ernest, no. 1071.

293 Baxter, James P., 3rd. "How Many Ships Make Security?" Christian Science Monitor Magazine, (March 9, 1938), 1-2.

293a Baxter, L. Leroy. "The Pioneer Fighter Everyone Forgot: The Grumman FF-1 Fighter." Air Classics, VIII (December 1971), 15-21.
    The U. S. Navy's first modern fighter, featuring retractable landing gear and an enclosed cockpit, was delivered in 1932. The article is well illustrated.

294 Baylen, J. O. "American Intervention in Nicaragua, 1909-1933: An Appraisal of Objectives and Results." Southwestern Social Studies Quarterly, XXXV (September 1954), 128-154.

295 _____. "Sandino: Death and Aftermath." Mid America, XXXVI (April 1954), 116-139.

296 _____. "Sandino: Patriot or Bandit?" Hispanic-American Historical Review, XXXI (1951), 394-419.

297 Baylis, Charles D., ed. Historical and Pictorial Review of the Harbor Defenses of San Francisco, 1941. Baton Rouge, La.: Army & Navy Publishing Company, 1941. 160p.

298 Beach, Samuel W. The Great Cruise of 1925: Activities of the Ships that Visited Australia and New Zealand. San Francisco: International Ptg. Co., 1925. 260p.

299 _____. "Tracking Submarines by Radio. " Popular
Mechanics, XXXIII (April 1920), 527-528.

300 _____. "The Warship's Wireless. " Popular Mechanics, XXXIII (February 1920), 231-232.

301 Beals, Carleton. Banana Gold. New York: Arno, 1973.
     A reprinting of the 1932 first edition in which the
     author denounces American imperialism and in the
     process reports on his visit with Nicaraguan guer-
     rilla leader Sandino.

302 Beard, Charles A. "The Big Navy Boys. " New Republic, LXIX (January 20-February 3, 1932), 258-
262, 287-291, 314-318.

303 _____. The Navy: Defense or Portent? New York:
Harper, 1932. 198p.

304 _____. "Our Confusion Over National Defense: Shall
We Listen to the Pacifists or the Admirals?" Harper's Monthly, CLXIV (February 1932), 257-267.
     The rejoinder by Charles F. Adams was printed
     in the same journal three months later.

305 _____. President Roosevelt and the Coming of the
War, 1941: A Study in Appearances and Realities.
New Haven: Yale University Press, 1948. 614p.
Rpr, 1968.

306 _____. "Rough Seas for the Super-Navy. " New Republic, XCIV (March 30, 1938), 210.

307 _____. "Sea Power and Land Power. " New Republic, XCIX (September 1940), 221-225.

308 _____. "Speech Before the House Committee on
Naval Affairs Urging that Congress Disregard the
President's Recommendations for an Increase in
Naval Appropriations. " Congressional Digest, XVII
(March 1938), 90-92.

309 _____. "What is This Sea Power?" Asia, XXXV
(January 1935), 4-9.

310 _____. _____. In: William H. and Kathryn Cor-

dell, eds. American Points of View, 1935. Garden
City, N. Y.: Doubleday, 1936. p. 32ε-336.

311 _____. and Alfred Vagts. "Sea Power and Land
Power. " New Republic, XCIX (June 28, 1939), 221-
225.

312 "Beard [Charles A.] Says Big Navy Policy Leads Only
to Aggression. " Christian Science Monitor Magazine,
(February 10, 1938), 5+.

313 Beard, William E. "Scraps from Old Sea Bags. " USNIP,
LIV (1928), 647-650.

314 Beaumont, Arthur. "Ships That Guard Our Ocean Ramparts, with Paintings. " National Geographic, LXXX
(September 1941), 328-337.

315 Beck, James R. Our Wonderland of Bureaucracy:
Study of the Growth of Bureaucracy in the Federal
Government, and its Destructive Effect Upon the
Constitution. New York: Macmillan, 1932. 272p.
Contains various comments on the U. S. Navy and
Coast Guard.

316 Bedford, Stephen R. "Making a Smart Ship. " USNIP,
LV (1929), 765-766.
Discipline.

317 Beers, Burton F. Vain Endeavor: Robert Lansing's
Attempts to End the American-Japanese Rivalry.
Durham, N. C.: Duke University Press, 1962.

318 Beers, Henry P. "The Bureau of Navigation, 1862-
1942. " American Archivist, VI (1943), 212-252.

319 _____. "The Development of the Office of the Chief
of Naval Operations. " Unpublished Paper, Individual
Personnel File, Operational Archives, U. S. Navy
Department, Naval History Division, n. d. 119p.
This account studies the position through the be-
ginning of World War II.

320 _____. _____. Military Affairs, X (Spring, Fall,
1946), 40-68, 10-38; XI (Summer-Winter 1947), 88-
99, 229-237.

320a _____. "Historical Sketch of the Bureau of Equipment." Unpublished paper, Files of the National
Archives Library, April 1941.

321 _____. U. S. Naval Forces in Northern Russia
(Archangel and Murmansk), 1918-1919. Administrative Reference Service Report, no. 5. Washington:
Administrative Office, Department of the Navy, 1943.
53p.

322 _____. U. S. Naval Detachment in Turkish Waters,
1919-1924. Administrative Reference Service Report, no. 2. Washington: Administrative Office, Department of the Navy, 1943. 29p.
Details on the appointment and duties of Rear
Admiral Mark L. Bristol as U. S. representative to
Constantinople and of the operations of the naval
forces under his command.

323 Beese, S. B. "Augusta, Cruiser Launched at Newport
News." Marine Engineering, XXXV (March 1930),
126-129.
CA-31, took F. D. R. to the Atlantic Charter Conference.

324 Beggs, A. H. "Big Brothers to the Fleet." Bureau of
Ships Journal, I (April 1952), 2-7.
The story of floating drydocks, 1904-1953.

325 "Being Generous to the Navy." Christian Century, L
(September 13, 1933), 1133-1134.

326 Belknap, Reginald R. "Life on board the U. S. S. Colo-
rado: Changes in Naval Sea Service from 1856-1923."
SciAmer, CXXX (January 1924), 30-31.
BB-45, launched in 1921 and scrapped in 1959.

327 _____. "Naval Preparedness: What Road Shall We
Take?" Vital Speeches, IV (April 1, 1938), 357-
359.

328 _____. "Squantum, the Victory Plant." USNIP,
XLVII (1921), 177-186.

329 _____. "The Study of Strategy." USNIP, XLIX
(1923), 1-17.

330 _____ . "What It Means to be an Officer." USNIP,
 (1926), 562-566.
 A November 6, 1925 speech before the Naval Academy preparatory class.

331 Bell, Archibald C. Sea Power and the Next War. New
 York: Longmans, Green, 1938. 172p.
 Chapters VII and VIII deal with the problems of a
 naval war with Japan.

332 Bell, Kensil. "Always Ready!" The Story of the United
 States Coast Guard. New York: Dodd, Mead, 1943.
 324p.

333 Bellairs, Carlyon M. P. The Naval Conference and
 After. London, 1930. 45p.
 The British view expressed by a Royal Navy com-
 mander.

334 Bellinger, Patrick N. L. "Flying in the Navy." Sci-
 Amer, CLIII (November 1935), 252-254.

335 _____ . "The Gooney Bird." Unpublished Paper, Individual Personnel File, Operational Archives, U. S.
 Navy Department, Naval History Division, ca. 1960.
 387p.
 The memoirs of this naval aviation pioneer, which
 cover the years 1912-1947, are primarily in rough
 draft form.

336 Bemis, Samuel F. The Latin American Policy of the
 United States. New York: Harcourt, Brace, 1943.
 470p. Rpr. 1967.
 Throws much light on the reasons for the Navy
 and Marine involvement in the banana wars.

337 Benjamin, Park. "David and Goliath." Independent,
 CV (April 23, 1921), 420-421.
 Airplanes vs. battleships.

338 Bennington, Charles W. "Isthmian Canal Routes in
 U. S. Naval Strategy." Unpublished MA Thesis, Ohio
 State University, 1951.

339 Benson, Rodney J. "Romance and Story of Pea Island--
 U. S. Coast Guard's Only all Colored Life Saving
 Crew." U. S. Coast Guard Magazine, VI (November
 1932), 52.

340 Bent, Silas. "Evading the Washington Treaty." Nation,
     CXXIII (July 21, 1926), 55-56.

341 Berg, Meredith W. "Admiral William H. Standley and
     the Second London Naval Treaty, 1934-1936." His-
     torian, XXXIII (1971), 215-236.

342 _____. "The United States and the Breakdown of
     Naval Limitations, 1934-1939." Unpublished PhD
     Dissertation, Tulane University, 1966.

343 Bergamini, David. Japan's Imperial Conspiracy. New
     York: Pocket Books, 1972. 1364p.

344 Berger, Meyer. "The Making of a Bluejacket." New
     York Times Magazine, (July 6, 1941), 3-4.

345 _____. "Men of the Convoys." New York Times
     Magazine, (August 3, 1941), 3-4.

346 _____. "Setter-Upper for Uncle Sam: Gene Tunney
     to Promote the Fitness of the Navy." New York
     Times Magazine, (June 8, 1941), 6.

347 Bermingham, John M. "Active Service." USNIP, LXV
     (1939), 551-554.

348 Bertrand, Kenneth J. Americans in Antarctica, 1775-
     1948. American Geographical Society Special Publi-
     cations, no. 39.
     Much on Admiral Byrd.

349 Beston, Henry B. "Wardens of Cape Cod." World's
     Work, XLVII (December 1923), 186-194.
     The U. S. Coast Guard.

350 Betancourt, Gilbert. "The Status of the Airship in
     America." American Society of Mechanical Engi-
     neers Transactions, LV (1933), AER-55-58, 61-64.

351 "Better Naval Defense." SciAmer, CLVIII (March 1938),
     137, 166.

352 Bichowsky, Francis R. Is the Navy Ready? New York:
     Vanguard Press, 1935. 328p.

353 Biddlecombe, Conrad H. "Some Scientific Aspects of

Commander Byrd's Transatlantic Flight. " Outlook,
CXLVI (July 27, 1927), 406-407.

354 "Bids Received for Building Twelve Naval Vessels. "
Marine Review, LXIV (September 1934), 14.

355 Bieg, Velentine N. "War and Naval Engineering. "
USNIP, XLVI (1920), 539-553.

356 Bienstock, Gregory. The Struggle for the Pacific. New
York: Macmillan, 1937. 299p. Rpr. 1971.
Pages 242-254 survey the problems of the U. S. in
a naval war with Japan.

357 "Big Battleships Triumph Over Bombing Planes in War
Game. " Popular Science, CXXII (June 1933), 18-19.

358 "A Big Deal: Warships for Naval and Air Bases. "
Time, XXXVI (September 16, 1940), 11-12.

359 "Big Navy. " Newsweek, XI (January 10, 1938), 11.

360 "Big Navy?" SciAmer, CLIII (July 1935), 9.

361 "The Big Navy Battle: Argument About the Relative
Value of Plane and Battleship. " Time, XXXI (March
7, 1938), 13.

362 "Big Navy Blues: U. S. Shipbuilding Facilities Fall Short
of Program Needs. " Newsweek, XVI (July 1, 1940),
49.

363 "A Big-Navy Congressman Hears from Home. " Literary
Digest, XCVI (March 3, 1928), 10-11.

364 "Big-Navy Nightmare. " New Republic, CII (January 22,
1940), 102-104.

365 "Big Navy Roosevelt. " New Republic, LXXVIII (March
7, 1934), 89-90.

366 "Big-Navy Staff. " Nation, CXLVI (February 19, 1938),
200-201.

367 "Big Navy: U. S. Citizens Now Beginning to Regard It
as a $550,000,000-a-Year Necessity. " Fortune,
XVII (March 1938), 54-65+.

368 "Bigger and Better Battlewagons. " Literary Digest,
     CXXI (February 15, 1936), 14.

369 "Bigger, Brighter Battleships. " New Republic, LXXXV
     (December 4, 1935), 90-91.

370 "Bigger Navies: The Vinson Bill. " Canadian Forum,
     XIV (April 1934), 244.

371 "Bigger Navy: The Construction of Twenty-Three Fight-
     ing Ships. " Commonweal, XXII (September 20,
     1935), 498.
         Cruisers and destroyers.

372 "The Biggest Roar Afloat: The U. S. S. North Carolina. "
     Time, XXXVIII (September 8, 1941), 28-29.
         BB-55 the first U. S. battleship completed since
     before the Washington Conference.

373 "The Bill for the Construction of Cruisers is Signed by
     President Coolidge. " Commercial and Financial
     Chronicle, CXXVIII (February 16, 1929), 999-1000.

374 Billard, Frederick C. "Good Samaritans of the Sea. "
     American Magazine, XCVIII (December 1924), 30-33.
         The Coast Guard.

375 "Billions Now Asked for a Huge Naval Program. " Lit-
     erary Digest, XCVI (January 28, 1928), 12-13.

376 Binder, Carroll. "On the Nicaraguan Front: How the
     American Intervention Looks to an Eye-Witness. "
     New Republic, L (March 16, 1927), 87-90.

377 Bingham, C. E. "At Sea with the Angel of the Arctic."
     U. S. Coast Guard Magazine, V (May 1932), 9.
         The cutter Northland.

378 Birkett, Frederick J. "Land of the Midnight Sun: Ob-
     servations from a Porthole in the Famous Old Coast
     Guard Cutter Bear. " USNIP, LV (1929), 427-431.

379 _____. "The Old Bear of the North. " U. S. Coast
     Guard Magazine, VIII (1935), 20.

380 Birn, D. S. "Britain and France at the Washington Con-
     ference, 1921-1922. " Unpublished PhD Dissertation,
     Columbia University, 1964.

381 "Birth of a Warship: Views." Newsweek, XI (February
     28, 1938), 22-23.

382 Bischoff, Lawrence P., comp. Naval Reciprocating En-
     gines: A Textbook for the Instruction of the Midship-
     men at the U. S. Naval Academy. Annapolis: U. S.
     Naval Institute, 1929. 208p.

383 Bisset, Guy A. "Navy Yards as Industrial Establish-
     ments." USNIP, XLVIII (1922), 1107-1124.

384 Bisson, Thomas A. American Policy in the Far East,
     1931-1940. I. P. R. Inquiry Series. New York: In-
     stitute of Pacific Relations, 1939. 146p.
          Chpt. IV summaries American naval policy since
     the London Conference.

385 _____. American Policy in the Far East, 1931-1941.
     Rev. ed. New York: Institute of Pacific Relations,
     1941. 206p.
          Contains a supplementary chapter by Miriam S.
     Farley with considerable data on naval problems.

386 _____. "America's Dilemma in the Far East."
     Foreign Policy Reports, XVI (July 1, 1940), 98-108.

387 _____. America's Far Eastern Policy. I. P. R. In-
     quiry Series. New York: Published for the Interna-
     tional Secretariat, Institute of Pacific Relations, by
     Macmillan, 1945. 235p.
          The road to Pearl Harbor.

388 Bixby, William. Track of the Bear. New York: David
     McKay, 1965. 309p.
          The Famous old vessel sank in 1963.

389 Black, Richard D. "Richard Evelyn Byrd." Geographic
     Review, XLVII (October 1957), 579-581.

390 Blackman, John L., Jr. "Navy Policy Towards the
     Labor Relations of Its War Contractors." Military
     Affairs, XVIII (Winter 1954), 176-187.
          Useful for the years 1940-1942.

391 Blakely, Charles A. "Our Sea Defenses." Institute of
     World Affairs Proceedings, XVIII (1940), 73-77.

392 Blakemore, Thomas L. and W. Watters Pagon. Pres-

sure Airships. New York: Ronald Press, 1927.
311p.
Blimp design and fabrication.

393 Blakeney, Ben B., jt. editor. See Togo, Shigenori,
no. 4026.

394 Blakeney, Jane. Heroes, U. S. Marine Corps, 1861-
1955: Armed Forces Awards, Flags. Washington:
Guthrie Lithograph, 1957. 621p.
Contains considerable data on our period.

395 Blakeslee, George H. "Hawaii: Racial Problems and
Naval Base. " Foreign Affairs, XVII (1939), 90-99.

396 _____, jt. author. See Quigley, Harold S., no.
3218.

397 Blakeslee, Victor F. "The Bomber Challenges the
Battleship. " Popular Mechanics, LXXVI (Nobember
1941), 17-24.

398 _____. Fighting Ships of the U. S. A. New York:
Random House, 1941. 76p.
A pictorial, with an introduction by retired ad-
miral and Newsweek commentator William V. Pratt.

399 Blandy, William H. P. "Elastic Strength of Radially Expanded Guns. " USNIP, XLVII (1921), 883-908.

400 _____. "From Rio to the Amazon in the DO-X. "
USNIP, LVIII (1932), 1432-1436.

401 _____. "The Manufacture of a Battleship's Turret
Guns. " SciAmer, CXXXVI (June 1926), 390-391.

402 "Bleak Bases: The Navy Looks North to Alaska for New
Bases. " Literary Digest, CXXI (May 16, 1936), 7.

403 Bleasdale, Victor F. "La Flor Engagement. " Marine
Corps Gazette, XVI (February 1932), 29-40.
By a Marine captain involved in this Nicaraguan
action.

404 Blessing, Arthur R. "Across the Seven Seas. " Library Journal, XLIX (March 1, 1924), 211-213.
The work of the Naval War College Library.

405   "Blimps for Subs. " Time XXXVIII (October 6, 1941),
      45.

406   Bliven, Bruce. "Mr. Roosevelt's Undeclared War. "
      New Republic, XCVII (January 11, 1939), 281-282.

407   Bloch, Kurt.   "Air Power Versus Sea Power in the
      South China Sea. " Far Eastern Survey, X (1941),
      124-130.
          Stresses importance of air power, but underesti-
      mates the Japanese capability.

408   Block, Everett M.   "Patrol Plane Navigation. " USNIP,
      LXV (1939), 1468-1472.

409   Bloomfield, Howard V.   The Compact History of the
      United States Coast Guard.   New York: Hawthorne,
      1966.   307p.

410   Blum, John M. , ed.   From the Morgenthau Diaries:
      Years of Decision, 1938-1941.   Boston: Houghton,
      Mifflin, 1964.   576p.

410a "The Boeing PB-1. " Air Classics, II (August-Septem-
      ber 1965), 58-66.
          A U. S. Navy seaplane of the mid-twenties. The
      piece is well illustrated.

411   "The Boeing Shipboard Fighter. " Aviation, XXIII
      (October 31, 1927), 1058-1059.

412   Boggs, Charles W. , Jr.   "Marine Aviation--Its Origins
      and Growth. " Marine Corps Gazette, XL (May 1951),
      14-20.
          From 1912-1933.

413   _____.   "Marine Aviation: Origin and Growth. "
      Marine Corps Gazette, XXXIV (November 1950), 68-
      75.
          Considerable references to its use in Nicaragua.

414   Bogusch, Harry R.   "Does the Navy Need a Naval Re-
      serve Force?" USNIP, XLIX (1923), 1419-1430.

415   Bolander, Louis H.   "A History of Regulations in the
      United States Navy. " USNIP, LV (1929), 491-494.

416 _____. "Training Midshipmen to Use the Library."
Libraries, XXXV (July 1930), 326-328.

417 Bolster, Calvin M. "Mechanical Equipment for Handling Large Rigid Airships." American Society of
Mechanical Engineers Transactions, LV (1933), AER-
55, 15, 113-119.

418 "The Bombing of Warships Proves Air Power." Aviation, XI (July 25, 1921), 96-98.

419 "The Bombing Tests and Our Naval Policy." SciAmer,
CXXV (August 6, 1921), 90.

420 "Bombing Tests of the U.S.S. Alabama." USNIP,
XLVII (1921), 1834-1838.

421 "Bombing the Alabama." Aerial Age, XIV (October 3,
1921), 85.

422 "Bombing the Old Battleship Indiana." SciAmer, CXXIII
(December 4, 1920), 575.
BB-1.

423 Boone, Andrew R. "The Eyes of the Fleet: Ranger."
SciAmer, CLIII (October 1935), 196-197.
CV-4, first U.S. carrier designed as such.

424 _____. "Flying Lifeboats Make Thrilling Rescues at
Sea." Popular Science, CXXXI (December 1937),
56-57.
The work of the Coast Guard.

425 _____. "How Swift Navy Planes Hit the Spot on a
Carrier's Deck." Popular Science, CXIX (December 1931), 56-58+.

426 _____. "Invisible Targets in Sea or Sky Hit by Navy
Miracle Guns." Popular Science, CXXV (August
1934), 49-52.

427 _____. "The Miracles of Surgery at Sea Performed
in the Navy's Floating Hospital, U.S.S. Relief."
Popular Science, CXXIX (October 1936), 24-25+.

428 _____. "Navy Business." California, (October
1937), 8-11.

Comments on the buildup contained in the publication of the California State Chamber of Commerce.

429 _____. "New Talking Ear Saves Men Trapped in
Submarine. " Popular Science, CXX (March 1932),
17-19+.

430 Border, Lee S.   "Planning and Estimating at Navy
Yards. " USNIP, LXI (1935), 809-811.

431 Borg, Dorothy.   The United States and the Far Eastern
Crisis of 1933-1938: From the Manchurian Incident
Through the Initial Stage of the Undeclared Sino-
Japanese War.   Cambridge, Mass.: Harvard Univer-
sity Press, 1964.   674p.
Contains details on the activities of the U.S. Navy
in those years.

432 _____. et al.   Pearl Harbor as History: Japanese-
American Relations 1931-1941.   Studies of the East
Asian Institute.   New York: Columbia University
Press, 1973.   801p.

433 Borton, Hugh.   Japan's Modern Century.   New York:
Ronald Press, 1955.   524p.
Contains some data on naval rivalry with America
during our period.   A second edition was issued in
1970.

434 "Both Captains are Blamed for Sinking the Submarine
S-4." Engineering News, C (March 1, 1928), 371+.

435 Bourgin, Simon.   "Public Relations of Naval Expansion. " Public Opinion Quarterly, III (January 1939),
113-117.

436 Boutwell, William D., ed.   American Prepares for
Tomorrow: The Story of Our Total Defense Effort.
New York: Harper, 1941.   612p.
Descriptive articles of a non-controversial nature.

437 Bowden, Adelphia D., Jr.   "The Disarmament Move-
ment, 1918-1935." Unpublished PhD Dissertation,
Columbia University, 1956.

438 Bowen, Harold G.   "The Navy Expansion Program and
Its Importance to Industry. " Machinery, XLV (No-

vember 1938), 145-147.

439 _____ . One Hundred Years of Steam in the U. S.
Navy. Princeton, N. J. : Princeton University Press,
1937. 30p.

440 _____ . Ships, Machinery and Mossbacks: The Auto-
biography of a Naval Engineer. Princeton, N. J. :
Princeton University Press, 1954. 397p.
The author was active in the period between the
World Wars.

441 Bowers, Peter M. The Boeing F4B-4 Hawks. Aircraft
Profiles, no. 27. Leatherhead, Surrey, England:
Profile Publications, n. d.

442 _____ . The Curtiss Navy Hawks. Aircraft Profiles,
no. 116. Leatherhead, Surrey, England: Profile
Publications, n. d.

443 _____ . Forgotten Fighters and Experimental Aircraft
of the U. S. Navy, 1918-1941. New York: Arco,
1971. 80p.

444 _____ , jt. author. See Swanborough, Gordon, no.
3867.

445 Bowers, Ray L. "The Twentieth Century Penchant for
the Offensive. " USNIP, XCIII (1967), 58-70.

446 Bowman, Josephine B. "Public Health Nursing in the
Navy. " American Journal of Public Health, XVII
(May 1927), 541-542.

447 Bowser, Alpha L. , Jr. "Light Artillery Support in
Landing Operations. " Marine Corps Gazette, XXII
(June 1938), 22-25, 74.

448 Bradshaw, Harvey D. "Marine Corps Aviation: Cunningham to Cu Lai. " USNIP, XCII (1966), 106-123.

449 Brailsford, Henry N. "Abolish the Battleship!" New
Republic, LXI (December 25, 1929), 132-134.

450 _____ . "Anglo-American Friendship. " New Republic, LIX (May 29, 1929), 39-41.

451 _____. "Battleships in the [1930 London] Confer-
    ence." New Republic, LXII (February 19, 1930), 16-
    18.

452 "The Brain of the Giant Dirigible, U. S. S. Macon, is in
    Her Control Room." Popular Mechanics, LX (August
    1933), 207.

453 Brainard, E. H. "Marine Corps Aviation." Marine
    Corps Gazette, XIII (March 1928), 25-26.
        The first use of dive-bombing in combat over
    Ocotal, Nicaragua.

454 _____. "Marines Take Wings: Nicaraguan Air Fight-
    ing." Collier's, LXXXI (June 23, 1928), 8-9.

455 Braisted, William R. The United States Navy in the
    Pacific, 1909-1922. Austin: University of Texas
    Press, 1971. 741p.

456 Brandenburg, Howard H. Navy Evidence: A Digest of
    the Law of Evidence as Stated in Navy Court-Martial
    Orders, 1916-1951. Washington, 1952. 179p.

457 Brandt, Edmund S. R. "Down Went McGinty to the
    Bottom of the Sea." USNIP, LVIII (1932), 67-72.

458 _____. "Naval Ratios and Neutrality." USNIP, LIX
    (1933), 1690-1694.

459 _____. "A Suggestion for Naval Reserve Training."
    USNIP, L (1924), 1786-1794.

460 _____. "Treaty Cruisers." USNIP, LVII (1931),
    1163-1168.
        Citation refers to the London Naval Treaty of 1930.

461 Brandt, George E. "The Economy of Naval Armament."
    USNIP, LVIII (1932), 1597-1609.

462 _____. "The Man-Overboard Problem as Applied to
    Destroyers." USNIP, LVI (1930), 419-425.

463 _____. "Newspaper Publicity for the Navy." USNIP,
    L (1924), 916-930.

464 _____. "Our Knowledge of the Earth's Natural Re-

sources: The Gulf of Mexico to be Base of Re-
searches Planned by the Naval Scientific Expedition. "
Manufacturing Record, LXXXVI (October 16, 1924),
67-71.

465 _____. "What Really Happened in the Hawaiian
Maneuvers. " Aviation, XIX (July 20, 1925), 66-68.

466 Brassey's Naval Annual.   London and New York: Various
publishers, 1886-1950.
Includes statistical data on navies.

467 "Breach with the Axis Widened by the Nazi Sinking of
the Robin Moor. " Newsweek, XVII (June 23, 1941),
13-16.

468 Breckel, Harry F.   "Guiding the Battle Fleet by Multi-
plex Radio Signaling. " Radio News, VIII (June
1927), 1420-1421.

469 _____. "Naval Radio Progress. " USNIP, LI (1925),
2279-2285.

470 _____. "The Vital Importance of Radio Communication in Modern Naval Warfare. " USNIP, XLVIII
(1922), 383-393.

471 Breckenridge, J. C.   "Why Quantico?" USNIP, LIV
(1928), 969-975.

472 Breese, James L.   "Precautions that Spelled Success:
Some Engineering Features of the First Flight
Across the Ocean. " SciAmer, CXXI (July 19, 1919),
55, 74.
That of the NC's.

473 Brewster, Ralph O.   "An Adequate Navy. " Delta Kappa
Epsilon Quarterly, LVI (May 1938), 57-59.

473a "The Brewster F2A Buffalo. " Air Classics, III (July
1967), 16-24.
Evolution of a Navy fighter of the 1930s, well
illustrated.

474 Breyer, Siegfried.   Battleships and Battle-Cruisers.
Garden City N. Y. : Doubleday, 1973. 922p.

475   Bridge, Cyprian A. G.   "American and British Naval
      Preparations. "   Current History, XIII (March 1921),
      377-380.

476   _____.   "The Capital Ship: Is It Doomed?"   19th
      Century, LXXXIX (February 1921), 307-315.
      In light of the airplane.

477   _____.   "The Naval Situation. "   Edinburgh Review,
      CCXXXIII (April 1921), 238-254.

478   _____.   "The Overrated Submarine. "   19th Century,
      XCIII (May 1923), 658-665.

479   "A Bridge to the Orient: The Navy's New Station on the
      Midway Islands. "   Time, XXXVIII (August 11, 1941),
      28.

480   Briggs, Henry W.   "Neglected Aspects of the Destroyer
      Deal: The Requirements of International Law Govern-
      ing the Transfer of Naval or Military Equipment. "
      American Journal of International Law, XXIV (Octo-
      ber 1940), 569-587.

481   Briggs, Raymonde.   New Submersible Battle Cruiser
      with Sixteen-Inch Guns.   New York, 1940.   28p.
         The idea for this submersible got no further than
      this pamphlet.

482   Bright, Joy.   "The History of Naval Aviation. "   In:
      William H. Fetridge, ed.   The Navy Reader.   Indi-
      anapolis: Bobbs-Merrill, 1943.   p. 109-120.   Rpr.
      1971.
         Written by a Wave officer formerly in charge of
      the Editorial Research Section of the Navy's Bureau
      of Aeronautics for a 1942 issue of Flying, this
      article discusses the pre-war and early World War
      II history of American naval flying, including air-
      ships.

483   Brine, pseud.   "Shall We Scrap Our Greatest Battle-
      ships?"   Current History, XIII (March 1921), 381-
      385.

484   "Bringing the Fleet Back to the Atlantic. "   Christian
      Century, L (November 15, 1933), 1429.

485 Brisay, Richard de. "Warships and Foodships." Cana-
     dian Forum, X (January 1930), 111-113.
          Comments on the London Naval Conference.

486 Bristol, Mark L. "Conditions in the Near East." Un-
     published Lecture, G-2 Course 1, Files of the U. S.
     Army Military History Research Collection, 1925.
          Rear Admiral Bristol was High Commissioner to
     Turkey after World War I. A word about these lec-
     tures, others of which are cited below. All are part
     of the curricular archives of the U. S. Army War
     College presently housed at the USAMHRC.   Dr. Ben-
     jamin F. Cooling, Chief of Research Studies, who
     prepared the introduction to Vol. IV of this series,
     has published A Suggested Guide to the Curricular
     Archives of the U. S. Army War College, 1907-1940,
     Special Bibliographic Series, no. 8. (Carlisle Bar-
     racks, Pa. : U. S. Army Military History Research
     Collection, 1973), 95p, (available free upon request),
     which may be used as a guide to this important
     source of pre-war military and naval thinking.

487 "Britain's Navy and Ours." New Republic, XC (March
     3, 1937), 97-98.

488 Britannica Book of the Year. Chicago: Encyclopedia
     Britannica, Inc. , 1938-1942.

489 "British-American Naval Rivalry." Literary Digest, LX
     (January 11, 1919), 12-13.

490 "British Destroyer Leader, We Have None." SciAmer,
     CXL (February 1929), 142-143.

491 "British Praise New American Cruisers." SciAmer,
     CLX (January 1939), 37.

492 "British Premier Reveals Three German U-boats Sunk:
     Nazi Warships Operating in American Waters."
     China Weekly Review, XCVI (March 22, 1941), 79.

493 Britton, Beverly L. , jt. author. See Kearns, William
     H. , Jr. , no. 1941.

494 "Broad Stripes for Mustangs: The Navy's New Officer-
     Training Program." Time, XXXVII (March 21, 1941),
     17.

495 Broadbent, Ernest W.   "Aircraft in Joint Military-Naval
     Operations. " USNIP, LVII (1931) 1056-1059.

496 _____. "The Fleet and the Marines. " USNIP, LVII
     (1931), 369-372.

497 _____. "Joint Military-Naval Operations: A Spe-
     cialty. " USNIP, LX (1934), 321-334.

498 Brodie, Bernard. A Guide to Naval Strategy. Rev. ed.
     Princeton, N. J. : Princeton University Press, 1958.
     315p. Rpr. 1965.

499 _____. "New Tests of Sea and Air Power. " Cur-
     rent History, New Series I (October 1941), 97-108.

500 _____. Sea Power in the Machine Age. 2nd ed.
     Princeton, N. J. : Princeton University Press, 1943.
     462p.

501 _____. "Sea Power in the Machine Age: Major
     Naval Inventions and Their Consequences on Interna-
     tional Politics, 1814-1940. " Unpublished PhD Dis-
     sertation, University of Chicago, 1941.

502 Brodie, F. , jt. author. See Lockwood, W. W. , no.
     2222.

503 Brookings, Delano. "The Navy's Flying Crow's Nests:
     Blimps for Patrol. " Christian Science Monitor Mag-
     azine, (May 17, 1941), 3.

504 Brooks, C. T. "War in Nicaragua. " Marine Corps
     Gazette, XVII (1933), 45-48.

505 Brooks, Charles B. , Jr. "Some Thoughts on Heavy
     Ships. " USNIP, LXXXIII (1957), 1250-1252.
     Mainly battleships.

506 Brooks, Stanley T. "Newfoundland, the Gibraltar of the
     North. " Christian Science Monitor Magazine, (Sep-
     tember 14, 1940), 6-8.

507 Brown, Alexander C. Monitor Class Warships of the
     United States Navy. New York: Society of Naval
     Architects and Marine Engineers, 1943. 7p.

508 _____. "Monitor-Class Warships of the United States
Navy." In: The Society of Naval Architects and
Marine Engineers. Historical Transactions, 1893-
1943. New York, 1945. p. 330-340.

509 Brown, C. H. "Naval Libraries." Library Journal,
XLV (1920), 169-170.

510 _____. "Naval Libraries: Present and Future."
Library Journal, XLIV (1919), 235-241.

511 Brown, Ernest W. "The Human Mechanism and the
Submarine." USNIP, LXVI (1940), 1608-1616.

512 _____. "The Navy League Dispute." Current History, XXXV (December 1931), 428-429.

513 _____. "Study of Lead Poisoning Among Oxyacetyline
Welders in the Scrapping of Naval Vessels." Journal
of Industrial Hygiene, VIII (March 1926), 113-140.

514 Brown, Marvin L., Jr. The United States Marines in
Iceland, 1941-1942. Marine Corps Historical Refer-
ence Series, no. 34. Washington: Historical
Branch, U. S. Marine Corps, 1961. 17p.

515 Brown, Paul. Insignia of the Services. New York:
Scribners, 1941. 63p.

516 Brown, Riley. The Story of the Coast Guard: Men,
Wind, and Sea: Garden City, N. Y.: Blue Ribbon
Books, 1943. 266p.
A brief account of the evolution of the service
from 1790.

517 Brown, Robert V. "The Navy's Mark 15 (Norden) Bomb
Sight: Its Development and Procurement, 1920-
1945." Unpublished Paper, Individual Personnel
File, Operational Archives, U. S. Navy Department,
Naval History Division, 1946. 321p.
Based on Bureau of Ordnance papers, complete
with appendices listing documents pertaining to the
bomb sight.

518 Brown, Stimson J. "A Method of Gun Construction by
Radial Expansion." USNIP, XLVI (1920), 1941-1970.

519   Brown, Wilson.   "Our Unofficial Diplomats Abroad. "
      USNIP, LXXVIII (1952), 868-875.
      On the behavior of Yankee sailors in foreign ports
      during the period ending with the outbreak of World
      War II.

520   Brownson, Howard G.   "Naval Policy in Peace and
      War. "   USNIP, LVII (1931), 1007-1017.

521   _____.   "The Naval Policy of the United States. "
      USNIP, LIX (1933), 975-987.

522   _____.   "The Price of Peace. "   USNIP, LVIII (1932),
      1771-1781.

523   _____.   "Sea Power and World Peace. "   USNIP,
      LXIII (1937), 1689-1701.

524   Bruce, Bryson.   "Natural Competition. "   USNIP, LXXIV
      (1948), 1367-1371.
      Concerns engineering competition in the Navy,
      1932-1934.

525   _____.   "River Gunboats for Yangtze Service. "   Far
      Eastern Review, XXIV (December 1928), 558-563.

526   Brune, Lester H.   "Foreign Policy and Air Power Dis-
      pute, 1919-1932. "   Historian, XXIII (1961), 449-464.
      Based on the William Mitchell and Dudley W.
      Knox papers in the Library of Congress.

527   Bryant, S. W.   "Office of Naval Operations. "   Unpub-
      lished Lecture, G-3 Course 5, Files of the U. S.
      Army Military History Research Collection, 1932.

528   Bryant, Stewart F.   "Should the Government of Samoa
      be Changed?"   USNIP, LVI (1930), 834-842.

529   Buchanan, A. E. , Jr.   "Cheap Helium Made Possible
      Novel Features of the Akron. "   SciAmer, CXLVI
      (January 1932), 52-53.

530   Buchanan, A. R.   The U. S. and World War II.   New
      American Nation Series.   2 vols.   New York: Harper,
      1964.
      Our interest here extends only through 1941.

531 Buchowsky, Francis R. Is the Navy Ready? New York:
     Vanguard Press, 1935. 328p.

532 Buckley, Franklin D. "Let's Try a New Weapon. "
     USNIP, LVII (1941), 691-694.
     Airships.

533 Buckley, Thomas H. "The United States and the Wash-
     ington Conference, 1921-1922. " Unpublished PhD
     Dissertation, Indiana University, 1961.

534 _____. _____. Knoxville: University of Tennessee
     Press, 1970. 222p.

535 Buel, K. L. "The Psychology of Pacifism. " USNIP,
     LIV (1928), 473-480.

536 Buell, Raymond L. U. S. Navy "Second to None. " New
     York: Foreign Policy Association, 1933. 2p.

537 _____. "The Washington Conference. " Unpublished
     PhD Dissertation, Princeton University, 1922.

538 _____. _____. New York: D. Appleton-Century,
     1922. 461p.

539 Buell, Thomas B. "Admiral Edward C. Kalbfus and
     the Naval Planner's 'Holy Scripture': Sound Military
     Decision. " Naval War College Review, XXV (May-
     June 1973), 31-41.
     During the 1930s.

540 _____. "Admiral Raymond A. Spruance and the
     Naval War College. " Naval War College Review,
     XXIII (July-August 1971), 30-51. 29-53.

541 Buenzle, Frederick J. Bluejacket, an Autobiography.
     New York: W. W. Norton, 1939. 368p.

542 "Building Alaska Bases for Naval Aircraft. " Engineer-
     ing News, CXXV (October 24, 1940), 556-557.

543 "Building the Navy to Treaty Strength. " Marine News,
     XXIII (December 1936), 37-45.

544 "Building the New Navy: Delays in the Program. " U. S.
     News, (November 7, 1938), 7.

545 "Building the United States Navy: Photographs. " Inde-
     pendent, CXV (October 24, 1925), 469-472.

546 "Building the United States Navy to Treaty Strength:
     Hobart College, Affirmative and Negative. " In: E. R.
     Nichols, ed. Intercollegiate Debates. New York:
     Noble & Noble, 1934. p. 301-339.

547 Bundel, Charles M. "Is Proper Provision Made for
     Cooperation of Army and Navy Air Forces in Coastal
     Warfare?" Unpublished General Staff Memorandum,
     Files of the U. S. Army Military History Research
     Collection, 1924.
        The author was a Brigadier General in the U. S.
     Army.

548 Bundy, McGeorge, jt. author. See Stimson, Henry L.
     no. 3802.

549 Bunkley, Joel W.   Military and Naval Recognition Books:
     A Handbook on the Organization, Insignia of Rank of
     the World's Armed Forces, Etiquette and Customs of
     the American Services.   New York: D. Van Nostrand,
     1941.   297p.
        Written by a naval captain.

550 "The Bureau of Aeronautics. " USNIP, LXXV (1949),
     85-95.
        A history from the days of Admiral Moffett.

551 "The Bureau of Ordnance. " USNIP, LXXV (1949), 213-
     224.
        A history from 1842-1949.

552 "The Bureau of Ships. " USNIP, LXXV (1949), 813-821.

553 "Bureau of Yards and Docks. " USNIP, LXXV (1949),
     577-587, 1293-1294.
        A history.

554 "The Bureau of Yards and Docks Reports on Navy Con-
     struction. " Engineering News, CXXVI (June 26,
     1941), 978-979.

555 Burgess, Charles P. Airship Design. New York:
     Ronald Press, 1927.   300p.

556 _____, et al.   "Aeronautics in Naval Architecture. "
Society of Automotive Engineers Journal, XL (January 1937), 13-18.

557 _____.   "Airships as Cruisers. "   U. S. Air Services,
XX (October 1935), 19-21.

558 _____.   "Mooring the U. S. Airship Shenandoah to
U. S. S. Patoka. " U. S. Air Services, IX (September
1924), 418-419.

559 _____.   "New 6, 000, 000 Cubic Foot Airship for Our
Navy. " SciAmer, CXL (December 1926), 418-419.

560 _____.   Progress in Airship Design from the U. S. S.
Shenandoah to the U. S. S. Akron. " Journal of the
American Society of Naval Engineers, XLIII (August
1933), 419-425.

561 _____.   "The Rigid Airship ZR-3. " Journal of the
American Society of Naval Engineers, XXXVI (November 1924), 553-572.

562 _____.   Some Airship Problems.   Akron, O. : Gug-
genheim Airship Institute, 1935.   9p.

563 _____.   "Water Recovery Apparatus for Airships. "
American Society of Mechanical Engineers Transactions, LIV (1932), AER 54-11, 83-92.

564 Burlingame, Roger.   General Billy Mitchell, Champion
of Air Defense.   New York: McGraw-Hill, 1952.
212p.
Foe of big battleships and even aircraft carriers.

565 Burn, North C.   "United States Base Rights in the
British West Indies, 1940-1942. "   Unpublished PhD
Dissertation, Fletcher School of Law and Diplomacy,
1964.
The destroyers-for-bases deal between President
Roosevelt and Prime Minister Churchill was con-
sumated in September 1940.

566 Burns, Richard D.   "Regulating Submarine Warfare,
1921-1941: A Case Study in Arms Control and Limited War. "   Military Affairs, XXXV (April 1971),
56-63.

567 _____ and Donald Urquidi. Disarmament in Per-
      spective: An Analysis of Selected Disarmament and
      Arms Control Agreements Between the World Wars,
      1919-1939. 4 vols. Washington: U. S. Arms Control
      and Disarmament Agency, 1968.

568 Burns, W. H. "Strategic Naval Bases Throughout the
      World. " USNIP, LV (1929). 65-69.
      Reprinted from the November 1928 issue of the
      Coast Artillery Journal.

569 Burrough, Edmund W. "Submarine Sizes. " USNIP,
      LII (1927), 1292-1294.

570 Burroughs, Polly. The Great Ice Ship Bear: Eighty-
      Nine Years in Polar Seas. New York: Van Nostrand
      Reinhold, 1970. 104p.

571 Burrows, Albert C. "A Brief for the Submarine. "
      USNIP, LIV (1928), 644-646.

572 Bursey, Jack. Antarctic Night: One Man's Story of '28,
      224 Hours at the Bottom of the World. New York:
      Rand McNally, 1957. 256p.
      Reminiscences of the author's Antarctic experi-
      ences beginning as a dog driver with the Byrd Ex-
      pedition of 1928-1930.

573 Burtness, Paul S. and Warren U. Ober. "Research
      Methodology: The Problem of the Pearl Harbor In-
      telligence Reports. " Military Affairs, XXV (Fall
      1961), 132-146.
      Or, who knew what before December 7!

574 Burton, Wilbur. "Panama: Defense Problem No. 1. "
      Current History, XLIX (December 1938), 34-37.

575 Bush, Harald. U-boats at War. Translated from the
      German by L. P. R. Wilson. London: Putnam, 1955.
      286p.
      Useful for the period of our 1941 undeclared naval
      war with Nazi Germany.

576 Bush, Vannevar. Modern Arms and Free Men: A Dis-
      cussion of the Role of Science in Preserving Democ-
      racy. New York: Simon and Schuster, 1949. 273p.
      Contains several sections relative to this compilation.

577 Bushey, Arthur C., Jr. "United States Navy Rubber
     Craft." Journal of the American Society of Naval
     Engineers, LXIV (August 1952), 621-625.
     Since 1930.

578 Buss, Claude A. War and Diplomacy in Eastern Asia.
     New York: Macmillan, 1941. 570p.

579 Butler, James R. M., ed. Grand Strategy. History of
     the Second World War--United Kingdom Military
     Series. 6 vols. London: H. M. Stationery Office,
     1957-1972.
         Contains some data relative to the late years of
     this study.

580 Butler, Jarvis. "The Aeronautical Board of the Army
     and Navy." USNIP, LII (1926), 2246-2254.

581 Butler, Smedley D. "American Marines in China."
     Annals of the American Academy, CXLIV (July 1929),
     128-134.

582 _____. "Historical Report of the Occupation of
     Tientsin by the Third Brigade, Under the Command
     of Brigadier General Smedley D. Butler, U. S. M. C.,
     from the First Part of June 1927 Until December
     1928." Unpublished paper, Subject File 1911-1927,
     ZK, Box 799, RG-45, National Archives, 1929. 29p.
         The operations of the author's command in pro-
     tecting U. S. citizens during the Civil War in China.

583 _____. "The Navy Bill a 'Bluff': Retired Marine,
     Advocating a 'Home Guard' Navy, Asks Defeat of the
     Measure." New Yorker, (April 9, 1938), 11.

584 _____, as told to Lowell Thomas. Old Gimlet Eye:
     The Adventures of Smedley D. Butler, Maj. Gen.,
     U. S. M. C. New York: Farrar & Rinehart, 1933.
     310p.

585 _____. War is a Racket. New York: Revisionist
     Press, n. d.

586 Butler, Thomas S. "America Misled by Five-Power
     Naval Treaty." Current History, XXVI (April 1927),
     86-92.

Butler   51

587 _____ . "Don't Give Up the Ships. " North American
     Review, CCXXIV (June 1927, 214-222.
     Cruiser-talk at Geneva.

588 Butman, C. H. "Naval Shore Establishments Need Air
     Stations. " Aviation, XIV (February 12, 1923), 186-
     187.

589 Butow, Robert J. C. "The Hull-Nomura Conversations:
     A Fundamental Misconception. " American Historical
     Review, LXV (1960), 822-836.

590 _____ . Tojo and the Coming of the War. Princeton,
     N. J.: Princeton University Press, 1961. 584p.

591 Butt, Marshall W. Norfolk Naval Shipyard: A Brief
     History. Portsmouth, Va.: The Yard, 1951.

592 Buzanski, Peter M. "Admiral Mark L. Bristol and
     Turkish-American Relations, 1919-1922. " Unpub-
     lished PhD Dissertation, University of California at
     Berkeley, 1960.

593 Buzzell, Francis. The Great Lakes Naval Training
     Station: A History. Boston: Small, 1919. 212p.

594 Byrd, Richard E. Alone. New York: G. P. Putnam,
     1938. Rpr. 1966.

595 _____ . "The Coming Age in Aviation. " World's
     Work, LIV (October 1927), 600-610.

596 _____ . "Conquering the Antarctic by Air: With Pre-
     sentation of Letters of Tribute from the School
     Children of America. " National Education Associa-
     tion Journal, XX (April 1931), 117-118.

597 _____ . "The Conquest of Antarctica by Air. " Na-
     tional Geographic, LVIII (August 1930), 127-227.

598 _____ . "Discovery: Abridged. " Reader's Digest,
     XXVIII (February 1936), 111-126.

598a _____ . Discovery: The Story of the Second Byrd
     Antarctic Expedition. Detroit: Gale Research, 1971.
     405p.
     Reprint of 1935 first edition.

599 _____. "Exploring the Ice Age in Antarctica. " National Geographic, LXVIII (October 1935), 399-474.

600 _____. Exploring with Byrd: Episodes from an Adventurous Life. New York: G. P. Putnam's, 1937. 241p. Rpr. 1972.

601 _____. "Facing Aviation's Critics. " Forum, LXXX (August 1928), 166-171.

602 _____. "Fertile Land of Ice. " Literary Digest, CXXIV (November 6, 1937), 28.

603 _____. "First Flight to the North Pole. " National Geographic, L (September 1926), 356-376.

604 _____. "Fly on! Fly on!" Collier's, LXXXI (May 12, 1928), 8-9.

605 _____. "Flying Over the Arctic. " National Geographic, XLVIII (November 1925), 519-532.

606 _____. "Flying Over the Polar Sea. " USNIP, LI (1925), 1319-1338.

607 _____. "How I Pick My Men. " Saturday Evening Post, CC (April 21, 1928), 12-13.

608 _____. "Is a Dark Age Ahead?" Rotarian, L (March 1937), 6-9.

609 _____. Little America: Aerial Exploration in the Antarctic and the Flight to the South Pole. New York: G. P. Putnam's, 1930. 422p.

610 _____. "Our Trans-Atlantic Flight. " National Geographic, LII (September 1927), 346-368.

611 _____. "Perils of Arctic Flying. " World's Work, LII (May 1926), 69-83.

612 _____. "Santa Claus at the North Pole. " Ladies' Home Journal, LIII (December 1926), 13.

613 _____. Skyward: Man's Mastery of the Air As Shown by the Brilliant Flights of America's Leading Air Explorer. New York: G. P. Putnam's, 1928. 359p.

614 _____. "This Hero Business!" Ladies' Home
    Journal, XLIV (January 1927), 21.

615 _____. "Trust Your Navigator. " Vital Speeches, IV
    (January 1, 1938), 162-165.

616 _____. "A Warning to Peace-at-Any-Price Groups."
    Literary Digest, CXXV (February 12, 1938), 16-17.

617 _____. "We Must Stand Behind the President. "
    Vital Speeches, VII (September 1, 1941) 683-685.

618 _____. "Why I Am Going to the South Pole. "
    World's Work, LV (December 1927), 158-167.

619 _____. "Why the Antarctic Again. " Rotarian, XLIV
    (February 1934), 9-11+.

620 _____. "Wings Over the Antarctic: Admiral Byrd's
    Plan. " Popular Mechanics, LXXVI (October 1941),
    28-31.

621 "The Byrd Antarctic Expedition. " Science, New Series
    XC (August 11, 1939), 131.

622 "Byrd Arrives, [Lincoln] Ellsworth Leaves Antarctica. "
    Newsweek, III (January 27, 1934), 26.

623 "Byrd Bags His Second Pole by Air. " Literary Digest,
    CIII (December 14, 1929), 8-9.

624 "Byrd Begins Solitary Vigil to Make Weather Study. "
    Newsweek, III (April 7, 1934), 19.

625 "Byrd Has Plane Trouble. " Newsweek, III (March 24,
    1934), 34.

626 "Byrd's Antarctic Igloo is Scientific Wonder. " Popular
    Mechanics, LXII (September 1934), 396.

627 "Byrd's Greatest Achievement. " Outlook, CXLVI (July
    27, 1927), 401-402.

628 "Byrd's Hermit Hut in Antarctica. " SciAmer, CLI
    (August 1934), 104-105.

629 Bywater, Hector C. "America and Britain: The Naval

Issue. " Forum, LXXVII (January 1927), 96-106.
The noted British commentator died in the summer
of 1940, thus missing the outcome of his prophesies.

630 _____. "American Naval Policy. " 19th Century,
CIII (March 1928), 322-332.

631 _____. _____. Review of Reviews, LXXVII (May
1928), 504.
For N. H. Goss' reply to the author's article, see
the citation above.

632 _____. "Are Huge Aircraft Carriers Worth While?"
SciAmer, LXXII (March 1923), 164.

633 _____. "The Battleship and Its Uses. " USNIP, LII
(1926), 407-426.

634 _____. "Battleship vs. Plane Still a Naval Puzzle. "
USNIP, LIV (1928), 710-712.

635 _____. "Britain on the Seas. " Foreign Affairs,
XVI (January 1938), 210-221.
Contains comments often relative to the American
navy of our period.

636 _____. "The Coming Struggle for Sea Power. "
Current History, XLI (October 1934), 9-16.

637 _____. "Dismal Prospect for Limiting Armaments."
Atlantic Monthly, CXXXIV (November 1924), 672-680.

638 _____. The Great Pacific War: A History of the
American-Japanese Campaign of 1931-33. London:
Constable, 1925. 317p.
Not designed as fiction but an imaginary account
of what might happen in a U. S. -Japanese naval conflict. By 1942, it was still regarded with startling
significance for its strategic conclusions.

639 _____. "High Speed Fighting Ships. " SciAmer,
CXXV (December 1921), 97.

640 _____. "The Influence of Material on Naval Operations. " USNIP, XLVIII (1922), 1677-1686.

641 _____. "Japanese and American Naval Power. "

Atlantic Monthly, CXXVIII (November 1921), 704-712.

642 _____. "Japanese and American Naval Power in the Pacific. " Foreign Affairs, VIII (1935), 168-175.

643 _____. "Japanese Naval Policy. " 19th Century, XCVIII (November 1925), 689-700.
In light of the disarmament conference and that of the United States.

644 _____. "The Limitation of Naval Armaments. " Atlantic Monthly, CXXIX (February 1922) 259-269.

645 _____. "Limitation of Navies. " Fortnightly, CXLII (December 1934), 673-682.

646 _____. "The London Naval Conference. " 19th Century, CVI (December 1929), 717-730.

647 _____. _____. Living Age, CCCXXXVII (January 15, 1930), 731-742.

648 _____. "Long Term Enlistment as a Naval Requisite. " USNIP, L (1924), 1724-1726.
Reprinted from the July 24, 1924 issue of the Baltimore Sun.

649 _____. "Naval Construction in 1932. " Engineer, CLV (January 6, 1933), 6-7.

650 _____. "Naval Construction in 1933. " Engineer, CLVII (January 5, 1934), 3-5, 7.

651 _____. "Naval Construction in 1934. " Engineer, CLIX (January 4, 1935), 18-21.

652 _____. "Naval Construction in 1935. " Engineer, CLXI (January 3, 1936), 10-12.

653 _____. "Naval Construction in 1936 " Engineer, CLXIII (January 1, 1937), 8-11.

654 _____. "Naval Construction in 1937. " Engineer, CLXV (January 7, 1938), 5-9.

655 _____. "Naval Construction in 1938 " Engineer,

CLXVII (January 6-13, 1939), 2-4, 45-47.

656 _____. "The Naval Outlook. " 19th Century, CXXI (January 1937), 116-128.

657 _____. "Navies Adrift. " Christian Science Monitor Magazine, (July 24, 1935), 1-2.

658 _____. Navies and Nations: A Review of Naval Developments Since the War. London: Constable, 1927. 285p.

659 _____. "Power in the Pacific. " Review of Reviews, XCIV (September 1936), 68. Japanese-American relations.

660 _____. Sea Power in the Pacific: A Study of the American-Japanese Naval Problem. Boston: Houghton, Mifflin, 1921. 334p. Rpr. 1973.

661 _____. "The Super-dreadnought as a Target. " SciAmer, CXXIV (May 21, 1921), 412.

662 _____. "Technical Elements Affecting Sea Power. " USNIP, L (1924), 115-118.

663 _____. "The Treaty Cruiser, is It Worth While?" SciAmer, CXXXV (November 1926), 326-328.

664 _____. "The Use of Airship in Time of War. " USNIP, XLIX (1923), 1053-1058. Reprinted from the April 13, 16-17, 1923 issues of the Baltimore Sun.

665 _____. "Value of the Battleship for Naval Defense." USNIP, L (1924), 2087-2092. Reprinted from the October 9-10, 1924 issues of the Baltimore Sun.

666 Cable, Frank T. The Birth and Development of the American Submarine. New York: Harper, 1924. 337p.

667 Cagle, Malcolm W. "Acey-deucy, a Navy Game. " USNIP, LXXVII (1951), 512-515.

668 _____. The Naval Aviation Guide. 2nd ed. Annap-

olis: U. S. Naval Institute, 1969. 415p.
Chapt. III: "History and Tradition of Naval
Aviation. "

669 Caidin, Martin. Golden Wings: A Pictorial History of
the United States Navy and Marine Corps in the Air.
New York: Random House, 1960. 232p.

670 Caidwell, E. S. "Riding the Navy's Thunderbolts. "
American Magazine, CXXXI (March 1941), 36-37.

671 Caldwell, Charles A. "Airplanes Can Sink Battleships!"
Aero Digest, XXX (June 1937), 28-30.

672 _____. "Airpower and Seapower Again. " Aero Digest, XXXIX (July 1941), 53-55+.

673 "California Man [Curtiss D. Wilbur] to Boss the Navy. "
Literary Digest, LXXX (March 29, 1924), 12-13.

674 Callender, Harold. "Our Vital Ditch: Mighty New Defenses of Panama. " New York Times Magazine,
(May 18, 1941), 8-9+.

675 Camden, B. H. "In Arctic Seas with the Coast Guard. "
Travel, XL (March 1923), 10-14.

676 Cameron, Theodore, "Suicide Boats. " Literary Digest,
CXXV (January 15, 1938), 14.
Motor Torpedo Boats.

677 "Camp Perry. " Leatherneck, XXIII (November 1940),
14-15.

678 Campbell, H. Denny. "Aviation in Guerrilla Warfare. "
Marine Corps Gazette, XV (May 1931), 35-42; XVI
(November 1931), 33-40.
As practiced in the various banana wars of the
1920s and early 1930s.

679 Campbell, John P. "Marines, Aviators, and the Battle-
ship Mentality, 1923-1933. " Journal of the Royal
United Service Institute, CIV (1964), 45-50.
Contains some data on the work of Admiral
Moffett.

680 "Can Naval Building Bring Prosperity?" Christian Cen-

tury, LV (March 9, 1938), 294-296.
Many now believe this answer was yes.

681   Canada.   National War Services.   Canada at War: A
      Summary of Canada's Part in the War.   Ottawa:
      Director of Public Information, 1941.   71p.
      Revised monthly.

682   Cant, Gilbert.   The War at Sea.   New York: John Day,
      1942.   340p.
      From September 1939 through Pearl Harbor.

683   "Capital Ships and Aircraft. "   Outlook, CXXX (January
      11, 1922), 60-63.

684   Capron, Walter C.   The U. S. Coast Guard.   New York:
      Franklin Watts, 1965.   218p.
      Provides in-depth treatment of the complex or-
      ganizational development of the service.

685   Carlson, Evans F.   "The Guardia Nacional de Nicara-
      gua. "   Marine Corps Gazette, XXI (August 1937),
      7-20.
      The organization and experiences of an outfit led
      by Marines which fought bandits under Sandino in
      Nicaragua, 1927.

686   Carlton, David.   "Great Britain [America] and the
      Coolidge Naval Disarmament Conference of 1927. "
      Political Science Quarterly, LXXXIII (1968), 573-
      598.
      That held at Geneva.

687   Carmichael, Andrew W.   Practical Ship Production.
      2nd ed.   New York: McGraw-Hill, 1941.   283p.
      Planned as an aid for men who must become
      shipyard workers without previous experience.

688   Carmody, Francis X.   "Our Lighter-than-Air Policy. "
      USNIP, LXVI (1940), 1586-1589.

689   Carney, J. Russell.   "Some Forgotten Naval History:
      The First Navy Day, 1922. "   USNIP, LXIX (1939),
      1441-1442.

690   Carney, Robert B.   "Damage Control. "   USNIP, LVI
      (1930), 623-625.

691 _____. "Gas Defense Afloat." USNIP, LVI (1930), 291-295.

692 _____. "Interior Control Board." USNIP, LVI (1930), 531-534.

693 _____. "Material Administration aboard Ship." USNIP, LXIV (1938) 963-968.

694 _____. "Selection, Security, and Morale." USNIP, LXI (1935), 814-817.

695 _____. "Staff Organization Afloat." USNIP, LXI (1930), 1113-1125.

696 _____. "Towing the Crane Ship." USNIP, LXIV (1938), 1776-1784.

697 Carpenter, William T. "The Influence of Aviaticn Upon Coast Defense." USNIP, LII (1926), 1417-1425.

697a "Carrier Tail Markings." Air Classics, IV (September 1967, February 1968), 40-46, 14-20.
On the distinctive markings painted on the aircraft belonging to different U. S. aircraft carriers. The article is well illustrated.

698 Carroll, Charles B. "Sea Duty for Voluntary Reserves." USNIP, LXIV (1938), 376-379.

699 Carse, Robert. Rum Row. New York: Rinehart, 1959. 251p.
The Coast Guard vs. the bootleggers during the Prohibition Era.

700 Carter, James. "Those Naval Maneuvers." New Republic, XLI (February 18, 1925), 338-349.

701 Carter, John. "The Economic Side of Sea Power." Commonweal, IX (April 24, 1929), 712-714.

702 _____. "Where do We go from Geneva?" Independent, CXIX (August 27, 1927), 198-200.
In the matter of naval disarmament.

703 Casey, Thomas J. "Again--the Engineering Competition." USNIP, LV (1929) 1023-1026.

704   _____. "Arms and the Man. " USNIP, LVI (1930),
        980-984.

705   _____. "The New Composition. " USNIP, LVI (1930),
        792-794.

706   Casey, Walter S. "Coastguarding the Detroit River. "
        Review of Reviews, LXXXI (February 1930), 86-87.

707   Cassidy, Edward J. "Conservation: King-Size. "
        Bureau of Ships Journal, I (May 1952), 2-9.
        The naval reserve fleet, 1939-1952.

708   Catton, Bruce. "The Marine Tradition. " American
        Heritage, X (February 1959), 24-35, 68-90.

709   Cave, Floyd A. The Origins and Consequences of
        World War II. New York: Dryden, 1948. 820p.
        The section on "origins" is useful.

710   "Censorship Changes: The Navy's Move. " Time,
        XXXVIII (September 29, 1941), 54.

711   Centner, Charles W. , Jr. "History of the U. S. Naval
        Operating Facility, Navy 120. " Unpublished Paper,
        Admin. Hist. Appen. 24, Operational Archives,
        U. S. Navy Department, Naval History Division,
        1945. 75p.
            Complete with appendices and photographs, the
        data concerns the activities at Recife, Brazil,
        which began in 1938 as a result of Nazi influence
        in the area.

712   Chadwick, Guy. "A Destroyer Engineering Department."
        USNIP, LVII (1931), 515-517.

713   Chaffee, Allen. Heroes of the Shoals. New York: Holt,
        1935. 196p.
        The Coast Guard.

714   "The Challenge to Sea Power. " Round Table, XXXI
        (June 1941), 450-456.

715   Chamberlain, J. "The Man Who Pushed Pearl Harbor."
        Life, XX (April 1 1946), 84-88.
        Admiral Yamamoto.

Chamberlin   61

716 Chamberlin, Waldo. "The Tradition of the Offensive in
     the U. S. Navy. " USNIP, LXVII (1941), 1375-1384.

717 Chamberlin, William H. Japan Over Asia. Rev. and
     enl. ed. Garden City, N. Y. : Blue Ribbon Books.
     1942. 463p.

718 _____. "Naval Bases in the Pacific. " Foreign
     Affairs, XV (April 1937), 484-494.

719 Chambers, E. T. R. "Naval Uses for Seaplanes and
     Flying Boats. " USNIP, LIV (1928), 414-417.

720 Chambliss, William C. "Air Bombardment Regulations."
     USNIP, LX (1934), 1577-1581.

721 Champie, Elmore A. A Brief History of the Marine
     Corps Recruit Depot, Parris Island, South Carolina,
     1891-1962. Marine Corps Historical Reference
     Series, no. 8. Rev. ed. Washington: Historical
     Branch, U. S. Marine Corps, 1962. 28p.

722 Chandler, C. deF. "Airships for Military Purposes. "
     U. S. Air Services, X (July 1925), 20-25.

723 Chandler, Charles D. and Walter S. Diehl. Balloon and
     Airship Gases. New York: Ronald Press, 1926.
     226p.

724 Chandler, Lloyd H. "Principles of Command. " USNIP,
     XLVIII (1922), 15-34, 233-250, 403-420.
         An abridged thesis prepared by the author in
     March 1920 when a student at the Naval War Col-
     lege.

725 Chandler, Theodore E. "American and British De-
     stroyers. " USNIP, LXVII (1922), 585-591.

726 Chaplin, Philip A. "The Reincarnation of the Four-
     Stackers. " USNIP, LXXXVI (1960), 95-103.
         Those given to Britain in the 1940 Destroyers-
     for-Bases arrangement.

727 _____. "Statistics of Submarine Warfare, 1939-
     1945. " USNIP, LXXXV (1959), 109-111.
         Our interest here is primarily in U. S.-German
     clashes late in 1941.

728 "Characteristics of the U. S. Navy Airship ZR-3. "
     Aviation, XIV (April 2, 1923), 366.

729 Charlton, Alexander M. "The Electrical Division
     Aboard Ship. " USNIP, XLV (1919), 987-1008.

730 _____. "Foundries on Our Men-of-War. " Foundry,
     LII (August 1, 1924), 584-588.

731 _____. "Ship Control on Modern Battleships. "
     Marine Engineering, XXVII (March 1922), 198-
     200+.

732 Chase, Henry. "The Navy's New Dirigible ZR-1 Com-
     pletes Trial Flight Successfully. " Automotive In-
     dustries, XLIX (September 6, 1923), 474-478.
     U. S. S. Shenandoah.

733 Chase, Jehu N. "Fleets: Their Composition and Use."
     USNIP, LVI (1930), 895-901.

734 Chatterton, Edward K. The Royal Navy, from Septem-
     ber 1939 to September 1945. 5 vols. London and
     New York: Hutchinson, 1942-1947.
         Vols. 4 & 5, by Kenneth Edwards, have the
     title: The Royal Navy and Allies. With some data
     relative to the late years covered in this compila-
     tion.

735 Cheatham, Joseph J. "Naval Methods of Supply. " Un-
     published Lecture, Files of the U. S. Army Military
     History Research Collection, 1931.
         Admiral Cheatham was Chief of the Bureau of
     Supplies and Accounts.

736 Cherry, Alexander H. Yankee R. N. : Being the Story
     of a Wall Street Banker Who Volunteered for Active
     Duty in the Royal Navy Before America Came Into
     the War. London: Jarrolds, 1951. 544p.

737 "Chief Constructor Selected to Take Office October 1:
     Emory S. Land. " Marine Review, LXII (October
     1932), 22.

738 Child, Richard W. "Disarmament and Our Navy. "
     Saturday Evening Post, CXCIX (April 16, 1927),
     14-15.

739 Chirol, Valentine, Herbert B. Elliston, and Archibald
     Hurd. "Anglo-American Relations and Sea Power."
     19th Century, CVI (November 1929), 577-606.

740 "Choppy Weather for Navy Boosters. " Literary Digest,
     LXXXVI (August 8, 1925), 12.

741 Christy, Joe, jt. author. See Shamburger, Page,
     no. 3601.

742 Churchill, Winston. "Japan Guesses Wrong. " Collier's,
     CII (July 30, 1938), 12-13+.

743 _____. "The U-boat Menace. " Liberty Magazine,
     (May 10, 1941), 15-18.

744 _____. "War Comes to America. " In: his The
     Grand Alliance. Vol. II of his The Second World
     War. Boston: Houghton, Mifflin, 1950. p. 377-
     713. Rpr. 1971.

745 "Civil Engineering and Construction in the United States
     Navy. " Engineering News, CX (March 23, 1933),
     368-371.

746 Clapp, Vernon O. "The Formation of Ice on Aircraft."
     USNIP, LVI (1930), 743-744.

747 Clark, A. W. "Air Cooperation with the Fleet. " USNIP,
     LIV (1928), 1011-1016.

748 Clark, Austin H. "The Navy's Oceanographic Program."
     Science, New Series LXI (March 13, 1925), 269-
     276.

749 Clark, Ellery H. , Jr. "Famous Swords at the U. S.
     Naval Academy. " USNIP, LXVI (1940), 1769-1772.

750 Clark, Francis E. "The Last Years of the Sailing
     Navy. " American Neptune, XX (March 1960), 134-
     145.
         Early 20th Century training, receiving, and sta-
     tion vessels and their operations.

751 Clark, Frank H. "Training of the U. S. Fleet for Its
     Most Probable Mission. " Unpublished Lecture,
     War Plans Course 7, Files of the U. S. Army Mili-

tary History Research Collection, 1931.
The author was a rear admiral.

752   Clark, George R.   "Here and There: Sketches from a
      Naval Officer's Notebook. " USNIP, LV (1929),
      1052-1056.

753   _____.   "This and That: Sketches from a Naval Offi-
      cer's Notebook. " USNIP, LVII (1931), 1205-1212.

754   Clark, V. E.   "Apparent Present Tendencies in Air-
      plane Design. " USNIP, LIII (1927), 808-813.

755   Clarke, Basil. History of Airships.   London: Jenkins,
      1961.   181p.

756   Clarke, Frank E.   "Half a Century of Progress in Naval
      Boiler Water Treatment, 1896-1955. " American
      Society of Naval Engineers Journal, LXVII (Feb-
      ruary 1955), 11-43.

757   Clarke, Reuben R.   "The Construction and Repair De-
      partment Afloat, Records of Work and the Hull
      Book. " USNIP, XLVI (1920), 1465-1475.

758   Clay, J. P.   "Pearl River Log: A Different Navy, A
      Different World. " USNIP, XCVI (1970), 58-67.
      Life on the Chinese river gunboats before World
      War II.

759   Cleary, F. J.   "The Navy and Foreign Trade. " Out-
      look, CXLVI (July 20, 1927), 376-377.

760   _____.   "The Relative Importance of Capital Ships
      and Aircraft. " Outlook, CXXIX (November 9,
      1921), 392-395.
      Capital ships rated far more important than
      planes.

761   Clifford, John G.   "The Odyssey of the City of Flint. "
      American Neptune, XXXII (April 1972), 100-116.
      Seized by the German pocket battleship Deutsch-
      land, October 9, 1939.

762   Clifford, Kenneth J. , ed.   The United States Marines
      in Iceland, 1941-1942.   Marine Corps Historical

Reference Pamphlets. Washington: Historical Division, U. S. Marine Corps, 1970. 22p.

763 Clifford, Nicholas R. "Britain, America, and the Far East, 1937-1940: A Failure in Cooperation. " Journal of British Studies, III (January 1968), 137-154.

764 Clizbe, Wilma. "Dances for Naval Trainees. " Recreation, XXXV (August 1941), 305-307.

765 Cluverius, Wat T. "Planting a War Garden. " USNIP, XLV (1919), 333-338.
In short, mining operations.

765a _____. Ralph Earle--Naval Officer and College President: A Newcomen Address. Princeton, N.J. : Princeton University Press, 1940. 20p.

766 _____. "To Youth in Uniform. " USNIP, LXIV (1938), 1601-1606.
Leadership development.

767 Coady, J. W. "F. D. R. 's Early Washington Years, 1913-1920. " Unpublished PhD Dissertation, St. John's University, 1968.
The future President was Assistant Secretary of the Navy under Woodrow Wilson.

768 Coakley, Robert W. , jt. author. See Leighton, Richard W. , no. 2156.

769 Coale, Griffith B. North Atlantic Patrol, the Log of a Seagoing Artist. New York: Farrar & Rinehart, 1942. 48p.
Highly illustrated story of life at a Newfoundland air base and aboard American destroyers in an Iceland convoy. Rough weather and submarine attacks, including the sinking of the Reuben James and rescue of her crew, provide the action.

770 "The Coast Guard Patrols the Sea Lanes. " Popular Science, CXXXVII (September 1940), 98.

771 Coffey, R. B. "A Brief History of the Intervention in Haiti. " USNIP, XLVIII (1922), 1324-1344.
From 1915 to the article's date.

772 Cohen, Lester, jt. author. See Gauvreau, Emile, no.
     1405.

773 Cole, A. P. "Destroyer Turning Circles. " Engineering,
     CXLV (April 22, 1938), 452-453.

774 Cole, Eli K. "Joint Overseas Operations. " USNIP, LV
     (1929), 927-942.
     Navy and Marines, pre-war thinking.

775 Cole, Wayne S. America First: The Battle Against In-
     tervention, 1940-1941. Madison: University of Wis-
     consin Press, 1953. 305p.
     The rush to naval preparedness was anathema to
     the America Firsters.

776 _____. "American Entry into World War II: A His-
     toriographical Appraisal. " Mississippi Valley His-
     torical Review, XLIII (October 1957), 595-617.

777 _____. Senator Gerald P. Nye and American Foreign
     Relations. Minneapolis: University of Minnesota
     Press, 1962. 293p.

778 Cole, William C. "Neutrality--Can It be Maintained by
     a World Power?" USNIP, LVIII (1932), 335-339.

779 Coleman, Charles H. "Shipbuilding Activities of the
     National Defense Advisory Commission and Office of
     Production Management: July 1940 to December
     1941. " Unpublished paper, Operational Archives,
     U. S. Navy Department, Naval History Division,
     1946. 148p.
     A study of the Commission's administration of
     the separate shipbuilding programs of the Navy and
     the Maritime Commission.

780 Colette, Paolo E. "Oceanography: Maury to Mohole. "
     USNIP, LXXXVI (1960), 98+.

781 Collier, James R. "Professionals: 1920-1940. " USNIP,
     XCIX (1973), 77-96.
     Abstracts of nine articles all of which are cited
     above and below with complete bibliographic data.

782 Collins, Elmer B. "Locating Surface Ships with Bubble
     Octant. " USNIP, LXVI (1940), 1138-1139.

783   Collins, Ross F.   "The Problems of a Reserve Battal-
      ion Commander. "   USNIP. LXV (1939), 539-541.

784   Colton, F. Barrows.   "Life in Our Fighting Fleet. "
      National Geographic Magazine, LXXIX (June 1941),
      671-702.

785   Colvin, F. H.   "The Naval Air Station at Pensacola. "
      American Machinist, LIII (July 29   1920), 197-199.

786   "Combat Operations in Nicaragua. "   Marine Corps
      Gazette, XIII (December 1928), 241-247.
          Subsequent reports appeared in the same journal
      for March, June, and September 1929.

787   "Coming, the ZR-3. "   Literary Digest, LXXXII (Sep-
      tember 20, 1924), 72-76.

788   Commager, Henry S.   "The Naval Base Trade and the
      Monroe Doctrine. "   Scholastic, XXXVII (September
      23, 1940), 7-10.

789   "The Commandant's House. "   Marine Corps Gazette,
      XXXVIII (May 1954), 32-39.

790   "Commander Byrd Receives the Hubbard Gold Medal. "
      National Geographic, L (September 1926), 377-388.

791   Commerce Clearing House.   The Conscription, Law and
      Regulation: Including Selective Training and Service
      Act of 1940, National Guard and Reserve Officers'
      Mobilization Act, Soldiers' and Sailors' Civil Relief
      Act of 1940.   Chicago, 1940.

792   "Comparative Cruiser Strength of the Five Great
      Powers. "   Literary Digest, CII (August 24, 1929),
      7.

793   "Comparative Naval Data for the Treaty Navies. "
      USNIP, LI (1925), 1954-1959.
          Correct as of September 1, 1925.

794   "Comparative Naval Strength of the Six World Powers. "
      Literary Digest, CXXV (February 12, 1938), 5.

795   "Comparative Naval Strengths. "   Foreign Affairs, VII
      (April 1929), 500-501.

796 "Comparison of Leading Navies. " Congressional Digest,
     VIII (October 1929), 239-240.

797 "Comparison of the U. S. and Japanese Navies. " Sci-
     Amer, CLXIV (March 1941), 148-149.

798 "Complete Text of the Naval Treaty of 1930. " USNIP,
     LVI (1930) , 560-565.

799 Compton, James V. The Swastika and the Eagle. Bos-
     ton: Houghton, Mifflin, 1967. 282p.
          U. S. -German relations from Munich to Pearl
     Harbor.

800 Compton, Lawrence. "Naval Policies and Development
     Since the World War. " Journal of the Franklin In-
     stitute, CCXXX (December 1940), 677-684.

801 Condit, Kenneth W. and Edwin T. Turnbladh. Hold
     High the Torch: A History of the 4th Marines.
     Washington: Historical Branch, U. S. Marine Corps.
     1960. 458p.

802 "Conditions in Nicaragua. " Marine Corps Gazette, XVII
     (November 1932), 88-93.

803 Cone, Hutchinson I. "Shipping for War Needs: Its Con-
     trols and Operation. " Unpublished Lecture, G-4
     Course 11, Files of the U. S. Army Military History
     Research Collection, 1928.

804 _____. "Shipping for War Needs: Its Control and
     Operation, the Merchant Marine. " Unpublished
     Lecture. G-4 Course 8, Files of the U. S. Army
     Military History Research Collection, 1929.
          The author was a Navy rear admiral.

805 "Congress and Our Naval Air Service. " SciAmer, CXXI
     (July 5, 1919), 4.

806 Congressional Record. Washington, 1874--.
          Within these volumes are much data on the Navy,
     including messages and reports by the President
     and Heads of Executive Departments, e. g., Navy
     Department.

806a Conn, Stetson. "Changing Concepts of National Defense

in the United States, 1937-1947. " Military Affairs,
XXVIII (Spring 1964), 1-7.

807 _____ and Byron Fairchild. The Framework of
Hemisphere Defense. U. S. Army in World War II:
The Western Hemisphere. Washington: Office of
the Chief of Military History, U. S. Army, 1960.
470p.

808 Connolly, James B. Navy Men. New York: John Day,
1939. 230p.

809 Conrad, Charles. "The Functions of the Bureau of
Supply and Accounts. " Unpublished Lectures, Files
of the U. S. Army Military History Research Collection, 1936 & 1937.
Two lectures by a Navy rear admiral.

810 Conrad, Robert D. "This Far Flung Navy. " USNIP,
LIII (1927), 674-679.

811 "The Consolidated XPB2Y-1: The Navy's Newest Big
[Flying] Boat. " Aviation, XXXVII (January 1938),
30-31.

812 "Construction Operations at the Naval Air Station, Pensacola. " Manufacturing Record, CI (June 2, 1932),
16-17.

813 "The Convoy System. " Popular Mechanics, LXXVI
(October 1941), 73-75.

814 "A Convoy to Iceland. " Newsweek, XVIII (September 1,
1941), 13-14.

815 "Convoys: Planes, Submarines and Raiders Make Their
Job Hard, but on Its Success Hangs the Fate of
Britain. " Life, X (June 16, 1941), 52-55.

816 Cook, Arthur B. "Aviation Activities of the United
States Navy. " Aero Digest, XXIX (December 1936),
16-20+.

817 _____. "Naval Aviation. " USNIP, LXII (1936),
1455-1458.

818 _____. "Naval Aviation and the Aircraft Industry. "

Unpublished Lecture, Files of the U.S. Army Military History Research Collection, 1938.
Another talk by a Navy rear admiral before his Army colleagues.

819 _____. "The Navy in 1936." Aviation, XXXVI (January 1937), 23+.
Refers to naval aviation.

820 Cook, Merlyn G. "The Proposal for an Independent Air Service." USNIP, LI (1925), 215-232.

821 Cook, Sterling S. "Efficacy of Typhoid Prophylaxis in the United States Navy." American Journal of Public Health, XXV (March 1935), 251-257.

822 Cooke, David C. War Wings: Fighting Planes of the American and British Air Forces. New York: McBride, 1941. 218p.
Fighters, bombers, flying boats, and training craft both army and navy. During the 1960s the author penned several aviation books too juvenile for inclusion here.

823 Cooney, David M. A Chronology of the U.S. Navy, 1775-1965. New York: Watts, 1965. 471p.

824 Coontz, Robert E. "Across the Continent with a Crazy Man." USNIP, XLVII (1921), 1749-1754.

825 _____. From the Mississippi to the Sea. Philadelphia: Dorrance, 1930. 485p.
Autobiography.

826 _____. "The Material Condition of the U.S. Fleet." Aviation, XVI (May 26, 1924), 571.

827 _____. "The Navy." USNIP, XLIX (1923), 747-757.
An address made over radio phone to the American Association Exposition at New York on November 9, 1922.

828 _____. "The Navy and Business." USNIP, XLVIII (1922), 987-1004.

829 _____. "The Navy as a Protective Investment." Current History, XVII (December 1922), 403-410.

830 _____. True Anecdotes of an Admiral. Philadelphia: Dorrance, 1935. 128p.

831 _____. "Why the United States Must Have an Adequate Navy." American Industries, XXII (June
1922), 16-17.

832 Cooper, Morris. "The Future of the Submarine in International Law." USNIP, XLVIII (1922), 337-346.

833 Cooper, Walter. "For the Coast Guard." Outlook,
CLIV (January 29, 1930), 169-171.

834 _____. "The Navy and the Next War: Why We Must
Go Down to the Bottom in Submarines." Independent, CXIV (June 6, 1925), 639-640.

835 Corbett, Charles H. "Growing Navies and Dwindling
Merchant Marine." Christian Century, LI (December 5, 1934), 1546-1548.

836 Corbett, Scott. The Sea Fox: The Adventures of Cape
Cod's Most Colorful Rumrunner. New York:
Crowell, 1956. 244p.
The author's autobiography.

837 Corey, Herbert. "Across the Equator with the American Navy." National Geographic, XXXIX (June
1921), 571-624.

838 _____. "America's Need of Sea Power." Current
History, XLI (December 1934), 264-272.

839 _____. _____. Far Eastern Review, XXXI (February 1935), 41-44.

840 _____. "The Coast Guard, a Business Man's Navy."
Nation's Business, XXVI (January 1938), 30-32+.

841 _____. "The Long Road to Preparedness: Items
Needed to Put the Army and Navy in Fighting
Trim." Nation's Business, XXVIII (July 1940), 15-
17+.

842 "Correspondence Concerning the Defense of Iceland by
United States Forces: Text of Message from the
President to the Congress, July 7, 1941, and Cor-

respondence with the Prime Minister of Iceland. "
American Journal of International Law, XXXV (October 1941), Supplement, 194-198.

843   "The Cost of the New Three-Year Naval Program. "
SciAmer, CXX (March 1, 1919), 204-205.

844   Coster, H. M.   "The Navy's Sulphuric Acid Plant. "
USNIP, LVII (1931), 317-319.

845   Cotten, Lyman A.   "Commerce Destroying in War. "
USNIP, XLV (1919), 1495-1516.
Principally a discussion of submarine operations.

846   _____.   "Unrestricted Commerce Destroying. " USNIP,
XLV (1919), 1517-1527.

847   Cottle, George F.   "The Turnover of Personnel. "
USNIP, LXV (1939), 379-382.

848   Courtney, W. B.   "Lighter than Air: ZRS-4, the U. S. S.
Akron. "   Collier's, LXXXVII (June 20, 1931), 17-
21.

849   _____.   "Navy Wings. "   Collier's, XCIX (June 12,
1937), 12-13+.
The Pensacola Naval Air Station and its training
of navy pilots.

850   Cowburn, Philip.   The Warship in History.   New York:
Macmillan, 1965.   364p.
Contains some useful chapters on our period.

851   Cox, Isaac J.   Nicaragua and the United States, 1909-
1927.   Boston, 1927.   887p.

852   Cox, Leonard M.   "The War on War. "   USNIP, LVII
(1931), 599-605.

853   Cox, Ormond L.   "The Problem of the Naval Design
Engineer as Affected by the Limitation of Armament
Treaty. "   USNIP, LIV (1928), 875-878.

854   _____   and Miles A. Libbey.   Naval Turbines.
Annapolis: U. S. Naval Institute, 1924.   241p. Rpr.
1931.

855 Cracknell, William H. U. S. S. Tennessee (BB-43). War-
     ship Profile Series, no. 2⁻. London: Ian Allen,
     1972. 136p.

856 Cragie, Robert. Behind the Japanese Mask. London:
     Hutchinson, 1945.
         Memoirs of the British ambassador to Japan con-
     cerning the road to Pearl Harbor. For the record,
     it might be noted here that unlike America, the
     United Kingdom did not receive a "note" and Japa-
     nese forces were pushing into Malaya hours before
     the Pearl Harbor attack.

857 Craig, Paul M. "Lexington and Saratoga, the Begin-
     ning. " USNIP, XCV (1969), 85-92.

858 Craige, John H. What the Citizen Should Know About
     the Marines. New York: Norton, 1941. 211p.

859 Cramer, Floyd. Our Neighbor Nicaragua. New York:
     Frederick A. Stokes, 1929.

860 Crane, John D. M. C. and James F. Kieley. The United
     States Naval Academy: The First Hundred Years.
     New York: McGraw-Hill, 1945. 58p.

861 Cranwell, John P. The Destiny of Sea Power and Its
     Influence on Land Power and Air Power. New
     York: Norton, 1941. 262p.
         A study of strategy and of the relations of naval
     tactics to aerial and land fighting. Warships have
     not been superseded, believes the author, but air-
     planes grow more important and all forces must be
     integrated.

862 Craven, Francis S. "Excellence of Naval Material. "
     USNIP, LI (1925), 1573-1631.

863 _____. "We Must Have It. " USNIP, XLIX (1923),
     949-955.

864 Craven, Thomas T. "Appropriation for Naval Aviation."
     Aerial Age, XII (February 7, 1921), 562-564.

865 _____. "Appropriations for Naval Aviation: State-
     ment of Capt. T. T. Craven, Director of Naval Avi-
     ation, Before the Naval Affairs Committee. " USNIP,

XLVII (1921), 612-618.
Reprinted from the February 7, 1921 issue of
Aerial Age.

866 _____. "Director of Naval Aviation, 1919-1921."
Unpublished paper, Subject File 1911-1927, ZGP,
Box 780, National Archives, 1922.   25p.
A short autobiography presenting a personal view
on an important early period in the development of
naval aviation.

867 _____. "Naval Air Service Independence." Aviation,
X (March 7, 1921), 304-305.

868 _____. "Naval Aviation." USNIP, XLVI (1920),
181-191.

869 _____. "Naval Aviation and a United Air Service."
Flying, X (April 1921), 96-100.

870 _____. _____. USNIP, XLVII (1921), 307-321.

871 _____. "Our Navy's Air Service." Review of Reviews, LXII (October 1920), 399-404.

872 _____. "Points to be Observed in the Advancement
of Naval Aviation." USNIP, L (1924), 1233-1248.

873 _____. "Recollections." USNIP, LXXIX (1953),
292-301.

874 Crawford, Rensen. "Three Men from Maryland." Outlook, CXLIII (August 4, 1926), 469.
The Coast Guard and Prohibition enforcement.

875 Crew, William H.   "An Academician in the Naval Pro-
fession." USNIP, LVIII (1932), 1110-1115.

876 Crivelli, Albert F. Shipfitter's Manual.   New York:
Pitman, 1941.   145p.

877 Croizat, Victor J.   "The Development of MCS." Marine
Corps Gazette, XXXVIII (September 1954), 36-43.
Emphasis on the Marine Corps Schools opened
at Quantico, Virginia, in 1922.

878 _____. "The Marine's Amphibian." Marine Corps

Gazette, XXXVII (June 1953), 40-49.
The use of the amtrack. 1924-1953.

879 Cronon, E. David, ed. See Daniels, Josephus, no. 911.

880 Cross, Wilber. Challengers of the Deep: The Story of
     Submarines. New York: W. Sloane, 1959. 258p.

881 Crosser, Robert. "Shall We Have a Naval Boundary?"
     Vital Speeches, IV (June 1, 1938), 501-502.

882 Crowell, David C. "Agriculture and the Navy." USNIP,
     LII (1926), 2067-2070.
        Reprinted from the Congregationalist of April
     29, 1926.

883 Crowl, Philip A. "Education Versus Training at the
     Naval War College: 1884-1972." Naval War Col-
     lege Review, XXVI (November-December 1973),
     2-11.

884 "The Cruiser Bill and the Freedom of the Seas." Com-
     mercial and Financial Chronicle, CXXVIII (Febru-
     ary 9, 1929), 783-784.

885 "Cruiser Louisville Launched at Puget Sound." Marine
     Review, LX (October 1930), 39.
        CA-28 scrapped 30 years later.

886 "Cruiser-Naval Base Deal Between the United States and
     Great Britain: Text of the Diplomatic Papers."
     Congressional Digest, XX (January 1941), 15-17.
        Destroyers, not cruisers, were swapped for the
     naval bases.

887 "Cruiser Victory That May Aid Disarmament." Literary
     Digest, C (February 16, 1929), 5-8.

888 "Cruisers, 1882-1958." In: U. S. Navy Department.
     Naval History Division. Dictionary of American
     Naval Fighting Ships. Washington: U. S. Govern-
     ment Printing Office, 1959--. I, 203-222.

889 Crumble, Frank, Jr. "Stirring Events on Voodoo
     Isle." In: Clyde H. Metcalf, ed. The Marine
     Corps Reader. New York: G. P. Putnam's, 1944.
     p. 46-56.

Marine activities on Haiti as recalled in a 1943
issue of Leatherneck.

890 Cuff, Samuel H. The Face of the War, 1931-1942.
New York: Messner, 1942. 290p.
A reference work, based on details then avail-
able, of the road to Pearl Harbor.

891 Cullen, Charles W. "From the Kriegsacademie to the
Naval War College: The Military Planning Process." Naval War College Review, XXII (January
1970), 6-18.

892 Cummings, Damon E. "Aviation or Naval Aviation:
Which?" USNIP, XLVI (1920), 177-180.

893 _____. "A Director Looks at the Naval Reserve."
USNIP, LXV (1939), 508-512.

894 _____. "Enlisted Training in the Navy." USNIP,
LV (1929), 878-886.

895 _____. "Use of Aircraft in Naval Warfare." USNIP,
XLVII (1921), 1677-1688.

896 Cummins, Lejeune. Quijote on a Burro: Sandino and
the Marines. Mexico City, Mexico, 1958. 207p.
Battles in Nicaragua in the late 1920s.

897 Cunningham, John C. "The Navy's Part in the Fur
Seal Industry." USNIP, LXII (1936), 236-240.
Mainly patrolling the hunting grounds.

898 Curran, Frederick M., Jr. "Midshipman, U.S. Naval
Reserve." USNIP, LXVI (1941), 1741-1749.

899 _____. "A Naval Reservist's Impressions of a
Shakedown Cruise." USNIP, LXV (1939), 563-566.

900 Current, Richard N. Secretary Stimson: A Study in
Statecraft. New Brunswick, N.J.: Rutgers University Press, 1954. 272p. Rpr. 1970.

901 "Current Opinion: Views Pro and Con on the Budget
Plan for More Warships and Less Relief." Literary Digest, CXXV (January 22, 1938), 3.

902 "Curtiss Builds New Navy Fighter. " Aviation, XXII
     (March 14, 1927), 514-515.

903 "The Curtiss Navy Command Helldiver. " Aero Digest,
     XVII (December 1930), 60.

904 "Curtiss Navy Dive Bomber Built for Shipboard Opera-
     tion. " Aviation, XL (April 1941), 67.

905 Custer, Benjamin S. "The Geneva Conference for the
     Limitation of Naval Armaments--1927. " Unpub-
     lished PhD Dissertation, Georgetown University,
     1948.

906 _____. "Naval Aviation and the Numbers Racket. "
     USNIP, LXIV (1938), 714-716.

907 Dacy, George F. "Marvelous Mechanical Bird, the
     Shenandoah. " St. Nicholas Magazine, LI (January
     1924), 314-315.

908 Daniels, Jonathan. The Time Between the Wars.
     Mainstream of America Series. Garden City, N.Y.
     Doubleday, 1966. 372p.

909 Daniels, Josephus. "Above All, Patriotism !" Foru
     LXIII (March 1920), 298-306.

910 _____. "Building the World's Most Powerful W
     ships. " Saturday Evening Post, CXCIII (Ma
     1921), 21-24.

911 _____. The Cabinet Diaries of Josephus D
     1913-1921. Edited by E. David Cronon
     University of Nebraska Press, 1973.

912 _____. "The Message of the Pacific
     set, XLIII (September 1919), 14-15

913 _____. "Native at Large: The Ne
     Press Relationship for the Arm
     tion, CLII (January 4, 1941),
     The author was Navy Secr
     Wilson.

     _____. "A Navy That Flie
     Post, CXCII (April 23,

915   _____. "The Navy's Future." Independent, CI (January 10, 1920), 51-52.

916   _____. "Secretary Daniels on Aeronautics." Aviation, IX (December 13, 1920), 414-416.
An excerpt from his annual report.

917   _____. "Training Men for the Navy and the Nation." Saturday Evening Post, CXCIII (April 9, 1921), 21-24.

918   _____. "Why the United States Needs a Big Navy." Saturday Evening Post, CXCIII (March 19, 1921), 8-10.

919   _____. "Why We Need a Great Navy." Independent, XCVII (January 25, 1919), 116.

_____. The Wilson Era: Years of War and After, 1917-1923. Chapel Hill: University of North Carolina Press, 1946. 654p.
The last of four volumes of autobiography during ⁓h the author finished out his term as Navy ⁓ary. Filled with personal commentary on ⁓nd minor matters and judgments on public ⁓ncluding Admiral Sims.

. "Indoctrinating Civilians in Matters of ⁓efense." USNIP, L (1924), 1854-1858.
⁓ussion included.

⁓rry G. "The U. S. Naval Medical School." ⁓urgeon, LXXX (1937), 53-60.

"History of the Port Director (NTS), ⁓ornia." Unpublished paper, Shore ⁓ Operational Archives, U. S. ⁓val History Division, 1945.

⁓nces from September

Jones: Submarines ⁓XXXI (February

⁓ew Flotill⁓

Curtiss 77

902 "Curtiss Builds New Navy Fighter. " Aviation, XXII
(March 14, 1927), 514-515.

903 "The Curtiss Navy Command Helldiver. " Aero Digest,
XVII (December 1930), 60.

904 "Curtiss Navy Dive Bomber Built for Shipboard Operation. " Aviation, XL (April 1941), 67.

905 Custer, Benjamin S. "The Geneva Conference for the
Limitation of Naval Armaments--1927. " Unpublished PhD Dissertation, Georgetown University,
1948.

906 _____. "Naval Aviation and the Numbers Racket. "
USNIP, LXIV (1938), 714-716.

907 Dacy, George H. "Marvelous Mechanical Bird, the
Shenandoah. " St. Nicholas Magazine, LI (January
1924), 314-315.

908 Daniels, Jonathan. The Time Between the Wars.
Mainstream of America Series. Garden City, N.Y.:
Doubleday, 1966. 372p.

909 Daniels, Josephus. "Above All, Patriotism !" Forum,
LXIII (March 1920), 298-306.

910 _____. "Building the World's Most Powerful Warships. " Saturday Evening Post, CXCIII (March 26,
1921), 21-24.

911 _____. The Cabinet Diaries of Josephus Daniels,
1913-1921. Edited by E. David Cronon. Lincoln:
University of Nebraska Press, 1973. 648p.

912 _____. "The Message of the Pacific Fleet. " Sunset, XLIII (September 1919), 14-15.

913 _____. "Native at Large: The Need for Intelligent
Press Relationship for the Army and Navy. " Na-
tion, CLII (January 4, 1941), 21.
The author was Navy Secretary under President
Wilson.

914 _____. "A Navy That Flies. " Saturday Evening
Post, CXCIII (April 23, 1921), 16-17.

915 _____. "The Navy's Future. " Independent, CI
(January 10, 1920), 51-52.

916 _____. "Secretary Daniels on Aeronautics. " Aviation, IX (December 13, 1920), 414-416.
An excerpt from his annual report.

917 _____. "Training Men for the Navy and the Nation."
Saturday Evening Post, CXCIII (April 9, 1921), 21-
24.

918 _____. "Why the United States Needs a Big Navy. "
Saturday Evening Post, CXCIII (March 19, 1921),
8-10.

919 _____. "Why We Need a Great Navy. " Independent,
XCVII (January 25, 1919), 116.

920 _____. The Wilson Era: Years of War and After,
1917-1923. Chapel Hill: University of North Carolina Press, 1946. 654p.
The last of four volumes of autobiography during
which the author finished out his term as Navy
Secretary. Filled with personal commentary on
major and minor matters and judgments on public
figures, including Admiral Sims.

921 Daniels, R. E. "Indoctrinating Civilians in Matters of
Naval Defense. " USNIP, L (1924), 1854-1858.
Discussion included.

922 Danilson, Harry G. "The U. S. Naval Medical School. "
Military Surgeon, LXXX (1937), 53-60.

923 Dashiell, G. W. D. "History of the Port Director (NTS),
San Pedro, California. " Unpublished paper, Shore
Establishment File, Operational Archives, U. S.
Navy Department, Naval History Division, 1945.
38p.
The author's reminiscences from September
1940 through October 1945.

924 Davenport, Walter. "Safe with Davy Jones: Submarines
and Safety Devices. " Collier's, LXXXI (February
18, 1928), 8-9.

925 _____. "Suicide Squadron: The New Flotilla of

Fighting Speedboats. " Collier's, CV (March 16, 1940), 13-15.
PT boats.

926 David, Evan J. Our Coast Guard: High Adventure with the Watchers of Our Shores. New York: D. Appleton, 1937. 298p.

927 Davidonis, Anthony C. J. The American Naval Mission to the Adriatic, 1918-1921. Administrative Reference Service Report, no. 4. Washington: Administrative Office, Navy Department 1943. 99p.

928 Davidson, Louis. United States Destroyers Waterline Shipmodelers Planbook, Series 1. Pensacola, Fla., 1968. 16p.

929 Davies, H. L. "Iceland: Key to the North Atlantic. " Journal of the Royal United Service Institute, CI (1956), 230-234.

930 Davis, Burke. The Billy Mitchell Affair. New York: Random House, 1967. 373p.

931 _____. Marine! The Life of Chesty Puller. Boston: Little, Brown, 1962. 403p.

932 Davis, Edward J. P. Historical San Diego. San Diego, Calif., 1953.

933 _____. The United States Navy and U. S. Marine Corps at San Diego. San Diego, Calif., 1955.

934 Davis, Ernest J. "Endurance Swimming. " USNIP, LXV (1939), 819-823.

935 Davis, Forrest. The Atlantic System: The Story of Anglo-American Control of the Seas. New York: Reynal & Hitchcock, 1941. 363p. Rpr. 1973.
A journalistic follower of Mahan proposes closer naval cooperation with Britain, naval preparedness, and an end to isolationism.

936 _____ and Ernest K. Lindley. How War Came, an American White Paper, from the Fall of France to Pearl Harbor. New York: Simon & Schuster, 1942. 342p.

Based on the few official reports then available,
the volume contains information on the destroyer-
bases deal, the Atlantic Charter, and negotiations
with South America, Russia, and Japan. A con-
densed version appeared in the Ladies' Home
Journal in 1942.

937   Davis, George T.   "Big Navy for What?"   Nation, CL
(May 4, 1940), 560-562.

938   _____.   A Navy Second to None: The Development of
Modern American Naval Policy.   New York: Harcourt, Brace, 1940.   508p.   Rpr. 1972.

939   Davis, Harold P.   Black Democracy: The Story of
Haiti.   Rev. ed.   New York: McBeagh, 1936.
360p.   Rpr. 1972.
Considerable data on the American intervention
and occupation.

940   Davis, Henry C.   "Military Government for a Latin-
American Country in the Light of Our Santo Domingo Experience."   Unpublished Lecture, Files
of the U. S. Army Military History Research Collection, 1924.

941   Davis, Henry F. D.   "The Effect of an Order to Increase Speed."   USNIP, LVII (1937), 757-760.
In the various sections of the particular vessel
involved.

942   _____.   "What is the Matter with Operating Engineering?"   USNIP, XLVI (1920), 1431-1436.

943   Davis, John W.   "Anglo-American Relations and Sea
Power."   Foreign Affairs, VII (April 1929), 345-
355.

944   Davis, Norman H.   "New Naval Agreement."   Foreign
Affairs, XIV (July 1936), 578-583.

945   Davis, Robert G.   "Aviation Medicine and Its Application to the Naval Service."   USNIP, LII (1926),
2011-2019.

946   _____.   "Some Physical Aspects of Flying."   USNIP,
LI (1925), 1225-1230.

947 Davis, Saville R. "Colonizing the Sixth Continent:
     Admiral Byrd Heads South in October to Stake
     United States Claims. " Christian Science Monitor
     Magazine, (July 29, 1939), 1, 3-6.

948 Davis, W. Jefferson. Japan, The Air Menace of the
     Pacific. New York: Arno, 1973.
         A reprinting of the 1928 first edition in which
     the author forecasts war between the Empire and
     America and begs for an up-to-date air force.

949 Davis, William S. G. "ABCs of the Naval Reserve. "
     USNIP, LXV (1939), 470-472.

950 _____. "Calling Your Shots of Sun and Stars. "
     USNIP, LIX (1933), 1463-1465.

951 _____. "How About the Naval Reserve?" USNIP,
     LXVI (1940), 352-360.

952 _____. "If a Modern Lexington, Why an Obsolete
     Patoka?" USNIP, LVII (1931), 1069-1070.
         Refers to the airship base Patoka, which handled
     among others the huge Shenandoah.

953 _____. "Radio Direction Finder, the Navigator's
     Friend. " USNIP, LVII (1931), 518-519.

954 Davison, Louis. United States Aircraft Carriers. Pen-
     sacola, Fla., 1971. 32p.
         From the days of the Langley.

955 Davison, Ralph E. "The Salvage of the U. S. S. Alle-
     gheny. " USNIP, XLIX (1923), 631-642.

956 _____. "The Training of Naval Aviators. " USNIP,
     XLVIII (1922), 1501-1505.

957 Day, Harry E. "Aviation and the Naval Educational
     System. " USNIP, LXV (1939), 57-62.

958 "Dead Dogfish: The Squalus Disaster and Rescue Appa-
     ratus. " Time, XXXIII (June 5, 1939), 18-19.
         Foundered on trials in May 1939, salvaged in
     1940, and renamed Sailfish.

959 Dear, Wilfred P. "America's Undeclared Naval War. "

USNIP, LXXXVII (1961), 70-79.
1940-1941 in the Atlantic.

960 "The Debate on Big Navy Plans. " Newsweek, XI (February 28, 1938), 14.

961 DeBoe, David C. "The United States and the Geneva Disarmament Conference, 1932-1934. " Unpublished PhD Dissertation, Tulane University, 1969.

962 DeBooy, H. Theodore. "The Naval Arm of Diplomacy in the Pacific. " Pacific Affairs, VIII (1935), 5-20.

963 _____. _____. Far Eastern Review, XXXI (1935), 201-204.

964 "A Decade of Grumman Progress. " Aero Digest, XXXVI (January 1940), 48-49, 52+.
Refers to the company's activities in turning out Navy fighter craft.

965 "Decision in the Pacific. " New Republic, LXXXI (January 9, 1935), 335.

965a _____. "Reply by J. D. Lewis. " New Republic, LXXXI (January 30, 1935), 335.

966 DeConde, Alexander. Herbert Hoover's Latin-American Policy. Stanford Books in World Politics. Palo Alto, Calif.: Stanford University Press, 1951. 154p. Rpr. 1970.

967 "Deep-Sea Cruise Trains Reserve Officers for the Navy. " Life, IX (August 12, 1940), 27-29.

968 Deese, Rupert R. "The Anti-Aircraft Machine Gun. " Marine Corps Gazette, XX (February 1936), 15, 39.

969 "Defense of the Hemisphere Eased by Action to Butress the Canal. " Newsweek, XVI (December 16, 1940), 32.

970 "A Defensive Sea Force Second to None is the Navy's Aim: Building of 32 New Ships to Mark First Step in Bringing the Fleet to the Limits Imposed by the Treaties. " US News (July 15-22, 1938), 8.

971 Del Valle, Pedro A. "Marine Corps Artillery." Marine
     Corps Gazette, V (December 1920), 353-355.

972 De M. C. Crane, John. The United States Marines.
     Baton Rouge, La.: Army & Navy Publishing Co.,
     1952. 72p.
     A pictorial history offered under the auspices of
     the Marine Corps War Memorial Foundation.

973 Demme, Robert E. "Evolution of the Hellcat." In:
     William H. Fetridge, ed. The Second Navy Reader.
     Indianapolis: Bobbs-Merrill, 1944. p. 193-203.
     Traces the story of the F6F from 1929.

974 "Democracies' Net Around Japan: U. S. and British
     Bases." Illustrated London News, CXCIX (October
     25, 1941), 533.

975 "Demosthenes and Hiram Johnson Advocate a Bigger
     and Better Navy." Golden Book, XX (October
     1934), 438-440.

976 Denby, Edward. "Fleet Aviation." Aerial Age, XVI
     (March 1923), 107-109.

977 Denlinger, Sutherland and Charles B. Gary. War in
     the Pacific: A Study of Navies, Peoples, and Battle
     Problems. New York: McBride, 1936. 338p.
     Rpr. 1970.

978 "Denmark-United States Agreement Relating to the De-
     fense of Greenland and Exchange of Notes, Signed
     at Washington, April 9, 1941: Text." American
     Journal of International Law, XXXV (July 1941),
     Supplement, 129-134.

979 _____. American Scandinavian Review, XXIX (July
     1941), 155-158.

980 Dennett, Tyler. "Why Bother About Japan." Current
     History, XLIII (February 1936), 467-472.

981 DeNogales, Rafael. The Looting of Nicaragua. New
     York: McBride, 1928. 304p. Rpr. 1970.

982 "The Departments [of the Naval Academy]." USNIP,
     LXI (1935), 1414-1440.

983 "Deplorable Cut in Naval Personnel. " SciAmer, CXLIII
     (December 1930), 429.

984 De Seversky, Alexander P.   "The Twilight of Sea
     Power. " American Mercury, LII (June 1941), 647-
     658.

985 "Design of the Navy's Great Airship ZR-1 Approved. "
     Aerial Age, XVI (January 1923), 36.

986 "The Destroyer Hammann Typifies New Power Era. "
     SciAmer, CLXI (September 1939), 157.

987 "The Destroyer: The Navy's Favorite Ship. " Life, X
     (February 24, 1941), 39-42.
     Illustrated.

988 "Destroyer vs. Submarine. " Popular Mechanics,
     LXXIII (March 1940), 347-351.

989 "Destroyers for Bases: The U. S. Trades 50 Old War-
     ships for Control of the North Atlantic. " Life, IX
     (September 16, 1940), 19-23.

990 "Destroyers in the U. S. Navy. " USNIP, LXXII (1951),
     976-987.

991 DeTreville, Davis.   "The Construction and Repair De-
     partment of a Battleship. " USNIP, LV (1929), 965-
     973.

992 "Development of the American Submarine. " SciAmer,
     CXXXI (November 1924), 320-321.

993 "The Development of the Mine-Laying Cruiser. " Engi-
     neering CXXII (December 24, 1926), 790-791.

994 "The Development of the NC Seaplanes. " Aviation, VI
     (June 1, 1919), 468-474.

995 "The Development of U. S Naval Aviation. " Aviation,
     VII (December 15, 1919), 424-428.

996 Devine, David A.   Uncle Sam's Trouble Shooters. Los
     Angeles: De Vorss, 1940.   36p.
     The Coast Guard.

997   Dewar, Kenneth G. B.   "The Naval Conference of
       1930. " 19th Century, CVII (March, May 1930),
       285-299, 606-619.

998   DeWeerd, H. A.   "Blockade--Ultimate Weapon of Sea
       Power. " USNIP, LIX (1933), 1141-1149, 1780-
       1782.

999   DeWeese, Wade.   "The Ninetieth Anniversary [Naval
       Academy] Class Ring Collection. " USNIP, LXII
       (1936), 514-518.

1000   "Dick Byrd as a Mercury of Modern Flying Science. "
       Literary Digest, XCIV (July 23, 1927), 34-42.

1001   Dickson, Belle L.   "The Choosing of Byrd's Crew. "
       Hygeia, XV (March 1937), 269-270.

1001a Diebold, William, Jr.   "The Wartime Use of Shipping."
       Foreign Affairs, XIX (July 1941), 751-763.

1002   Diehl, Walter S.   A Study of the Effect of a Diving
       Start on Airplane Speed.   U. S. National Advisory
       Committee for Aeronautics Report, no. 228.
       Washington: Government Printing Office, 1925. 9p.

1003   _____ .   Three Methods of Calculating Range and
       Endurance of Airplanes.   U. S. National Advisory
       Committee for Aeronautics Report, no. 234.
       Washington: Government Printing Office, 1926.
       18p.

1004   _____ ., jt. author.   See Chandler, Charles D. ,
       no. 723.

1005   "Diesel Propulsion for Warships. " Marine Engineer-
       ing, XXXVII (March 1932), 127-128.

1006   Dieter, H. B.   "Armor, Speed and Freeboard in Battle-
       ships. " SciAmer, CXXII (March 27, 1920), 333.

1007   "The Dilemma of Sea Power. " New Republic, LI
       (July 20, 1927), 213-215.

1008   Dillingham, Albert C.   "Our Divided Personnel. "
       USNIP, XLVI (1920), 1921-1924.

1009 Dillingham, Walter F.   "Pearl Harbor. "   USNIP, LVI
      (1930), 403-410.

1010 Dimick, Chester A.   "Coast Guard Academy Formally
      Dedicated. "   U. S. Coast Guard Magazine, VI
      (June 1933), 4.

1011 Dinger, Henry C.   "The Inspection of Naval Material."
      American Machinist, LXVII (July 14, 1927), 59-
      60.

1012 _____.   "Our Post-War Navy: Maintaining the Fleet
      on the Treaty Basis. "   SciAmer, CXXXI (Novem-
      ber 1924), 314-315.

1013 Diogenes, pseud.   "The Threat of Hostilities Aboard
      Brings Isolationists to the Fore as the President
      Weights British Reaction to a Naval Program
      Calling for 10, 000 Ton, Six-Inch-Gun Cruisers. "
      Literary Digest, CXVI (January 6, 1934), 11.

1014 DiPalma, Louis.   "A Plea for the Merchant Marine
      Naval Reserve. "   USNIP, LXIII (1937), 477-479.

1015 _____.   "Training the Merchant Marine Naval Re-
      serve. "   USNIP, LXIII (1937), 1760-1761.

1016 "Disaster to One of Our Latest Submarines: How an
      Air Valve, Left Open, Caused the S-5 to Plunge
      to the Bottom. "   SciAmer, CXXIII (September 25,
      1920), 298+.

1017 "Disaster to the [Airship] Shenandoah. "   Science, New
      Series LXII (September 11, 1924), 14.

1018 "Disciplining [Thomas P.] Magruder. "   Outlook,
      CXLVII (November 9, 1927), 304.

1019 _____. _____.   Literary Digest, XCV (Novem-
      ber 5, 1927), 9.

1020 "A Disgraceful Naval Bill. "   Nation, CXII (June 15,
      1921), 836.

1021 "Disney Designs Army and Navy Insignia. "   Life, X
      (May 26, 1941), 10-13.

1022 Disraeli, Robert. "The Treasury's Navy. " In: his
      Uncle Sam's Treasury. Boston: Little, Brown,
      1941. p. 114-119.
      The Coast Guard.

1023 "Dividing the Fighting Fleet. " World's Work, XXXVIII
      (September 1919), 461-462.

1024 Divine, Robert A. The Reluctant Belligerent: Ameri-
      can Entry into World War II. America in Crisis.
      New York: Wiley, 1965. 172p.

1025 _____. Roosevelt and World War II. Baltimore:
      Johns Hopkins University Press, 1969. 107p.
      The role of the President in the road to Pearl
      Harbor.

1026 Dixon, Benjamin F. Seeing the World Through a Port-
      hole: the Cruise of the U.S.S. Asheville. Hong-
      kong, China: The Newspaper Enterprise, 1923.
      81p.

1027 "Do We Need the Largest Navy in the World?" Sci-
      Amer, CXXII (March 13, 1920), 268.
      Yes, answer the editors.

1028 Dodds, Harold W. "American Supervision of the Nica-
      raguan Election. " Foreign Affairs, VII (April
      1929), 488-496.

1029 "Dollars and Ships at London. " Nation, CXXX (Janu-
      ary 29, 1930), 122-123.

1030 Domville, Barry. "The Strategical Realities of the
      Pacific. " Fortnightly, CXLIX (April 1938), 438-
      444.

1031 Domville-Fife, Charles W. Submarines and Seapower.
      Philadelphia: Lippincott, 1919. 250p.

1032 _____, ed. Evolution of Sea Power: Studies of
      Modern Naval Warfare and the Effect of Evolution
      on the Basis and Employment of Sea Power.
      London: Rich & Cowan, 1939. 258p.

1033 Donald, Harry G. "Operation of a Destroyer at Full
      Power. " USNIP, LI (1925), 15-27.

1034 Donitz, Karl. <u>Memoirs: Ten Years and Twenty Days.</u>
      Translated by R. H. Stevens, in collaboration with
      David Woodward. London: Weidenfeld and Nicol-
      son, 1959. 500p. Rpr.
      The English edition of the U-boat commander's
      <u>Zehn Jahre und Zwanzig Tage.</u> Contains some
      data relative to this compilation.

1035 "Don't Scuttle the Navy. " <u>National Republic,</u> XXI
      (September 1933), 9

1036 Dorling, Henry T. "The Navy and the Air. " <u>19th</u>
      <u>Century,</u> CX (November 1931), 570-579.

1037 Doty, William K. , ed. <u>Anchors Aweigh: Verses by</u>
      <u>Midshipmen of the United States Navy.</u> Baltimore:
      Norman, Remington Company, 1924. 195p.
      Sponsored by the Trident Society.

1038 Doughty, Leonard. "The Effect of Depth Charges on
      Submarines. " <u>USNIP,</u> LXI (1935), 353-357.

1039 Douglas, Louis H. "Submarine Disarmament in the
      Interwar Period. " Unpublished Paper, Individual
      Personnel File, Operational Archives, U. S. Navy
      Department, Naval History Division 1968. 19p.
      A summary of the series of international
      disarmament conferences from 1924-1936 with the
      positions of each power on the submarine issue.

1040 _____ . "Submarine Disarmament, 1919-1938. " Un-
      published PhD Dissertation, Syracuse University,
      1970.
      An unsuccessful effort.

1041 Douglas, Paul H. "The American Occupation of Haiti."
      <u>Political Science Quarterly,</u> XLII (June-September
      1927), 228-258, 368-396.

1042 Dow, Harry E. "The True Meaning of the Phrase,
      'An Officer and a Gentleman. ' " <u>USNIP,</u> XLVIII
      (1922), 2071-2073.

1043 Downes, John. "Navigation Versus the Junior Naval
      Officer. " <u>USNIP,</u> XLIX (1923), 469-478.
      Traditionally one of the most difficult of naut-
      ical subjects has been navigation.

1044   Doyle, Walter E.   "The Education and Training of
       Midshipmen. "   USNIP, LIX (1933), 1438-1441;
       LXI (1935), 252.

1045   _____. "Elementary Points of the [Washington]
       Treaty Limiting Armaments. " USNIP, L (1924),
       195-207.

1046   "Drawing Based on Latest Information Showing Ameri-
       can Battleships, Cruisers, Aircraft Carriers, De-
       stroyers, Submarines, Patrol and Auxiliary Ves-
       sels. " Illustrated London News, CXCVIII (Janu-
       ary 18, 1941), 70-71.

1047   Dreller, Lawrence.   "Electricity in the United States
       Navy. " Electrical Engineer, LIX (July 1940),
       267-270.

1048   Drexel, Henry W. , trans.   See Raeder, Erich, no.
       3222.

1049   The Drift of the United States Navy to Third Place.
       Washington: Navy League of the United States,
       1933.   4p.
       Behind Britain and Japan.

1050   Driggs, Laurence L.   "Daughter of the Stars! The
       Destruction of the [Airship] Shenandoah. "   Out-
       look, CXLI (September 16, 1925), 78-79.

1051   Drummond, Donald F.   The Passing of American Neu-
       trality, 1937-1941.   History and Political Science.
       Ann Arbor: University of Michigan Press, 1955.
       409p.   Rpr. 1968.

1052   Drury, Clifford N.   The History of the Chaplain Corps
       United States Navy.   6 vols.   Washington: U. S.
       Government Printing Office, 1949-1960.
       Compiled under the sponsorship of the Bureau
       of Naval Personnel, Vols. I & II are narrative
       histories to 1949, Vols. III-V contain biographic
       and service records, and Vol. VI deals with the
       Korean War.

1053   Drury-Lowe, Sidney R.   "The Naval Conference and
       After. " Contemporary Review, CXXXVII (May
       1930), 545-554.

1054 _____. "Prospects of the Five Power Naval Con-
       ference." Contemporary Review, CXXXVII (Jan-
       uary 1930), 7-12.

1055 DuBois, Isabell. "Organization of Libraries of the
       U. S. Navy." Library Journal, XLIX (June 1,
       1924), 519-524.

1056 Ducey, D. F. "Our New Scout Cruisers." Marine
       Engineering, XXVI (April 1921), 274-277.

1057 Duddy, Frank E., Jr. "Cruisers in the U. S. Navy."
       USNIP, LXXVIII (1952), 304-317.

1058 Dudley, Ernest. Monsters of the Purple Twilight: The
       Life and Death of the Zeppelins. London: Har-
       rap, 1961. 218p.

1059 Dugan, Mary C. "Even the Birds." USNIP, LX
       (1934), 44-49.
       Concerns the airship Akron.

1060 Dulles, Allan W. "Cash and Carry Neutrality: The
       Pittman Act." Foreign Affairs, XVIII (January
       1940), 179-195.

1061 _____. "The Threat of Anglo-American Naval Ri-
       valry." Foreign Affairs, VII (January 1929),
       173-182.

1062 Dulles, Foster R. America's Rise to World Power,
       1898-1954. New American Nation Series. New
       York: Harper, 1955. 314p.

1063 _____. Forty Years of American-Japanese Rela-
       tions. New York: D. Appleton-Century, 1937.
       289p.

1064 Dunbar, Ralph M. "Library Work Aboard Naval Ves-
       sels." Library Journal, XLVIII (December 1,
       1923), 995-998.

1065 Dunn, H. H. "American Submarines on the High
       Seas." Travel, LX (December 1932), 43-44+.

1066 Dunn, Lucius C. "Draft Convention of 1932 Armament
       Limitation Conference." USNIP, LVII (1931), 889-
       891.

1067 _____. "The United States Navy and 104 Years of the Monroe Doctrine. " USNIP, LIV (1928), 1067-1079.

1068 _____. "What Price Leadership. " USNIP, LVI (1930), 323-325.

1069 Dupree, A. Hunter. Science in the Federal Government: A History of Policies and Activities to 1940. Cambridge, Mass : Harvard University Press, 1957. 460p.

1070 Dupuy, E. "Six Days in a Submarine. " St. Nicholas Magazine, LI (May 1924), 686-691.

1071 Dupuy, R. Ernest and William H. Baumer. The Little Wars of the United States: A Compact History from 1798-1920. New York: Hawthorne, 1969. 226p.

1072 Durand Special Committee on Airships. General Review of Conditions Affecting Airship Design and Construction with Recommendations as to Future Policy. Report No. 1. Palo Alto, Calif. : Stanford University Press, 1936. 12p.

1073 _____. The Metalclad Type of Airship Construction with Recommendations. Report No. 4. Palo Alto, Calif. : Stanford University Press, 1937. 4p.

1074 _____. The Respess Type of Airship Construction with Recommendations. Report No. 5. Palo Alto, Calif. : Stanford University Press, 1937. 4p.

1075 _____. Review and Analysis of Airship Design, Past and Present. Report No. 2. Palo Alto, Calif. : Stanford University Press, 1937. 127p.

1076 _____. Technical Aspects of the Loss of the Macon. Report No. 3, Palo Alto, Calif. : Stanford University Press, 1937. 32p.

1077 Dutton, Benjamin. Navigation and Nautical Astronomy: A Textbook on Navigation and Nautical Astronomy Prepared for Use at the United States Naval Academy. 4th ed. Annapolis: U. S. Naval Institute, 1932. 457p.

1078 DuVal, Ruby R.   "The Charm of Old Annapolis. "
      USNIP, LVII (1931), 713-721.

1079 _____.   "Fort Severn: The Battery at Windmill
      Point. "   USNIP, LIX (1933), 843-848.

1080 _____.   "The Naval Academy Cemetery on 'Straw-
      berry Hill. ' "   USNIP, LXXI (1945), 75-77.

1081 _____.   "The Perpetuation of History and Tradition
      at the United States Naval Academy Today. "
      USNIP, LXIV (1938), 669-677.

1082 Duvall, William H.   "Excerpts from the Log of the
      U. S. S. Indianapolis. "   USNIP, LXIII (1937), 685-
      687.

1083 Dyer, George C.   "Naval Amphibious Landmarks. "
      USNIP, XCII (1966), 50+.

1084 Dziuban, Stanley W.   Military Relations Between the
      United States and Canada, 1939-1945.   U. S. Army
      in World War II: Special Studies, Washington:
      Office of the Chief of Military History.   Depart-
      ment of the Army, 1959.   432p.

1085 _____.   United States Military Collaboration with
      Canada in World War II.   Washington: Office of
      the Chief of Military History, Department of the
      Army, 1954.   830p.

1086 Earle, Edward M.   "American Military Policy and
      National Security. "   Political Science Quarterly,
      LIII (March 1938), 1-13.

1087 _____.   "The Navy's Influence on Our Foreign Re-
      lations. "   Current History, XXIII (February 1926),
      648-655.

1088 Earle, Ralph.   "Some Mutual Relations of Gunnery and
      Tactics. "   USNIP, XLVIII (1922), 917-952.

1089 Eberle, Edward W.   "The Elements of Sea Power and
      the Future of the Navy. "   USNIP, LI (1925), 1832-
      1837.

1090 _____.   "A Few Reflections on Our Navy and Some

of Its Needs. " USNIP, L (1924), 1400-1407.

1091 _____. "The Navy and the Merchant Marine. "
USNIP, LII (1926), 1931-1935.

1092 _____. "The Office of Naval Operations. " USNIP,
LIII (1927), 1153-1157.

1093 Eckhardt, George H. "The Government of the United
States Naval Home, Philadelphia. " USNIP, LVI
(1930), 636-638.

1094 _____. "The Police of Our Foreign Trade, the
Navy. " USNIP, LVIII (1932), 366-367.

1095 Edison, Charles. "The Naval Construction Program. "
Marine Engineering, XLV (January 1940), 46-48.

1096 _____. "New Engineering in the Navy. " SciAmer,
CLXII (March 1940), 138-139.

1097 Edson, Merritt A. "The Coco Patrol. " Marine Corps
Gazette, XX (August, November 1936), 18-23, 38-
48, 40-41, 60-72; XXI (February 1937), 35-43,
57-63.
Action in Nicaragua.

1098 _____. "Training a Match Team. " Leatherneck,
XXIII (August 1940), 10-13.

1099 Edwards, F. A. The United States Fleet. Annapolis:
U. S. Naval Institute, 1929. 80p.

1100 Edwards, H. W. "The Case for the Enlisted Pilot. "
Marine Corps Gazette, XXXVIII (November 1954),
12-18.
Otherwise known as the Naval Aviation Pilot,
1915-1945.

1101 Edwards, Kenneth. "The Naval Situation in the Far
East. " Navy, XLIV (1939), 289.

1102 _____. Uneasy Oceans. London: Routledge, 1939.
382p.
Chapt XXI: "The United States vs. Japan, I";
Chapt XXII: "The United States vs. Japan, II. "

1103   Edwards, Walter A.   "Incentive in the Junior Grades."
       USNIP, LIII (1927), 962-964. 1000-1002.

1104   _____. "The U. S. Naval Air Force in Action. "
       USNIP, XLVIII (1922), 1863-1882.

1105   "Effect of the Naval Halt on Industry. " Literary Di-
       gest, LXXIII (June 10, 1922), 23.

1106   "The Effect of Treaties on Naval Strength. " Marine
       Engineering, XXXVIII (November 1933), 398-401.

1107   "Efficient This Time: The Army and Navy Working
       Together, Using the Same Designs and Testing
       for Each Other. " Business Week, (November 16,
       1940), 44.

1108   Egan, Robert S.   "The U. S. S. Wasp (CV-7) in Re-
       trospect. " Warship International, III (1966), 142-
       146, 159.
       Launched in April 1939.

1109   Eggert, Ernest F.   "The Battleship. " USNIP, XLV
       (1919), 877-893.

1110   _____. "The Battle-Cruiser. " USNIP, XLV (1919),
       719-728.

1111   Eggleston, Frederic W.   "Sea Power and Peace in the
       Pacific. " Pacific Affairs, VIII (1935), 325-358.

1112   Eliot, George F.   "Against a Separate Air Force: The
       Record. " Foreign Affairs, XX (October 1941),
       30-48.

1113   _____. "American Military and Foreign Policies:
       Their Interdependence and What to Do About It. "
       Harper's Magazine, CLXXIX (November 1939),
       619-628.

1114   _____. "American Sea Power and the Indian
       Ocean. " Marine Corps Gazette, XLI (December
       1957), 8-18.
       An historical review.

1115   _____. Are We Headed for War with Japan? New
       York: World Peaceways, 1939. 3p.

1116   . Defending America. World Affairs Pamphlets, no. 4. New York: Foreign Policy Association, 1939. 33p.

1117   . "Defense in Two Oceans. " Academy of
Political Science Proceedings, XIX (May 1941),
277-283.

1118   . "The Defense of America. " Harper's Magazine, CXXVIII (December 1938), 74-83.

1119   . "The Defense of America: A Choice of
Hemisphere Defense or Sea Command. " Life, IX
(July 8, 1940), 70-73.

1120   . "For Impregnable Defense. " New Republic,
XCIV (March 30, 1938) 240-249.

1121   . "Impossible War with Japan. " American
Mercury, XLV (September 1938), 16-25.

1122   . The Ramparts We Watch: A Study of the
Problems of American National Defense. New
York: Reynal, 1938. 370p.
Chpt X: "The Composition of the United States
Fleet"; Chpt XI: "Our Many-sided Navy. "

1123   . "U. S. Senate Committee on Naval Affairs
Hearings, April 15-23, 1940: Text of Statement."
Amerasia, IV (June 1940), 192-196.

1124   . "World of Water: Naval Geography Shows
Control of the Sea. " Life, IX (November 25,
1940), 52-55.
Includes several maps.

1125   , et al. Must We Fight Japan? Town Meeting Series, v. 7, no. 4. New York: Columbia
University Press, 1941. 29p.

1126 Eller, Ernest M. "Japan's Rising Sun. " USNIP,
LXIV (1938), 949-962.

1127   . "Launching U. S. Power from the Sea: The
Saga of U. S. Combined Operations Since 1775. "
Army Information Digest, XVI (July 1961), 44-55.
Contains several references to our period.

1128 _____. "Naval Strategy: Some Material and Moral
          Aspects. " USNIP, LXV (1939), 945-957.

1129 _____. "Navy Life Begins. " USNIP, LXI (1935),
          1515-1528.
          At the U. S. Naval Academy.

1129a _____. "The Nimitz Memorial Museum. " Ship-
          mate, (April 1969), 2-5.
          Contains vignettes of the late admiral's early
          naval career.

1130 _____. "The Philippines and the Pacific. " USNIP,
          LXIV (1938), 1467-1480.

1130a _____. "The Postwar Follies. " Seapower, (May
          1973), 31-35.
          The American navy after wars.

1130b _____. "The Scientific Navy. " Navy, (May 1958),
          20-27.
          Much on our period.

1131 _____. "Submarine Passage to Hongkong. " Asia,
          XXIX (October 1929), 778-783.

1131a _____. "Thank the Lord They're Over. " USNIP,
          LXI (1935), 169-172.

1132 _____. "The Three Craftsmen and the Part of
          the Naval Academy in the Mould of a Man. "
          USNIP, LI (1925), 2049-2061.

1133 Ellicott, John M.   "The Passing of the Cadet Engi-
          neers. " USNIP, LXIV (1938), 1123-1134.

1134 _____. "Some Psychological Phases of Discipline."
          USNIP, LIX (1933), 334-338.

1135 Elliott, A. Randle.   "U. S. Strategic Bases in the
          Atlantic. " Foreign Policy Reports, XVI (January
          15, 1941), 258-268.

1136 Elliott, Charles F.   "The Genesis of the Modern
          United States Navy. " USNIP, XCII (1966), 62-69.
          The story of the Vinson-Trammel Naval Ship
          Replacement Act of 1934.

1137   Elliott, Maud H.   "The Navy at Newport. "   USNIP,
       LIX (1933),   833-842.

1138   Ellis, E. H.   "Bush Brigades. "   Marine Corps Gazette,
       VI (March 1921),   1-15.

1139   Ellis, Ezra M.   "New Gunboat Construction at Shang-
       hai. "   USNIP, LV (1929),   783-785.

1140   Ellis, Lewis E.   Republican Foreign Policy, 1921-33.
       New Brunswick, N. J. :   Rutgers University Press,
       1968, 404p.
          The banana wars, naval conferences, and gen-
       eral foreign intercourse of the administrations of
       Harding, Coolidge, and Hoover.   Some material
       on the role of the navy therein.

1141   Ellis, Richard W.   "Battleships of the United States
       Navy. "   USNIP, LXXXIX (1963),   94-114.

1142   Elliston, Herbert B.   "The President as Diplomat:
       Note to Japan's Emperor on the Panay Incident. "
       Christian Science Monitor Magazine. (January 19,
       1938),   3-6.

1143   _____, jt. author.   See   Chirol, Valentine, no. 739.

1144   Ellsberg, Edward.   Men Under the Sea.   New York:
       Dodd, 1939.   365p.

1145   _____.   On the Bottom.   New York: Dodd, Mead,
       1929.   324p.
          An account of the raising of the S-51.

1146   _____.   "Releasing Gear for Launching as Used on
       U. S. S. Whitney [AD-4]. "   USNIP, L (1924), 1281-
       1291.

1147   _____.   "Safety for Our Submarines. "   World's
       Work, LV (March 1928),   493-500.

1148   _____.   _____.   Review of Reviews, LXXVII
       (March 1928),   311-312.

1149   _____.   "Salvage of the S-51. "   SciAmer, CXXXV
       (October 1926),   257-259.

1150 _____ . "Salvaging the United States Submarine
      S-51. " Marine Engineering, XXXI (August 1926),
      443-448.
            Sunk in collision with S. S. City of Rome off
      Block Island, September 25, 1925.

1151 _____ . "Ten Thousand Tons of Fighting Cat: What
      a New Set of Rules Did to Naval Design--U. S. S.
      Indianapolis. " Fortune, VII (March 1933), 56-61.

1152 Ellsworth, Harry A. One Hundred Eighty Landings of
      United States Marines, 1800-1934. Washington:
      U. S. Marine Corps, 1934. 163p.

1153 Ellsworth, Lincoln. Across Antarctica: An Epic of
      Air Adventure, with Notes on Byrd's Second Ant-
      arctic Expedition. Newport News, Va. : Mariner's
      Museum, 1939. 130p.

1154 _____ . Beyond Horizons. Garden City, N. Y. :
      Doubleday, 1938. 408p.
            Arctic and Antarctic exploration.

1155 "The Employees in Manufacturing Plants of the United
      States War and Navy Departments. " Monthly
      Labor Review, XIV (May 1922), 987-997.

1156 "End of the [Geneva] Naval Conference. " Outlook,
      CXLVI (August 17, 1927), 497-498.

1157 Enders, Dalvin W. "The Vinson Navy. " Unpublished
      PhD Dissertation, Michigan State University, 1970.
            The Georgia congressman, longtime chairman
      of the House Naval Affairs Committee, played an
      important role in the rebuilding of the American
      navy during the New Deal years.

1158 Engel, Leonard H. "Antarctic Ho! The First Fed-
      erally Sponsored Expedition to Antarctic. "
      Science News Letter, XXXVI (August 26, 1939),
      138-140.
            The author is off by about 100 years. Charles
      Wilkes' voyage in the 1840s was the first. The
      citation refers to the 1939-1941 Byrd Expedition.

1159 Engely, Giovanni. The Politics of Naval Disarma-
      ment. London: Williams and Norgate, 1932. 301p.

1160 Engeman, George H. "Progress Underseas. " New
Outlook, CLXIV (August 1934) 26-30.
In submarine warfare.

1161 England, R. A. J. "Preliminary Account of the United
States Antarctic Expedition, 1939-1941. " Geo-
graphic Review, XXXI (July 1941), 466-478.
The Byrd Expedition.

1162 "England Calls a Conference for Further Naval Limitations: Official Text of the British and American
Notes. " Congressional Digest, VIII (October
1929), 243-244.

1163 "Epic of the Illustrious: The British Carrier's Heroic
Odyssey from the Mediterranean to Norfolk, Va."
Life, XI (September 15, 1941), 29-35.
Where she was repaired.

1164 Erickson, C. L. The Navy in Review. New York:
Dutton, 1941. 212p.

1165 Ericsson, Edward L. "Maneuvering Aircraft in
Formation. " USNIP, XLIX (1923), 79-89.

1166 Eskew, Garnett L. The Cradle of Ships. New York:
Putnam, 1958. 279p.
The Bath (Maine) Iron Works.

1167 Esler, J. L. "Scout Cruiser: The U. S. S. Salt Lake
City. " Marine Engineering, XXXV (September
1930), 500-507.

1168 Esler, Jay K. "Preparing the Engineer Department
[aboard ship] for Battle. " USNIP, XLIX (1923),
1085-1096.

1169 _____ . "A Suggestion Concerning Battleship Organization. " USNIP, XLIX (1923), 1805-1817.

1170 Esposito, Vincent J. The West Point Atlas of American Wars. 2 vols. New York: Praeger, 1959.

1171 Estaves, Paul E. "The 19th Dive. " New Hampshire
Profiles, (August-September 1959), 10-13, 14-17.
On the rescue of the crew of U. S. S. Squalus
in 1939.

1172   Esthus, Raymond A.   "President Roosevelt's Commit-
       ment to Britain to Intervene in a Pacific War."
       Mississippi Valley Historical Review, L (1963),
       28-38.

1173   Etherton, Percy T. and H. Hessell Tiltman.   The
       Pacific: A Forecast.   New York: Arno, 1973.
       A reprinting of the 1928 first edition in which
       the authors predict war between America and
       Japan.

1174   Etzold, Thomas H., jt. author.   See Silver, Steven
       M., no. 3651.

1175   "Europe's Wet Blanket on Our Naval Idealism."   Lit-
       erary Digest, CII (July 6, 1929), 14-15.

1176   Evans, Edward J.   "Time on Target--177 Years."
       Marine Corps Gazette, XXXVIII (February 1954),
       36-39.
       A brief history of Marine artillery with data on
       our period.

1177   Evans, Frank E., jt. author.   See Jackson, Orton,
       P., no. 1855.

1178   Evans, Holden A.   One Man's Fight for a Better Navy.
       New York: Dodd, Mead, 1940.   398p.
       The autobiography of a retired Lieutenant-Com-
       mander and naval constructor which tells of his
       battle for economy and efficiency in the fleet.

1179   _____.   "Our Muscle-Bound Navy."   Collier's, CI
       (June 11, 1938), 9-10+.
       Wants construction of more escort vessels and
       fewer battleships.

1180   Evans, Stephen H.   The United States Coast Guard,
       1790-1915: A Definitive History (With a Post-
       script, 1915-1949).   Annapolis: U.S. Naval Insti-
       tute, 1949.   228p.
       The postscript of two pages relates the earlier
       period to the developmental phase, 1915-1949.

1181   Evans, Sydney D.   "As 'Holy Joe' Sees It: Leaflet
       Issued November 27, 1926."   USNIP, LIII (1927),
       733.

1182   _____. "Religion in Leadership." USNIP, LIII (1927), 639-645.

1183 Evans, Thomas C. "Creep, or Latitude Error, in Torpedo Fire." USNIP, LXII (1936), 1593-1596.

1184 Evans, Waldo. "The Development and Growth of the American Navy." USNIP, LI (1925), 1897-1915.

1185 "Events in Nicaragua." Marine Corps Gazette, XIII (June, September 1928), 143-146, 204-205.

1186 "Every Day is Navy Day: The Warships Launched This Week are Part of a Huge Building Program." Business Week, (November 2, 1935), 36-37.

1187 "Everything's Not All Right with Our Navy: Reply to C. D. Wilbur." Collier's, LXXIX (March 26, 1927), 8-9.
    For Wilbur's original remarks, see the interview conducted by C. W. Gilbert cited below.

1188 "Exchange of Naval and Air Bases for Over-age Destroyers: Official Documents." American Journal of International Law, XXXIV (October 1940), 183-186.

1189 "The Expansion Program of the Navy is Now Under Way." U. S. News, II (July 29-August 5, 1933), 9.

1190 "The Expedition to the Antarctic Under Admiral Byrd Finds 900 Miles of New Coastline." Life, IX (July 8, 1940), 27-33.

1191 "Experts in the U. S. Have a Plan for Defeating the Nazi U-boat Campaign." China Weekly Review, XCVII (June 28, 1941), 113+.

1192 "Explorers [of Byrd's Expedition] See Antarctic by Plane and Sled." Popular Mechanics, LXXIII (June 1940), 814-815

1193 "Exploring a Frozen Continent." Popular Mechanics, LXXV (January 1941), 50-53.
    Admiral Byrd.

1194 "Exploring the Last Frontier: Drawings of the North
      Star and Equipment for Exploring." Popular
      Mechanics, LXXIII (March 1940), 366-367.

1195 "F. D. R. Scores Nazi Acts of Piracy: Radio Address,
      September 11--Excerpts, with Replies from the
      German and Japanese Press." China Weekly Re-
      view, XCVIII (September 20, 1941), 71-73.

1196 Fagan, George V. "Anglo-American Naval Relations,
      1927-1937." Unpublished PhD Dissertation, Uni-
      versity of Pennsylvania, 1954.

1197 _____. "Franklin D. Roosevelt and Naval Limita-
      tion." USNIP, LXXXI (1955), 411-418.

1198 Fagen, Melvin M. "The High Cost of Ships." New
      Republic, CIV (January 6, 1941), 10-12.

1199 Fahey, James C. The Ships and Aircraft of the U. S.
      Fleet, 1939. New York: Herald-Nathan Press,
      1939.

1200 Fahle, Robert S. "The Panama Canal--An Auxiliary
      of the Fleet." USNIP, LXXXIV (1954), 494-503.

1201 Fahrney, Delmer S. "The History of Pilotless Air-
      craft and Guided Missiles." Unpublished paper,
      Shore Establishment-BUAER File, Operational
      Archives, U. S. Navy Department, Naval History
      Division, n. d. 1345p.
      Much space is given to the pre-war develop-
      ment pushed by the Navy.

1202 "Failure of the Geneva [Naval] Conference." World's
      Work, LIV (September 1927), 468-471.

1203 "Fair Exchange: American Destroyers for Leased
      Naval Bases." Economist, CXXXIX (September
      7, 1940), 299-300.
      A British view of the deal.

1204 Fairbanks, Andrew J. Pressure Distribution Tests on
      PW-9 Wing Models Showing Effects of Biplane In-
      terference. U. S. National Advisory Committee
      for Aeronautics Report, no. 271. Washington:
      Government Printing Office, 1927. 13p.

1205   Fairchild, Byron. "The Decision to Land United States
       Forces in Iceland, 1941. " In: Kent R. Greenfield,
       ed. Command Decisions. Washington: Office of the
       Chief of Military History, Department of the Army. ,
       1960.   p. 73-97.

1206   _____ jt. author. See Conn, Stetson, no. 807.

1207   Fairlamb, George R.   "The Destroyer Engineer in
       Battle. "   USNIP, LI (1925), 2289-2292.

1208   _____. "The Independent Air Force. " USNIP, LI
       (1925), 381-385, 807-809.
       Discussion included.

1209   "Faith, Hope and Parity at London. " Literary Digest,
       CIV (February 22, 1930), 11-12.

1210   Falk, Edwin A.   From Perry to Pearl Harbor, the
       Struggle for Supremacy in the Pacific.   New York:
       Doubleday, Doran, 1943.   362p.

1211   Falls, Cyril.   A Hundred Years of War, 1950.   New
       York: Collier Books, 1962.   480p.
       A general survey with several sections relative
       to our present compilation.

1212   Farago, Ladislas.   Broken Seal: "Operation Magic"
       and the Road to Pearl Harbor.   New York: Ran-
       dom House, 1967.   439p.

1213   Farley, Miriam S.   America's Stake in the Far East.
       New York: American Council Institute of Pacific
       Relations, 1938.   23p.

1214   Farnham, D.   W.   "Portrait of the Navy Academy:
       Reply to Fletcher Pratt. "   American Mercury,
       XLII (September 1937), 127-128.
       The "offending" Pratt article is cited below.

1215   Farwell, Raymond F.   "Conflicting Signals: A Critical
       Analysis. "   USNIP, LX (1934), 333-344.

1216   Fassett, Frederick G.   The Shipbuilding Business in
       the United States of America.   2 vols.   New York:
       Society of Naval Architects and Marine Engineers,
       1948.   Rpr. 1970.

1217   "Fast Airplane Tested for the Navy: The New Scout
       Bomber, SBU-1. " SciAmer, CLIII (November
       1935), 267.

1218   Fawcett, L. H.   "Saving Tonnage in Cruisers. " Metal
       Progress, XIX (April 1931), 39-43.

1219   Fea, Lawrence.   "Washington Conference Influences on
       Warship Design. " Engineering, CXIV (July 7,
       1922), 28-30.

1220   Fechet, J. E.   "More Aircraft Carriers Needed. "
       Aero Digest, XX (May 1932), 23+.

1221   _____.   "Navy Torpedo and Bombing Planes. "
       Aero Digest, XXII (May 1933), 14-15.

1222   _____.   "Observation and Scouting Planes of the
       U. S. Navy. " Aero Digest, XXI (December 1932),
       18-19.

1223   _____.   "U. S. Navy Fighting Airplanes. " Aero Di-
       gest, XXII (February 1933), 16-17.

1224   Federal Writers' Program.   Maryland.   A Guide to
       the U. S. Naval Academy.   New York: Devin-
       Adair, 1941.

1225   Fehrenbach, T. R.   FDR's Undeclared War, 1939-1941.
       New York: David McKay, 1967.   344p.

1226   Feipel, Louis W.   "The Rise and Development of Li-
       braries on board Vessels of the United States Navy."
       Library Journal, XLIV (1919), 638-644.

1227   Feis, Herbert.   The Road to Pearl Harbor: The Com-
       ing of the War Between the United States and Japan.
       Princeton, N. J.: Princeton University Press, 1950.
       356p.   Rpr. 1962.

1228   _____.   "War Came at Pearl Harbor: Suspicions
       Considered. " Yale Review, XLV (March 1956),
       378-390.

1229   Fenner, Edward B.   "Discipline. " USNIP, XLVII
       (1921), 1371-1385.

1230   Ferguson, Otis C. "The Old Navy Game. " New Re-
       public, LXXIX (June 13, 1934), 131.

1231   Ferguson, W. B. "Unusual Features Involved in Launch-
       ing the U. S. S. Mahan. " Marine Engineering, XL
       (November 1935), 421-424.

1232   Ferraby, Hubert C. "Mahan and the Present War. "
       19th Century, CXXVII (April 1940), 456-463.
       Suppositions on what the great naval philosopher,
       whose works are cited in Vol. IV of this series,
       would have thought of early World War II.

1233   _____ . "Sea Power in the Pacific. " 19th Century,
       CXXXI (February 1942), 56-60.
       Relates to the results of the Washington Confer-
       ence of 1922.

1234   Ferrell, H. C. , Jr. "Claude A. Swanson of Virginia. "
       Unpublished PhD Dissertation, University of Vir-
       ginia, 1964.
       The subject was Secretary of the Navy from 1933
       to 1939.

1235   Ferrell, Robert H. "Pearl Harbor and the Revision-
       ists. " Historian, XVII (1955), 215-233.
       Causes as well as consequences.

1236   Fey, Harold E. "Armaments and the Defense Myth. "
       Christian Century, LVI (March 15, 1939), 346-348.

1237   _____ . "Behind the Fleet Maneuvers. " Christian
       Century, LII (May 22, 1925), 695-698.

1238   _____ . "Cancel the Naval Maneuvers!" Christian
       Century, LII (March 6, 1935), 298-300.

1239   Field, J. A. , Jr. "Admiral Yamamoto. " USNIP,
       LXXV (1949), 1105-1113.

1240   Field, R. J. "A Trip Through the Panama Canal. "
       USNIP, XLVI (1920), 405-408.
       Aboard U. S. S. South Carolina, BB-26.

1241   Field, Richard S. "Spalato, 1919. " USNIP, LI
       (1925), 775-789.

1242 _____. "Training Reservists Aboard Destroyers. "
       USNIP, LV (1929), 502-504.

1243 Fiennes, Gerald Y.   "Naval Problems of To-day. "
       19th Century, XCVIII (July 1925), 80-93.

1244 "A 52-Knot Aluminum Destroyer Developed as the U-
       boat Answer. " Newsweek, XVIII (December 1,
       1941), 39-40.

1245 Figgis, D.   "The Cart Before the Horse: Mr. Side-
       botham's Proposal for a High Seas Fleet. " New
       Republic, XXI (February 18, 1920), 354.

1246 "Fight for Life: Excerpts from Admiral Byrd's Diary
       of Self-Exile, with Commentary by C. J. V. Mur-
       phy. " American Magazine, CXX (October 1935),
       32-33+.

1247 "Findings of the S-51 Naval Court. " Literary Digest,
       LXXXVIII (January 23, 1926), 9.

1248 "Findings of the Shenandoah Court of Inquiry. " In:
       U. S. Congress. House. Naval Affairs Committee.
       Hearings on Sundry Legislation Affecting the Naval
       Establishment, 1925-1926.   69th Cong. , 1st sess. ,
       1925-1926. p. 217-224.

1249 Finney, B.   "Millions to be Spent Preparing Ship Yards
       to Build Battleships. " American Machinist,
       LXXXII (March 9, 1938), 190a-190b.

1250 Fioravanzo, Guisseppe.   "The Japanese Military
       [Naval] Mission to Italy in 1941. " USNIP, LXXXI
       (1955), 24-31.
           The Italians were interested in learning about the
       operations of U. S. carriers while the Japanese de-
       sired details on British naval tactics which might
       be useful in planning the Pacific war.

1251 "The Fire-Control Tower is the Battleship's Brain. "
       Popular Mechanics, LXXIV (August 1940), 238-239.

1252 "A Firm Position on the Suspension of Work on Naval
       Cruisers Taken by President Hoover. " Commercial
       and Financial Chronicle, CXXIX (August 3, 1929),
       740.

1253 "First Blood to Germany: The Destroyer Kearny Tor-
      pedoed. " Scholastic, XXXIX (October 27, 1941), 4.

1254 "The First Fifty Years of U. S. Submarines. " USNIP,
      LXXXII (1956), 1212-1225.
      A pictorial.

1255 "The First Trial Flight of the U. S. Navy Airship ZR-
      1. " Aviation, XV (September 10, 1923), 311.
      The Shenandoah.

1256 "First U. S. Ship Torpedoed by Germany: Odyssey of
      the Robin Moor's Survivors. " Illustrated London
      News, CXCIX (July 26, 1941), 120.

1257 Fish, Hamilton. "America Safe from Attack. " In:
      H. B. Summers, ed. Anglo-American Agreement.
      Vol. XII of The Reference Shelf. New York: H. W.
      Wilson, 1938. p. 331-332.
      A speech by the New York congressman in which
      he quotes a statement by Admiral Sims: "No foreign
      power or group of powers can operate across the
      oceans and stand a chance in combat with the
      American Navy and planes operating from home
      bases. " Reprinted from the January 4, 1938 issue
      of Congressional Record.

1258 _____ . A Navy for Defense, but not for Aggression.
      Washington, 1938. 4p.
      A reprinting of his speech in the House of Repre-
      sentatives on the subject.

1259 Fisher, Alvan. "Selective Recruiting for the Naval
      Reserve. " USNIP, LXV (1939), 1161-1164.

1260 Fisher, Charles W. "Industrial Organization of Navy
      Yards. " USNIP, XLVIII (1922), 761-787.

1261 Fisher, George J. B. "Naval Tactics for Land War-
      fare. " USNIP, LXII (1936), 1295-1299.

1262 Fisher, Helen. "The Future of Naval Limitation. "
      Foreign Policy Reports, XII (October 1, 1936),
      178-188.

1263 Fiske, Bradley A. "Disarmament and Foreign Trade."
      USNIP, XLVII (1921), 1539-1542.

1264 _____. From Midshipman to Rear Admiral.   New
      York: Century, 1919. 694p.
      The author was one of the most inventive and
      interesting characters of our period.   He was most
      noted for his numerous inventions, including the
      naval telescopic sight adopted by all the world's
      navies.   He was also an early exponent of torpedo
      planes.   After his retirement, he resided at New
      York's Waldorf Astoria where he died April 7, 1942.

1265 _____. "How We Shall Lose the Next War and
      When. " World's Work, LIII (April 1927), 626-635.
      By disarming the fleet.

1266 _____. "Limitation of Armaments: Uncensored
      Statement. " Harper's Monthly, CLI (July 1925),
      129-138.

1267 _____. "The Relative Importance of the Philippines
      and Guam. " USNIP, XLVII (1921), 595-602.

1268 _____. "Strongest Navy: Reply to Wester-Wemyss
      and Admiral Sims. " Current History, XVI (July
      1922), 557-563.
      Both the articles by Sims and Wester-Wemyss
      are cited in their proper alphabetical locations
      below.

1269 _____. "Torpedo Plane and Bomber. " USNIP,
      XLVIII (1922), 1473-1478.

1270 _____. "The United States Naval Institute. " USNIP,
      XLV (1919), 197-200.
      A century old in 1974.

1271 _____. "The Warfare of the Future. " USNIP,
      XLVII (1921), 157-167.

1272 Fishe, Leon S. "The Naval Rhodes Scholar. " USNIP,
      LVI (1930), 328-332.

1273 Fitsgerald, Kenyon B. "The Merchant Officer's Place
      in the Naval World. " USNIP, LXVI (1940), 224-
      234, 719-721, 1631-1632.

1274 Fitzgerald, Helen M. "A History of the USN Nurse
      Corps from 1934 to the Present. " Unpublished MS

Thesis, Ohio State University, 1968.

1275 Fitzgerald, Paul A. "Anti-Aircraft Defense. " Leatherneck, XXIII (January 1940), 14-18.

1276 "Five Navies as the Conference Meets. " Scholastic,
XXVII (January 4, 1936), 20-21.

1277 Flamm, Oliver. "The Armored Submarine Cruiser. "
Mechanical Engineering, XXXVI (June 1931), 265-
267.

1278 Fleesom, David. "Growing Navy and Other Capital
News. " Independent Woman, XVII (April 1938), 111.

1279 "Fleet Base: Model Operating Base, Navy Yard, Destroyer, Submarine, and Naval Air Station. " Fortune, XXII (December 1940), 61-67.

1280 "The Fleet in Review. " Marine Engineering, XXXIX
(July 1934), 256-259.

1281 "The Fleet Passes Through the Panama Canal. " Newsweek, III (May 5, 1934), 7.

1282 Fleisher, Wilfred. "How Japan Kept the U. S. Fleet
out of the Mandated Islands in 1929. " USNIP,
LXX (1944), 726.
Reprinted from the New York Herald-Tribune,
April 23, 1944.

1283 Fleming, H. Kingston. "The Admirals See the Point."
Nation, CXXXIII (September 2, 1931), 228-229.

1284 Fletcher, Frank J. "Scope and Application of the
Monroe Doctrine. " General Staff Memorandum,
Files of the U. S. Army Military History Research
Collection, 1931.
The Navy captain's view as expressed to his
Army colleagues.

1285 Fletcher, H. C. "Pensacola, Cruiser Launched at New
York. " Marine Engineering, XXXIV (June 1929),
298-301.
CA-24, with her sistership Salt Lake City (CA-
25), were the first U. S. cruisers built subject to
the limitations of the Washington Naval Treaty.

1286 "Flint's Mystery Voyage Rouses Washington Protest."
      Scholastic, XXXV (November 6, 1939), 9-10.
      The City of Flint taken by a German raider.

1287 "Flitting City of Flint." New Republic, CI (November
      8, 1939), 5.

1288 "Floating Airfields: U. S. Carriers." Time, XXXVIII
      (November 3, 1941), 32.

1289 "Floating Hospital for Warships: ARD-3: The Navy's
      Seagoing Base Will Even Have Its Own Movies."
      Literary Digest, CXXII (November 28, 1936), 35.

1290 "Floating Landing Field Aviation's Latest Marvel: The
      Saratoga." Dunn's International Review, XLVI
      (January 1926), 57-58.

1291 Floherty, John J. Aviation from Shop to Sky. Phila-
      delphia: Lippincott, 1941. 214p.
      Contains some data on the naval air service.

1292 _____. Guardsmen of the Coast. Garden City,
      N. Y.: Doubleday, Doran, 1935. 100p.
      The Coast Guard.

1293 _____. Men Without Fear. New York: Lippincott,
      1940. 224p.
      Describes a number of Coast Guard rescue
      operations during the late 1930s.

1294 _____. Sons of the Hurricane. New York: Lippin-
      cott, 1938. 224p.
      Coast Guard rescues, including the personnel of
      the S. S. Morro Castle in 1934.

1295 _____. White Terror: Adventures with the Ice
      Patrol. New York: Lippincott, 1947. 183p.
      The Coast Guard's exploits in the ice fields with
      the International Ice Patrol, the Marion Expedition,
      and the World War II Greenland Patrol. Contains
      biographical data on ice expert Edward H. Smith.

1296 "Flying Marines Over Florida Palms." Literary Di-
      gest, CXXII (December 12, 1936), 32.

1296a "Flying Sergeants." Air Classics, I (Fall 1964), 32-40.

Enlisted Marine Corps pilots of our period.

1297 Flynn, John T. "The Brainbuster and His Son: Why
      We are to Have a Large Army and Navy." New
      Republic, XCVII (November 23, 1938), 74-75.
      The Panay incident.

1299 Fogg, A. K. "Engineering in the Navy." Society of
      Western Engineers Journal, XXXIV (December
      1929), 688-691.

1300 Foley, Paul. "The Naval Research Laboratory."
      USNIP, LI (1925), 1925-1932.

1301 Folk, Winston P. "Basic Education of Officers."
      USNIP, LI (1925), 274-279.

1302 _____. "Uniforms That Are and Uniforms That
      Aren't." USNIP, LVII (1931), 745-750.

1303 "The Folly of a Divided Fleet." SciAmer, CXXIII
      (July 17, 1920), 56.

1304 Foote, Percy W. "Engineering Experiences--Its
      Value to the Captain." USNIP, XLIX (1923), 1243-
      1253.

1305 "For a Huge Fleet, Steel or Paper?" Literary Digest,
      XCVI (January 7, 1928), 12-14.

1306 "For an Independent Naval Air Service." SciAmer,
      CXXIII (October 9, 1920), 372.

1307 "For Speed, the New Omaha." Literary Digest,
      LXXVI (March 24, 1923), 44-46.
      A fast American cruiser, the four-stacker was
      designated CL-4.

1308 "For Tomorrow's Navy." American Machinist,
      LXXXIII (March 22, 1939), 178a-178p.

1309 Ford, Frederick W., comp. Review of the Conference
      on Limitation of Armament, in Connection with the
      Pacific and Far Eastern Questions. Boston: Even-
      ing Transcript, 1922. 142p.

1310 "Foreign Policy and Cruiser Folly." Nation, CXXVIII

(January 30, 1929), 122.

1311 Foreign Policy Association. The London Naval Con-
      ference. New York, 1929. 31p.

1312 Forster, Guito F. "Building an Effective Naval Re-
      serve." USNIP, LIX (1933), 387-396.

1313 Fortune, Editors of. The Background of War. New
      York: A. A. Knopf, 1937. 296p.

1314 "Four Years at Annapolis." Popular Mechanics, XLIV
      (August-November 1925), 193-200, 417-424, 577-
      584, 753-600.

1315 "4,500 Mile Chain: The Way Opened for the Conver-
      sion of Seven Destroyer-Deal Bases." Newsweek,
      XVI (December 2, 1940), 30-31.

1316 "$458,000 Naval Appropriations Bill Passed by the
      House Without Record Vote: Provides for the
      Largest Peace-Time Naval Program in History with
      Early Approval by the Senate Expected." Com-
      mercial and Financial Chronicle, CXL (May 4,
      1935), 2964-2965.

1317 "Forty Fathoms Down: The Epic of the Submarine
      Squalus Poses New Problems for the Navy." News-
      week, XIII (June 5, 1939), 14-15.

1318 Fox, Edward J. "If Independence is Granted the
      Philippine Islands, Should a Naval Base be Re-
      tained?" General Staff Memorandum, Files of the
      U.S. Army Military History Research Collection,
      1932.

1319 _____. "Joint Army and Navy Training." Unpub-
      lished Lecture, G-3 Course 7, Files of the U.S.
      Army Military History Research Collection, 1937.

1320 _____. "Naval Intelligence." Unpublished Lecture,
      G-2 Course 4, Files of the U.S. Army Military
      History Research Collection, 1939.

1321 _____. "Naval Logistics." Unpublished Lecture,
      G-4 Course 12, Files of the U.S. Army Military
      History Research Collection, 1937.

1322   Fradin, Morris. "Cruising in a Submarine." Travel,
       LXIV (March 1935), 48-50+.

1323   France, Beulah. "The Health of Our Navy at Sea."
       Hygeia, XIII (October 1935), 891-893.

1324   Francke, Frederick R. "Naval Reserve Liaison Of-
       ficer." USNIP, LIX (1933), 669-670.

1325   Frank, M. R. "In Praise of the Coast Guard." New
       Republic, LXI (February 12, 1930), 330.

1326   Frank, W. C. , Jr. "Sea Power and Politics and the
       Onset of the Spanish War. 1936." Unpublished
       PhD Dissertation, University of Pittsburgh, 1969.

1327   Frank, Wolfgang. The Sea Wolves: The Story of the
       German U-boats at War. Translated by R. O. B.
       Long. New York: Rinehart, 1955. 340p. Rpr.
       1972.
       Some data relative to this work.

1328   Fraser, Chelsea. Heroes of the Sea. New York:
       Thomas Y. Crowell, 1924. 390p.
       Many were Coast Guard personnel.

1329   Frazier, Charles E. , Jr. "The Dawn of Nationalism
       and Its Consequences in Nicaragua." Unpublished
       PhD Dissertation, University of Texas, 1958.
       U. S. Marines vs. Sandino.

1330   Fredericksen, Paul. "War with the Icy Unknown."
       New York Times Magazine, (April 7, 1940), 6-9.
       The Byrd Expedition.

1331   Freeman, Charles S. "The Exercise of Command
       Afloat." USNIP, LVI (1930), 779-791.

1332   Freeman, Kathleen, ed. What They Said at the Time:
       A Survey of the Causes of the Second World War
       and the Hopes for a Lasting Peace, as Exhibited in
       the Utterances of the World's Leaders and Some
       Others from 1917-1944. London: Muller, 1945.
       470p.

1333   Freeman, Lewis R. "The 1929 Naval Manoeuvres."
       USNIP, LV (1929), 341-348.

Reprinted from the February 14, 1929 issue of
the New York Times.

1334 French, Burton. "Naval Reduction: What It Means in
      Money." Current History, XXXI (January 1930),
      711-717.

1335 _____. "Our Navy, Shall We Build to the Limit?"
      Saturday Evening Post, CCIV (October 31, 1931),
      21-25.

1336 Friedel, Frank. "World War II: Before Pearl Har-
      bor." Current History, XXXV (1958), 211-215.
      The hardening of U.S. opinion for the Allies.

1337 Friedlander, Saul. Prelude to Downfall: Hitler and the
      United States, 1939-1941. New York: Knopf, 1967.
      328p.

1338 Fritsche, Carl B. "A Comparative Examination of the
      Airplane and the Airship." American Society of
      Mechanical Engineers Transactions, L (1928), AER
      50-20, 9-20.

1339 _____. "The Metalclad Airship." American Society
      of Mechanical Engineers Transactions, LI (1929),
      AER 51-36, 245-266.

1340 Frolkingham, Thomas G. "Our Naval Building Pro-
      gram." USNIP, LV (1929), 804-806.
      Reprinted from the Boston Herald.

1341 "From Atlantic to Pacific in Single File in 42 Hours."
      Newsweek, IV (November 3, 1934), 11.

1342 Frost, Holloway H. The Battle of Jutland. Annapolis:
      U.S. Naval Institute, 1936. 571p. Rpr. 1970.
      Although a study of a subject not directly re-
      lated to our period, it is entered here for the les-
      sons it aimed at American naval officers of the
      late Interwar years and the maxim, "every mistake
      in war is excusable except inactivity and refusal to
      run risks."

1343 _____. "National Strategy." USNIP, LI (1925),
      1353+.

1344   _____.   "Naval Aircraft in Coastal Warfare. "
            USNIP, LVII (1931), 1-16.

1345   _____.   "Naval Operations of a Red-Orange Cam-
            paign. " Unpublished Lecture G-2 Course 36, Files
            of the U. S. Army Military History Research Col-
            lections, 1920.

1346   _____.   "Naval Personnel Plans for Mobilization. "
            Unpublished Lecture, G-1 Course 2, Files of the
            U. S. Army Military History Research Collection,
            1925.
                The same paper was presented in 1926 and 1927.

1347   _____.   "The Naval Service. " USNIP, L (1924),
            31-39.

1348   _____.   "A New Deal for the Naval Reserve. "
            USNIP, LII (1926), 51-61.

1349   _____.   "Night Scouting with Listening Devices. "
            USNIP, XLVI (1920), 1449-1463.

1350   _____.   "Our Cruise in the Kuriles. " USNIP, L
            (1924), 1665-1686.

1351   _____.   "The Present Strength of the United States
            Navy. " Current History, XXV (November 1926),
            185-189.

1352   _____.   "Some Torpedo Problems for Destroyers. "
            USNIP, XLVIII (1922), 2087-2099.

1353   _____.   "The Spirit of the Offensive. " USNIP,
            XLIX (1923), 285+.

1354   _____.   "Strategy of the Atlantic. " Unpublished
            Lecture, G-2 Course 39, Files of the U. S. Army
            Military History Research Collection, 1919.

1355   Frothingham, Thomas G.   "The American Naval Build-
            ing Program. " Fortnightly, CXV (March 1921),
            384-387.

1356   _____.   "The Increased Strength of the United
            States on the Sea. " Current History, XII (Septem-
            ber 1920), 943-952.

1357 _____. "Our Naval Building Program." USNIP, LV
      (1929), 804-806.

1358 _____. "The Power Behind Naval Disarmament."
      Independent, CXX (May 5, 1928), 422-424.

1359 Fry, M. G. "Anglo-American-Canadian Relations with
      Special Reference to Far Eastern and Naval Issues,
      1918-1922." Unpublished PhD Dissertation, Uni-
      versity of London, 1964.

1360 Fugate, Robert T. "Chow Down." Leatherneck,
      XXXVII (July 1954), 24-31.
         A history of Marine rations with some data on
      our period.

1361 Fukuda, Teizaburo. "A Mistaken War." USNIP, XCIV
      (1968), 42-48.
         On the opposition of some Japanese to war with
      America.

1362 Fullam, W. F. "Air Power and Naval Conservatism."
      Aviation, XVI (March 10, 1924), 256-260.
         For the rebuttal, see the article by Dudley W.
      Knox cited below.

1363 _____. "The Use and Abuse of Submarines." North
      American Review, CCXVI (October 1922), 467-469.

1364 Fulton, Garland. "Airship Progress and Airship Prob-
      lems." Journal of the American Society of Naval
      Engineers, XLI (February 1929), 30-63.

1365 _____. "Improving Airship Performance." Ameri-
      can Society of Mechanical Engineers Transactions,
      LVI (1934), AER 56-8.   301-303.

1366 _____. "Rigid Airships." USNIP, XLVII (1921),
      1565-1591, 1697-1723.

1367 _____. "Some Features of a Modern Airship-U. S. S.
      Akron." Society of Naval Architects and Marine
      Engineers Transactions, XXXIX (1931), 135-157.

1368 _____. "Some Features of a Modern Airship: U. S. S.
      Akron." Marine Review, LXI (December 1931), 16.

1369 _____. "Some Matters Relating to Large Airships."
Society of Naval Architects and Marine Engineers
Transactions, XXXIII (1925), 187-207.

1370 Fumihiko, Togo, jt. editor. See Togo, Shigenori,
no. 4026.

1371 "Funds for Naval Air Stations." Aero Digest, XVI
(May 1930), 108.

1372 Funnell, Charles L. "Second Alma Mater." USNIP,
LXII (1936), 1231-1237.
The navy.

1373 Fuqua, Stephen O. Americans Wanted: Your Place in
Our Military Structure. New York: Smith & Dur-
rell, 1940. 183p.

1374 "The Fur Flies in Air vs. Seapower Attack." Current
Opinion, LXXVIII (April 1925), 400-401.

1375 Furer, Julius A. "Drydocking and Major Repairs in a
Campaign in the Western Pacific." Unpublished
Lecture, Files of the U. S. Army Military History
Research Collection, 1921.
The Navy captain was explaining the difficulties
facing the fleet to his colleagues at the Army War
College.

1376 _____. "History of the Office of the Coordinator of
Research and Development, from 12 July 1941 to
19 May 1945." Unpublished paper, Shore Establishment File, Operational Archives, U. S. Navy Department, Naval History Division, 1945.   28p.
Memories by the Office's Chief.

1377 _____. "The Structure of Naval Appropriation
Acts." USNIP, LXXIV (1948), 1517-1527.
A History.

1378 Gainard, Joseph A. "Voyage of the Flint." Life,
VIII (March 4, 1940), 78+.
Gainard was awarded the Navy Cross for gal-
lantry in the episode; unfortunately, both he and
the City of Flint were destroyed in 1942-43.

1379 _____. Yankee Skipper: The Life Story of Joseph
A. Gainard, Captain of the City of Flint. New
York: Frederick A. Stokes, 1940. 265p.
How the Coast Guard cutters Bibb and Campbell
rescued 236 survivors of the S. S. City of Flint in
1939 is related on p. 169-188.

1380 Galbraith, W. H. "A Raft of Trouble." USNIP, XCVII
(1971), 74-75.
The U. S. S. Tracy (DD-214) at target practice
off Manila Bay in 1922.

1381 Gale, Esson M. "The Yangtze Patrol." USNIP,
LXXXI (1955), 306-315.
By U. S. Navy gunboats, China, during the 1920s
and 1930s.

1382 Gallagher, Thomas. Fire at Sea: The Story of the
Morrow Castle. New York: Rinehart, 1959. 280p.
The Coast Guard played an important role in
saving lives during this 1934 disaster.

1383 Gally, Benjamin W. "A History of U. S. Fleet Land-
ing Exercises." Unpublished Paper, Discontinued
Commands File, Operational Archives, U. S. Navy
Department, Naval History Division, n. d.   14p.
A brief study of five exercises conducted at
Culebra Island, Puerto Rico, and near San Pedro,
California, 1934-1939.

1384 Gantenbein, James W. "The Doctrine of Continuous
Voyage as Applied to Contraband and Blockade."
Unpublished PhD Dissertation, Columbia University,
1931.

1385 _____. Documentary Background of World War II,
1931-1941. New York: Columbia University Press,
1948. 1112p. Rpr. 1973.

1386 Gardiner, Leslie. The British Admiralty. Annapolis:
U. S. Naval Institute, 1968. 418p.
A history with some information relative to this
compilation.

1387 Gardiner, William H. The American Navy and World
Peace: An Address Before the Boston Branch,
Foreign Policy Association, Feb. 23, 1931. Wash-

ington: Navy League of the United States, 1931.
13p.

1388 _____. "Elements and Outlook of American Sea
Power." USNIP, LIV (1928), 823-827.

1389 _____. "The Functions of Naval Power." USNIP,
LV (1929), 839-846.

1390 _____. "Insular America." Yale Review, New
Series, XIV (April 1925), 509-524.

1391 _____. "National Policy and Naval Power." USNIP,
LII (1926), 229-248.

1392 _____. Naval Fleet Building and Replacement.
Washington: Navy League of the United States, 1931.
8p.

1393 _____. "Naval Fleet Ratios." Review of Reviews,
LXIX (March 1924), 305-308.
As a result of the Washington Conference.

1394 _____. "Naval Parity? The Outlook After Geneva."
Harper's Monthly, CLVI (January 1928), 211-219.

1395 _____. "Present Naval Programs." Review of Reviews, LXVII (January 1923), 45-48.

1396 _____. Treasury Deficit and a Treaty Navy. Washington: Navy League of the United States, 1932.
17p.

1397 _____. "What the United States Navy Costs and Who
Pays for It." USNIP, XLIX (1923), 828-842.

1398 Gardner, Kinlock N. "The Beginning of the Yangtze
River Campaign of 1926-1927." USNIP, LVIII
(1932), 40-44.

1399 Gary, Charles B., jt. author. See Denlinger, Sutherland, no. 977.

1400 "Gas Bags on Patrol." Popular Mechanics, LXXVI
(December 1941), 50-53.
Refers to the activities of Navy blimps.

120   The American Navy, 1918-1941

1401 Gatch, Thomas L.   "How Peace?" USNIP, LVI (1930),
      820-826.

1402 _____ . "The Naval Mind. " USNIP, LXI (1935),
      617-625.

1403 Gates, Thomas S.   The United States Navy: Its Influ-
      ence Upon History.   New York: Newcomen Society,
      1958. 40p.

1404 Gatewood, Richard D.   "Sea Power and American
      Destiny. " USNIP, LIII (1927), 1076-1080.

1405 Gauvreau, Emile and Lester Cohen.   Billy Mitchell:
      Found of Our Air Force and Prophet Without Honor.
      New York: Dutton, 1942. 318p.
      Ample discussion of his tests on naval vessels.

1406 Gayhart, E. L.   "U. S. Naval Requirements for Ship
      Heating and Ventilation. " Heating-Piping, III (Octo-
      ber 1931), 878-881.

1407 Gayn, Mark J.   The Fight for the Pacific.   New York:
      Morrow, 1941. 378p.
      Written before Pearl Harbor.

1408 Gehres, Leslie E.   "The Navy Cruises Inland. " USNIP,
      LVI (1930), 727-730.
      With its aircraft.

1409 Geiger, Roy S.   "The Relation of the Army and Navy
      Air Components in Joint Operations. " Unpublished
      General Staff Memorandum, Files of the U. S. Army
      Military History Research Collection, 1929.

1410 General Electric Company.   The Electric Ship.
      Schenectady, N. Y. , 1919. 37p.
      The battleship New Mexico, BB-40.

1411 "General Mitchell Drops Some Bombs. " Literary Di-
      gest, LXXXIV (February 21, 1925), 5-7.

1412 "General Mitchell Explains. " Independent, CXIV
      (April 4, 1925), 391.

1413 "General Smith [USMC] Does a Job at Guantanamo, on
      the Southeast Coast of Cuba. " Time, XXXVII

(May 5, 1941), 23.

1414   "The Geneva Conference and Submarines." Engineer-
       ing, CXXIV (July 22, 1927), 112-113.

1415   "The Geneva Conference for the Limitation of Naval
       Armaments." Commercial and Financial Chronicle,
       CXXIV (June 25, 1927), 2682-2684, 3723-3726.

1416   "Geneva Experts Define the Meaning of Armaments. "
       USNIP, LII (1926), 1889-1895.
              Reprinted from the Army & Navy Journal for
       July 31, 1926.

1417   Germains, Victor W.   "Command of the Sea." Con-
       temporary Review, CLVIII (November 1940), 528-
       536.

1418   Gerould, James T.   "Disagreement at [the Geneva]
       Conference on Naval Disarmament." Current His-
       tory, XXVI (August 1927), 792-797.

1419   _____. "Failure of the Three-Power Naval Confer-
       ence." Current History, XXVI (September 1927),
       945-949.
              That held in Geneva.

1420   _____. "The Problem of Naval Needs." Current
       History, XXXI (February 1930), 977-981.

1421   Gervasi, Frank.   "Our Gibraltar on Sand: Building the
       Most Important Base in Our Caribbean Defense
       System on Puerto Rico." Collier's, CVII (Febru-
       ary 22, 1941), 18-20.

1422   Gherardi, Walter R.   "A Pioneer Flight: St. Lucia, St.
       Vincent, and Granada by Air." USNIP, LV (1929),
       706-708.

1423   Ghormley, R. L.   "Execution of Naval Plans, Security
       in Formations, and the Naval Battle." Unpublished
       Lecture, Files of the U. S. Army Military History
       Research Collection, 1939.

1424   "The Giant Reduction Gear Used on U. S. Navy Tend-
       ers." Popular Mechanics, XL (July 1923), 84.

1425 Gibson, Henry. "U. S. Navy Diesel Engine Require-
      ments. " Mechanical Engineer, LIII (December
      1931), 871-875.

1426 Gibson, K. S. "Address at Geneva Naval Conference
      Contrasting the American and British Proposals. "
      Commercial and Financial Chronicle, CXXV (Sep-
      tember 3, 1927), 1276-1278.

1427 Gilbert, C. W. "I'm Proud of the Navy: An Interview
      with [Navy Secretary] C. D. Wilbur. " Collier's
      LXXIX (March 19, 1927), 8-9.
          For an anonymous reply, see "Everything's not
      All Right with Our Navy" cited above.

1428 Gill, Charles C. "The New Far East Doctrine. "
      USNIP, XLVIII (1922), 1479-1486.

1429 _____. "The Realism of Sea Power. " USNIP, LIX
      (1933), 1260-1268.

1430 Gillon, John F. "Naval Academy Flying Squadron. "
      USNIP, LV (1929), 703-705.

1431 _____. "Naval Patrol and Bombing Flying Boats. "
      USNIP, LVI (1930), 695-699.

1432 _____. "The Problem in Navigating Small Air-
      planes. " USNIP, LVIII (1932), 506-508.

1433 Gilman, Kenneth. "When the Roads Give Out. " Marine
      Corps Gazette, XXXVIII (March 1954), 32-36.
          The use of pack animals in the Caribbean during
      the banana wars.

1434 Gilmer, Francis H. "Preparing an Advance Base. "
      USNIP, L (1924), 1073-1081.

1435 _____. "Questions and Answers Concerning Air-
      ships. " USNIP, LXII (1936), 176-177.

1436 _____. "Why Should the United States Have Air-
      ships. " USNIP, LXIII (1937), 806-809.

1437 Glad, Betty. Charles Evans Hughes and the Illusions
      of Innocence: A Study in American Diplomacy.
      Urbana: University of Illinois Press, 1966.

Details provided on the Washington Conference.

1438   Gladden, Charles T. S.   "Uses of Aircraft in Naval
       Warfare. "   USNIP, LV (1929), 121-130.

1439   Glasgow, George.   "The American Navy. "   Contem-
       porary Review, CXXXIII (February 1928), 238-241.

1440   _____.   "Freedom of the Seas. "   Contemporary Re-
       view, CXXXV (May 1929), 645-653.

1441   _____.   "Humanizing the Submarine. "   Contempo-
       rary Review, CXXXVII (March 1930), 373-375.

1442   _____.   "A Naval Conference. "   Contemporary Re-
       view, CXLVI (September 1934), 357-368.

1443   _____.   "Naval Conference. "   Contemporary Re-
       view, CXLVIII (December 1935), 742-748.

1444   _____.   "The Naval Conference. "   Contemporary
       Review, CXXXVII (March-May 1930), 373-388, 509-
       515, 645-654.

1445   _____.   "Naval Disarmament. "   Contemporary Re-
       view, CXXXII (August 1927), 237-249.

1446   _____.   "The Naval Limitation Conference. "   Con-
       temporary Review, CXXXII (September 1927), 373-
       385.

1447   Glass, S. F.   "Excess Profit on War Materials Under
       the Vinson Act. "   Marine Engineering and Shipping
       Review, XLIII (October 1938), 445-447.

1448   Glassford, W. A.   "The U. S. Would Require Two
       Fleets if Britain Lost the War. "   China Weekly
       Review, XCII (March 2, 1940), 2.

1449   Gleason, Edmund H.   "The Advance of Naval Preven-
       tive Medicine. "   USNIP, LXXXIV (1958), 66-71.

1450   Gleason, S. Everett, jr. author.   See   Langer, William
       L. , nos. 2095 and 2096.

1451   Gleaves, Albert.   "Has Sea Power Passed? An Authori-
       tative Exposé of the Extravagant Claims of the Air

Enthusiasts. " SciAmer, CXXIX (November 1923), 313-314+.

1452 _____ . "Leadership. " USNIP, LVIII (1938), 1-14.

1453 _____ . "Libraries for the Navy. " Library Journal, XLIV (1919), 499-501.

1454 _____ . "The United States Naval Home, Philadelphia. " USNIP, LVII (1931), 473-476.

1455 _____ . "Will Seapower be Displaced by Airpower?" In: John O. Beaty, et al. , eds. Facts and Ideas for Students of English Composition. New York: Crofts, 1930. p. 175-177.

1456 Glenn, Bess. Demobilization of Civilian Personnel by the U. S. Navy After the First World War. Administrative Reference Service Report, no. 8. Washington: Administrative Office, Navy Department, 1945. 43p.

1457 Glickert, Robert W. "Quantico's Other Schools. " Marine Corps Gazette, XXXVIII (October 1954), 49-53.
     The Extension, Communications, and Ordnance schools begun in the mid-1920s.

1458 "Gloomy Prospects for Naval Conference: London Invites Four Nations to Sessions in December. " Literary Digest, CXX (November 2, 1935), 9.

1459 "The Glory--and Some of the Humor--of the Marines. " Literary Digest, LX (January 22, 1919), 42-50.

1460 Glover, Hamilton F. "The Desirability and Practicability of a Supply Line in Suez for a War in the Western Pacific. " Unpublished Staff Memorandum, Files of the U. S. Army Military History Research Collection, 1934.

1461 Glover, Robert O. "Practical Hints on Handling a Destroyer. " USNIP, XLVII (1922), 57-67.
     One wonders if those faced with "handling" four-stackers in World War II dipped back to read this article.

1462   Godfrey, J. L.   "Anglo-American Naval Conversations
       Preliminary to the London Naval Conference of
       1930. "   South Atlantic Quarterly, XLIX (July 1950),
       303-316.

1463   Godfrey, Vincent H.   "A Destroyer Division Com-
       mander's Inspection. "   USNIP, LI (1925), 2293-2297.

1464   _____.   "Form H for Destroyers. "   USNIP, LIII
       (1927), 1290-1291.

1465   Goerner, Fred.   The Search for Amelia Earhart.
       Garden City, N. Y.: Doubleday, 1966.   326p.
       Contains information on the U. S. Navy's role in
       the quest.

1466   Goldsborough, Washington L.   "The Aleutians, Their
       Strategic Importance. "   USNIP, LXVII (1941), 830-
       831.

1467   Golovin, Nikolai N. , in collaboration with Admiral A.
       D. Bubnov.   The Problem of the Pacific in the
       Twentieth Century.   New York: Arno. , 1973.
          A reprinting of the 1922 first edition in which
       another forecast of an American-Japanese war is
       made.   A Russian view of the strategical conditions
       is presented, with particular attention paid to the
       role of the U. S. fleet.

1468   "Good Neighbors: Japan Pays Itemized Bill. "   Time,
       XXXI (May 2, 1938), 14.
          The Panay incident.

1469   "Good Will and the Navy. "   Outlook, CXXXVIII (De-
       cember 24, 1924), 668.

1470   Goodall, S. V.   "American Warship Practice. "   En-
       gineering, CXIII (February 10, March 17-24, 1922),
       178, 320-323, 371-373.

1471   Goodhart, Philip.   Fifty Ships that Saved the World:
       The Foundation of the Anglo-American Alliance.
       Garden City, N. Y.: Doubleday, 1965.   267p.

1472   Goodrich, Casper F.   "The Navy and Its Owners. "
       North American Review, CCXIII (January 1921),
       25-35.

1473 _____. "The Navy's Paper Work. " USNIP, XLIX
      (1923), 465-468.

1474 _____. "The Princeton Naval Unit. " USNIP, XLV
      (1919), 1227-1232.

1475 Gordon, Arthur. "The Day the Astral Vanished. "
      USNIP, XCI (1965), 76-83.
           Sunk by U-43, December 2, 1941.

1476 Gordon, Bob. "The Coast Guard to the Rescue. "
      Popular Mechanics, LXII (July 1934), 56-58+.

1477 Gordon, Robert W.   "The Experimental Pack. " Leath-
      erneck, XXIII (October 1940), 21.

1478 Gorry, William A.   "Training Divers. " USNIP, LXI
      (1935), 1674-1676.

1479 Goslin, Ryllis A. , jt. author. See Stone, William T.
      no. 3835.

1480 Goss, Nathaniel H.   "Case for the Navy: A Reply to
      H.C. Bywater. " Review of Reviews, LXXVII (May
      1928), 86-92.

1481 _____. "Have We a Navy?" North American Re-
      view, CCXXVII (April 1929), 449-456.

1482 _____. "Naval Adequacy. " SciAmer, CXXXIX
      (September-December 1928), 220-224, 320-324, 418-
      422, 519-523; CXL (January 1929), 38-42.

1483 _____. "Naval Officer on the Pending Program. "
      Iron Age, CXXI (February 9, 1928), 424-425.

1484 Goss, Nelson H.   "Amalgamation. " USNIP, XLVII
      (1921), 231-233.

1485 Goude, Stephen.   "Battleships and Navy Officers. "
      Christian Century, XLVII (March 12, 1930), 338-
      339.

1486 Gould, Laurence M.   Cold: The Record of an Ant-
      arctic Sledge Journey. New York: Brewer, War-
      ren & Putnam, 1931.   275p.
           The second Byrd expedition.

1487 _____. "Some Geographical Results of the Byrd
      Antarctic Expedition. " In: Smithsonian Report.
      Washington, 1932. p. 235-250.

1488 Graham, S. V. "The Navy and International Relations."
      Institute for International Relations Proceedings, V
      (1930), 82-93.

1489 Grahame, Arthur. "Our Billion-Dollar Juggernaut. "
      American Magazine, CXXVII (March 1939), 20-21₊.

1490 Grant, Robert M. "Heroes of the Coast Guard. "
      Popular Mechanics, LXXII (December 1939), 892-
      896.

1491 _____. "How Many U-boats Have Been Sunk?"
      USNIP, LXVII (1941), 1598-1600.

1492 _____. "The Use of Mines Against Submarines. "
      USNIP, LXIV (1938), 1275-1279.

1493 Grantham, Emery A. "Drum and Bugle Corps [of the
      Naval Academy]. " USNIP, LXI (1935), 1492-1493.

1494 _____. "Extra-curricular Activities [at the Naval
      Academy]. " USNIP, LXI (1935), 1537-1543.

1495 Gray, George W. "Q-R-T, S. O. S. " U. S. Coast
      Guard Magazine, II (March 1929), 3.
         A rescue at sea by the cutter Manning.

1496 _____. "When Tempests Last the Cradle of the
      Deep: The [Coast Guard] Cutter Manning Aids Ships
      in Distress." American Magazine, CVI (November
      1928), 46-48.

1497 Gray, J. A. C. Amerika Samoa: A History of Ameri-
      can Samoa and Its United States Naval Administra-
      tion. Annapolis: U. S. Naval Institute, 1960. 295p.

1498 Gray, John A. "The Second Nicaraguan Campaign. "
      Marine Corps Gazette, XVII (February 1933), 36-
      41.

1499 Graybeal, C. W. "Bombing the Navy: A Pilot Tells
      His Story. " Independent, CXIV (March 7, 1925),
      263-264.

Mitchell's bombing tests and their results.

1500 "Great Britain and France Join the United States in
       Increasing the Limit for the Size of Battleships to
       45,000 Tons." Commercial and Financial Chron-
       icle, CXLVII (July 9, 1938), 202.
       The Japanese had already begun building the
       Yamato-class of superbattleship.

1501 "Great Britain-United States Agreement for the Use and
       Operation of Naval and Air Bases, Signed at Lon-
       don, March 27, 1941, Text." American Journal of
       International Law, XXXV (July 1941), 134-159.

1502 "Great Britain-United States Exchange of Notes Con-
       cerning the British Fleet: Text." American Journal
       of International Law, XXXV (January 1941), Supple-
       ment, 37+.

1502a "The Great Sky Ships: Navy Rigid Airships." Air
       Classics, VII (July 1971), 38+.
       Very well illustrated.

1503 "Greatest Weakness of the Navy: Scandalous Treatment
       of Bluejackets is Charged." Current Opinion,
       LXXVIII (April 1925), 452-453.

1504 Greathouse, R. H. "King of the Banana War." Marine
       Corps Gazette, XLV (June 1960), 28-33.

1505 Green, Fitzhugh. "Dick Byrd, Gentleman." American
       Magazine, CIV (December 1927), 16-17.

1506 _____. "Floating Citadels." St. Nicholas Maga-
       zine, XLVI (July 1919), 835-837.
       Battleships.

1507 _____. "Science and the Navy." USNIP, XLVIII
       (1922), 1697-1706.

1508 _____. Uncle Sam's Sailors. New York: D. Apple-
       ton, 1928. 284p.

1509 Green, Joseph A. "Would a Joint Army and Navy
       General Staff for War be Preferable to the Joint
       Board and the Joint Planning Committee?" Unpub-
       lished General Staff Memorandum, Files of the
       U. S. Army Military History Research Collection, 1925.

1510   Greenberg, Daniel S. "U. S. Destroyers for British
        Bases: Fifty Old Ships Go to War. " USNIP,
        LXXXVIII (1962), 70-83.

1511   Greene, A. B. "What the Sailors Read. " Forum,
        LXXV (1926), 89-98.
        Naval libraries.

1512   Greene, Frank L. The Grumman F4F-3 Wildcat. Air-
        craft Profiles, no. 53. Leatherhead, Surrey, Eng-
        land: Profile Publications, n. d.

1513   _____ . The Wildcat Story: History of the Grumman
        F4F "Wildcat. " Bethpage, N. Y. ; Grumman Air-
        craft Engineering Corp. , n. d.
        The mainstay of Navy and Marine fighter squad-
        rons for the first two years of the war.

1514   "The Greene's Cruise. " U. S. Coast Guard Magazine,
        IV (October 1931), 28.
        In the far north.

1515   Greenlee, Halford R. "Short Range Battle Practice
        for the Engineers of the Navy. " USNIP, XLVI
        (1920), 1443-1449.

1516   Greenman, W. G. "Entrance Requirements, United
        States Naval Academy. " USNIP, LIII (1927), 722-
        732.

1517   Greenslade, John W. "America's Naval Policy. " U.S.
        News and World Report, VIII (May 10, 1940), 9-11.

1518   _____ . "Command U. S. Navy. " USNIP, LVIII
        (1932), 805-822.

1519   _____ . "The Development of the Faculty of Com-
        mand. " USNIP, LVIII (1932), 721-731.

1520   _____ . "The International Naval Situation. " Un-
        published Lecture, G-2 Course 8, Files of the
        U. S. Army Military History Research Collection,
        1935.
        As seen by a Navy rear admiral.

1521   "The Greer Incident. " New Republic, CV (September
        15, 1941), 338.

1522 Gregory, H. B.   "U. S. S. New Mexico. " SciAmer,
      CXX (April 5, 1919), 340-341.
      BB-40, launched in 1917 and sold out 30 years
      later.

1523 Gregory, Luther E.   "Naval Civil Engineering--Its
      Place in National Defense, and Its Value to the
      Engineering Profession. " USNIP, LIII (1927), 1097-
      1101.

1524 Grenfell, Russell.   Sea Power in the Next War. Lon-
      don, 1938.   183p.

1525 Grew, Joseph C.   Ten Years in Japan: A Contemporary
      Record Drawn from the Diaries and Private and
      Official Papers of Joseph C. Grew, United States
      Ambassador to Japan, 1932-1942.   New York: Simon
      and Schuster, 1944.   554p.   Rpr. 1972.

1526 Grierson, John.   Challenge to the Poles: Highlights of
      Arctic and Antarctic Aviation.   Hamden, Conn.:
      Archon Books, 1964.   695p.
      Our concern here is with Admiral Byrd.

1527 Griffin, Alexander.   Here Come the Marines: The Story
      of the Devil Dogs from Tripoli to Wake Island.
      New York: Howell, Soskin, 1942.   219p.

1528 Griffith, Samuel B. , 2nd.   "Amphibious Warfare: Yes-
      terday and Tomorrow. " USNIP, LXXVI (1950),
      871-875.

1529 Grigore, Julius, Jr.   "The 0-5 (SS-66) is Down. "
      USNIP, XCVIII (1972), 54-60.
      Sunk in collision with S. S. Abangarez in Limon
      Bay, Panama, October 28, 1923.

1530 Grimminger, George and W. C. Haines.   "Meterological
      Results of the Byrd Antarctic Expeditions, 1928-
      1930, 1933-1935. " Geographic Review, XXX (Jan-
      uary 1940), 162.

1531 _____ . _____ . Nature, CXLV (January 6, 1940),
      34-35.

1532 Griswold, A. Whitney.   The Far Eastern Policy of the
      United States.   New York: Harcourt, 1938.   517p.
      Rpr. 1962.

1533 _____ . "The Influence of History Upon Sea Power:
      A Comment on American Naval Policy. " American
      Military Institute Journal, IV (1940), 1-8.

1534 Groeling, Dorothy T. "Submarines, Disarmament, and
      Modern Warfare. " Unpublished PhD Dissertation,
      Columbia University, 1950.
      During the years between World Wars I & II,
      there was much discussion about outlawing the use
      of submarines in future wars; in the end, that is
      all it amounted to--just talk.

1535 Grosvenor, Gilbert H. "Byrd: The Explorer and the
      Man. " National Education Association Journal, XX
      (January 1931), 19-21.

1536 Grow, Harold B. "Bombing Tests on the Virginia and
      New Jersey. " USNIP, XLIX (1923), 1987-1996.

1537 "Growing Strength of the U. S. Navy: Diagrammatic
      Drawing. " Illustrated London News, CXCIX (De-
      cember 20, 1941), 778.

1538 "Growing War Fleets of the World's Great Powers. "
      Literary Digest, CXVII (March 24, 1934), 16.

1539 Gruening, Edward H. "The Conquest of Haiti and Santo
      Domingo. " Current History, XV (March 1922),
      885-896.

1540 _____ . "Haiti Under American Occupation. " Cen-
      tury, CIII (April 1922), 836-845.

1540a "The Grumman F3F Fighter. " Air Classics, VII (May
      1971), 20-36.
      An illustrated piece on the development of a
      carrier fighter.

1541 "The Grumman F2F-1 Single-Seater Fighter. " Aero
      Digest, XXIX (February 1936), 56.

1542 Grunder, Garel A. and William E. Livezey. The
      Philippines and the United States. Norman: Uni-
      versity of Oklahoma Press, 1951. 315p. Rpr. 1973.

1543 "Guam. " In: Julia E. Johnsen, ed. The United States
      and War. Vol. XII of The Reference Shelf. New

York: H. W. Wilson, 1939.   p. 119-129.
Excerpts from the Report of the Naval Board on
naval bases.

1544   Guam: The Last Straw for Japan.   New York: World
       Peaceways, 1939.   3p.

1545   "Guardians of the Sea: The [Coast Guard] Training
       Ship Alexander Hamilton. " Popular Mechanics, L
       (October 1928), 546-550.

1546   Guiler, Robert P.   "The Naval Gun Factory. " USNIP,
       L (1924), 1107-1121.

1547   Gulick, J. W.   "Cooperation Between Army and Navy. "
       Unpublished Lecture, War Plans Division Course 2,
       Files of the U. S. Army Military History Research
       Collection, 1922.
       As seen by an Army major general, Chief of the
       Coast Artillery.

1548   _____. "Coordination of Indoctrination and Training
       of the Army and Navy in the Interest of Combined
       Action in Combat. " Unpublished General Staff
       Memorandum, Files of the U. S. Army Military His-
       tory Research Collection, 1924.

1549   _____. "Would a Joint Army and Navy General
       Staff for War Planning be Preferable to the Joint
       Board and the Joint Planning Committee?" Unpub-
       lished General Staff Memorandum, Files of the
       U. S. Army Military History Research Collection,
       1924.
       This presentation brought Coast Artillery Major
       Joseph Green's reply cited above, no. 1509.

1550   Gullett, William M.   "Malta, Focal Point of Mediter-
       ranean Control. " USNIP, LXVII (1941), 15-20.
       The author was an American naval lieutenant
       and observer.

1551   Gulliver, Louis J.   "Plane Carriers vs. Dive Bom-
       bers. " Christian Science Monitor Magazine,
       (March 29, 1941), 5.

1552   _____. "The Yangtze U. S. Gunboats. " USNIP,
       LXVIII (1942), 1285-1287.

1553   "The Gun Elevation Tangle." Independent, CXIV (January 24, 1925), 87-88.

1554   Gunn, Sidney. "The Naval Academy Collection of Paintings." USNIP, XLVI (1920), 245-252.

1555   Gunning, M. F. "Naval Limitation from a Technical Point of View." USNIP, LIX (1923), 1433-1437.

1556   Gurley, Ralph R. "Flying Boats." USNIP, LXIII (1937), 1302-1304.

1557   Gurney, Gene. The United States Coast Guard: A Pictorial History. New York: Crown, 1972. 288p.

1558   Guthrie, Harry A. "The Cause of Battery Explosions." USNIP, LVI (1930), 629-633.

1559   Guthrie, Woody. The Sinking of the Reuben James. New York: Leeds Music Company, 1941. 3p.
        A ballad of the undeclared U.S.-German naval war of 1941.

1560   Guyton, Boone T. Air Base. New York: Whittlesey House, McGraw-Hill, 1941. 295p.
        By a dive bomber pilot attached to U.S.S. Lexington operating out of the North Island Naval Air Base at San Diego.

1561   _____. "The Making of a Pilot: How the Navy Trains Its Airmen." New York Times Magazine, (January 12, 1941), 6-7, 12-13.

1562   Gwynn, Stephen. "Abolition of the Submarine: The National Viewpoint." Fortune, CXXXIII (March 1930), 406-409.

1563   Gwynne, Clarence L. The 1931-1934 Cruise of the U.S. Frigate Constitution. Boston: The Author, 1949. 285p.

1564   _____. "The Naval Conference." Fortune, CXXXIII (February 1930), 258-260.

1565   Hadaway, Richard B. "Course Zero Nine Five." USNIP, LXXXIII (1957), 40-47.
        The Honda Point disaster.

1566 Hagood, Johnson. "Our Defenseless Coast. " Collier's,
      CV (June 22, 1940), 18-19.

1567 _____ . We Can Defend America. Garden City,
      N. Y. : Doubleday, Doran, 1937. 321p.

1568 Haig, R. A. deH. "Large Airships as Aircraft Car-
      riers. " Aviation, XXII (March 28, 1927), 611-614.

1569 Haight, John M. , Jr. "Franklin D. Roosevelt and a
      Naval Quarantine of Japan. " Pacific Historical Re-
      view, XL (1971), 203-226.
          A mutual plan with England, 1937-1938, which
      was eventually shelved.

1570 Hailey, Foster. "Their Mission was to Begin a War:
      A Reconstruction of Events that Lead to Japan's
      Attack on Pearl Harbor. " New York Times Maga-
      zine, (December 2, 1945), 8-9+.

1571 _____ and Milton Lancelot. Clear for Action: The
      Photographic Story of Modern Naval Combat, 1898-
      1964. New York: Duell, Sloan, & Pearce, 1964.
      320p.

1572 Haines, C. Grove and Ross J. S. Hoffman. The Ori-
      gins and Background of the Second World War.
      New York: Oxford University Press, 1943. 659p.

1573 Haines, W. C. , jt. author. See Grimminger, George,
      no. 1530.

1574 "Haiti and Its Regeneration by the United States. "
      National Geographic, XXXVIII (December 1920),
      397-512.

1575 Hale, Frederick. "How the U. S. Navy Stands Today."
      Congressional Digest, XIII (April 1934), 118, 122.

1576 Hale, William H. "Hold the Pacific!" New Republic,
      CV (September 29, 1941), 394-396.
          The author printed a "Correction" on page 439
      of the October 6, 1941 issue.

1577 _____ . "The Oceans Are Ours. " New Republic,
      CV (November 24, 1941), 690-693.
          Not for long!

1578 Hall, John. "The Battle of Bermuda: American Military and Naval Forces Delayed by the Petty Tactics of the Islanders. " New Republic, CV (August 4, 1941), 157-158.

1579 Hall, Norman B. "Coast Guarding the Air. " U. S. Coast Guard Magazine, IV (August 1931), 10.

1580 Hallet, Richard. "Destroyer, a Million a Minute. " Science Digest, X (July 1941), 1-4.

1581 Halsey, William F. Admiral Halsey's Story. New York: Whittlesey House, 1947. 310p.
       Also covers his pre-war career.

1582 _____. "The Carrier. " In: William H. Fetridge, ed. The Navy Reader. Indianapolis: Bobbs-Merrill, 1943. p. 69-76. Rpr. 1971.
       A useful general history which includes the story of the first carrier operations, some discussion of naval planes in modern war, and a carrier's organization and operation.

1583 _____. "Japan's Attitude at the Forthcoming Naval Conference. " Unpublished Staff Memorandum, Files of the U. S. Army Military History Research Collection, 1934.
       The future fleet admiral was referring to the London Conference of 1935.

1584 Hamilton, Charles. "American Naval Autographs. " Hobbies, LIX (April 1954), 131-133.

1585 _____. "The Navy's Future Fuel Problem. " USNIP, LIX (1933), 1400-1412.

1586 _____. "This Naval Race. " USNIP, LXIV (1938), 1013-1020.

1587 Hammond, Paul S. "The Secretaryships of War and Navy: A Study of Civilian Control of the Military. " Unpublished PhD Dissertation, Harvard University, 1953.

1587a Hammond, Paul Y. Organizing for Defense: The American Military Establishment in the Twentieth Century. Princeton, N. J. : Princeton University

Press, 1961. 403p.
Contains several essays relative to our subject
and period.

1588 Hancock, J. B. "Our Flying Navy." Popular Mechanics, LXXIII (June 1940), 817-824; LXXIV (July
1940), 17-24.

1589 Hanna, James. "The Merchant Naval Reserve."
USNIP, LVII (1931), 1187-1191.

1590 _____. "Safety Third." USNIP, LXIII (1927), 1144-
1146.

1591 Hanneken, Herman H. "A Discussion of the Voluntario
Troops in Nicaragua." Marine Corps Gazette,
XXVI (November 1942), 120, 247-266.
Marine led native troops which battled Sandino's
bandits during the American occupation of Nicaragua.

1592 Hansen, Emil M. Modern Marine Pipefitting. New
York: Cornell Maritime Press, 1941. 434p.

1593 Hansen, Harry J. "Resultant Course Method of
Course Angle Plotting." USNIP, LII (1926), 1163-
1171.

1594 Hard, William. "Continuous Instead of Spasmodic Naval
Parleys." World's Work, LIX (July 1930), 58-61.

1595 _____. "Dollars and Sense of Naval Reduction."
World's Work, LIX (January 1930), 83-87.

1596 _____. "Naval Conference Consequences." Saturday Evening Post, CCII (June 7, 1930), 14-15.

1597 _____. "Politics and Fleets." World's Work, LIX
(February 1930), 57-61.
At the London Naval Conference.

1598 Hardy, Alfred C. Warships at Work: A Naval Note-
book Explaining in Text and by Profile Some Functions of the Principal Warship Types of the World.
New York: Penguin Books, 1940. 144p.

1599 Hargreaves, Reginald. "Sweethearts and Wives--a
Tribute." USNIP, LXXXVI (1960), 63-69.
Since the earliest days.

Harriman   137

1600   Harriman, Florence J. (Hurst).   Mission to the North.
       Philadelphia: Lippincott, 1941. 331p.
       Reminiscences of the U.S. Ambassador to Nor-
       way, 1937-1941, including the 1939 City of Flint
       episode.

1601   Harrington, Samuel M.   "The Strategy and Tactics of
       Small Wars." Marine Corps Gazette, VI (Decem-
       ber 1921), 474-491.

1602   Harris, Brayton. The Age of the Battleship, 1890-
       1922. New York: Franklin Watts, 1965.   212p.

1603   Harris, Frank S.M.   "Naval Reserve Cruising."
       USNIP, LVII (1931), 1533-1539.

1604   _____. "Naval Reserve Discipline." USNIP, LXIV
       (1938), 369-375.

1605   _____. "The Navy and the Diplomatic Frontier."
       USNIP, LXII (1936), 473-486.

1606   Harris, Harold D.   "Anti-Aircraft Problems and a
       Solution." Marine Corps Gazette, XIX (May 1934),
       14-15.

1607   Harris, Henry W.   Naval Disarmament.   London: Allen
       & Unwin, 1930.   124p.

1608   Harris, Seymour E.   The Economics of American De-
       fense. New York: Norton, 1941.   350p.

1609   Harsch, Joseph C.   "Farewell to Naval Limitation."
       Christian Science Monitor Magazine (December 23,
       1936), 3-5.

1610   _____. "Saving the Keel of Naval Limitations."
       Christian Science Monitor Magazine, (April 1, 1936),
       8-9.

1611   _____. "The United States Checks Its Defenses:
       What are American Vital Interests? Navy Adequate
       for What?" Christian Science Monitor Magazine
       (December 28, 1938), 1-2+.

1612   Hart, Albert B.   "President Hoover's Challenge to Big
       Navy Propaganda: The Shearer Case." Current

History, XXXI (October 1929), 156-158.

1613 Hart, Thomas C.   "Problems of Combined Expedi-
      tions. " Unpublished Lecture, Files of the U. S.
      Army Military History Research Collection, 1925.
      The future admiral would see these first hand
      with his ABDA forces in the Pacific in the early
      months of the Second World War.

1614 _____. "Sea Power. " Unpublished Lecture, War
      Planning Division Course 3, Files of the U. S. Army
      Military History Research Collection, 1924.

1615 _____. "Some Naval Strategic Considerations. "
      Unpublished Lecture, War Planning Division Course
      22, Files of the U. S. Army Military History Re-
      search Collection, 1925.

1616 _____. "Submarines. " Unpublished Lecture, Files
      of the U. S. Army Military History Research Col-
      lection, 1919.

1617 Hartley, Livingston. Our Maginot Line: Defense of the
      Americas. New York: Carrick & Evans, 1939.
      315p.

1618 Hatcher, Charles H.   "A Navy Homebuilding and Fi-
      nancial Co-operative. " USNIP, LXV (1939), 1465-
      1467.

1619 Haughen, Lawrence T.   "Naval Trial Course and
      Trials. " USNIP, LXIV (1938), 821-830.

1620 Havens, B. S.   "America's All-Electric Battle Fleet."
      American Industries, XXIV (February 1924), 5-10.

1621 Havill, Clinton H.   "Aircraft Propellers. " USNIP,
      LIV (1928), 314-318.

1622 "Hawaii: Sugar-Coated Fort, Pearl Harbor is Our Sing-
      apore. " Fortune, XXII (August 1940), 30-37.

1623 Hawley, Paul R. and J. S. Simmons.   "Effectiveness
      of the Vaccines Used for the Prevention of Typhoid
      Fever in the United States Army and Navy. "
      American Journal of Public Health, XXIV (July
      1934), 689-709.

1624   Hawthorne, Randolph. "Wings for the Catalinas: The
       Brewster Aeronautical Corporation. " Aviation, XL
       (October 1941), 74-76.

1625   Hayden, Reynolds. Elementary Hygiene, General and
       Naval. Annapolis: U. S. Naval Institute, 1939.
       417p.
       Prepared as a Naval Academy textbook.

1626   Hayes, John D. "Admiral Joseph Mason Reeves,
       U. S. N. (1872-1948). " Naval War College Review,
       XXIII (November 1970), 48-57; XXIV (January 1972),
       50-64.

1627   _____. "Dudley W. Knox, 1877-1960, USN (Rt)."
       USNIP, LXXXVI (1960), 103-105.

1628   "Hazards of the Submarine. " Engineer, CXLII (August
       27, 1926), 225-226.

1629   Hazelrigg, Hal. "Great Armada Comes East to Salute
       the President. " Literary Digest, CXVII (May 19,
       1934), 11-13.

1630   Hazlett, Edward E. "Submarines and the London
       Treaty. " USNIP, LXII (1936), 169-1694.

1631   "Headquarters Hut for Admiral Byrd in the Antarctic:
       V. H. Czegka, Designer. " Architectural Record,
       LXXVI (July 1934), 54-55.

1632   Heffernan, John B. "A Building Program for the Naval
       Academy. " USNIP, LXI (1935), 364-368.

1633   Heinl, Robert D. , Jr. "The Cat With More Than Nine
       Lives. " USNIP, LXXX (1954), 658-671.
       Various unsuccessful attempt to abolish the
       Marine Corps.

1634   _____. "Damage Control School. " USNIP, LXVII
       (1941), 382-383.

1635   _____. Dictionary of Military and Naval Quotations.
       Annapolis: U. S. Naval Institute, 1966.   367p.
       A unique and most useful item.

1636   _____. "The Last Banana War. " Leatherneck,

XLIII (October-November 1960), 38-43+, 58-62.
Nicaragua.

1637   . "The Old Slouch Hat." Marine Corps Gazette, XXXVI (June 1952), 30-33.
The Marine Corps field hat.

1638   . "On the Mobility of Base Defense Artillery." Marine Corps Gazette, XXV (September
1941), 23-24, 42-43.
Suggests interchanging 5" naval guns for 155mm
guns to secure mobility when needed.

1639   . "Slouch and the Spring: A Footnote on Discipline." USNIP, LXVII (1941), 1709-1711.

1640   . Soldiers of the Sea: A Definitive History of
the U. S. Marine Corps, 1775-1962. Annapolis:
U. S. Naval Institute, 1962. 693p.
Considerable data on our period.

1641   . "Training the Landing Force." USNIP,
LXVII (1941), 1452-1457.

1642   . "What is the Naval R. O. T. C. ?" USNIP,
LXII (1936), 702-704.

1643 Heite, Edward F. "Naval Honors at Mount Vernon. "
Virginia Cavalcade, XIV (1964), 40-41.
The continuing tradition of saluting the home of
our first President by warships enroute up or down
the Potomac River.

1644 Helkerington, William, Jr. "Modern Deck Winches for
U. S. Battleships." Marine Engineering, XXXVI
(September 1931), 431-432.

1645 Hellweg, Julius F. "The United States Naval Observa-
tory. " USNIP, LXII (1936), 1464-1468.

1646   .   . Natural History, XXXI (Septem-
ber-October 1931), 488-499.

1647 "Hemisphere Defense Map: Showing the Location of
Army and Navy Bases and Indicating the Extent of
Border Air Defenses. " Aviation, XXXIX (August
1940), 74-75.

1648   Hendricks, Daniel E., Jr.   "History of the U. S. Naval
        Reserves Participation in the Cuban Revolt of 1933."
        Unpublished Paper, Individual Personnel File,
        Operational Archives, U. S. Navy Department, Naval
        History Division, n. d.   3p.
            How the reserve destroyer U. S. S. Claxton, DD-
        140, was sent from New Orleans in response to the
        civil disturbances as seen by one of the ship's
        officers.

1649   Henry, Walter O.   "A Six-Year Course at the Naval
        Academy. "   USNIP, XLVIII (1922), 725-735.

1650   Hepburn, Arthur J.   "The United States Fleet. " USNIP,
        LXII (1936), 1443-1446.

1651   "Hepburn, Fleet's New Four Star Commander. "   News-
        week, VII (January 18, 1936), 14.

1652   Herbster, Victor D.   "The Offensive Power of Air-
        craft. "   USNIP, LII (1926), 1701-1703.

1653   _____.   "United Air Service. "   USNIP, L (1924),
        886-892.

1654   Heritage, Gordon W.   "Forced Down in the Jungles of
        Nicaragua. "   Leatherneck, XV (May 1932), 13-15.

1655   Herold, Frank C.   "The Coast Guard as a Naval
        Asset. "   USNIP, LXVII (1941), 969-976.

1656   Herromg, George C., Jr.   "Experiment in Foreign
        Aid: Lend-Lease, 1941-1945. "   Unpublished PhD
        Dissertation, University of Virginia, 1965.
            Contains some information relative to this work.

1657   Hertel, Frank M.   "The Naval Academy and Naval
        Aviation. "   USNIP, LXXIV (1948), 37-41.

1658   Herwig, Holger H.   "Prelude to Weltblitzkrieg: Ger-
        many's Naval Policy Towards the United States of
        America, 1939-1941. "   Journal of Modern History,
        XXXIII (December 1971), 649+.

1659   Herzog, Bobo.   "Top Submarines in Two World Wars."
        USNIP, LXXXVII (1961), 90-99.
            Our concern here is with 1939-1941.

1660 Herzog, James H. Closing the Open Door: American-
      Japanese Diplomatic Negotiations, 1936-1941.
      Annapolis: U. S. Naval Institute, 1973. 296p.
      Covered in detail are U. S. and Allied strategic
      planning in the Pacific, the effect of the economic
      sanctions against Japan, and the U. S. efforts at
      adopting deterrence as a strategic concept. Based
      on the dissertation cited below.

1661 _____. "The Role of the United States Navy in the
      Evolution and Execution of American Foreign Policy
      Relative to Japan, 1936-1941. " Unpublished PhD
      Dissertation, Brown University, 1963.

1661a Hewes, James E. , Jr. "Management vs Bureaus. "
      Marine Corps Gazette, LI (February 1967), 39-41.
      Navy Department administration.

1662 Hezlet, Arthur. "The Development of U. S. Naval Avi-
      ation and the British Fleet Air Arm and Coastal
      Command Between the Wars. " Aerospace Histor-
      ian, XVIII (1971), 116-122.

1663 _____. The Submarine and Sea Power. New York:
      Stein & Day, 1967. 278p.

1664 Hice, Charles. The Last Hours of Seven Four-Stack-
      ers. Miamisburg, Ohio: Ohioian Newspaper, 1968.
      Wrecked on the California coast in the 1920s.

1665 Hickman, Albert. "Sea Sleds vs. Battleships. " Re-
      view of Reviews, XCIII (February 1936), 66-69.
      Concerns the development of torpedo boats.

1666 Hicks, Norman W. , author. See U. S. Marine Corps. ,
      no. 4728.

1667 Hicks, T. H. "Tested Methods for an Accurate Inven-
      tory: Storehouses of the United States Navy. "
      Manufacturing Industries, XIV (July-August 1927),
      37-40, 107-110.

1668 "High Seas Flying Patrol. " Popular Mechanics, LXXII
      (August 1939), 4-7.
      Maintained by the U. S. Navy.

1669 Hilbert, William E. "The Three-Mile Limit of Territorial Waters. " USNIP, LXIV (1938), 804-812.

1670 Hiles, C. C.   "The Kita Message: Forever a Mystery?"
      Chicago Tribune Special Supplement, (December 7,
      1966), 6-8.
      A message from Japanese consul general Nagoa
      Kita in Honolulu to Tokyo intercepted by U. S. naval
      intelligence four days before Pearl Harbor.

1671 Hill, Charles E.   Purser's Manual and Marine Store-
      keeping.   New York: Cornell Maritime Press, 1941.
      194p.

1672 Hill, Henry W.   "Can Our Present Navy be Reduced?"
      World's Work, XLIV (May 1922), 106-109.

1673 _____ .   President-Elect Herbert Hoover's Good Will
      Cruise to Central and South America, Being the
      Log of the Trip aboard the U. S. S. Maryland.   San
      Francisco: Priv. print. , 1929.   90p.

1674 Hill, Norman L.   "Was There an Ultimatum Before
      Pearl Harbor?"   American Journal of International
      Law, XLII (April 1948), 355-367.

1675 Hilliard, Robert B.   "The Salvage of S-19. " USNIP,
      LI (1925), 1408-1414.

1676 Hilmar, H. O.   The Development of Underseas Craft.
      Boston: Society of Naval Architects and Marine
      Engineers, 1952.   29p.

1677 Hinds, Alfred W.   "Better Preparation for War. "
      USNIP, LII (1926), 1496-1508.

1678 _____ .   "Naval Disarmament is a Gamble. " Marine
      Review, LVI (December 1926), 11-12+.

1679 Hinkamp, Clarence N.   "Bringing in the Sheaves. "
      USNIP, XLV (1919), 1117-1133.

1680 _____ .   "Pipe Sweepers. " USNIP, XLVI (1920),
      1477-1484.
      Removing the mine fields in European Waters
      after World War I.

1681 Hinman, George W. , Jr.   "The Submarine Menace. "

Forum, LXXIII (April 1925), 555-561.

1682 Hinsley, Francis H. Command of the Sea: The Naval
     Side of British History from 1918 to the End of the
     Second World War. London: Christophers, 1950.
     104p.
        With several comments on the American navy
     relative to this period.

1683 Hinton, Harold B. Cordell Hull: A Biography. Garden
     City, N. Y. : Doubleday, 1942. 377p.
        Very sympathetic, with the book ending with
     Pearl Harbor.

1684 Hironori, Mizuno. "America's Pacific Maneuvers. "
     Living Age, CCCXXV (April 11, 1925), 87-91.
        The great cruise of 1925.

1685 Hirst, Francis W. Armaments: The Race and the
     Crisis. London: Cobden-Sanderson, 1937. 171p.

1686 Hishida, Seji G. Japan Among the Great Powers: A
     Survey of Her International Relations. New York:
     Longmans, Green, 1940. 405p.
        Contains discussions of her role in and after the
     Washington Conference and the naval problems of
     the Pacific.

1687 "History of the United States Navy War College, 1884-
     1963. " Unpublished paper, Files of the U. S. Naval
     War College Library, 1966.

1688 "Hits and Duds in the Hoover-Navy League Fight. "
     Literary Digest, CXI (November 14, 1931), 8-10.

1689 Hittle, James D. "20th Century Amphibious Warfare."
     Marine Corps Gazette, XXXVIII (January 1954), 14-
     21.
        A general review.

1690 Hobbs, Ira E. , jt. author. See Knight, Richard H. ,
     no. 2012.

1691 Hobbs, William H. "Centenary Celebration of the
     Wilkes Exploring Expedition. " Scientific Monthly,
     L (April 1940), 372-377.
        For more information on that pioneering U. S.

Navy expedition to the South Seas and Antarctica,
see the many references in Volume II of this series.

1692 _____. "The Defense of Greenland. " Annals of the
Association of American Geographers, XXXI (June
1941), 95-104.

1693 _____. "The Early Attempted Flights to Europe
Over Greenland. " USNIP, LXXV (1949), 38-45.

1694 _____. "Professor W. H. Hobbs Urges Bases on
Greenland for Planes and Submarines. " Science
News Letter, XXXIX (January 11, 1941), 30.

1695 Hobsen, F. M. "The U. S. Navy's Rubber Lung. " India
Rubber Weekly, LXXX (June 1929), 63-66.
For submarine rescues and escapes.

1696 Hoehling, Adolph A. America's Road to War: Nineteen
Thirty-nine to Nineteen Forty-one. New York:
Abelard, 1970. 178p.

1697 _____. The Week Before Pearl Harbor. New York:
W. W. Norton, 1963. 238p.

1698 Hoffman, Ross J. S., jt. author. See Haines, C.
Grove, no. 1572.

1699 Hoffman, Roy C. "Report on Lend-Lease Activities in
the Department of the Navy Before and During
World War II. " Admin. Hist. Appen. Procurement
and Material 22, Operational Archives, U. S. Navy
Department, Naval History Division, 1948. 16p.

1700 Hogg, William S. and A. P. H. Tawresey. "Naval Communications and Governmental Reorganization. "
USNIP, LII (1926), 1285-1299.

1701 Holcomb, Richard C. A Century with Norfolk Naval
Hospital, 1830-1930: A Story of the Oldest Naval
Hospital, the Medical Department of the Navy, and
the Progress of Medicine Through the Past One
Hundred Years. Portsmouth, Va.: Printcraft, 1930.
543p.

1702 "Hold Up Naval Contracts!" Christian Century, LII
(February 20, 1935), 230-232.

1703 Holden, E. C. , Jr. "Sea Power and Our Navy. "
      Weekly Underwriter, CXLIII (December 14, 1940),
      1387-1389.

1704 Holmes, Wilfred J. "The Foundation of Naval Policy."
      USNIP, LX (1934), 457-469.

1705 _____. "Naval Research. " USNIP, LXII (1936),
      178-185.

1706 _____. "Tactical Horsepower of Submarines. "
      USNIP, LVII (1931), 1616-1620.

1707 "Holystone for the Navy's Vocabulary. " Literary Di-
      gest, CXV (June 10, 1933), 16.
          Could it have been too salty?

1708 Home of the Commandants, 801 G. St. , S. E. , Wash-
      ington, D. C. Washington: Leatherneck Association,
      1956.   137p.
          A history of the home plus biographies of all
      commandants, including those from our period.

1709 Honan, William H. "Japan Strikes, 1941: Prophesies
      in Books by Hector C. Bywater. " American Heri-
      tage, XXII (December 1970), 12-15+.

1710 Hooker, Richard. "The Geneva Naval Conference. "
      Yale Review, New Series XVII (January 1928), 263-
      280.

1711 "Hooking an Airplane to an Airship. " Aviation, XVIII
      (April 6, 1925), 378-379.

1712 Hooper, Stanford C. "The Naval Radiotelegraph in
      Peace and War, with a Review of International Law
      with Respect to Radio. " Annals of the American
      Academy, Supplement, CXLII (March 1929), 90-94.

1713 _____. "The Navy and Its Communications. " USNIP,
      LV (1929), 847-851.

1714 Hoover, Herbert. "National Defense and World Dis-
      armament. " In: his The Cabinet and the Presi-
      dency, 1920-1933. Vol. II of The Memoirs of
      Herbert Hoover. New York: Macmillan, 1952.
      p. 338-359.

1715 _____. "The Naval Arms Agreement: A Great Step
in World Peace." Commercial and Financial
Chronicle, CXXX (April 19, 1930), 2681.

1716 _____. "Summary of [London] Naval Conference
Results." Current History, XXXII (May 1930), 356-
358.

1717 "Hopeful Experiment: New Rigid Airship for the Navy."
Time, XXXII (November 14, 1938), 20.

1718 Hopkins, John J. We Work for Freedom. New York:
Newcomen Society in North America, 1950. 28p.
History of the Electric Boat Company.

1719 Horka, Archie. "The Merchant Marine Reserve Cruise
of 1937." USNIP, LXIV (1938), 975-980.

1720 Horne, Frederick J. "Report of the Board to Study
Matters Concerning Regular and Reserve Personnel
of the Navy and Marine Corps." Unpublished
paper, Individual Personnel File, Operational
Archives, U. S. Navy Department, Naval History
Division, 1940. 57p.
An analysis of personnel needs and requirements
in the preparedness period.

1721 Hough, Frank O., jt. author. See Pierce, Philip N.,
no. 3053.

1722 Hough, Richard. Dreadnought. New York: Macmillan,
1964. 268p.
A heavily-illustrated history of the battleship,
with considerable data from our period.

1723 "House Approves Naval Appropriations Bill." Commercial and Financial Chronicle, CXLVI (January
29, 1938), 681-682.

1724 "House Committee Favorably Reports $1,000,000,000
Naval Expansion Bill." Commercial and Financial
Chronicle, CXLVI (March 5, 1938), 1479-1480.

1725 "House Concludes Debate on the Naval Expansion Bill."
Commercial and Financial Chronicle, CXLVI
(March 19, 1938), 1807-1808.

1726   "House Naval Affairs Committee Hearings on Vinson
           Bill. " Commercial and Financial Chronicle,
           CXLVIII (January 28-February 4, 1939), 515, 663.

1727   "House Passes 20 Per Cent Naval Expansion Bill. "
           Commercial and Financial Chronicle, CXLVI (March
           26, 1938), 1966-1967.

1728   "House Passes Vinson Bill Providing for New Naval Air
           Bases with Provisions for the Improvements at
           Guam Island Stricken Out. " Commercial and Fi-
           nancial Chronicle, CXLVIII (February 25, 1939),
           1101-1102.

1729   "House Votes Treaty Navy for the U. S. " Scholastic,
           XXIV (February 17, 1934), 19.

1730   Hovgaard, William.   "After the Akron: Should We Con-
           tinue to Build Airships?" Forum, LXXXIX (June
           1933), 338-340.

1731   _____. "Airships for Naval Service. " USNIP, LXII
           (1936), 362-366.

1732   _____. Biographical Memoir of David Watson Tay-
           lor, 1864-1940.   Biographical Memoirs, Vol. XXII,
           7th Memoir.   Washington: National Academy of
           Sciences, 1941.   18p.

1733   _____. The Structural Design of Warships.   Annap-
           olis: U. S. Naval Institute, 1940.   410p.

1734   _____. "The Value of Naval Aeroplanes. "   Engin-
           eering, CXVI (December 14, 1923), 743-744.

1735   "How Big a Navy?" Forum, C (December 1938), 292-
           295.
               A debate, with the topic "Keep the Navy for De-
           fense" expounded by Ernest Lundeen and the topic
           "An Inadequate Navy is Worse than None" expounded
           by Millard E. Tydings.

1736   "How Coast Guard Planes Save Lives and Spot Smug-
           glers. " Literary Digest, CIV (February 22, 1930),
           57-60.

1737   "How the Navy Trains Sailors on Dry Land. " Popular

Science, CXXIV (February 1934), 22-23.

1738 "How to Get Heating Business in Navy Ships, With a
List of Ships Under Construction as of January 7. "
Heating and Ventilation, XXXVIII (February 1941),
11-14.

1739 "How to Reach a Naval Agreement. " New Republic,
LVI (October 10, 1928), 192-193.

1740 "How Warships are Scrapped. " Literary Digest, LXXIV
(August 12, 1922), 20-21.
Using those units designated under the terms of
the Washington Treaty as examples.

1741 Howard, Herbert. "Battleship vs. Airplane. " Independent, CXIV (March 21, 1925), 325-326.
A reply to this article, written by Admiral Sims,
appeared on page 241 of Vol. IV of the Congressional Digest for April 1925.

1742 _____. "The Light Cruiser. " USNIP, LII (1926),
1733-1745.

1743 _____. "What the Naval Building Program Means
to Design. " USNIP, LIV (1928), 879-882.

1744 Howard, Michael. "Military Intelligence and Surprise
Attack: The 'Lessons' of Pearl Harbor. " World
Politics, XV (1963), 701-711.

1745 Howarth, David. "Secrets of the Unknown War. "
Saturday Evening Post, CCXXX (August 3-31, 1957),
13-15+, 32-33+, 34+, 30+.
Greenland.

1746 Howe, H. , ed. "Key to the Americas: The Problem
of Hemisphere Defense. " Commonweal, XXXII
(August 23, 1940), 366-369.

1747 Howe, Hartley E. , jt. author. See Pratt, Fletcher,
no. 3134.

1748 Howe, Quincy. "Roosevelt Drifts Towards War. "
Living Age, CCCXLVII (February 1935), 480-486.

1749 _____. "The United States Checks Its Defenses: A

Navy Adequate for What?" Christian Science Monitor Magazine, (December 28, 1938), 1-2.

1750 Howe, Walter B. "Why the United States Asks Naval Equality. " USNIP, LIII (1927), 1056-1059.

1751 _____. "Why the United States Should Maintain a Full Strength Treaty Navy. " USNIP, LVI (1930), 919-922.

1752 Howell, Glenn F. "Army-Navy Game; or, No Rules of the Road. " USNIP, LXIV (1938), 1435-1438.

1753 _____. "Chungking to Ichang. " USNIP, LXIV (1938), 1312-1316.

1754 _____. "Lost, Strayed, or Stolen--Four Gunboats." USNIP, LVI (1930), 281-284.

1755 _____. "Neptune Rex. " USNIP, LII (1926), 2485-2486.
         The traditional initiation when first crossing the equator.

1756 _____. "Operations of the United States Navy on the Yangtze River--September '26 to June 1927. " USNIP, LIV (1928), 273-286.

1757 _____. "Opium Obligato. " USNIP, LXIV (1938), 1729-1735.
         Concerns the adventures of the China river gunboat U. S. S. Palos.

1758 Howeth, Lindwood S. A History of Communications-Electronics in the U. S. Navy. Washington: U. S. Government Printing Office, 1963. 657p.

1759 Howland, Charles P. "Navies and Peace. " Foreign Affairs, VIII (October 1929), 20-40.

1760 Howland, Felix. "The Naval Officer as a Teacher. " USNIP, LXVII (1941), 9-14.

1761 Hoyt, Edwin P. From the Turtle to the Nautilus: The Story of Submarines. Boston: Little, Brown, 1963. 134p.

1762 _____ . The Last Explorer: The Adventures of
         Admiral Byrd. New York: John Day, 1968. 380p.

1763 Hubbard, N. M. , Jr. "The Navy League of the United
         States Explains Our Naval Policy to the Navy League
         of the British Empire. " Marine Engineering and
         Shipping Age, XXXVIII (November 1933), 402-404.

1764 "A Hucksters' Treaty. " Nation, CXXX (May 28, 1930),
         615-616.

1765 Huff, B. F. "The Maritime History of San Francisco
         Bay. " Unpublished PhD Dissertation, University of
         California at Berkeley, 1956.
         Including its relationship with the navy.

1766 "Huge Naval Program Planned. " Marine Engineering
         and Shipping Review, XLIII (December 1938), 547.

1767 Hughes, Charles E. "Address of Secretary Hughes
         Proposing Ten Years Naval Holiday. " Commercial
         and Financial Chronicle, CXIII (November 19, 1921),
         2138-2140.

1768 _____ . "American Naval Proposals as Stated by
         Secretary Hughes. " Review of Reviews, LXIV
         (December 1921), 646-648.

1769 Hughes, Charles P. "A Modern Naval Cruiser and Its
         Varied Uses. " Congressional Digest, VIII (Janu-
         ary 1929), 4-5.

1770 Hughes, James J. "The United States Naval Academy,
         1918-1926. " USNIP, LII (1926), 2500-2509.

1771 _____ and W. E. Tanner. "Naval Radio in Africa."
         USNIP, LXII (1936), 373-374.

1772 Hughes, James P. "Making Sailors: San Diego Naval
         Training Station. " Sunset, LIX (July 1927), 26-28.

1773 Hughes, Wayne P. , Jr. "Speed Characteristics of the
         Treaty Cruisers. " USNIP, LXXIX (1953), 182-193.
         Those built between 1922 and 1936.

1774 Hugli, W. C. , Jr. A Motor Torpedo Boat Comparison
         Based on Published Data (Not Stevens Model Tests),

Nov. 18, 1940. Technical Memorandum, no. 54.
Hoboken, N. J.: Stevens Institute of Technology,
1940. 6p.

1775 Hule, William B. The Case Against the Admirals:
Why We Must Have a Unified Command. New
York: E. P. Dutton, 1946. 216p.
Takes a historical view over the previous half
century.

1776 Hull, Cordell. Memoirs of Cordell Hull. 2 vols.
New York: Macmillan, 1948.

1777 _____. "Pan American Relations: The Havana Conference Results." Vital Speeches, VI (August 15,
1940), 648-650.

1778 Hull, George D. "The New Destroyers." USNIP,
LVII (1931), 464-467.

1779 Hull, Merlin. "Millions for What?: The Cost of War
Preparation." Vital Speeches, IV (April 1, 1938),
376-377.
Opposes the big navy preparedness.

1780 "Hull Triumph: Basis for Collective Action by Americas Set up at Havana." Newsweek, XVI (August 5,
1940), 29-31.

1781 "The Human Side of the Shenandoah Disaster." Literary Digest, LXXXVI (September 26, 1925), 36-
48.

1781a Humble, Richard. "Towards the Abyss." In: his
Japanese High Seas Fleet. Ballantine's Illustrated
History of World War II. New York: Ballantine,
1973. p. 24-44.
The road towards Pearl Harbor as taken by the
Imperial Navy.

1782 "Hunger Gets a Brush Off: The Great Improvements in
the Battle of the Atlantic." Time, XXXVIII (November 24, 1941), 26.

1783 Hunnewell, Frederick A. United States Coast Guard
Cutters. New York: Society of Naval Architects
and Marine Engineers, 1937. 29p.

1784 _____. "Typical Vessels and Boats of the U. S. Coast Guard. " USNIP, LV (1929), 401-405.

1785 Hunsaker, Jerome C. Aeronautics in Naval Architecture. New York: Society of Naval Architects and Marine Engineers, 1924. 17p. Paper presented at the 1924 General Meeting.

1786 _____. "Airship Engineering Progress in the United States. " Aviation, VII (August 15, September 1, 1919), 72-76, 123-128.

1787 _____. "The Day of the Dirigible. " North American Review, CCXXIX (April 1930), 432-436.

1788 _____. "How American Ingenuity Designed the NC Boats. " Automotive Industries, XLI (July 10-24, 1919), 68-72, 120-123, 172-176.

1789 _____. "Naval Airships. " Society of Automotive Engineers Transactions, XIV (1919), 578-598.

1790 _____. "Naval Architecture in Aeronautics. " Journal of the Royal Aeronautical Society, XXIV (July 1920), 321-405.

1791 _____. "The Navy's First Airship. " USNIP, XLV (1919), 1347-1368.

1792 _____. "Progress in Naval Aircraft. " Society of Automotive Engineers Transactions, XIV (1919), 236-252.

1793 _____. "U. S. Naval Aircraft. " Journal of the Franklin Institute, CLXXXIX (June 1920), 715-736.

1794 _____. "Uses of Airships with the Fleet. " U. S. Air Services, I (April 1919), 6-9.

1795 Hunter, F. T. "Kings, Princes, and American Sailors. " World's Work, XXXVIII (June 1919), 184-194.

1796 Hunter, Harold O. "A Suggested Base for the Scouting Fleet. " USNIP, LIII (1927), 843-845.

1797 Hurd, Archibald. "American Fleet's Cruise in the

Pacific." Fortnightly, CXXIV (July 1925), 92-103.
The great cruise of 1925.

1798 _____. "America's Increasing [Naval] Armaments."
Fortnightly, CXXVII (March 1927), 364-375.

1799 _____. "Are Submarines Worth While?" Fortnightly, CXXV (January 1926), 78-90.

1800 _____. "Are We Losing Faith in Sea Power?"
Fortnightly, CXXV (May 1926), 657-667.

1801 _____. "Great Ships or--?" Fortnightly, CXV
(February 1921), 240-254.
Airplanes vs. Battleships.

1802 _____. "Is the Battleship Doomed?" Fortnightly,
CXIII (February 1920), 222-235.

1803 _____. _____. Review of Reviews, LXI (April
1920), 431-432.

1804 _____. "Naval Supremacy: Great Britain or the
United States?" Fortnightly, CXIV (December
1920), 916-930.

1805 _____. "The United States and Sea Power: A Challenge." Fortnightly, CXI (February 1919), 175-
189.

1806 _____. "The Washington Conference and the Naval
Issue." Fortnightly, CXVI (November 1921), 717-
726.

1807 _____, jt. author. See Chirol, Valentine, no. 739.

1808 Hurley, Alfred F. "The Aeronautical Ideas of General
William Mitchell." Unpublished PhD Dissertation,
Princeton University, 1961.

1809 _____. Billy Mitchell: Crusader for Air Power.
New York: Watts, 1965. 140p.

1810 "Hurricane-Test for the Shenandoah." Literary Digest,
LXXX (February 2, 1924), 52-57.
Trials of the giant Navy airship.

1811 Huse, John O. "Diesel Driven Surface Craft. " USNIP,
      LX (1934), 1564-1576.

1812 Hutchinson, M. M. "When Nature Goes to Sea: Birds,
      Fishes, and Stars Give Names to the U. S. Navy. "
      Nature Magazine, XXXII (November 1939), 497-498.

1813 Hutchison, Isobel W. Stepping Stones from Alaska to
      Asia. London: Blackie & Son, 1937. 246p.
      The author, a British botanist, tells of her
      cruise around the Aleutian Islands aboard the
      U. S. C. G. cutter Chelan during the summer of 1936,
      p. 116-193.

1814 Hyde, Charles C. "The City of Flint. " American
      Journal of International Law, XXXIV (January 1940),
      89-95.

1815 "The Hydrographic Office. " SciAmer, CXXIV (April
      2, 1921), 262.

1816 Hynd, Alan. Betrayal from the East: The Inside Story
      of Japanese Spies in America. New York: R. M.
      McBride, 1943. 287p.

1817 "Iceland--Occupied by American Forces to Release
      British Troops. " Illustrated London News, CXCIX
      (July 12, 1941), 36.

1818 Icenhower, Joseph B. The Panay Incident, December
      12, 1937: The Sinking an American Gunboat Worsens
      U. S. -Japanese Relations. A Focus Book. New
      York: Watts, 1971. 81p.

1819 _____, ed. Submarines in Combat. New York:
      Watts, 1964. 207p.
      Includes U-boats.

1820 Ichihashi, Yamato. The Washington Conference and
      After: A Historical Survey. Palo Alto, Calif. :
      Stanford University Press, 1928. 443p. Rpr. 1969.

1821 Ickes, Harold L. "F. D. R. and the Decision for War."
      Look, XVIII (December 14, 1954), 61+.

1822 Iden, Virginius G. "New Ways to Float Sunken Ships."
      USNIP, XLV (1919), 2087-2091.

1823 "If Britain Should Lose: The Development of a Hypo-
      thetical Case which Alters the Outlook for U. S.
      National Security. " Time, XXXVI (July 22, 1940),
      19-22.

1824 Ihrig, Russell M.   "A Pass Defense for the Battle
      Line. " USNIP, LXIII (1937), 1117-1121.

1825 Ikle, Frank W.   German-Japanese Relations, 1936-
      1940. New York: Bookman Associates, 1956. 243p.

1826 "Important Treaties That Affect Naval Armaments,
      1920-1930. " USNIP, LVIII (1932), 150-171.

1827 "Increases in Naval Expenditures as Proposed by the
      President. " Congressional Digest, XIX (February
      1940), 40.

1828 Ingalls, Davis D.   "Naval Aviation To-day and in
      Prospect. " USNIP, LVI (1930), 891-894.

1829 Ingraham, Charles N.   "Radio Communications from an
      Operator's Standpoint. " USNIP, XLVII (1921),
      1201-1208.

1830 Ingram, Jonas H.   "Air-Minded First Line of De-
      fense. " SciAmer, CLIX (July 1938), 9-11.
      Comments on the Navy air service.

1831 _____.   "Fifteen Years of Naval Development. "
      SciAmer, CLIII (November 1935), 231-236.

1832 _____.   "The Growth of the Navy. " Marine News,
      XX (September 1933), 36-40.

1833 _____.   "Why the Battleship?" SciAmer, CLI
      (August-September 1934), 82-84.

1834 "An International Armament Free-for-All?" Literary
      Digest, CXVII (March 17, 1934), 8.

1835 "Into Action with the U. S. Fleet. " Life, IX (October
      28, 1940), 23-39.
      Many interesting photographs.

1836 "Inventors Save Sunken Subs. " Popular Mechanics, LI
      (March 1929), 361-364.

1837 "Investigation by Congress Should be Expanded to the
        Navy. " New Republic, LXXVIII (February 28,
        1934), 57.

1838 "Invitation to the Naval Disarmament Conference. "
        Current History, XXXI (November 1929), 359-361.
        Held at London in 1930.

1839 "Is It to be Bomb or Battleship?" SciAmer, CXXV
        (July 2, 1921), 4-5.

1840 "Is Our Navy Headed for the Rocks?" Literary Digest,
        LXXXI (May 17, 1924), 8-10.
        As a result of the Washington Conference.

1841 "Is Our Navy in Jeopardy?" SciAmer, CXXVII (No-
        vember 1922), 306-307.
        As a result of the Washington Conference.

1842 "Is President Roosevelt's Deal with Great Britain for
        Naval Bases Legal?: Pro and Con Discussion. "
        Congressional Digest, XX (January 1941), 19-32.

1843 Ishimaru, Tōta. The Next World War. Translated
        from the Japanese by B. Matsukawa. London, 1937.
        352p.
        The Japanese equal of the Bywater work cited
        above as written by a Lt. Cmdr. in the Imperial
        Navy.

1844 Ito, Masanori. "The American Navy Under Survey. "
        Contemporary Japan, IX (1940), 387-395.
        An English language article with a Japanese
        point of view.

1845 _____ . _____ . Far Eastern Review, XXXVI
        (May 1940), 170-171.

1846 _____ . "Future of the Two-Ocean Fleet. " Far
        Eastern Review, XXXVII (July 1941), 227-229.

1847 _____ . "Japan Wants Ten to Ten: Reply to W. V.
        Pratt. " Asia, XXXIV (December 1934), 720-727.
        The Pratt article is cited below.

1848 _____ . "A Japanese Writer on Naval Limitation. "
        USNIP, LVIII (1932), 1393-1396.

Reprinted from the June 25-29, 1932 issues of
Japan Advertiser.

1849 Jablonski, Edward. Atlantic Fever. New York: Mac-
      millan, 1972. 325p.
      Early efforts by the NC's, Byrd, etc. to cross
      the Atlantic by air.

1850 _____. Sea Wings: The Saga and Romance of Fly-
      ing Boats. New York: Macmillan, 1972. 259p.

1851 Jackson, Elmer M. Annapolis. Annapolis: Capitol
      Gazette, 1936. 200p.

1852 Jackson, George G. The World's Aeroplanes and Air-
      ships. London: S. Low, Marston, 1930. 244p.

1853 Jackson, John P. "Employment and Tactics of Air-
      craft in Naval Warfare." USNIP, XLVIII (1922),
      1263-1297, 1779-1780, 2135-2138; XLIX (1923), 117-
      120.
      Various discussions are included in the citation.

1854 Jackson, Lon. "Our Billion Dollar Rock: Oahu, Key
      of The Hawaiian Islands Has Become a Strategic
      Fort." Current History, LI (March 1940), 36-38.

1855 Jackson, Orton P. and Frank E. Evans. The New
      Book of American Ships. New York: Frederick A.
      Stokes, 1926. 428p.
      Contains data on warships and Coast Guard units.

1856 Jackson, Robert. Airships: A Popular History of
      Dirigibles, Zeppelins, Blimps, and Other Lighter
      Than Air Craft. Garden City, N.Y.: Doubleday,
      1973. 277p.

1857 _____. Airships in Peace and War. New York:
      International Publications Service, 1971. 272p.

1858 Jackson, Robert H. "Opinion on the Exchange of Over-
      age Destroyers for Naval and Air Bases, With Dis-
      cussions." American Journal of International Law,
      XXXIV (October 1940), 569-587, 680-697, 728-736.

1859 Jacobs, A. M. "Over the Sea in Planes." St. Nicholas
      Magazine, LIII (July 1926), 852-856.

1860   Jacobsen, Arnold A.   "Do We Need Artillery in Small
       Wars?"   Marine Corps Gazette, XIX (August 1935),
       28-29.
       Favors the howitzer.

1861   Jacobus, Melancthon.   "Six Fighting Ships."   Con-
       necticut Historical Society Bulletin, XXI (October
       1956),   112-116.
       Commissioned in 1906, the last battleship Con-
       necticut was sold for scrap in November 1923 under
       the terms of the Washington Treaty.

1862   Jahncke, Ernest L.   "Naval Contributions to Industry."
       USNIP, LVI (1930), 888-890.

1863   James, Jules.   "Hints on Tactical Maneuvers." USNIP,
       XLVIII (1922), 2117-2127.

1864   Janes Fighting Ships.   London: S. Low, Marston,
       1898--.
       An annual publication, issues of which are now
       being commercially reprinted.

1865   Jansson, A. H.   "The Cruiser Program."   Marine Re-
       view, LIX (September 1929), 25-26.

1866   "Japan and Our Navy."   SciAmer, CXLIX (December
       1933), 257.

1867   "Japan on the American Navy."   Living Age,
       CCCXLVIII (August 1935), 553-554.

1868   "Japan Using Navy as Weapon to Test the Patience of
       the Powers."   Newsweek, XIII (June 5, 1939), 17-
       18.

1869   "Japanese Alarm at the American Navy."   Literary
       Digest, LXV (May 22, 1920), 30-31.

1870   "The Japanese Fret While [Ramsey] MacDonald and
       [John W.] Davis Discuss Warships."   Newsweek,
       III (June 30, 1934), 9.

1871   "Japanese Naval Intelligence."   The ONI Review, I
       (July 1946), 36-40.

1872   "The Japanese Navy at a Glance."   SciAmer, CLIX

(August 1938), 66-67.

1873 "The Japanese Oil Plan Gums up the Strained Machinery of Naval Discussions. " Newsweek, IV (November 3, 1934), 12-13.

1874 Jenkins, James C. "Chronology of Outstanding Events of the American Marines. " Marine Corps Gazette, XXIV (1940), 15, 81-90.

1875 _____. "The Tenth Marines. " Marine Corps Gazette, XXVII (March-April 1943), 37-42. During the years 1919-1938.

1876 _____. "The United States Marine Corps: A Brief Outline of Its History and Activities. " Marine Corps Gazette, XXIV (1940), 18, 54-61.

1877 Jenkins, P. A. "The World's Largest Trade School Trains Mechanics for the U. S. Naval Air Service. " Popular Mechanics, XXXIV (July 1920), 41-44.

1878 Jessop, Earl D. "Repair Ships, Advance Bases, and Fleet Mobility in War Time. " USNIP, LVIII (1932), 1138-1142.

1879 _____. "Searchlight Barrage in Night Landings. " USNIP, LXII (1936), 839-841.

1880 "Jingoism and the Navy. " Current Opinion, LXXVIII (January 1925), 10-12.

1881 Joerg, Wolfgang L. G. Brief History of Polar Exploration Since the Introduction of Flying. Special Publication, no. 11. New York: American Geographical Society, 1930. 50p.

1882 _____, ed. The Work of the Byrd Antarctic Expedition, 1928-1930. New York: American Geographical Society, 1930. 71p.

1883 John, Walton C. "Schools for [Navy] Enlisted Men. " School Life, XXV (May 1940), 234-235.

1884 _____. "Schools Under the Federal Government: The Department of the Navy. " School Life, XXV (May 1940), 232-235.

1885 _____ . "Schools Under the Federal Government:
The United States Coast Guard Academy. " School
Life, XXV (January 1940), 99-100.

1886 John Fritz Medal Board of Award. Presentation of
the John Fritz Gold Medal to Rear Admiral David
Watson Taylor ... at the Annual Dinner of the
American Society of Mechanical Engineers, Hotel
Astor, New York, Wednesday Evening. Dec. 3,
1930. New York: Society of Naval Architects and
Marine Engineers, 1930. 23p.

1887 Johns, A. W. "Aircraft Carriers. " Marine Engineering, XXXIX (July 1934), 264-267.

1888 Johnson, Alfred W. "Naval Aviation. " Unpublished
Lecture, Command Course 73, Files of the U. S.
Army Military History Research Collection, 1925.
The captain was Assistant Chief of the Bureau
of Aeronautics under Admiral Moffett.

1889 _____ . "Naval Policy of Maritime Powers: United
States, British Empire, and Japanese Empire. "
Unpublished Lecture, G-2 Course 3, Files of the
U. S. Army Military History Research Collection,
1938.

1890 _____ . "The Proposal for a United Air Service. "
USNIP, L (1924), 1422-1442.

1891 Johnson, Felix L. "The Asiatic Station. " USNIP,
LVIII (1932), 697-700.

1892 _____ . "Naval Activities on the Yangtse. " USNIP,
LIII (1927), 506-514.

1893 Johnson, Gerald A. "Junior Marines in Minor, Irreg-
ular Warfare. " Marine Corps Gazette, VI (June
1921), 152-163.

1894 Johnson, Harvey F. The United States Coast Guard--
Some Adventures. Princeton, N. J. : Princeton
University Press for The Newcomen Society, 1941.
64p.
Text of an address November 13, 1941.

1895 Johnson, Hugh S. "Anchors Away. " Saturday Evening

Post, CCXIII (October 5, 1940), 14-15+.

1896 Johnson, Lucius W. "An Adventure in Disaster Be-
lief. " USNIP, LXXIII (1947), 1044-1047.
Following the great storm of Santo Domingo in
1930.

1897 _____. "The Navy Builds a Medical Center. "
Military Surgeon, CVII (October 1950), 261-270.
The Naval Medical Center, Bethesda, Maryland,
1938-1950.

1898 _____. "The Fleet Hospital Ship. " USNIP, LXIII
(1937), 1225-1234.

1899 Johnson, Robert E. Thence Round Cape Horn: The
Story of U. S. Naval Forces on Pacific Station,
1818-1923. Annapolis: U. S. Naval Institute, 1963.
276p.
Based on the dissertation cited below.

1900 _____. "United States Forces on Pacific Station,
1818-1923. " Unpublished PhD Dissertation, Clare-
mont Graduate School and University Center, 1957.

1901 Johnson, Theodore. "Naval Aircraft Radio. " Institute
of Radio Engineers Proceedings, VIII (February-
April 1920), 3-58, 87-141.

1902 _____. "Naval Radio Tube Transmitters. " Institute of Radio Engineers Proceedings, IX (October
1921), 381-433.

1903 Johnson, William S. "Naval Diplomacy and the Failure
of Balanced Security in the Far East, 1921-1935. "
Naval War College Review, XXIV (February 1972),
67-88.

1904 Johnston, James. "The NC-4 Preserved. " USNIP,
XCV (1969), 94-105.
A pictorial.

1905 Johnston, Rufus Z. "'Arms and the Men. '" USNIP,
LIV (1928), 26-30.

1906 Johnston, Samuel P. Flying Fleets: A Graphic History
of U. S. Naval Aviation. New York: Duell, Sloan &

Pearce, 1941. 188p.

1907 _____. "Our Air Defenses--Navy." Aviation,
XXXVII (November 1938), 26-29, 76+.

1908 _____. "Riding Fence: Patrolling Zones to Hemi-
spheric Defense is but One of the Jobs for the
Navy's Flying Fleet." Technical Review, XLIII
(June 1941), 360-361+.

1909 Johnstone, William C. The United States and Japan's
New Order. New York: Oxford University Press,
1941. 382p.

1910 Jonas, Manfred. Isolationism in America, 1935-1941.
Ithaca, N. Y.: Cornell University Press, 1966.
315p.

1911 Jones, C. A. Marine and Naval Boilers. New York:
Society of Naval Arctictects and Marine Engineers,
1934. 20p.

1912 _____. "The Problem of the Naval Design Engineer
as Affected by the Limitation of Armament Treaty."
USNIP, LIV (1928), 875-878.

1913 Jones, Chester L. The Caribbean Since 1900. New
York: Prentice-Hall, 1936. 511p. Rpr. 1970.
Throws light on the Navy and Marine involve-
ments in the various banana wars.

1914 Jones, Hilary P. "The Limitation of Armaments."
Unpublished Lecture, G-2 Course 13, Files of the
U. S. Army Military History Research Collection,
1928.
As seen by a Navy admiral.

1915 Jones, John P. "The Fleet's In." Christian Century,
LI (June 20, 1934), 831-833.

1916 Jones, Louis B. "Recollections of the Early History
of Naval Aviation: A Session in Oral History."
Technology and Culture, IV (1963), 149-153.

1917 Jordan, J. N. "Scrapping Uncle Sam's Warships."
Marine Engineering, XXIX (December 1924), 697-
702.

The specifics of complying with the terms of the
Washington Treaty.

1918   Jordan, Ralph B.   Born to Fight: The Life of Admiral
        [William F.] Halsey.   Philadelphia: David McKay,
        1946.   208p.

1919   Judson, Harold C.   "The Necessity for Anti-Aircraft
        Defense of Advanced Bases and Naval Stations, Es-
        pecially as Regards Searchlights, and a Short Dis-
        cussion of the Necessary Characteristics of the
        Lights. "   Marine Corps Gazette, IV (June 1919),
        111-131.

1920   "Jumping Devildogs. "   Time, XXXVIII (August 11,
        1941), 30.
        Marine parachutists.

1921   Jurika, Stephen, Jr.   "Pilots, Man Your Planes:
        Hawaiian Maneuvers from the Saratoga. "   Saturday
        Evening Post, CCXI (January 21, 1939), 23+.

1922   Kaempffert, Waldemar.   "The Transatlantic Flight--A
        Magnificent Scientific Experiment. "   U. S. Air
        Services, I (July 1919), 10-14.
        The NC's.

1923   Kalinowski, L. B.   "General Aviation's 'Antares': New
        Flying Boat for the U. S. Coast Guard. "   Aviation
        Engineering, VII (August 1932), 10-12.

1924   Kamman, William.   The Search for Stability: United
        States Diplomacy Toward Nicaragua, 1925-1933.
        International Studies Series.   South Bend, Ind. :
        University of Notre Dame Press, 1968.

1925   Kaplan, H. R.   "A Toast to the Rum Fleet. "   USNIP,
        XCIV (1968), 84-90.
        Activities of the U. S. Coast Guard during the
        Prohibition era.

1926   _____, jt. author.   See   Rankin, Robert H. , no.
        3248.

1927   Kaplan, Laurence.   "The Launching of the U. S. S.
        North Carolina. "   Marine Engineering, XLV
        (September 1940), 59-64.

1928   Karig, Walter. "U. S. Navy Report on Guam, 1899-
       1950: History of Guam Under Naval Administra-
       tion. " Unpublished Paper, Individual Personnel
       File, Operational Archives, U. S. Navy Department,
       Naval History Division, 1950. 41p.

1929   _____, et al. Battle Report: The Atlantic War.
       New York: Published in Co-operation with the
       Council on Books in Wartime by Farrar & Rine-
       hart, 1946. 558p.
          The American Navy's role beginning with the
       first attacks of the U-boats on U. S. shipping and
       the Neutrality Patrol. Based on official sources,
       this volume is part of a larger series the other
       works of which are not relative to this work.

1930   Karker, Maurice H. "Business and Navy Food. "
       USNIP, XLVIII (1922), 81-91.

1931   Karsten, Peter. The Naval Aristocracy: Mahan's
       Messmates and the Emergence of Modern American
       Navalism. Riverside, N. J. : Free Press, 1972.
       460p.
          Based on the dissertation cited below, this
       volume has received somewhat controversial atten-
       tion.

1932   _____. "The Naval Aristocracy: U. S. Naval Officers
       from 1840s to the 1920s: Mahan's Messmates. " Un-
       published PhD Dissertation, Univ. of Wisconsin, 1968.

1933   Kasai, Jinji G. The United States and Japan in the
       Pacific: American Naval Maneuvers and Japan's
       Pacific Policy. Tokyo: Kokusai Press, 1935. 148p.
       Rpr. 1970.
          An English language text giving a Japanese view
       of U. S. Pacific naval maneuvers.

1934   Kauffman, D. L. "German Naval Strategy in World
       War II. " USNIP, LXXX (1954), 1-12.
          Some data on Nazi attempts to avoid trouble with
       the U. S. , 1939-1941.

1935   Kauffman, James L. Philadelphia's Navy Yards. New
       York: Newcomen Society of England, American
       Branch, 1948. 36p.
          A brief history.

1936 Kaufman, John B. "Advice to Fellow Middle-Graders."
     USNIP, LX (1934), 50-55.

1937 Kawakami, Kuyoshik. "Hidden Conflict at the Three-
     Power Naval Conference." Current History, XXVII
     (October 1927), 106-111.

1938 _____. "The London Naval Conference." 19th Cen-
     tury, CVI (December 1929), 731-742.

1939 Kay, Howard N. "The Fifty Old Maids Come
     Through." USNIP, LXXVI (1950), 976-979.
     The Roosevelt-Churchill destroyers for bases
     deal of 1940 and how the old U. S. four-stackers
     aided the British in their darkest hour.

1940 Kean, John W. "Navy Building Battleships of New
     Design." Popular Mechanics, XXXV (March 1921),
     331-334.
     The title is misleading as the article, in fact,
     concerns the carrier Langley.

1941 Kearns, William H., Jr. and Beverly L. Britton.
     The Silent Continent. New York: Harper, 1955.
     237p.
     Data on Byrd's expeditions included.

1942 Keen, Walter H. "A Midshipman's Day." USNIP,
     LXI (1935), 1533-1535.
     At the Naval Academy, Annapolis.

1943 "Keeping Fit in a Submarine." Literary Digest, LXXIV
     (August 26, 1922), 54.

1944 Keleher, T. J. and F. M. McGeary. "Purchase on a
     Weak Factor Basis: Standard Tests for Industrial
     Supplies Bought by the United States Navy." Manu-
     facturing Industries, XVI (July-September 1928),
     193-196, 281-284, 373-374.

1945 Kell, C. O. "Structural Characteristics of the De-
     stroyers Preston and Bruce: Abstract." Engineer-
     ing, CLI (January 24, 1941), 76.

1946 Kellogg, Frank B. "The Position of the United States
     in the Preliminary Discussions at Geneva." Com-
     mercial and Financial Chronicle, CXXIII (Septem-

ber 4, 1926), 1196-1198.
Concerning naval disarmament.

1947 Kelly, Ralph. "Fifteen Days for Training. " USNIP,
L (1924), 40-47.
Aboard the Navy's first aircraft carrier, U. S. S.
Langley.

1948 Kelly, Samuel G. "Motion Pictures in Naval Train-
ing--an Overlooked Essential. " USNIP, LXVII
(1941), 489-496.

1949 Kelsey, Charles. "American Intervention in Haiti and
the Dominican Republic. " Annals of the American
Academy, C (March 1922), 109-202.

1950 Kendall, Park and John Viney. , comps. A Dictionary
of Army and Navy Slang. New York: M. S. Mill,
1941. 26p.

1951 Kennaday, John M. "Physical Prowess and Leadership. " USNIP, LX (1934), 947-948.

1952 Kennan, George F. American Diplomacy, 1900-1950.
Chicago: University of Chicago Press, 1950. 103p.
Rpr. 1970.

1953 Kennedy, H. A. S. "Flight to Hawaii. " Outlook, CXLI
(September 16, 1925), 77-78.
A largely overlooked epic of early naval aero-
nautical history.

1954 Kennedy, Malcolm D. "Japan and the Pacific: A
Reply. " 19th Century, CXVII (April 1935), 421-
430.
A rejoinder to the article by Joseph M. Strabolgi
cited below.

1955 Kennedy, Thomas C. "Beard vs. FDR on National Defense and Rearmament. " Mid America, L (1968),
22-41.

1956 _____. "Charles A. Beard and the 'Big Navy
Boys. '" Military Affairs, XXXI (February 1967),
65-73.
A discussion of the historian's opposition to a
large fleet.

1957 Kenney, William. The Crucial Years, 1940-1945.
      New York: McFadden, 1962. 204p.

1958 Kenworthy, James M. "The International Naval Race."
      Nation, CXXIV (February 23, 1927), 203-204.

1959 Kerley, Jay L. California and the Navy. San Diego:
      Priv. print, 1935.
      A brief history.

1960 Kerr, Evor S., Jr. The United States Coast Guard:
      Its Ships, Duties, Stations. New York: Robert W.
      Kelly, 1935. 103p.

1961 Kerrigan, Evans E. American War Medals and Deco-
      rations. New York: Viking, 1964. 149p.
      Featuring some honoring naval achievements.

1962 Ketcham, Elizabeth. Armed Forces of the United
      States: The Ranks, Pay, and Insignia of the Army,
      Navy, Marines, and Coast Guard Fully Described
      and Their Historical Background. Washington:
      Washington Service Bureau, 1942. 32p.

1963 Kieffer, Henry M. "Control of the Seas by an Air De-
      partment." USNIP, LI (1925), 2265-2275.
      Further opposition to "Billy" Mitchell's call for
      a Unified Air Force.

1964 _____. "Last Days of the U.S.S. Quirros." Ship-
      mate, XXXVI (April 1973), 18-21.
      A Yangtze river gunboat.

1965 Kieley, James F., jt. author. See Crane, John
      D.M.C., no. 860.

1966 Kimball, Warren F. The Most Unsordid Act: Lend-
      Lease, 1939-1941. Baltimore: Johns Hopkins Uni-
      versity Press, 1969. 281p.

1967 Kincaid, Earle. The History and Cruises of the United
      States Ship Whipple, Destroyer Number 217. Con-
      stantinople, Turkey: Zellitch, 1921. 106p.
      A cruise book covering her tour of the Near
      East in 1920.

1968 King, Edward L. "Command." USNIP, LII (1926),

114-122.
Reprinted from the November 1925 issue of
Coast Artillery Journal.

1969 King, Ernest J. "The Progress in Naval Aviation."
Mechanical Engineering, LVI (October 1934), 613-
615.

1970 _____. "Recent Activities of Our Naval Air Service." Aero Digest, XXVI (January 1935), 10-13.

1971 _____. "Salvaging U. S. S. S-51." USNIP, LIII
(1927), 137-152.

1972 _____. "Some Ideas About the Effects of Increasing
the Size of Battleships." USNIP, XLV (1919), 807-
809.

1973 _____. The U. S. Navy at War, 1941-1945; Official
Reports to the Secretary of the Navy. Washington:
Navy Department, 1946. 305p.
The early pages contain data useful for the last
year of this period.

1974 _____. "A 'Wrinkle or Two' in Handling Men."
USNIP, XLIX (1923), 427-434.

1975 _____ and W. M. Whitehill. Fleet Admiral King: A
Naval Record. New York: W. W. Norton, 1952.
674p.
Very useful for the admiral's pre-World War II
career.

1976 King, William H. "Condemnation of United States
Naval Policy." Current History, XXII (May 1925),
167-177.
Commodore Knox's reply is cited below.

1977 Kinkaid, Thomas C. "Naval Corps, Specialization and
Efficiency." USNIP, XLVIII (1922), 1491-1500.

1978 Kiralfy, Alexander. "The Armed Strength of the United
States in the Pacific." Pacific Affairs, XI (1938),
208-223.

1979 _____. "Coral Isles as Naval Bases." Asia,
XXXVIII (1938), 681-685.

1980   . "The Imperial Japanese Navy. " Asia,
          XXXIX (January 1939), 51-54.

1981   . "Japan's Strategic Problem. " Far Eastern
          Survey, X (February 12, 1941), 15-20.

1982   . "A Naval Base in the Pacific. " Asia,
          XXXIX (1939), 655-658.
          Advocates retention of a naval base in the Phil-
          ippines.

1983   Kirchwey, Freda. "After the Greer. " Nation, CLIII
          (September 13, 1941), 212-213.
          Written under the author's pen name, her real
          name being Mrs. Evans Clark.

1984   Kirk, Alan G. "New Methods of Exterior Ballistic
          Computation. " USNIP, XLVI (1920), 1777-1784.

1985   Kirk, Neville T. "Sentinel for a Century: The Pro-
          ceedings, The Navy, and the Nation, 1873-1973. "
          USNIP, XCIX (1973), 96-115.

1986   Kirkpatrick, James J. "Promotion for Enlisted Men."
          USNIP, LVIII (1932), 15-17.

1987   . "Submarine Service for Profit and Plea-
          sure. " USNIP, LV (1929), 193-194.

1988   Kitchens, Joseph H. , Jr. "The Shearer Scandal and
          Its Origins: Big Navy Politics and Diplomacy in the
          1920s. " Unpublished PhD Dissertation, University
          of Georgia, 1969.

1989   Kittler, Glenn D. , jt. author. See Steirman, Hy,
          no. 3774.

1990   Kittredge, Tracy B. "Historical Monograph: U. S. -
          British Naval Cooperation, 1940-1945. " Unpub-
          lished Paper, Individual Personnel File, Operational
          Archives, U. S. Navy Department, Naval History
          Division, ca. 1941.   1, 022p.
          Despite its title, the study, one of the most im-
          portant on the subject, was completed only through
          the end of 1941.   Although it has no index, it is
          divided into five separate areas: I Policy and Stra-
          tegy Background of U. S. Action in World War II;

II U. S. -British Relations, 1939-1940; III Problems
of U. S. Naval Aid to Britain, 1940; IV Preparation
of American-British War Plans; V Strategic Concepts
and Victory Requirements, (July-November 1941).

1991 _____. "The Muddle Before Pearl Harbor. " U. S.
News and World Report, XXXVII (December 3,
1954), 52-63, 110-139.
See Admiral Theobald's reply cited below.

1992 Klachko, M. "Anglo-American Naval Competition,
1918-1922. " Unpublished PhD Dissertation, Columbia University, 1962.

1993 Klemin, Alexander. "An Aerial Torpedo. " SciAmer,
CLV (July 1936), 32.

1994 _____. "Airships Still Hold Possibilities for Military Purposes. " SciAmer, CLXIII (September
1940), 138.
Anti-submarine patrol, for instance.

1995 _____. "Deck Flying. " SciAmer, CXLIV (June
1931), 408-409.
Aboard an American carrier.

1996 _____. "Dive Bomber, the Curtiss XSB2C-1. "
SciAmer, CLXV (July 1941), 35.

1997 _____. "Finishing the [Airship] Macon. " SciAmer,
CXLVIII (June 1933), 334.

1998 _____. "High-Speed Naval Aircraft Carrier. " Sci-
Amer, CLV (July 1936), 32.

1999 _____. "Navy Flight to the [Panama] Canal. " Sci-
Amer, CXLIX (December 1933), 281.

2000 _____. "Navy Seaplane Record. " SciAmer, CLIV
(January 1936), 33.

2001 _____. "Navy Torpedo Boat. " SciAmer, CLVIII
(June 1938), 351.

2002 _____. "The World's Largest Naval Patrol Bomber."
SciAmer, CLVIII (March 1938), 162.
Catilina PB-Y.

2003 Knapp, Harry S. "An International Outlook. " USNIP,
      XLVII (1921), 1023-1027.

2004 _____. "The Limitation of Armament at the Con-
      ference of Washington. " USNIP, XLIX (1923), 767-
      776; L (1924), 1473-1491.
      Reprinting of a speech by an American rear
      admiral before the American Society of International
      Law meeting in Washington on April 27, 1922.

2005 _____. "The Naval Officer in Diplomacy. " USNIP,
      LIII (1927), 309-317.
      A brief history with several examples from our
      period.

2006 _____. "Onward and Upward. " USNIP, XLVII
      (1921), 1509-1517.

2007 _____. "Treaty No. 2 of the Washington Conference
      Relating to Submarines and Noxious Gases. " Polit-
      ical Science Quarterly, XXXIX (June 1924), 201-
      217.

2008 Knight, Austin M. "Treaty Cruisers. " Outlook,
      CXLIV (December 29, 1926), 565-566.

2009 Knight, Bruce W. "How a Navy Kills People. "
      American Mercury, XXXIV (February 1935), 137-
      144.

2010 Knight, Melvin M. The Americans in Santo Domingo.
      New York: Vanguard Press, 1928.

2011 Knight, Richard H. "Seismology and the Navy. "
      USNIP, LX (1934), 1110-1120.

2012 _____ and Ira E. Hobbs. Tactical Graphics for Air-
      craft Operations. Washington: U. S. Hydrographic
      Office, 1935. 112p.

2013 Kniskern, Leslie A. "A Cruiser Program. " USNIP,
      LVII (1931), 1229-1237.
      Growing out of the 1930 London Naval Treaty.

2014 Knox, Cornelius V. "The Metal Clad Airship. " USNIP,
      LVI (1930), 741-742.

2015 Knox, Dudley W. "Another Side of the 5-5-3 Agreement." USNIP, LI (1925), 1985-1988.

2016 _____. "Another Side of the 5-5-3 Argument: Reply to J. B. Walker." SciAmer, CXXXIII (August 1925), 100-101.
For Walker's original article and his rejoinder, see the citations in the proper alphabetical locations below.

2017 _____. "Aspects of Military and Naval Aviation." Unpublished Lecture, Command Course 25, Files of the U. S. Army Military History Research Collections, 1923.

2018 _____. "Defense of United States Naval Policy." Current History, XXII (June 1925), 339-344.
A reply to the article by William King cited above.

2019 _____. "The Disturbing Outlook in the Orient." USNIP, LXIV (1938), 797-303.

2020 _____. The Eclipse of American Sea Power. New York: American Army & Navy Journal, 1922. 140p.
Gives the American version of the proceedings of the Washington Naval Limitations Conference.

2021 _____. A History of the United States Navy. New York: Putnam, 1936. 481p.

2022 _____. _____. Rev. ed. New York: Putnam, 1948. 704p.
Still very useful and authoritative. The Commodore wrote the first edition while chief of what is now the Naval History Division, U. S. Navy Department.

2023 _____. "The Japanese Situation." USNIP, LXI (1936), 1277-1280.

2024 _____. "The London Naval Treaty and American Naval Policy." USNIP, LVII (1931), 1079-1088.

2025 _____. "Naval Power and Sea Borne Commerce." USNIP, LV (1929), 852-854.

174 The American Navy, 1918-1941

2026 _____ . "Naval Power as a Preserver of Neutrality." USNIP, LXIII (1937), 619-626.

2027 _____ . "Naval Reduction and Parity." SciAmer,
CXLI (October 1929), 320-322.

2028 _____ . "The Navy and Public Indoctrination. "
USNIP, LV (1929), 479-490.

2029 _____ . "The Navy and the National Life." USNIP,
LX (1934), 774-783.

2030 _____ . "On the Importance of Leadership." USNIP,
XLVI (1920), 335-353.

2031 _____ . "Our Post War Mission." USNIP, XLV
(1919), 1293-1303.

2032 _____ . "Our Stake in Sea Power." USNIP, LIII
(1927), 1087-1089.

2033 _____ . "Peace and the Navy." Atlantic Monthly,
CLXI (April 1938), 495-503.

2034 _____ . "Problems of Defense in the Panama Zone."
USNIP, L (1924), 647-649.
Reprinted from the January 30, 1924 issue of
the Baltimore Sun.

2035 _____ . "Recent Development in Limitation of Naval
Armament." USNIP, LII (1926), 1985-1992.

2036 _____ . "The Relation of Air Power to Sea Power."
Aviation, XVI (March 3, 1924), 225-227.

2037 _____ . "Reply to Admiral Fullam." Aviation, XVI
(March 31, 1924), 334-335.
The original Fullman article is cited above.

2038 _____ . "Sea Power and Pocketbooks." USNIP, LI
(1925), 2231-2241.

2039 _____ . "The Ships that Count." USNIP, LIX
(1933), 959-968.

2040 _____ . _____ . USNIP, LXII (1936), 1419-1426.

2041   . "Some Comments on the Washington Trea-
        ties. " USNIP, LVIII (1932), 319-320.

2042   . "Some Naval Aspects of the War Debt
        Question. " USNIP, LVIII (1932) 685-688.

2043   Knox, Franklin. "Clear the Atlantic of the German
        Menace. " Vital Speeches, VII (July 15, 1941),
        590-592.

2044   . "Hands Off Navy Planes! Why the Navy
        Needs Its Own Air Arm. " Collier's, CVIII (1941),
        13-17.

2045   . "The Navy is Ready: It Has Been Ordered
        into Action. " Vital Speeches, VII (October 1, 1941),
        741-745.

2046   . The United States Navy in National Defense.
        Washington: American Council on Public Affairs,
        1941. 40p.

2047   Koch, Ralph A. "Our Present Naval Situation. "
        USNIP, XLIX (1923), 287-302.

2048   Koenig, Louis W. The Presidency and the Crisis:
        Powers of the Office from the Invasion of Poland
        to Pearl Harbor. New York: King's Crown Press,
        1944. 166p.
            Considerable discussion of the destroyer bases
        deal and Lend Lease.

2049   Koginos, Emmanuel T. "The Panay Incident: Prelude
        to War. " Unpublished PhD Dissertation, American
        University, 1966.

2050   .   . West Lafayette, Ind. : Purdue
        University Studes, 1967. 154p.

2051   Kohn, George F. "Disarmament. " Annals of the
        American Academy, Supplement, CXIV (July 1924),
        38-45.

2052   Konoye, Fumimaro. The Memoirs of Prince Fumimaro
        Konoye. Tokyo: Okuyama Service, [195?], 62p.

2053   Kopplemann, Herman P. "The Japanese Apologize. "

In: H. B. Summers, ed. Anglo-American Agreement. Vol. XII of The Reference Shelf. New
York: H. W. Wilson, 1938, p. 78-79.
A speech by the Connecticut Congressman concerning Japanese attacks on the Augusta and Panay
as reprinted from the December 21, 1937 issue of
Congressional Record.

2054 Krafft, Herman F.   "The Long Cruise of a Squadron
of Naval Academy Ship Models. " USNIP, LVI
(1930), 301-303.

2055 _____. "Memorials and Naval Heroes. " USNIP,
LV (1929), 1047-1051.
At the Naval Academy.

2056 _____. "Seapower and American Destiny. " USNIP,
LXVII (1921), 473-486.

2057 _____. "Ship Models at the United States Naval
Academy. " USNIP, L (1924), 1257-1265.

2058 _____. "Slogans of the Navy. " USNIP, LIII (1927),
519-522.

2059 Krause, Roland E.   "The Human Factor in War. "
USNIP, LXI (1935), 1065-1074.

2060 _____. "Morale for Our New Navy. " USNIP,
XLVII (1921), 519-524.

2061 _____. "Torpedo Fire from Surface Craft. " USNIP,
LIV (1928), 1051-1059.

2062 _____. "The Trend of Naval Affairs. " USNIP, LI
(1925), 521-561.

2063 _____. "War and Peace. " USNIP, LXIII (1937),
1724-1731.

2064 Kreh, William R.   Citizen Sailors: The U. S. Naval
Reserve in War and Peace. New York: David
McKay, 1969. 270p.

2065 Kuenne, Robert K.   The Attack Submarine: A Study in
Strategy. New Haven: Yale University Press, 1965.
207p.

2066 Kumao, Harada. Fragile Victory: Prince Saionji and
      the 1930 London Treaty Issue, from the Memoirs
      of Baron Harada Kumao. Detroit: Wayne State
      University Press, 1968. 330p.

2067 Kune, Thomas W. "Champion of the Fleet. " Popular
      Mechanics, L (November 1928), 786-788.

2068 Lademan, Joseph U. "A New Type for the Navy. "
      USNIP, LVIII (1932), 865-868.
      Concerns destroyers.

2069 _____. "U. S. S. Gold Star--Flagship of the Guam
      Navy. " USNIP, XCIX (1973), 67-79.
      The story of the pre-war converted tramp and
      Guam station ship as recalled by her commander.

2070 LaFollette, Philip F. Should America Clear the Seas
      of the Nazis? Round Table Pamphlets, no. 175.
      Chicago: University of Chicago Press, 1941. 29p.

2071 Lahn, J. A. "The Navy and Its Air Requirements. "
      USNIP, LII (1926), 1481-1491.

2072 Laidlaw, Frederick B. "The History of the Prevention
      of Fouling. " USNIP, LXXVIII (1952), 768-779.
      A discussion of U. S. Navy experiments during
      our period.

2073 Laing, Alexander K. American Ships. Annapolis: U.S.
      Naval Institute, 1971. 560p.

2074 Lake, Simon. Submarine: The Autobiography of Simon
      Lake. New York: D. Appleton, 1938. 303p.

2075 _____. "Vest-Pocket Submarine. " Popular
      Mechanics, LVII (April 1932), 618-621.

2076 Lamb, Scott G. "The U. S. Navy and the Japanese
      Earthquake. " USNIP, LI (1925), 963-974.

2077 Lancelot, Milton, jt. author. See Hailey, Foster,
      no. 1571.

2078 Land, Emory S. "Annual Report of the Bureau of
      Construction and Repair. " Marine Engineering,
      XLII (January 1937), 5.

2079 _____. "Comments on Aviation--Naval and Com-
       mercial. " Marine Engineering, XXVIII (December
       1923), 748-750.

2080 _____. Development in Ground Tackle for Naval
       Ships. New York: Society of Naval Architects and
       Marine Engineers, 1934. 4p.
       Speech given before the Society, November 15-
       16, 1934.

2081 _____. "The Navy Develops Improved Ground
       Tackle. " Marine Engineering, XXXIX (December
       1934), 455-457.

2082 _____. Some Policies of the United States Maritime
       Commission. New York: Society of Naval Archi-
       tects and Marine Engineers, 1940. 13p.
       Speech delivered November 14-15, 1940.

2083 _____. "What is Naval Aviation Doing?" Marine
       Engineering, XXXII (December 1927), 692-694.

2084 _____. Winning the War With Ships: Land, Sea
       and Air--Mostly Land. New York: McBride, 1958.
       310p.
       The author's autobiography; concerned primarily
       with the period after he became "Chief Construc-
       tor. "

2085 "Landing-field That Goes to Sea, U. S. S. Langley. "
       SciAmer, CXXXI (August 1924), 94-95.

2086 Lane, Carl D. What the Citizen Should Know About
       the Merchant Marine. New York: Norton, 1941.
       201p.

2087 Lane, Donald R. "Hard Scrapping. " Sunset, XLIX
       (December 1922), 40-41.
       Reducing the American fleet in lines with the
       terms of the Washington Treaty.

2088 _____. "Is Our Navy Fit to Fight?" Sunset, LIV
       (March 1925), 10-13.

2089 Lane, H. F. "Thirty-Seven Ships to be Built Under
       Naval Program. " Marine Engineering, XXXVIII
       (July 1933), 238-239.

2090 _____. "Trammell Bill Authorizing Naval Construct-
      ion." Marine Engineering. XXXVIII (May 1933),
      160-161.

2091 Lane, Rufus H. "Civil Government in Santo Domingo
      in the Early Days of the Military Occupation."
      Marine Corps Gazette, VII (June 1922), 127-146.
      The author was a Marine colonel fresh from the
      scene.

2092 Lang, Robert G. "The Supply Ship." USNIP, LI
      (1925), 268-273.

2093 Langen, Thomas D. F. "This Admiral Business."
      USNIP, LVI (1930), 973.

2094 Langenberg, William H. "Destroyers for Naval Bases:
      Highlights of an Unprecedented Trade." Naval War
      College Review, XXII (September 1970), 80-92.

2095 Langer, William L. and S. Everett Gleason. The
      Challenge to Isolation. The World Crisis and
      American Foreign Policy. New York: Harper,
      1952. 794p. Rpr. 1964.

2096 _____. _____. The Undeclared War, 1940-1941.
      The World Crisis and American Foreign Policy.
      New York: Published for the Council on Foreign
      Relations by Harper, 1953. 963p. Rpr. 1970.

2097 Laning, Harris. "The Naval Expansion Program." In:
      Julia E. Johnson, ed. Peace and Rearmament.
      Vol. XI of The Reference Shelf. New York: H. W.
      Wilson, 1938. p. 131-133.

2098 _____. "The Practical Application of the Principles
      of High Command." USNIP, XLVIII (1922), 2041-
      2060.

2099 Lansdowne, K. B. "The United States Navy Aims at
      Indestructible Steel for Building Warships." Steel,
      LXXXVIII (March 12, 1931), 44+.

2100 Lansdowne, Zachery. "The Birth of an Industry."
      Aero Digest, IV (May 1924), 200-201.

2101 _____. "Helium: An Important National Asset."

U. S. Air Services, VII (February 1922), 13-16.

2102 _____. "The Story of the R-34 Flight." Flying,
VIII (August 1919), 608-609.
The future skipper of the Shenandoah was the
U. S. Navy's observer on the voyage and thus the
first American to fly the Atlantic non-stop.

2103 _____. "With the Shenandoah." Saturday Evening
Post, CXCVIII (October 1925), 7, 214, 217-218.

2104 Lansdowne, Mrs. Zachary. "Daughter of the Stars."
Collier's, LXXVII (January 9-16, 1926), 5-6, 9-10.
On the loss of the airship Shenandoah.

2105 LaPlante, John B. "The Evolution of Pacific Policy
and Strategic Planning: June 1940-July 1941."
Naval War College Review, XXV (May-June 1973),
57-72.

2106 "A Larger Navy in the Pacific: The North Carolina
State College Affirmative vs. The University of
Pennsylvania Negative." In: Egbert R. Nichols,
ed. Intercollegiate Debates. New York: Noble and
Noble, 1938. p. 187-204.

2107 "The Largest Dirigible: A Description of the U. S. S.
Akron's Design and Construction." Aviation, XXX
(October 1931), 599-600.

2108 Larkins, William T. U. S. Marine Corps Aircraft,
1914-1959. Concord, Calif.: Aviation History Publications, 1959. 199p.
Mostly pictorial, with commentary on each aircraft type.

2109 _____. U. S. Navy Aircraft, 1921-1941. Concord,
Calif.: Aviation History Publications, 1961. 391p.

2110 Larmour, R. F. "Chief Petty Officers' School of the
Line." USNIP, LXIII (1937), 355-358.

2111 "Last Review: The Mounted Marines in China Dis-
banded." Time, XXXI (March 7, 1938), 17.

2112 "Last Word." Time, XXXI (January 10, 1938), 25.
On the Panay incident.

2113   "The Last Word in American Naval Construction: The
       Dewey Type of Destroyer. " SciAmer, CLIII
       (September 1935), 140-141.

2114   "Last Word on the Shenandoah. " SciAmer, CXXXIV
       (March 1926), 156.

2115   Lathrop, Mrs. Constance D.   "Seagoing Customs. "
       USNIP, LV (1929), 11-16, 528-529, 1066-1067.

2116   _____.   "Vanished Ships. " USNIP, LX (1934), 949-52.
       Lost U. S. warships, 1780-1930.

2117   _____.   "A Vanishing Naval Tradition--the Figure-
       head. " USNIP, LIII (1927), 1166-1168.

2118   Latimer, Hugh.   Naval Disarmament.   London: Royal
       Institute of International Affairs, 1930.   112p.

2119   _____.   "The Setting for the Naval Conference. "
       Bulletin of International News, XII (1935-1936),
       383-392.

2120   _____.   "Some Figures of Naval Strengths. " Bulle-
       tin of International News, XII (1935-1936), 426-427.

2121   "The Launch of the United States Airplane Carrier
       Saratoga. " USNIP, LII (1926), 2319-2325.

2122   "Launching New Dreadnoughts for Our Air Armada:
       The Dirigible Macon. " Literary Digest, CXIV
       (August 13, 1932), 24-26.

2123   "The Launching of the Airplane Carrier U. S. S. Sara-
       toga. " Engineer, CXXI (January 8, 1926), 56-60.

2124   "The Launching of the Ranger. " Marine Engineering,
       XXXVIII (April 1933), 145-146.

2125   "Launching the Cruiser Minneapolis at the U. S. Navy
       Yard. " Marine Review, LXIII (October 1933), 27.

2126   "Launching the Cruiser Tuscaloosa at the Camden Ship-
       yard. " Marine Review, LXIII (December 1933), 10.

2127   "Launching the Cruiser Vincennes. " Marine Engineer-
       ing, XLI (July 1936), 387.

2128   "Launching the Destroyer-Leader U. S. S. Clark."
       Marine Engineering, XL (November 1935), 426.

2129   "Launching the First Destroyer-Leader, U. S. S. Phelps."
       Marine Engineering, XL (August 1935), 299+.

2130   "Launching the Scout Cruiser U. S. S. Quincy." Marine
       Engineering, XL (July 1935), 269+.

2131   "Launching the U. S. Destroyer Gridley." Marine En-
       gineering. XLII (January 1937), 30.

2132   "Launching the U. S. S. Farragut." Marine Engineering,
       XXXIX (April 1934), 141.

2133   Lavender, Robert A.   "The Radio Equipment on NC
       Seaplanes." USNIP, XLVI (1920), 1601-1607.

2134   "Law." Time, XXXIV (November 6, 1939), 16-17.
       Concerns the City of Flint episode.

2135   Lawrence, Charles L.   "Aircraft and Navy Treaty
       Strength." SciAmer, CXLVI (April 1932), 206-
       208+.

2136   Layton, H. G.   "Scrapping the Warships of the United
       States Navy." Popular Mechanics, XXXVII (June
       1922), 835-841.

2137   League of Nations.   Armaments Yearbook: General and
       Statistical Information. 15 vols.   Geneva, Switzer-
       land, 1924-1939.
       Contains information on navies world wide.

2138   Leahy, William D.   I Was There: The Personal Story
       of the Chief of Staff to Presidents Roosevelt and
       Truman, Based on His Notes and Diaries Made at
       the Time.   New York: Whittlesey House, 1950.
       527p.

2139   _____.   "The National Defense Program." In: Julia
       E. Johnson, ed.   Peace and Rearmament.   Vol. XI
       of The Reference Shelf.   New York: H. W. Wilson,
       1938.   p. 111-117.

2140   _____.   "Speech Before the House Committee on
       Naval Affairs Urging Adoption of President Roose-

velt's Program for Increases in the Navy. " Congressional Digest, XVII (March 1938), 79-82.

2141 Leary, Herbert F. "Fleet Training. " Unpublished
      Lecture, War Plans Course 8, Files of the U. S.
      Army Military History Research Collection, 1937.

2142 _____. "Military Characteristics and Ordnance De-
      sign. " USNIP, XLVIII (1922), 1125-1137.

2143 LeBreton, Davis. "The Organization, Activities, and
      Objective of the Office of Naval Intelligence. " Un-
      published Lecture, Files of the U. S. Army Military
      History Research Collection, 1927.

2144 Lederer, William J. All the Ships at Sea. New York:
      William Sloan, 1950. 292p.
      Memoirs of naval life, 1930-1949.

2145 _____. "Running a Cruiser Wardroom Mess. "
      USNIP, LXIV (1938), 1567-1568.

2146 Lee, Henry. How Dry We Were: Prohibition Re-
      visited. Englewood Cliffs, N. J. : Prentice-Hall,
      1963. 244p.
      Contains numerous references to the work of the
      Coast Guard during the 13 years the 18th Amend-
      ment was the law of the land.

2147 Lee, Jermome A. "Between Wars in the Far East. "
      USNIP, LXV (1939), 63-73.

2148 _____. "The Perennial Philippine Problem. "
      USNIP, LXIV (1938), 1257-1261.

2149 LeGette, Curtis W. "On the Way. " Marine Corps
      Gazette, XVI (November 1931), 41-44.
      The 75mm pack howitzer for landing forces.

2150 _____. "Pack Howitzer Battery in Landing Attack."
      Marine Corps Gazette, XX (May 1936), 12-14, 55-
      57.

2151 Leigh, Richard H. "Naval Personnel. " USNIP, LV
      (1929), 855-860.

2152 _____. "A Plea for the Merchant Marine Naval Reserve. " USNIP, LIII (1927), 1068-1071.

2153 _____. "Training in the Navy. " USNIP, LIV
(1928), 883-886.

2154 _____. "Why a Peace Time Navy?" National Republic, XVII (October 1929), 5-7.

2155 Leighton, Bruce G. "The Relation of Aircraft to Sea
Power. " USNIP, LIV (1928), 731-741.

2156 Leighton, Richard M. and Robert W. Coakley. Global
Logistics and Strategy, 1940-1943. United States
Army in World War II--The War Department.
Washington: Office of the Chief of Military History,
U. S. Army, 1955. 780p.
Appropriate commentary on the naval efforts in
these areas.

2157 Lejeune, John A. "Esprit de Corps and Leadership. "
Unpublished Lecture, Leadership Course 1, Files
of the U. S. Army Military History Research Collection, 1921.

2158 _____. "The Marine Corps, 1926. " USNIP, LII
(1926), 1961-1969.

2159 _____. The Reminiscences of a Marine. Philadelphia: Dorrance, 1930. 488p.

2160 _____. "The United States Marine Corps. " USNIP,
LI (1925), 1858-1870.

2161 _____. "The United States Marine Corps. " Current History, XXXV (November 1931), 216-219.

2162 _____. "The U. S. Marine Corps, Present and
Future. " USNIP, LIV (1928), 859-861.

2163 _____. "War. " USNIP, LVII (1931), 1605-1611.

2164 Lemly, W. C. "Aerial Photography. " Leatherneck,
XXIII (July 1940), 19-22.
As understood by the Navy and Marines prior to
World War II.

2165 Lennox, Joseph J. "Training the Reserve Supply

Corps. " <u>USNIP</u>, LX (1934), 647-650.

2166 Lenton, Henry T.   <u>American Battleships, Carriers,</u>
      <u>and Cruisers.</u>   Navies of the Second World War.
      Garden City, N. Y. : Doubleday, 1968.   160p.

2167 _____ . <u>American Fleet and Escort Destroyers.</u>
      Navies of the Second World War.   2 vols. Garden
      City, N. Y. : Doubleday, 1971.

2168 _____ . <u>American Submarines.</u>   Navies of the
      Second World War.   Garden City, N. Y. : Double-
      day, 1973.   128p.
      Excellent source for material on those ships
      launched and/or active during our period.

2169 Leopold, Richard W.   "Fleet Organization, 1919-1941."
      Unpublished Paper, Individual Personnel, Opera-
      tional Archives, U. S. Navy Department, Naval His-
      tory Division, 1945.   42p.
      The distinguished diplomatic historian was a
      naval lieutenant when this synopsis was written.

2170 _____ . <u>The Growth of American Foreign Policy: A</u>
      <u>History.</u>   New York: Knopf, 1962.   848p.
      The author has much to say about the role of
      the American navy in diplomacy.

2171 Lescarboura, Austin C.   "The Battle of Rum Row. "
      <u>Popular Mechanics</u>, XLV (June 1926), 955-959.
      The Coast Guard vs. the booze smugglers.

2172 Letcher, John S.   <u>One Marine's Story.</u>   Verona, Va. :
      McClure Press, 1970.   387p.
      Follows the General's career from Nicaragua
      through the Pacific theatre of World War II.

2173 "Let's Build a Navy 'Second to None, ' Says the House."
      <u>U. S. News</u>, (February 5, 1934), 7.

2174 "Letters to Byrd. "   <u>National Education Association</u>
      <u>Journal</u>, XX (May 1931), 151-152.

2175 Leutze, J. R.   "If Britain Should Fail: Roosevelt
      Churchill, and British-American Naval Relations,
      1938-1940. "   Unpublished PhD Dissertation, Duke
      University, 1970.

2176 Levine, Isaac D. Mitchell: Pioneer of Air Power.
      New York: Duell, 1943. 420p. Rpr. 1971.

2177 Lewis, Charles L. "Description of the United States
      Naval Academy. " USNIP, LXI (1935), 1443-1467.

2178 _____. "Imaginative Aeronautics. " USNIP, LXII
      (1936), 544-552.

2179 Lewis, David D. The Fight for the Sea: The Past,
      Present and Future of Submarine Warfare in the
      Atlantic. Cleveland: World, 1961. 350p.

2180 "The Lexington and Saratoga. " Aviation, XXIV (Janu-
      ary 9, 1928), 94-95.

2181 Ley, Willie. Bombs and Bombing. New York: Modern
      Age Books, 1941. 124p.
      Data on planes, attack and defense techniques.

2182 _____. "How About Penetration Bombs?" USNIP,
      LXVII (1941), 1712-1716.

2183 _____. "Rocket Airplanes. " USNIP, LXVII (1941),
      835-840.

2184 Libbey, Miles A. , jt. author. See Cox, Ormond L. ,
      no. 854.

2185 Libby, F. F. An Open Letter to the President on the
      Navy. Washington: National Council for the Pre-
      vention of War, 1934. 1p.

2186 Libby, Frederick J. Statement to the House Naval
      Affairs Committee. Washington: National Council
      for the Prevention of War, 1939. 8p.
      Opposing the naval improvement of Guam.

2187 "The Library of the U. S. S. Tennessee. " Library
      Journal, XLV (1920), 634.

2188 Liddell Hart, B. H. "Marines and Strategy. " Marine
      Corps Gazette, XLIV (July 1960), 10-17.

2189 "Life on a Submarine. " Popular Science, CXXXII
      (April 1938), 48-49.

2190 Liljencrantz, Eric. "Aviation Medicine, Its Responsi-
      bilities and Problems. " USNIP, LXIV (1938), 1753-
      1760.

2191 "The Limitation of Navies. " Engineer, CXLII (Novem-
      ber 19, 1926), 555-556.

2192 Lincke, Jack. "Airplanes Can't Sink Battleships. "
      Saturday Evening Post, CCIX (April 10, 1937), 12-
      13+.

2193 Lindley, Ernest K. "American Newspapers Are Re-
      sponsible for the Cruiser-Naval Base Swap. " Con-
      gressional Digest, XX (January 1941), 17-18.
         Actually, Roosevelt traded Churchill 50 World
      War I four stacker destroyers, not cruisers.

2194 _____., jt. author. See Davis, Forrest, no. 936.

2195 Linklater, Eric. The Northern Garrisons: The Defense
      of Iceland and the Faeroe, Orkney, and Shetland
      Islands. Garden City, N.Y.: Garden City Publish-
      ing Co., 1941. 71p.
         The British were relieved by the Yanks.

2196 Linville, T.M. "First Trip Aboard a Submarine. "
      Marine Engineering, XLV (October 1940), 69.

2197 Lippmann, Walter. "The Atlantic and America: The
      Why and When of Intervention. " Life, X (April 7,
      1941), 84-88+.
         A reply to this article appeared in the Christian
      Century, LVIII (April 16, 1941), 529-521, under
      the title "The War for Seapower. "

2198 _____. "England and America. " Saturday Review
      of Literature, V (February 9, 1929), 662-663.
         For replies, see the articles by F.H. Simonds
      and J.T. Shotwell cited below.

2199 _____. "London Naval Conference: An American
      View. " Foreign Affairs, VII (July 1930), 499-518.

2200 _____. "Weapon of Freedom. " Life, IX (October
      28, 1940), 44-46.
         Seapower.

2201 Lisle, B. Orchard. "Boycotts, Sanctions, or Block-
      ades--Economics in the War of To-day. " USNIP,
      LXVII (1941), 227-230.

2202 _____. "Eliminating Bottlenecks in National De-
      fense. " USNIP, LXVII (1941), 802-806.

2203 _____. "Tankers as Naval Auxiliaries. " USNIP,
      LXIV (1938), 1249-1256.

2204 Litchfield, Paul W.   "The Case for the Super-Dirig-
      ible. " World's Work, LI (January 1926), 248-262.

2205 _____. "Establishing an Airship Building Industry."
      U. S. Air Services, XVII (April 1932), 24-26.

2206 _____. "Lighter-Than-Air-Craft. " Annals of the
      American Academy, CXXXI (May 1927), 79-85.

2207 Livermore, Seward.   "American Naval Base Policy in
      the Pacific. " Pacific Historical Review, XIII
      (June 1944), 113-135.

2208 _____. "American Strategic Diplomacy in the South
      Pacific. " Pacific Historical Review, XII (March
      1943), 42-49.

2209 Livezey, William E. , jt. author. See Grunder, Garel
      A. , no. 1542.

2210 Livingston, Brockholst. "Are We Ready?" USNIP,
      LXVI (1940), 629-641.

2211 _____. "Build No Freaks: Warships Can be Better
      Designed to Meet the Needs of Their Own Classes."
      SciAmer, CLXIII (September 1940), 130-132.

2212 _____. "Capital Ship Replacements. " USNIP, LIII
      (1927), 841-842.

2213 _____. "The Naval Publicist's Aim. " USNIP, L
      (1924), 1255-1256.

2214 _____. "Our Shipping Renaissance. " USNIP, LXV
      (1939), 1554-1558.

2215 _____. Types and Tactics. " USNIP, LXV (1939),
      311-323.

2216 _____. "Whither? Some Aspects of Our Present
      Policy." USNIP, LIII (1927), 289-294.

2217 _____. "A World Divided." USNIP, LXIV (1938),
      1612-1623.

2218 Ljunggren, Lawrence. "The Side Launching of Sub-
      marines." Engineering, CLII (September 26, 1941),
      258-259.

2219 Lobdell, G. H. "A Biography of Frank Knox." Unpub-
      lished PhD Dissertation, University of Illinois, 1954.
      Navy Secretary 1940-1944.

2220 Lockwood, Charles A. Down to the Sea in Subs. New
      York: W. W. Norton, 1967. 367p.
      The late vice-admiral's memoirs of his sub-
      marining days.

2221 _____ and Hans C. Adamson. Tragedy at Honda.
      Philadelphia: Chilton, 1960. 243p.
      When seven U. S. four-piper destroyers ran
      aground off the California coast in the late 1920s.

2222 Lockwood, W. W. and F. Brodie. Our Far Eastern
      Record. 2 vols. New York: American Council of
      the Institute of Pacific Relations, 1941.
      1937-1941.

2223 Lodge, Henry C. "The Power of the U. S. Fleet."
      USNIP, LVI (1930), 924-931.
      Reprinted from a speech given by the senator
      before his death in 1924.

2224 Lodge, John E. "Biggest American Navy Promised by
      New Fighting Ships." Popular Science, CXXXIII
      (September 1938), 21-23+.

2225 _____. "Riding Heard on a Million Seals." Popu-
      lar Science, CXXX (January 1936), 22-23+.
      Another chore of the Coast Guard--guarding
      against poachers.

2226 Loeb, Richard B. "The Honda Point Disaster."
      USNIP, LXXXIV (1958), 109-111.
      The loss of Destroyer Squadron Eleven on the
      California coast in 1927.

2227 "The London Naval Parley. " Catholic World, CXXXI
       (May 1930), 238-239.

2228 "The [London] Treaty of Naval Limitation. " Engineer-
       ing, CXXIX (May 2, 1930), 575-577.

2229 Long, F. R. "What the Navy is Doing to Protect Its
       Personnel Against Venereal Disease. " American
       Journal of Public Health, XXXI (October 1941),
       1032-1039.

2230 Long, Henry F. "What is Modern Navigation?" USNIP,
       LXII (1936), 1750-1754.

2231 Long, R. O. B. , trans. See Frank, Wolfgang, no. 1327.

2232 Longquest, Theodore C. "Aircraft Instruments. "
       USNIP, LIV (1928), 403-411.

2232a Lonsdale, A. L. "The Battle of Rum Row. " Sea
       Classics, V (March 1972), 18-32.
              The Coast Guard vs. the booze smugglers.

2233 "Looking Back on the Shenandoah. " American Indus-
       tries, XXVI (December 1925), 8+.

2234 Loomis, Alfred F. "Are There Any Sailors in the
       Navy?" USNIP, LVIII (1932), 1267-1268, 1795-
       1798; LIX (1933), 109, 270-272.
              A question which brought much discussion.

2235 Lord, Clifford L. "The History of Naval Aviation,
       1898-1939. " Unpublished paper, Individual Person-
       nel File, Operational Archives, U. S. Navy Depart-
       ment, Naval History Division, 1946. 1438p.
              The rough draft for the undocumented version
       the author and Archibald D. Turnbull had published
       by Yale University Press in 1948.

2236 _____, jt. author. See Turnbull, Archibald D. ,
       no. 4083.

2237 Lord, Walter. Day of Infamy. New York: Holt, 1957.
       254p.
              The first two chapters relate to Japan's prepa-
       rations for and America's lack of adequate defenses
       for December 7, 1941.

2238   "The Los Angeles Completes 4,400-Mile Round Trip to
        the Canal Zone. " Aviation, XXIV (March 12, 1928),
        644.

2239   "The Loss of the United States Navy Submarine S-51. "
        Engineering, CXX (October 2, 1925), 420-421.

2240   Lothrop, Cummings L.   "The United States Naval
        Proving Grounds. " USNIP, XLV (1919), 779-792.

2241   Lott, Arnold S.   A Long Line of Ships, Mare Island's
        Century of Naval Activity in California.   Annapolis:
        U. S. Naval Institute, 1954.   268p.

2242   Loud, George A.   "A Strong and Adequate Navy. "
        SciAmer, CXX (February 8, 1919), 117.

2243   Loukins, Alexander.   "The Submarine Mine-Layer
        Krab. " USNIP, LX (1934), 197-201.

2244   Lovette, Leland P.   "The First Line Strengthens Pan-
        American Policy. " USNIP, LXV (1939), 1687-
        1697.

2245   _____.   Naval Customs, Tradition, and Usage.
        Annapolis: U. S. Naval Institute, 1934.   371p.

2246   _____.   "Naval Policy at the Crossroads. " USNIP,
        LVI (1930), 269-280.

2247   _____.   Naval Policy in Its Relation to National
        Policy.   University, Va.: Institute of Public Affairs,
        1939.   21p.

2248   _____.   School of the Men: The Annapolis Tradition
        in American Life.   New York: Frederick A. Stokes,
        1941.   382p.
            Includes the Navy songs "Anchors Aweigh" and
        "Navy Blue and Gold. "

2249   _____.   "The United States Looks to Her Future on
        the Sea. " USNIP, LXVI (1940), 1383-1393.

2250   _____.   "What Price Victory? " USNIP, LX (1934),
        1073-1082.

2251   _____.   "Why Should the Naval Officer Study Ameri-

can Foreign Policy?" USNIP, LVI (1930), 426-
434.

2252 _____ . "The World's Biggest Chess Game. " Popular Mechanics, LXXIII (April 1940), 497-504.
Fleet maneuvering.

2253 Low, Archibald M. Mine and Countermine. New
York: Sheridan House, 1940. 224p.

2254 _____ . The Submarine at War--The Contributions
of the Inventors of the Submarine. New York:
Sheridan House, 1942. 305p.

2255 "Low Pay Drives Army and Navy Officers from the
Service. " Current Opinion, LXVII (October 1919),
264-265.

2256 Lowell, Joan. Gal Reporter. New York: Farrar and
Rinehart, 1933. 304p.
The author had the chance to join the Coast
Guard on several anti-rum patrols and saw a
smuggler captured and another sunk by gunfire.

2257 Lowry, Edward G. "The Three-Plane Navy. " Saturday Evening Post, CXCIII (June 11, 1921), 16-17.

2258 Lu, David J. From the Marco Polo Bridge to Pearl
Harbor: Japan's Entry into World War II. Washington: Public Affairs Press, 1961. 274p.

2259 Lucier, Roland O. "Marking of Enlisted Men. "
USNIP, LXII (1936), 1689; LXIII (1937), 708-709.

2260 Luck, John R. "Radio. " Leatherneck, XXIII (August
1940), 9-12.

2261 Luckel, Frank H. " 'The Bank.' " USNIP, LIX (1933),
204-206.

2262 _____ . "Ice Seamanship. " USNIP, XLIX (1923),
91-95.
Aboard U. S. S. Saturn in the ice at Vladivostok
in 1918-1919.

2263 _____ . "Public Speaking. " USNIP, LXII (1936),
537-543.

2264 _____. "Trans-Pacific Communication." USNIP,
XLVI (1920), 1274-1275.

2265 Luckey, Robert B. "Three Decades of Marine Education." Army Information Digest, V (May 1950),
7-10.
The Marine Corps Institute.

2266 Luichinger, M. J. "I Saw the Indiana Launched."
Indiana Telephone News, XXXII (January 1942),
18-21.
A happy event of November 21, 1941, when
BB-58 went down the ways at Newport News.

2267 Lyman, Henry. "A Survivor Talks: The True Story
of the U. S. S. Kearny." Time, XXXVIII (November
10, 1941), 25.

2268 Lynch, Joseph B. "Notes on U. S. Naval Reserve
Aviation." USNIP, LXV (1939), 473-478.

2269 Lyons, Edgar O. "The U. S. Navy Gets Crewless
Ghost Fleet for War and Peace." Popular Science,
CXX (February 1932), 5-10.

2270 Mable, Janet. "Nostalgia for the Antarctic: Admiral
Byrd Feels the Urge to go South Again." Christian
Science Monitor Magazine, (April 6, 1938), 3.

2271 McAdie, A. "Fliers Aspects of Aerology: The Shenandoah and the Squall." Aviation, XXII (January 31,
1927), 215-216.

2272 Macaulay, Neill. The Sandino Affair. New York:
Quadrangle Press, 1971.

2273 _____. "Sandino and the Marines." Unpublished
PhD Dissertation, University of Texas, 1965.

2274 McCain, John S. "A Personal Survey." USNIP, XLIX
(1923), 19-37.

2275 _____. "Selection à la Race Track Method."
USNIP, LVI (1930), 401-402.

2276 _____. "Service Since Graduation vs. Age in Grade
Retirement." USNIP, LI (1925), 737-745.

2277   . "The Staff Equalization Bill." USNIP, L
         (1924), 417-423.

2278 McCain, William D. The United States and the Re-
        public of Panama. Durham, N.C.: Duke Univer-
        sity Press, 1937. 278p. Rpr. 1965.

2279 McCarthy, Charles J. "Naval Aircraft Design in the
        Mid-1930s. " Technology and Culture, IV (1963),
        165-173.

2280 McCartin, Edward F. "The Administration of Enlisted
        Personnel. " USNIP, LXIII (1937), 1272-1274.

2281   . "'Fried Egg and Baker Sardine. '" USNIP,
         LXIV (1938), 326-328.

2282 McClellan, Edwin N. "Artillery in Marine Corps His-
        tory. " Marine Corps Gazette, XVI (August 1931),
        26-30.
        Our interest is in the years 1919-1930.

2283   . "An Air-Minded Corps. " Marine Corps
         Gazette, XVII (February 1933), 64.

2284   . "'A Branch of the Executive Not the Judi-
         cial. '" USNIP, LII (1926), 99-102.
         Naval courts-martial.

2285   . "Down in the Dominican Republic. " Marine
         Corps Gazette, XVII (May 1932), 39-40.

2286   . "He Remembered His Mission. " Marine
         Corps Gazette, XV (November 1930), 30-32, 51-52.
         Action in Nicaragua.

2287   . "History of the United States Marine Corps."
         2 vols. Unpublished Paper, Files of the Historical
         Section, U.S. Marine Corps, 1925-1932.
         Although never published, the major's work
         comes the closest to being the definitive history of
         the Corps to that time. Microfilm copies of the
         work may be purchased from the New York Public
         Library.

2288   . "The Nueva Segovia Expedition. " Marine
         Corps Gazette, XVI (May, August 1931), 21-25, 8-

11, 59.
Action in Nicaragua.

2289 _____. "Operations Ashore in the Dominican Republic." USNIP, XLVII (1921), 235-245.

2290 _____. "The Saga of the Coco." Marine Corps Gazette, XV (November 1930), 14-17, 71-79.

2291 _____. "Supervising Nicaraguan Elections, 1928." USNIP, LIX (1933), 33-38.

2292 McClellan, Willard C. "A History of American Military Sea Transportation." Unpublished PhD Dissertation, American University, 1953.

2293 McClelland, William. "Analysis of the Standardization Trials of the U.S. Battleships Maryland, West Virginia, and Colorado." Marine Engineering, XXXI (December 1926), 693-696, 711, 713.

2294 McClench, Donald. "Comments on Navigational Aspects of the Disaster (to Destroyer Squadron Eleven)." USNIP, LXXXIII (1957), 47-48.

2295 McClintic, William S. "The Engineering Officer-Personnel Problem." USNIP, XLVII (1921), 1355-1370.

2296 McClintock, Robert M. "American Foreign Policy and Naval Power." USNIP, LXV (1939), 791-798.

2297 McConnell, Burt M. "Our Fourth-Estate Looks at the Navy: A Survey of the Nation's Newspapers Reveals Little Unanimity on the Question of the New Naval Program." Current History, XLVIII (April 1938), 31-34.

2298 McCorkle, Edith M. "Nursing in the Navy." American Journal of Nursing, XLI (November 1941), 1326-1327.

2299 McCormick, George W. "The Merchant Marine Naval Reserve." USNIP, LXIV (1938), 1338-1342.

2300 McCormick, Olive. "Calling All Landlubbers! The Language of the Sea and Its Etiquette." Recreation,

XXXIII (July 1939), 213-218.

2301   McCracken, Alan R.   "Book Learnin' Leadership. "
       USNIP, LXII (1936), 790-792.

2302   _____.   "Canton Flower Boat. "   USNIP, LXXVIII
       (1952), 368-377.
       The 1941 adventures of the Yangtze River gun-
       boat U. S. S. Mindanao, which the author commanded.

2303   _____.   "The Church Pennant. "   USNIP, LVI
       (1930), 717-719.

2304   _____.   "Quotable Principles of War. "   USNIP,
       LXI (1936), 1826-1828.

2305   _____.   "Sealubbers. "   USNIP, LVI (1930), 132-136.

2306   _____.   "The Selection and Use of Binoculars. "
       USNIP, LI (1925), 1446-1451.

2307   _____.   "Ship Model Building as a Naval Officer's
       Hobby. "   USNIP, LX (1934), 974-976.

2308   _____.   "Strictly Private Thoughts on Naval Public-
       ity. "   USNIP, LXI (1935), 381-383.

2309   McCrocklin, James.   Garde d'Haiti, 1915-1934: Twenty
       Years of Organization and Training by the United
       States Marine Corps.   Annapolis: U. S. Naval In-
       stitute, 1956.   262p.

2310   MacDonald, Scot.   The Evolution of Aircraft Carriers.
       Washington: U. S. Government Printing Office, 1964.
       73p.

2311   _____.   "The Tailhook Navy. "   USNIP, LXXXIX
       (1963), 94-113.
       On the development of carriers since the
       Langley.

2312   McDowell, Clyde S.   "Acoustic Aids to Navigation. "
       USNIP, XLVI (1920), 231-236.

2312a _____.   "Model Making. "   USNIP, XLV (1919),
       1743-1750.

2313 _____ . "Naval Research." Science, New Series
        LXIX (June 14, 1929), 607-609.

2314 _____ . "A Naval Research Reserve." USNIP, LIV
        (1928), 976-978.

2315 McDowell, William. The Shape of Ships: Being the
        Story of the Development of Ships from the Earliest
        Times to the Present Day. London: Hutchinson,
        1950. 232p.
        Some data relative to our period.

2316 McElduff, Daniel A. "Wardroom of the U. S. S. Tusca-
        loosa." USNIP, LXI (1935), 944-948.

2317 McGeary, F. M., jt. author. See Keleher, T. J., no.
        1944.

2318 McGowan, Leo J. "Officer Education at Home and
        Aboard." USNIP, LVI (1930), 634-635.

2319 McGuire, Henry D. "Ball Bearings." USNIP, XLV
        (1919), 973-986.

2320 _____ . "Navigational Antecedents." USNIP, LIX
        (1933), 705-717.

2321 MacHatton, Robert P. "Evolution and Introduction of
        Chain Cables." USNIP, LXVI (1940), 361-368.

2322 _____ . "The Red Cross at the Masthead." USNIP,
        LXVI (1940), 1407-1411.

2323 McHugh, F. D. "Could America's Third-Rate Navy
        Fight Japan?" China Weekly Review, LXIV (May
        27, 1933), 516-519.

2324 _____ . "The Navy's Contribution to Industry."
        SciAmer, CXLVI (May 1932), 262-266.

2325 _____ . "Our Third-Rate Navy Could Not Fight
        Japan." SciAmer, CXLVIII (May 1933), 268-271.

2326 _____ . "Status of the World's Navies." SciAmer,
        CLVI (January 1937), 25.

2327 McIntosh, Kenneth C. "Afterwards!" USNIP, XLV
        (1919), 1-18.

2328 _____. "Economics and the Navy." USNIP, LIII
     (1927), 1263-1266.

2329 _____. "In Lacquer and Silk." USNIP, L (1924),
     77-85.

2330 _____. "Playing Safe with Books." USNIP, LX
     (1934), 615-622.

2331 _____. "Putting 'em Across." USNIP, XLV
     (1919), 793-805.

2332 _____. "Salient Features of the Law Maritime."
     USNIP, LVI (1930), 991-996.

2333 _____. "Some Notes on Training Men for Clerical
     and Commissary Rates." USNIP, XLV (1919),
     223-232.

2334 _____. "The Supply Corps School of Application."
     USNIP, XLVIII (1922), 953-957.

2335 _____. "'U. S. C. N.'" USNIP, XLV (1919), 1699-
     1724.
     United States Commerce Navy.

2336 _____. "When I was on the Old U. S. S. Biftick."
     USNIP, XLVI (1920), 383-404.

2337 Macintyre, Donald. "Shipborne Radar." USNIP, XCIII
     (1967), 70-84.
     From the early days.

2338 _____. The Thunder of the Guns: A Century of
     Battleships. New York: Norton, 1960. 352p.

2339 _____. U-boat Killer. London: Weidenfeld and
     Nicolson, 1956. 179p.

2340 _____ and B. W. Bathe. Man of War. New York:
     McGraw-Hill, 1969.
     A history of warships, including those in use
     during our period.

2341 McIntyre, M. H. "Battleship Holds Lead Against the
     Plane." USNIP, XLIX (1923), 1377-1381.

2342 _____. "The Naval Air Battle of the Future."
Aviation, XVIII (June 1, 1925), 608.

2343 _____. "Naval Aircraft Investigation: Finish Fight
Looms in Battleship-Airplane Controversy." Aviation, XVII (November 10, 1924), 1249-1250.

2344 MacKay, Robert A. "Political Implications of the
London [Naval] Conference." Queen's Quarterly,
XXXVII (July 1930), 532-543.

2345 Mackaye, Milton. "Modern Bluejackets, no Longer
Recruited from the Nation's Riffraff." Outlook,
CLII (July 31, 1929), 532-533.

2346 McKee, Andrew I. The Development of Submarines in
the United States. New York: Society of Naval
Architects and Marine Engineers, 1943. 12p.

2347 McKee, I. "Captain Edward Howe Watson and the
Honda Disaster." Pacific Historical Review, XXIX
(August 1960), 287-305.

2348 McKee, Oliver, Jr. "America's New [Coast Guard]
Cutter Fleet." National Republic, XX (May 1932),
5-6+.

2349 _____. "Training Our Coast Guard." National Republic, XVIII (August 1930), 5-7.

2350 _____. "Uncle Sam's Chinese Patrol." National
Republic, XVII (May 1929), 14-15+.

2351 _____. "Uncle Sam's Navy on Land." National
Republic, LXXI (April 1930), 5-7.
Navy yards and stations.

2352 _____. "The World's Navies." Commonweal, XXI
(November 9, 1934), 51-53.

2353 Mackey, Donald M. "The Control of Airship Planes."
American Aviation Historical Society Journal, VIII
(Spring 1963), 13-22.

2354 McKinley, Ashley C. "Mapping the Antarctic from the
Air." National Geographic, LXII (October 1932),
470-485.

Part of the mission of the 1928-1930 Byrd Expedition.

2355 Macklin, Thomas. "Navigating the Inland Waterways of Alaska. " USNIP, LVI (1930), 827-828.

2356 McLaren, William A. "The Navy as an Effective Agency in Diplomacy. " Current History, XXI (January 1925), 570-573.

2357 McLaughlin, C. H. "Neutral Rights Under International Law in the European War, 1939-1941. " Minnesota Law Review, XXVI (1941-1942), 1-49, 177-222.

2358 McLean, Ephrim R. "The Airplane in International Law. " USNIP, LXII (1936), 1533-1543.

2359 _____. "The Caribbean, an American Lake. " USNIP, LXVII (1941), 947-952.

2360 McLean, Ridley. "Analysis of United States Proposals for the Limitation of Armaments. " Unpublished Lecture, Files of the U. S. Army Military History Research Collection, 1921.
      Refers to the Washington Naval Conference.

2361 _____. "The Control of Transportation Overseas in Case of a Major War. " Unpublished Lecture, G-4 Course 44, Files of the U. S. Army Military History Research Collection, 1922.

2362 _____. "Naval Communications. " USNIP, LII (1926), 2029-2042.

2363 Macliesh, Archibald F. Strategy of the Americas. New York: Duell, Sloan and Pearce, 1941. 247p. Hemisphere defenses.

2364 McMillan, I. E. "The Development of Naval Gunfire Support of Amphibious Operations. " USNIP, LXXIV (1948), 1-15.

2365 McMillen Frederick E. "Banking Aboard a Battleship. " American Banker's Association Journal, XXI (January 1929), 663-664+.

2366 _____. "San Juan de Ulua Under the American

Flag. " USNIP, LXII (1936), 1155-1166.

2367 _____ . "Some Haitian Recollections. " USNIP, LXII
(1936), 522-528.
Both articles by a U. S. naval captain recall the
American intervention.

2368 McMurtrie, Francis E. "Naval Construction in 1939."
Engineer, CLXIX (January 5-12, 1940), 2-3, 35-37.
For earlier entries in this series, see the cita-
tions entered under Hector C. Bywater above.

2369 _____ ., jt. author. See Bacon, Reginald H. S. ,
no. 208.

2370 McNair, Frederick V. Handbook for Naval Officers:
An Aid to Examinations for Promotion. Van Nos-
trand's Nautical Manuals. 2nd ed. , rev. New York:
D. Van Nostrand, 1921. 243p.

2371 McNamee, Luke. "Aviation and the Navy. " Aviation,
XV (November 12, 1923). 604-608.

2372 _____ . _____ . USNIP, XLIX (1923), 2072-2075.

2373 _____ . "Keep Our Navy Strong. " USNIP, XLIX
(1923), 801-810.
An April 4, 1922 talk before the Woman's Republican Club of Massachusetts.

2374 _____ . "Naval Intelligence. " Unpublished Lecture,
Files of the U. S. Army Military History Research
Collection, 1923.

2375 _____ . _____ . USNIP, L (1924), 1443-1452.
A March 9, 1923 talk given aboard the U. S. S.
Henderson.

2376 _____ . "The Navy and the 5-5-3-Ratio. " USNIP,
XLVIII (1922), 1139-1148.

2377 _____ . "Types of Ships and Why. " USNIP, LVI
(1930), 907-912.

2378 _____ . "What the Navy Does for Industry. " American Industries, XXIII (March 1923), 5-12.

2379 McNulty, R. R.   "A Plan for Federal Merchant Marine
      Training. " USNIP, LVI (1930), 648-650.
      Reprinted from the May 24, 1930 issue of the
      Nautical Gazette.

2380 _____. "Plight of the Merchant Marine Naval Re-
      serve. " USNIP, LV (1929), 335-337.
      Reprinted from the February 15, 1929 issue of
      Marine Journal.

2381 "The Macon Makes Its First Trial Voyage. " News-
      week, I (April 29, 1933), 25.

2382 "Macon to Carry Defense Planes. " Newsweek, I
      (March 11, 1933), 24.

2383 McPherson, Guy and Mary Walls.   Fixing Wages and
      Salaries of Navy Civilian Employees in Shore Es-
      tablishments, 1862-1945.   Administrative Reference
      Service Reports, no. 9. Washington: Administra-
      tive Office, Navy Department, 1945.   13p.

2384 McPherson, O. H. M.   "The Navy's Relation to Com-
      mercial Shipping: A Proposal to Further Shipping."
      USNIP, LV (1929), 190-192.

2385 Maddox, R. J.   "Borah and the Battleships. " Idaho
      Yesterdays, IX (1965), 20-27.
      The senator sponsored naval conferences in the
      1920s in lieu of joining the League of Nations.

2386 Magdeburger, E. C.   "The Diesel Engine in the United
      States Navy, 1898-1948. " American Society of
      Naval Engineers Journal, LXI (February 1949),
      45-93.

2387 _____. "The U. S. Navy's Participation in Diesel
      Engine Development. " Mechanical Engineering,
      LIX (September 1937), 659-667.

2388 "Magic at Quantico. " Time, XXXVII (March 3, 1941),
      19.
      Marine Corps boot training.

2389 "Magic was the Word for It. " Time, XLVI (Decem-
      ber 17, 1945), 20-22.
      Operation Magic and the Japanese codes before
      Pearl Harbor.

2390   Magruder, P. M.   "Japanese Aviation. "   Aero Digest,
        XXX (May 1937), 26-29.

2391   Magruder, Thomas P.   "Aircraft Carriers. "   Saturday
        Evening Post, CC (June 23, 1928), 25.

2392   _____ .   "Battleships and Battle-Cruisers. "   Satur-
        day Evening Post, CC (March 24, 1928), 10-11.

2393   _____ .   "Destroyers. "   Saturday Evening Post, CC
        (February 4, 1928), 16-17.

2394   _____ .   "Light Cruisers. "   Saturday Evening Post,
        CC (July 2, 1927), 3-4.

2395   _____ .   "The Navy and the Economy. "   Saturday
        Evening Post, CC (September 24, 1927), 6-7.
        This article received discussion from the Lit-
        erary Digest, XCV (October 8, 1927), 14-15.

2396   _____ .   "Our Pressing Naval Problem. "   Forum,
        LXXX (December 1928), 882-889.

2396a   _____ .   "Participation of the Navy in the Sesqui-
        centennial International Exposition at Philadelphia,
        1926. "   Unpublished paper, Subject File 1911-1927,
        ZU, Box 842, National Archives, 1927.   36p.

2397   _____ .   "Submarines. "   Saturday Evening Post, CC
        (November 19, 1927), 8-9.

2398   _____ .   The United States Navy.   Philadelphia:
        Dorrance, 1928.   179p.
        The author was a rear admiral.

2399   "Maintaining the Navy's Efficiency. "   Outlook, CXXXII
        (October 4, 1922), 177-178.

2400   Maitland, E. M.   The Log of H. M. A. R-34, Journey
        to America and Back.   London: Hodder & Stoughton,
        1920.   168p.

2401   Mallory, Walter H.   "Security in the Pacific. "   Foreign
        Affairs, XIII (1935), 82-90.
        A resume of the effects of the Washington
        Treaties between 1921 and 1934.

2402 Mandeville, Ernest W.   "Most Amazing Story of Cor-
      ruption: The U. S. Coast Guard and Smuggling. "
      Outlook, CXLV (January 19, 1927), 81-82.
      A little salt water muckraking.

2403 Mang, L. H.   "Strength Tests at the U. S. Naval
      Academy. " USNIP, LVIII (1932), 91-96.

2404 Mann, Richard R.   "Chart Study and Preparation. "
      USNIP, XLV (1919), 1887-1888.

2405 Mann, William L.   A Manual on Foot Care and Shoe
      Fitting for Officers of the U. S. Navy and Marine
      Corps.   Philadelphia: Blakiston, 1920.

2406 _____.   "A Suggested Smoke Screen Indicator. "
      USNIP, LII (1926), 2221-2224.

2407 Manning, George C.   "The Case for the Capital Ship."
      USNIP, LII (1926), 2473-2484.

2408 _____.   "Congress Should Authorize Battleship Re-
      placements. " Marine Engineering, XXXIV (June
      1929), 295-297.

2409 _____.   "Financial Control of Ships' Overhauls. "
      USNIP, LVI (1930), 296-298.

2410 _____.   "Inclining Experiment--U. S. S. Florida. "
      Marine Engineering, XXXII (May 1927), 279.

2411 _____.   "Inclining Experiment--U. S. S. Utah. "
      Marine Engineering, XXXII (October 1927), 561.

2412 _____.   "The Modernization of Capital Ships. "
      Marine Engineering, XXXIII (April 1928), 215-216.

2413 _____.   "The Navy Material Inspection Service. "
      USNIP, LXII (1936), 1143-1146.

2414 _____.   "New Capital Ships. " Marine Engineering,
      XXXIII (October 1928), 528-529.

2415 _____.   "Recent Trends of U. S. Capital Ship De-
      signs. " Marine Engineering, XXXIII (January 1928),
      5-7.

2416   _____. "Yangtze: A Naval Constructor Goes to Sea
        with the Fresh Water Navy. " USNIP, LX (1934),
        221-229.

2417   _____ and T. L. Schumacher. Principles of Naval
        Architecture and Warship Construction, Especially
        Prepared to Furnish in Compact Form the Informa-
        tion Required by the Operating Personnel of the
        U. S. Navy. Annapolis: U. S. Naval Institute, 1930.
        395p.

2418   Manning, Harry. '"Ten Minutes. '" USNIP, LXVI
        (1940), 1590-1592.

2419   Manning, William R. , ed. Diplomatic Correspondence
        of the United States: Inter-American Affairs. 12
        vols. Washington: Carnegie Endowment for Inter-
        national Peace, 1934.

2420   Marchant, W. A. "A Landsman's Model of the U. S. S.
        Texas. " USNIP, LX (1934), 985-986.

2421   Marcosson, Isaac F. "Peace and Parity. " Saturday
        Evening Post, CCII (November 23, 1929), 6-7.

2422   Marder, Arthur J. Portrait of an Admiral: The Life
        and Papers of Sir Herbert Richmond. London:
        Cape, 1952. 407p.

2423   _____. "Sea Power: Democracy's Shield, Ships and
        Bases are the Two Fundamentals of Our Security."
        Christian Science Monitor Magazine, (March 22,
        1941), 1-4.

2424   "Marine Aviation, A Record of Achievement. " Marine
        Corps Gazette, XV (November 1930), 33-41.
                Principally a discussion of its application in the
        various banana wars.

2425   "Marine Aviators in Nicaragua. " Leatherneck, XI
        (March 1928), 25.

2426   "Marines and Machine Guns in Nicaragua. " Independ-
        ent, CXVIII (January 22, 1927), 90-91.

2427   "Marines on Teapot Dome. " Nation, CXVIII (March
        12, 1924), 274-275.

Concerns the oil reserves, not the political
scandal.

2428 "Marines Rapidly Boosted for Modern First-Line Warfare. " Newsweek, XVII (June 23, 1941), 31-32.

2429 Markey, Morris. "A Deckload of Flying Dynamite. "
American Magazine, CXVI (December 1933), 30-
33.
Planes aboard American carriers.

2430 _____. "Our Floating Frontier. " Reader's Digest,
XXVIII (March 1936), 47-51.
The U. S. Navy.

2431 Markland, H. B. "What Shall We Do About Japan?"
North American Review, CCXXXIX (February 1935),
170-176.

2432 Marshall, Elliott E. "Our Navy in Peace. " USNIP,
LVIII (1932), 191-196.

2433 Martienssen, Anthony K. Hitler and His Admirals.
New York: E. P. Dutton, 1949. 275p.
Contains some information relative to this work,
including the German leader's decision not to
antagonize the U. S. at sea in 1939-41.

2434 Martin, Harold M. "Service Aircraft. " USNIP, LVII
(1931), 1039-1043.

2435 Martin, Harrison P. "Small Arms and the Navy. "
USNIP, LXIII (1937), 1753-1759.

2436 Martin, James J. American Liberalism and World
Politics, 1931-1941: Liberalism's Press and Spokes-
men on the Road Back to War Between Mukden and
Pearl Harbor. 2 vols. New York: Devin-Adair,
1964.

2437 Martin, Laurence W. The Sea in Modern Strategy.
New York: Praeger, 1967. 190p.

2438 Martin, Robert E. "Balloon Flights Train Navy Airmen. " Popular Science, CXXXVII (November 1940),
86-89.

2439 "Marvelous Rescue of the Mosquito Fleet. " Saturday
      Evening Post, CCXIII (August 3, 1940), 28.

2440 Marvin, George. "Making Midshipmen. " Outlook,
      CXXXVIII (December 3, 1924), 538-542.

2441 "The Maryland, Our First 16-inch Gun Battleship. "
      SciAmer, CXXII (June 26, 1920), 600.

2442 Masek, William. "Operations of the Navy's Safest
      [Air] Squadron. " Aviation, XXVIII (February 22,
      1930), 373-375.

2443 Maskelyne, Jasper. Magic--Top Secret. New York:
      Paul, 1949. 191p.
           Breaking the Japanese codes before Pearl Har-
      bor.

2444 Masland, John W. "Public Opinion and American
      Pacific Naval Policy. " USNIP, LXVII (1941), 985-
      990.

2445 Mason, David. U-boat: The Secret Weapon. Ballan-
      tine's Illustrated History of World War II. New
      York: Ballantine, 1972. 160p.

2446 Mason, Francis K. Air Facts and Feats: A Record
      of Aerospace Achievement. Garden City, N. Y. :
      Doubleday, 1970. 223p.
           Two chapters apply to our period: Chpt. III,
      "Maritime Aviation, " and Chapter V, "Lighter-
      than-Air. "

2447 Matloff, Maurice. "Pre-War Military Plans and Pre-
      parations, 1939-1941. " USNIP, LXXIX (1953), 740-
      748.

2448 _____ and Edwin M. Snell. Strategic Planning for
      Coalition Warfare, 1941-1942. United States Army
      in World War II--The War Department. Washing-
      ton: Office of the Chief of Military History, U. S.
      Army, 1953. 454p.

2449 Matsukawa, B. , trans. See Ishimaru, Tōta, no. 1843.

2450 Matt, Paul R. "Grumman FF-1. " Aero Album, III
      (1970), 32-37.

The first Grumman plane sold to the American
Navy, 1931.

2451 _____, comp. United States Navy and Marine Corps
Fighters, 1918-1962. Los Angeles: Aero Publications, 1963. 248p.

2452 Maverick, Maury. "Should Congress Approve a Pro-
gram for the Expansion of the Army and Navy?:
Representative Maverick's Answers. " U. S. News,
VI (February 28, 1938), 7+.

2453 _____. "War Built to Order. " Collier's, CII
(July 2, 1938), 12-13+.

2454 Maxim, Hiram P. "The Next War on the Sea. "
Popular Mechanics, LXV (March 1936), 360-366.

2455 "Maximum Range of Guns in the United States and
British Navies. " SciAmer, CXXXVI (March 1927),
196.

2456 Maxon, Yale C. Control of Japanese Foreign Policy:
A Study of Civil-Military Rivalry, 1930-1945.
Berkeley: University of California Press, 1957.
286p. Rpr. 1973.

2457 May, C. Welles. "Sequel to the Squalus. " Southern
Literary Messenger, II (January 1940), 48-52.

2458 Mayo, Claude B. "Library Service for the Permanent
Naval Establishments. " ALA Bulletin, XIII (1919),
267-269, 349.

2459 _____. "Naval Intelligence. " Unpublished Lecture,
G-2 Course 27, Files of the U. S. Army Military
History Research Collection, 1924.

2460 _____. "Some Notes on Ship Administration. "
USNIP, LVII (1931), 57-62.

2461 "Meaning of ZR-1 [Shenandoah] to the Aeronautic
World. " Current Opinion, LXXV (November 1923),
602-603.

2462 "The Mechanics of Modern Naval Warfare. " Popular
Mechanics, LXXIII (January 1940), 40-47.

2463   Meese, Harry.   "Supply and Assault with Landing
       Ships. "   Bureau of Ships Journal, I (November
       1952),   2-8.
       A study of the Marine activity from 1935
       through 1952.

2464   Megee, Vernon E.   "The Evolution of Marine Aviation:
       Part I. "   Marine Corps Gazette, XLIX (August
       1965),   20-26.
       From the end of World War I to 1941.

2465   _____ .   "The Genesis of Air Support in Guerrilla
       Operations. "   USNIP, XCI (1965),   48-59.
       Mainly a study of Marine aviators in Nicaragua.

2466   _____ .   "United States Military Intervention in
       Nicaragua. "   Unpublished M. A. Thesis, University
       of Texas,   1963.

2467   "The Menace of Anglo-American Naval Rivalry. "   Lit-
       erary Digest, C (January 5,   1929),   5-7.

2468   Mencken, Henry L.   "The Downfall of the Navy. "   In:
       his Prejudices.   New York: Knopf, 1923.   p. 253-
       261.   Rpr.   1970.

2469   _____ .   "Hands Across the Sea. "   American Mer-
       cury, XX (May 1930),   27-28.
       Acid comments on the naval disarmament con-
       ference.

2470   Mendenhall, William K.   "Retardation of Ships' Speed
       Due to Turning. "   USNIP, LI (1925),   1719-1722.

2471   Merrill, James M. ,   ed.   Quarter-deck and Fo'c's'le:
       the Exciting Story of the Navy.   Chicago: Rand
       McNally, 1963.   500p.
       Selections from letters, eye-witness accounts,
       ballads, journals, log books, and war diaries.

2472   Merrill, Robert T.   "A Merchant Marine Naval Re-
       serve. "   USNIP, LXV (1939),   463-469.

2473   Merrill, Taylor.   "A Fire Sale on Sanity?"   Christian
       Century, LV (April 13, 1938),   458-461.
       With regard to new naval building programs.

2474 Merz, Charles, ed. Days of Decision: Wartime Edi-
      torials from the New York Times. Garden City,
      N. Y. : Doubleday, Doran, 1941. 278p.
      Between September 1939 and late 1941.

2475 "Metal-Clad Airship for the U. S. Navy. " Engineering,
      CXXII (December 31, 1926), 806-807.

2476 "Metal vs. Fabric: The All-Metal Naval Airship. "
      SciAmer, CXXXV (September 1926), 196-197.

2477 Metcalf, Clyde H. "The Marines in China. " Marine
      Corps Gazette, XXII (September 1938), 35-37, 53-
      58.
          Following their exploits in the Boxer Rebellion,
      cited in Vol. IV of this series, U. S. Marines
      served in that divided nation in 1924-1925, 1927-
      1929, and 1931-1938.

2478 "Me-too Boats and Their Brood. " Popular Mechanics,
      LVI (November 1931), 770-773.
      Treaty cruisers.

2479 Meyer-Oakes, F. F. "Prince Saionji and the London
      Naval Conference, Being Part of Volume One of
      the Memoirs of Harada Kunaio Translated into Eng-
      lish with Annotations. " Unpublished PhD Disserta-
      tion, University of Chicago, 1955.

2480 _____, ed. See Kumao, Harada, no. 2066.

2481 Meyers, George J. "The Characteristics of Naval
      Bases. " Unpublished Lecture, War Planning Divi-
      sion Course 8, Files of the U. S. Army Military
      History Research Collection, 1927.

2482 _____. "Combined Expeditions. " Unpublished Lec-
      ture, War Planning Division Course 8, Files of the
      U. S. Army Military History Research Collection,
      1927.

2483 _____. "The Elements of Sea Power. " Unpublished
      Lecture, War Planning Division Course 8, Files of
      the U. S. Army Military History Research Collec-
      tion, 1926.

2484 _____. "Finding Operations Against a Hostile

Coast. " Unpublished Lecture, War Planning Division Course 8, Files of the U. S. Army Military History Research Collection, 1927.

2485 _____ . "General Strategic Considerations. " Miscellaneous Course 7, Files of the U. S. Army Military History Research Collection, 1923.
As seen by a naval captain.

2486 _____ . "Naval Strategy in Relation to Seacoast Fortification. " Unpublished Lecture, War Planning Division Course 8, Files of the U. S. Army Military History Research Collection, 1927.

2487 _____ . "The Problems of a Modern Combined Expedition. " Unpublished Lecture, Miscellaneous Course 11, Files of the U. S. Army Military History Research Collection, 1924.

2488 _____ . "The Role of Aviation in Naval and Combined Operations. " Unpublished Lecture, War Planning Division Course 8, Files of the U. S. Army Military History Research Collection, 1927.

2489 _____ . "Sea Power. " Unpublished Lecture, Miscellaneous Course 5, Files of the U. S. Army Military History Research Collection, 1923.

2490 _____ . "Some Effects of the Treaty on Limitation of Naval Armaments in Naval Strategy. " Unpublished Lecture, War Planning Division Course 8, Files of the U. S. Army Military History Research Collection, 1927.

2491 _____ . "The Strategy of the Atlantic and the Pacific. " Unpublished Lecture, War Planning Division Course 8, Files of the U. S. Army Military History Research Collection, 1926.

2492 _____ . "The United States as a Sea Power. " Unpublished Lecture, War Planning Division Course 8, Files of the U. S. Army Military History Research Collection, 1926.

2493 "Midnight with the Battlefleet. " Popular Mechanics, LVII (January 1932), 82-86.

2494 Miles, Alfred H. "Navy Mine Depot, Yorktown, Virginia. " USNIP, LIV (1928), 299-304.

2495 Milius, Helen C. "Seagoing Surgeon from Virginia. "
      Commonwealth, XXVII (February 1960), 22-24, 39.
      Herbert L. Pugh, 1923-1956.

2496 Miller, Charles J. "Diplomatic Spurs: Our Experiences in Santo Domingo. " Marine Corps Gazette,
      XIX (February, May, August 1935), 43-50, 19-25,
      52-55, 35-55.

2497 _____. "Marine Corps Schools, 1934-1935. "
      Marine Corps Gazette, XIX (August 1934), 57-60.

2498 Miller, Daniel G. "History and Symbolism of the
      Naval Medical Corps Insignia. " U. S. Armed Forces
      Medical Journal, III (February 1952), 226-239.
      Also includes uniform developments, 1798-1952.

2499 Miller, Francis T. The Fight to Conquer the Ends of
      the Earth: Byrd's Great Adventure. Chicago: John
      C. Winston, 1930. 883p.

2500 Miller, Harold B. "The Airplane Carrier. " Mechanical Engineer, LIV (June 1932), 388-392.

2501 _____. "Covered Wagons of the Sea. " USNIP,
      LVII (1931), 1461-1468.
      Aircraft carriers.

2502 _____. "Navy Skyhooks. " USNIP, LXI (1935), 234-
      240.
      Airships.

2503 _____. Navy Wings. New York: Dodd, Mead,
      1937. 323p.

2504 _____. "Shooting the Catapult. " USNIP, LIX
      (1933), 345-354, 1481-1483.
      Discussion is included concerning this article on
      carrier takeoffs.

2505 _____. "Training the Naval Air Reserve. " Aero
      Digest, XVI (June 1930), 75-76+.

2506 Miller, Max. Fog and Men on Bering Sea. New York:

E. P. Dutton, 1936. 272p.
Aboard the U. S. C. G. cutter Northland off Alaska
in the mid-1930s.

2507 Miller, Norman M. I Took the Sky Road, as Told to
Hugh B. Cave. New York: Dodd, Mead, 1945.
212p.
Memoirs of a Navy flier from the 1930s through
the Big War.

2508 Miller, Richard T. "Sixty Years of Destroyers: A
Study of Evolution. " USNIP, LXXXVIII (1962), 93-
111.

2509 Miller, William D. "The Background and Development
of Naval Signal Flags. " Massachusetts Historical
Society Proceedings, LXVIII (1952), 60-71.

2510 Million, Paul E., Jr. "The Influence of the Washington Naval Conference Upon American Sea Power. "
Unpublished PhD Dissertation, Georgetown University, 1956.

2511 Millis, Walter. Arms and Men: A Study in American
Military History. New York: Putnam, 1956. 382p.
Rpr. 1967.

2512 _____. The Future of Sea Power in the Pacific.
World Affair Pamphlets, no. 9. New York: Foreign
Policy Association, 1935. 51p.

2513 _____. "Prepare, Prepare, Prepare!" Atlantic
Monthly, CXLIX (June 1932), 753-769.

2514 _____. This is Pearl!: The United States and
Japan, 1941. New York: Morrow, 1947. 384p.
Rpr. 1971.

2515 Millspaugh, Arthur C. Haiti Under American Control.
Boston: World Peace Foundation, 1931.

2516 Minckler, Campbell H. "Punishments Humanized. "
USNIP, LVI (1930), 582-587.

2517 "Minecraft, 1917-1969. " In: U. S. Navy Department.
Naval History Division. Dictionary of American
Naval Fighting Ships. Washington: U. S. Govern-

214   The American Navy, 1918-1941

        ment Printing Office, 1959--. V. 442-525.

2518 "Mine-Laying Submarine the Latest in War Craft."
       Popular Mechanics, LXX (November 1938), 698-
       699.

2519 "Miracle-Working Ships Keep the Navy Fit at Sea."
       Popular Science, CXX (May 1932), 33.

2520 "Misleading the American Public as to the Navy."
       SciAmer, CXXXII (February 1925), 84.
           Some harsh words from a friendly publication.

2521 "Mr. Hoover and Naval Disarmament." New Republic,
       LVII (November 28, 1928), 28-29.

2522 "Mr. Hoover and the Atlantic Pact." New Republic,
       LXII (February 26, 1930), 31-32.

2523 Mitchell, Donald W. History of the Modern American
       Navy from 1883 through Pearl Harbor. New York:
       Knopf, 1946. 477p.

2524 _____. "The History of the United States Navy."
       Unpublished PhD Dissertation, University of Southern
       California, 1938.

2525 _____. "How to Beat Japan." Nation, CLIII
       (August 30, 1941), 177-179.
           Embargo.

2526 _____. "Our First Line of Defense." Yale Review,
       New Series XXIX (March 1940), 565-588.

2527 _____. "What Our Warships Cost." Nation, CXLIX
       (September 23, 1939), 320-323.
           For the rejoinder, see the article by P. H. Van
       Gelder cited below.

2528 _____. "What the Maneuvers Showed." Nation,
       CLIII (November 22, 1941), 504-506.

2529 _____. "What's Wrong with Our Navy?" New Re-
       public, CIII (September 30, 1940), 437-439.

2530 Mitchell, John B. "Admiral [Samuel] McGowan, the
       Man Who Takes Care of Our 300,000 Sailor Boys."

Forum, LXI (January 1919), 92-99.

2531 Mitchell, John C. "A Chronological History of the
      F9C-2 and Its Use on the Akron and the Macon. "
      American Aviation Historical Society Journal, III
      (April-June 1958), 100-109.

2532 Mitchell, Jonathan. "What the Admirals Think. " Out-
      look, CLII (August 7, 1929), 563-567.

2533 Mitchell, R. J. "Marine Corps Aviation. " Aero Digest,
      XXXVI (February 1940), 81-82+.

2534 Mitchell, Ruth. My Brother Bill: The Life of General
      "Billy" Mitchell. New York: Harcourt, Brace,
      1953. 344p.

2535 Mitchell, William. "Aircraft Dominate Seacraft. "
      Saturday Evening Post, CXCVII (January 24, 1925),
      22-23.

2536 _____. "Air Power vs. Sea Power. " Review of
      Reviews, LXIII (March 1921), 273-277.

2537 _____. "Brig. General Mitchell's Startling Testi-
      mony: Claims Aircraft can Render Big Naval Bat-
      tleships Obsolete. " Aviation, X (February 7, 1921),
      164-167.

2538 _____. "Building a Futile Navy. " Atlantic Monthly,
      CXLII (September 1928), 408-413.

2539 _____. "The Mitchell Plan for a United Air Force."
      USNIP, LI (1925), 2372-2377.

2540 _____. "When the Air Raiders Come. " Collier's,
      LXXVII (May 1, 1926), 8-9.

2541 _____. "Will Seapower be Displaced by Airpower?"
      In: John O. Beaty, et al., eds. Facts and Ideas
      for Students of English Composition. New York:
      Crofts, 1930. p. 171-174.

2542 _____. Winged Defense: The Development and
      Possibilities of Modern Air Power--Economic and
      Military. Port Washington, N.Y.: Kennikat, 1973.
      261p.

Reprint of the 1925 edition by the army aviator
who tried out some of his theories on obsolescent
battleships.

2543   . "World's Largest Airship, the Dirigible
Akron. " Woman's Home Companion, LVIII (November 1931), 18-19+.

2544 Mizrahi, J. V.   Carrier Fighters.   2 vols. Northridge,
Calif. : Sentry Books, 1969.
From the Curtis TS-1 to the Chance Vought Cor-
sair F4U.

2545   . Dive and Torpedo Bombers.   Northridge,
Calif. : Sentry Books, 1967.   66p.
From the early days.

2546 Mock, Richard M.   "[Airplane] Engine Exhaust Si-
lencers. "   USNIP, LIV (1928), 701-706.

2547 "Modern American Destroyers. "   Engineer, CXXXIII
(March 10, 1922), 264-265.

2548 Moffett, J. A.   "The Akron Rescue. "   USNIP, LIX
(1933), 1717-1719.
Refers to the airship of that name.

2549 Moffett, William A.   "Admiral Moffett Claims All Sea
Flying for the Navy. " Aviation, XVI (May 26,
1924), 558-560.

2550   . "Admiral Moffet's Report on Aviation. "
Aviation, XIII (December 18, 1922), 800-804.

2551   . "The Aeronautical Engine: Some Differ-
ences Between the Airship and the Airplane Power
Plant. "   U. S. Air Services, VIII (March 1923),
13-15.

2552 No Entry

2553   . "Air Service Versus Air Force. "   Forum,
LXXV (February 1926), 179-185.
The Navy's top aeronautical expert takes on
"Billy" Mitchell over the General's idea for a uni-
fied air service.

2554 _____ . "The Aircraft Carrier Saratoga Launched."
Aviation, XVIII (April 20, 1925), 434-435.

2555 _____ . "Airships of the Future." American Magazine, XLII (November 1929), 187-192.

2556 _____ . "Airmada." USNIP, LXVII (1941), 73-74.
Published posthumously.

2557 _____ . "Annual Report on Naval Aviation." Aviation, XIX (December 21, 1925), 870-871.

2558 _____ . _____ . Aviation, XXII (January 3, 1927),
26-28.

2559 _____ . "Aviation in National Defense." USNIP,
LII (1926), 752-755.
An address delivered before the National Repub-
lican Club of New York on February 6, 1926.

2560 _____ . "Five Progressive Years of Naval Aviation." Aero Digest, XVIII (March 1931), 34-37.

2561 _____ . "How Disarmament Affects Steel Makers."
Iron Age, CVIII (November 17, 1921), 1279-1280.

2562 _____ . "The Naval Air Service." Unpublished
Lecture, G-3 Course 10, Files of the U. S. Army
Military History Research Collection, 1925.

2563 _____ . "Naval Aviation." USNIP, LIII (1927),
1081-1083.

2564 _____ . "Naval Aviation in 1921." Aviation, XI
(December 19-26, 1921), 715-716, 733-734.

2565 _____ . "Navy Plans for Scrapping Battleships."
Iron Age, CVIII (December 22, 1921), 1605-1606.

2566 _____ . "The Organization and Function of Naval
Aviation." Aviation, XIII (August 28, 1922), 248-
251.

2567 _____ . "Progress in Naval Aviation." USNIP,
LIV (1928), 840-842.

2568 _____ . "The Progress of Naval Aviation." Airway Age, XII (January 1931), 52-55.

2569 _____. "Recent Technical Development of Naval
Aviation. " USNIP, LVII (1931), 1181-1186.

2570 _____. "Rigid Airship Building and Operations in
This Country Originated with the U. S. Navy. "
Aero Digest, III (December 1923), 402-403.

2571 _____. "Rigid Airship Development and the U. S. S.
Akron. " National Aeronautical Magazine, X (January 1932), 6-12.

2572 _____. "Some Aviation Fundamentals. " USNIP,
LI (1925), 1871-1881.

2573 _____. "Statement of RAdm. William A. Moffett. "
In: U. S. Congress. House. Naval Affairs Committee. Hearings on Sundry Legislation Affecting
the Naval Establishment, 1925-1926.   69th Cong. ,
1st sess. , 1925-1926.   p. 455-464.

2574 _____. "The Stub Mast for Airships. " Slipstream,
IX (June 1928), 14-15.

2575 _____. "Testimony Before the Joint Military and
Naval Affairs Committee, May 1924. " USNIP, L
(1924), 1364-1370.
Reprinted from Aviation, May 26, 1924.

2576 _____. "The U. S. Airship Shenandoah. " Aero
Digest, IV (January 1924), 25-26.

2577 _____. "The United States Naval Air Service. "
Aviation, XIV (May 21, 1923) 556-557.

2578 Moley, Raymond. After Seven Years. New York:
Harper, 1939. 446p. Rpr. 1970.

2579 _____. "Appeal to Heaven. " Newsweek, X (December 27, 1937), 44.
The Panay incident.

2580 "Monster Seagoing Dry Docks. " Popular Science,
CXXX (February 1937), 42-43.

2581 Montague, Ludwell L.   Haiti and the United States,

1914-1938.   Durham,   N. C. :   Duke University Press,
1940.   Rpr.   1973.

2582   Montgomery, A. E.   "Aircraft Carrier Operations. "
Aero Digest, XXXVI (February 1940), 52, 54, 57.

2583   Montross, Lynn.   "The Marine Autogiro in Nicaragua."
Marine Corps Gazette, XXXVII (February 1953),
56-61.
Trials of an experimental aircraft.

2584   _____.   "The Mystery of Pete Ellis. "   Marine
Corps Gazette, XXXVIII (July 1954), 30-33.
The disappearance of a Marine Corps amphibious
warfare theorist while on a clandestine reconnais-
sance of the Palaus Islands in 1923.   Shades of the
Amelia Earhart mystery.

2585   _____.   "1917-1927--Forty Years Pass in Review."
Leatherneck, XL (November 1957), 16-23.
A summary of Marine activity in the early
Banana Wars.

2586   _____.   The United States and Haiti, 1800-1938.
New York: Holt, 1959.   242p.

2587   _____.   The United States Marines: A Pictorial
History.   New York: Rinehart, 1959.   242p.

2588   Moon, Don P.   "Recommissioning the Destroyers. "
USNIP, LVII (1931), 162-166.

2589   Moore, Charles G. , Jr.   "International Relations of
Our Navy in Peacetime. "   DAR Magazine, LXX
(1936), 1105-1109.

2590   Moore, Frederick.   America's Naval Challenge.   New
York: Macmillan, 1929.   166p.

2591   Moore, George F.   "Report on Philippine Coast Artillery Command and the Harbor Defenses of Manila
and Subic Bays, Corregidor, 14 February 1941-6
May 1942. "   Unpublished paper, Individual Personnel File, Operational Archives, U. S. Navy Department, Naval History Division, 1946.   148p.

2592   Moore, John W. and A. P. H. Tawresey.   "Small Boat

Sailing as a Character Builder in the Navy. "
USNIP, LVI (1930), 500-502.

2593 Moore, Samuel T.   "Fifteen Years Under the Sea. "
Popular Mechanics, XLVI (August 1926), 228-233.
Submarines.

2594 _____. "Fighting Rum Row. " Independent, CXIV
(January 10-24, 1925), 34-36, 67-72, 92-94.
The activities of the Coast Guard in enforcing
the 18th Amendment.

2595 _____. "Lesson of the Shenandoah. " Independent,
CXV (October 24, 1925), 465-467.

2596 Moore, Warren L.   "A Labor Saving and More Efficient Method of Daily Analysis of Engineering Performance. " USNIP, XLVII (1921), 1049-1058.

2597 Moran, Charles.   "Appraising Our Neutrality. " USNIP,
LXIV (1938), 1705-1715.

2598 _____. "From Greenland's Icy Mountains. " USNIP,
LXVI (1940), 1261-1268.

2599 _____. "The Genesis of Naval Policies. " USNIP,
9-18.

2600 _____. "Security by Enactment. " USNIP, LXXIV
(1948), 403-415.
American pre-war isolationism.

2601 Moran, Cyril G.   "Sea Power: The Senate and the
Air. " USNIP, XLVII (1921), 1676-1702.
A special supplement.

2602 Moray, Alastair.   The Diary of a Rum-Runner.
London: P. Allan, 1930.   250p.

2603 More, K.   The Submarine in War.   New York: Stech-
ert, 1931.   185p.

2604 "More Battleships or More AAA Money?" Wallaces'
Farmer, LXIII (January 29, 1938), 65.

2605 "More Guns and Men at the Canal is the Need Put up
to the Nation. " Newsweek, XV (March 11, 1940), 15-
16.

2606 "More Ways than One to Scrape a Navy. " Outlook,
       CXXX (April 12, 1922), 580-582.

2607 Morgan, Allan E.   "The Naval Reserve Aviation Base,
       Long Beach (Calif.), 1929-1942. " American Avia-
       tion Historical Society Journal, XVII (Winter 1971-
       Fall 1972), 280-285, 30-35, 191-199.

2608 Morgenstern, George.   "The Actual Road to Pearl
       Harbor. " In: Harry E. Barnes, ed. Perpetual
       War for Perpetual Peace. Caldwell, Idaho: Caxton
       Printers, 1953. p. 315-407.

2609 _____ . Pearl Harbor: The Story of the Secret War.
       New York: Devin-Adair, 1947. 425p.

2610 Morgenthau, Henry.   "The Morgenthau Diaries. "
       Collier's CXX (October 4, 1947), 20-21, 45, 48-
       49; (October 11, 1947), 20-21, 72-79; (October 18,
       1947), 16-17, 71-75; (October 25, 1947), 24-25,
       83-86.

2611 Morison, Elting E.   Admiral Sims and the Modern
       American Navy. Boston: Houghton, Mifflin, 1942.
       547p. Rpr. 1968.
          Sims relinquished command of U. S. naval forces
       in European waters on March 31, 1919 and retired
       with the permanent rank of rear admiral on Octo-
       ber 14, 1922. From that date until his death on
       September 25, 1936, he resided at Newport, R. I. ,
       where he wrote most of the articles cited herein.

2611a _____ . "Naval Administration: Selected Documents
       on Navy Department Organization, 1915-1940. "
       Unpublished paper, Files of the Navy Department
       Library, n. d.

2612 _____ . Turmoil and Tradition: A Study of the Life
       and Times of Henry L. Stimson. Boston: Hough-
       ton, Mifflin, 1960. 686p. Rpr. 1964.

2613 Morison, Samuel E.   History of United States Naval
       Operations in World War II. 15 vols. Boston:
       Little, Brown, 1947-1962.
          Two volumes contain data of value to our inter-
       war compilation: I The Battle of the Atlantic,
       September 1939-May 1943, and III The Rising Sun

[Japan] in the Pacific, 1931-April 1942.

2614   _____. "Notes on Writing Naval (Not Navy) Eng-
          lish. " American Neptune, IX (January 1949), 5-
          10.
          A delightful essay very useful to all writers of
          nautical affairs.

2615   _____. "The Twenty Years' Peace, 1919-1939. "
          In: his The Two-Ocean War. Boston: Little,
          Brown, 1963. p. 3-26.
          A succinct and useful examination of our period.

2616 Morris, Frank D. "Zoome Town, Corpus Christi,
          Texas: How the Navy Gets Its Pilots Fast. " Col-
          lier's, CVII (June 7, 1941), 16-19.

2617 Morrison, Joseph L. Josephus Daniels: The Small-d
          Democrat.   Chapel Hill: University of North Caro-
          lina Press, 1966. 316p.

2618 Morrison, M. R. "The Navy's Attitude Towards
          American Diesels. " Power, LXXIV (July 7, 1931),
          14-18.

2619 Morrow, Lacy. "Parris Island Hurricane. " Leather-
          neck, XXIII (October 1940), 17-18.

2620 Morse, R. W. "Naval Economies. " Current History,
          XXXV (November 1931), 265-266.

2621 Morton, C. G. "The Defense of Hawaii. " Unpublished
          Lecture, Files of the U. S. Army Military History
          Research Collection, 1921.
          The author was an Army major general.

2622 Morton, Charles G. "Landing in Force. " Infantry
          Journal, XVI (May 1920), 981-988, 1077-1083.
          Marine Corps preparations.

2623 Morton, Henry C. V. Atlantic Meeting. New York:
          Dodd, Mead, 1943. 196p.
          The author, a guest of the British minister of
          information, took passage on the Prince of Wales
          with Churchill for the August 2, 1941 meeting with
          Roosevelt off Newfoundland.   Of life at sea and the
          Prime Minister's interest in it, the author has

much to say, including the observation that Churchill "pink and cherubic" twice had the great ship's
course altered so he could pass through a convoy.

2624   Morton, Louis. "Germany First: The Basic Concept
of Allied Strategy in World War II. " In: Kent R.
Greenfield, ed. Command Decisions. Washington:
Office of the Chief of Military History, U. S. Army,
1960.   p. 11-47.
Understood even before Pearl Harbor.

2625   _____. "The Japanese Decision for War. " USNIP,
LXXX (1954), 1325-1337.

2626   _____. "War Plan Orange: The Evolution of a
Strategy. " World Politics, XI (January 1959), 221-
250.
U. S. Army/Navy planning, 1903-1938.

2627   _____, ed.   The Wars of the United States.   8 vols.
New York: Macmillan, 1970--.
An ongoing series.   Volumes of interest in pre-
paration, with their authors, include: Raymond G.
O'Connor, History of the United States Navy; Al-
fred F. Hurley, History of the United States Air
Force; Louis Morton, World War II (Pacific); and
Hugh M. Cole, World War II (Europe and North
Africa).

2628   Moseley, H. W. "The 'Cash and Carry' Section of the
1937 Neutrality Act. " Unpublished PhD Dissertation, Harvard University, 1939.

2629   Moses, M. J. "The Home-coming of the Fleet. " Bell-
man, XXVI (January 11, 1919), 39-44.
From European waters after World War I.

2630   Moses, Radford. "An Early Episode. " USNIP, LXIII
(1937), 1391-1392.
With the submarine K-2.

2631   _____. "The Naval Reserve Officer, a War-Time
Specialist. " USNIP, LXV (1939), 560-562.

2632   _____. "The San Marcos. " USNIP, LXIV (1938),
989.
An incident concerning the battleship Texas.

2633 _____ . "The Tale of the Lost Torpedo. " USNIP,
      LIV (1928), 381-384.
      Concerns the battleship Texas.

2634 Moses, Stanford E.   "Life on the Shenandoah. " Satur-
      day Evening Post, CXCVII (December 20, 1924), 5.

2635 _____ . "Preventive Discipline. " USNIP, XLIX
      (1923), 1441-1446.

2636 Mosley, Leonard.   Hirohito: Emperor of Japan. Engle-
      wood Cliffs, N. J. : Prentice-Hall, 1966.   371p.
      His career before and after Pearl Harbor with
      considerable data on his role in Japanese military
      and naval matters.

2637 Moss, L. Q.   Practical Mathematics for Shipfitters and
      Other Shipyard Workers.   New York: Pitman, 1941.
      126p.

2638 "Motor Torpedo Boats for the Philippines. " Engineer-
      ing, CXLVII (March 31, 1939), 368-369.
      These PT boats were shipped out aboard large
      U. S. Navy transports and would prove very useful
      in a couple of years.

2639 Moulton, Harold G.   "The Economic Necessity for Dis-
      armament. " Yale Review, New Series XI (January
      1922), 269-283.

2640 Moulton, Warren R.   "Rescue at Sea: A Coast Guards-
      man's Story of the Morrow Castle. " New Republic,
      LXXX (October 31, 1934), 332-333.

2641 Mulcahy, Francis P.   "Marine Corps Aviation in the
      Second Nicaraguan Campaign. " USNIP, LIX (1933),
      1121-1132.

2642 Munro, Dana G.   The United States and the Caribbean
      Area.   Boston: World Peace Foundation, 1934.
      322p.   Rpr. 1966.

2643 _____ . The Latin American Republics.   New York:
      Appleton-Century-Crofts, 1950.

2644 Murphy, C. J. V.   "Byrd a Big-Business Explorer. "
      Readers' Digest, XXXV (January 1940), 58-61.

2645 Murphy, William B.   "They Sailed to the Flying Boat's
      Future. "   USNIP, XCI (1965), 82-91.
      The voyage of PN-9. No. 1, from the U. S.
      mainland to Hawaii in 1925.

2646 Murray, G. D.   "Naval Aviators for Naval Aviation. "
      Aero Digest, XXXVI (February 1940), 44-45+.

2647 Musser, Neil B.   "Philadelphia's Naval Reserve
      Armory. "   USNIP, LVI (1930), 220-224.

2648 "The NC-4: History Preserved. "   USNIP, XCV (1969),
      94-106.
      A pictorial.

2648a "The NC-4 Transatlantic Flight. "   Air Classics, VI
      (August 1970), 42-52.

2649 Nalty, Bernard C., author.   See   U. S. Marine Corps.,
      no. 4737.

2650 "Names of the 50 Destroyers Transferred to Great
      Britain. "   USNIP, LXVII (1941), 301-302.
      Reprinted from the December 1940 issue of
      Navy.

2651 "Naming the Navy. "   Popular Science, CXXXIV (Janu-
      ary 1939), 58.

2652 Nash, Vernon.   "The Japanese-American War Myth. "
      International Conciliation, CCCXIX (April 1936),
      208-212.

2653 _____.   _____.   Nation, CXLI (December 11,
      1935), 671-672.

2654 National Council of American Shipbuilders.   Com-
      mercial Shipyards and the Navy. New York, 1937.
      105p.
      "The following study challenges the soundness of
      the Majority Recommendation of the Nye Munitions
      Committee for a government monopoly of naval
      shipbuilding. "--p. 7.

2655 National Geographic Society.   "Society's Special Medal
      is Awarded to Dr. T. C. Poulter. "   National Geo-
      graphic, LXXII (July 1937), 105-108.

For his work with the 1933-1935 Byrd Antarctic
Expedition.

2656 "The National Geographic Society Honors the Byrd Ant-
       arctic Expedition. " National Geographic, LXVIII
       (July 1935), 107-114.

2657 "The Nation's Greatest Ships. " Popular Mechanics,
       XLIX (March 1928), 442-446.
       The carriers Lexington and Saratoga.

2658 "The Naval Academy: A Glance at Yesterday, Today,
       and Tomorrow: 1845-1970. " Shipmate, (Septem-
       ber-October 1970), 14-46.

2659 "Naval Academy Cheers and Songs. " USNIP, LXI
       (1935), 1482-1491.

2660 "Naval Academy Curriculum. " USNIP, LVIII (1932),
       1668-1670.

2661 "Naval Aeronautics--1929. " Airway Age, XI (January
       1930), 51-54.

2662 "Naval Air Appropriations, 1922-1923. " Aviation, XII
       (April 24, 1922), 476-477.

2663 "The Naval Airship C-5 Makes 1100-Mile Flight. "
       Aviation, VI (June 1919), 475-476.

2664 "The Naval Airship ZR-1 Visits New York City. "
       Aviation, XV (September 24, 1923), 362-364.
       The Shenandoah.

2665 "Naval Armaments and the Washington Conference. "
       Engineer, CXXXII (October 28 & November 25,
       1921), 443-445, 570-571.

2666 "Naval Aviation. " SciAmer, CXXXIV (January 1926),
       54-55.

2667 "Naval Aviation. " SciAmer, CL (April 1934), 177.

2668 "Naval Aviation Activities in 1921. " Aerial Age, XIV
       (December 26, 1921), 367-368.

2669 "Naval Aviation: The U. S. Has the Best in the World."

Life, IX (October 28, 1940), 70-78.
Illustrated.

2670 "Naval Bases, Stations, etc., of the British Empire,
the United States, and Japan." USNIP, LVI (1930),
948.

2671 "Naval Board Urges Wide Defense Plan." Journal of
Commerce, (January 4, 1939), 26.

2672 "Naval Conference." Outlook, CXLVI (June 1929),
267-270.
That held at Geneva in 1927.

2673 "Naval Construction." SciAmer, CLVIII (March 1938),
166-167.

2674 "Naval Construction in 1940." USNIP, LXVII (1941),
439-444.
Reprinted from the January 10, 1941 issue of
The Engineer.

2675 "A Naval Crisis." Nation, CXXXIX (February 28,
1934), 579.

2676 "The Naval-Cuts Battle." Literary Digest, CXV (May
20, 1933), 5.

2677 "A Naval Decision to be Viewed with Disquiet: A
Permanent European Naval Squadron." Christian
Century, LIII (September 30, 1936), 1277.

2678 "Naval Economies." SciAmer, CXLVIII (February
1933), 75.

2678a "Naval Enlisted Flight Training: 1938." Air Classics,
VII (October 1970), 32-42.

2679 "The Naval Establishment." Washington Information
Service of the National Peace Conference, I (June
1, 1938), 5-8.

2680 "The Naval Establishment." In: Julia E. Johnson, ed.
Peace and Rearmament. Vol. XI of The Reference
Shelf. New York: H. W. Wilson, 1938, p. 82-86.

2681 "The Naval Expansion Program." In: Julia E. John-

son, ed. Peace and Rearmament. Vol. XI of The
Reference Shelf. New York: H. W. Wilson, 1938.
p. 120-122.

2682 "The Naval Expansion Program. " In: U. S. Congress.
House. Naval Affairs Committee. Hearings on
Sundry Legislation Affecting the Naval Establishment, 1937-1938. 75th Cong. , 3rd sess. , 1938.
p. 1937-2889.

2683 "The Naval Junk Pile Receives Three Subs. " Popular
Mechanics, LIV (July 1930), 16.

2684 "Naval Libraries. " Library Journal, XLVII (1922),
463-464.

2685 "The Naval Limitation Treaty. " Engineer, CXLIX
(April 25, 1930), 463-464.

2686 Naval Machinery. 3rd ed. Annapolis: U. S. Naval
Institute, 1941. 187p.

2687 "Naval Mania in America. " Literary Digest, XCII
(February 19, 1927), 20.

2688 "Naval Mission: The Stolen Plans of the New Japanese
Naval Program. " Current History, XLVIII (April
1938), 57.

2689 Naval Officer. "The 1933 Naval Building Program. "
Marine News, XX (September 1933), 44.

2690 "Naval Oil Reserves: Correspondence Taken from the
Hearings Before the [U S. Senate] Committee on
Public Lands and Surveys. " USNIP, L (1924),
1182-1207.
Teapot Dome.

2691 Naval Ordnance: A Textbook Prepared for the Use of
the Midshipmen of the United States Naval Academy,
by Officers of the United States Navy. Annapolis:
U. S. Naval Institute, 1933. 725p.

2692 "Naval Parity by Construction. " World's Work, LV
(February 1928), 348.

2693 "Naval Policies at Geneva. " Engineering, CXXIII (July

1, 1927), 17-19.

2694 "The Naval-Preparedness Program. " Nation,
      CXXXVIII (March 21, 1934), 315.

2695 "The Naval Program as Pacifism. " New Republic,
      XXXIV (February 9, 1938), 17-18.

2696 "The Naval Program of the United States. " Current
      History, XIII (February 1921), 189-191.

2697 "Naval Proposals at Geneva. " Nation, CXXIV (June
      29, 1927), 710.

2698 "The Naval Race. " Literary Digest, CXXIII (January
      9, 1937), 5-6.

2699 "Naval Realities. " Quarterly Review, CCLIV (January
      1930), 1-14.
      A hard-nosed British view on the eve of the
      London Naval Conference.

2700 "Naval Reserve Aviation Policy. " Aviation, XVI
      (March 10, 1924), 256-257.

2701 "Naval Reserve Maintenance: Floyd Bennett Base. "
      Aviation, XXXIX (December 1940), 42-43.

2702 "The Naval Reserve Nurse Corps. " American Journal
      of Nursing, XLI (April 1941), 385-386.

2703 "Naval Shipbuilding, Large Programs Now Underway. "
      Marine Review, LXV (April 1935), 42-43.

2704 "Naval Shipbuilding Program Contracts Awarded. "
      Marine Review, LXIII (September 1933), 11-12.
      An abstract of this article appeared in Marine
      Engineering and Shipping Age, XXXVIII (September
      1933), 352.

2705 "The Naval Situation in the Pacific: Japan's Battleships,
      America's Battleships. " Illustrated London News,
      CXCIX (October 25, 1941), 530-531.

2706 "The Naval Transatlantic Flight Expedition. " Aviation,
      VI (May 15, 1919), 420-422.
      The NCs.

2707 "The Naval War College. " Life, IX (October 28,
      1940), 59-61.

2708 "Navies and Peace. " Nation, CXXVII (August 15,
      1928), 151.

2709 "Navies and the Pacific. " Roundtable, XXIV (1934),
      693-716.

2710 "The Navy Absorbs the Marine Corps. " Newsweek,
      II (December 23, 1933), 6.

2711 "The Navy Air Bill. " Aviation, XXI (July 19, 1926),
      86.

2712 "The Navy Air Force Acts as a Unit with Ships of the
      Fleet. " Life, XI (December 8, 1941), 113-121.
      Must have made very interesting reading to
      Americans on the day after Pearl Harbor!

2713 "The Navy Airship Akron. " Aero Digest, XIX (Septem-
      ber 1931), 52-55.

2714 "The Navy as a Business Investment. " Outlook,
      CXXXI (May 24, 1922), 140-142.

2715 "The Navy Asks Aid of Psychiatrists in Selecting Men. "
      Science News Letter, XXXVII (June 1, 1940), 340.

2716 "Navy Bill Launched. " Newsweek, III (February 3,
      1934), 11.

2717 "Navy Blimps Can Spot and Sink Submarines. " Life,
      XI (August 18, 1941), 42-46.

2718 "Navy Budget Cuts Shipyards and Personnel. " News-
      week, I (May 20, 1933), 8.

2719 "The Navy Bureau of Engineering--1920. " Aviation, X
      (January 17, 1921), 76-77.

2720 "The Navy Calls for Airship Designs. " Aviation, XXII
      (January 31, 1927), 230.

2721 "Navy Close-Up. " Life, IX (October 28, 1940), 23-40.

2722 "The Navy Combat Trainer: Curtiss SNC-1. " Aviation,

XL (August 1941), 105-106.

2723 "The Navy Cruiser Bill, with Pro and Con Discussion."
      Congressional Digest, VIII (January 1929), 1-19.

2724 "Navy Day Brings Home to the U. S. the Stern Might
      of the Biggest Fleet. " Newsweek, XVIII (October
      27, 1941), 31-32.

2725 "The Navy Department Is Installing Diesels in Ships'
      Boats. " Marine Engineering, XLI (June 1936), 323.

2726 "The Navy Department Retires 4800 Men and 49 Ships
      in Conformity with the London Naval Treaty Limi-
      tations. " Commercial and Financial Chronicle,
      CXXXI (October 11, 1930), 2326.

2727 "The Navy Department to Form New Atlantic Force of
      125 Ships. " Commercial and Financial Chronicle,
      CLI (October 19, 1940), 2287.

2728 "Navy Dirigibles and the Eclipse. " Science, New
      Series, LX (December 19, 1924), 10.

2729 "The Navy Dollar. " Business Week (March 28, 1936),
      35-36.

2730 "A Navy for War. " Nation, CXXXVIII (February 28,
      1934), 236.

2731 Navy League of the United States. Navy Day, October
      27, 1941. Washington, 1941. 512p.

2732 "The Navy Looks and Learns: Finding and Sinking the
      Bismarck. " Collier's, CVIII (August 23, 1941), 12.

2733 "Navy Notes: A Fighter, an Observation and Two
      Scout Planes. " Aviation, XXXIV (September 1935),
      35.

2734 "Navy Nurses on the U. S. S. Solace. " American
      Journal of Nursing, XLI (October 1941), 1173-1175.

2735 "Navy Orders Mean More Shipyards. " Business Week,
      (July 27, 1940), 16-18.

2736 "Navy Pay and a Fifty-Cent Dollar. " SciAmer, CXXI

(November 8, 1919), 456.

2737 "Navy Race: Japan Passes the Buck to Mr. Roosevelt."
      Newsweek, XI (February 21, 1938), 9-10.

2738 "Navy Ready for Hawaiian Flight on August 28." Avi-
      ation, XIX (August 17, 1925), 174-175.

2739 "The Navy Repudiates Admiral Mahan." World's Work,
      XXXVIII (October 1919), 569-571.

2740 "Navy Reviewed by the President." Newsweek, III
      (June 2, 1934), 6-7.

2741 "A Navy Second to None." Literary Digest, CXXV
      (January 8, 1938), 3-4.

2742 "The Navy Should Have a Bureau of Aeronautics."
      SciAmer, CXXIV (April 16, 1921), 302.

2743 "The Navy Starts Convoying in the Western Atlantic."
      Scholastic, XXXIX (September 29, 1941), 4.

2744 "The Navy Submarine 0-9 Sinks." Commercial and
      Financial Chronicle, CLII (June 28, 1941), 4052.
      In the same area as the Squalus with the loss
      of all 33 aboard.

2745 "Navy Tapping the Treasury." New Republic, LXXVII
      (February 7, 1934), 348.

2746 "The Navy Wants Guam Fortified." Christian Century,
      LVI (January 18, 1939), 75.

2747 "The Navy Wants More Battleships." Christian Cen-
      tury, LVI (July 26, 1939), 915.

2748 "Navy Yards: The Decision of the Departmental Wage
      Board." Monthly Labor Review, XIII (October
      1921), 828-839.

2749 "The Navy's Army." Life, XI (July 7, 1941), 45-47.
      The Marines.

2750 "Navy's Emergency Bill Founders." Business Week,
      (January 13, 1940), 17.

2751   The Navy's General Store." New York Times Maga-
       zine, (October 5, 1941), 23.

2752   "The Navy's Huge Test Basin is Now Nearing Comple-
       tion." Science News Letter, XXXVI (August 26,
       1939), 134-135.

2753   "The Navy's Machine Tool Program for Yards and on
       Ships." American Machinist, LXXXIII (March 22,
       1939), 178g-178j.

2754   "The Navy's Mammoth Snake Hunt Puts the War in the
       U. S. Front Yard." Newsweek, XVIII (September
       22, 1941), 13-16.
       Anti U-boat operations.

2755   "Navy's Miracle Motor is Direct Descendant of the
       Famous 1917 Liberty: The Packard 4M-2500 Marine
       Engine." Popular Science, CXXXVIII (April 1941),
       118-119.
       An aircraft motor.

2756   "The Navy's New Brewster Dive Bomber, SB2A-1."
       Popular Science, CXXXIX (September 1941), 50.

2757   "The Navy's New Silver Whale of the Air: The Dirig-
       ible ZR-1 [Shenandoah]." Literary Digest, LXXVIII
       (September 22, 1923), 42-46.

2758   "The Navy's New Submarine." Outlook, CXXXVIII
       (December 31, 1924), 705-706.

2759   "The Navy's Newest Floating Airport." Literary Di-
       gest, CXIV (October 15, 1932), 42-43.
       U. S. S. Hornet.

2760   "The Navy's Patrol Planes." USNIP, LXXVIII (1952),
       1356-1365.

2761   "Navy's Roll Call Keeps Track of Far-Flung Fighting
       Ships." Popular Science, CXXIX (November 1936),
       46.

2762   "The Navy's Super-Airship Nears Completion." Sci-
       Amer, CXLIV (May 1931), 296-300.

2763   Needham, Ray C.   "Officer Evaluation and Promotion."

USNIP, LXXXVI (1960), 60-69.
1938-1960.

2764   Neeser, Robert W.   "Historic Ships of the Navy--
       Hornet. "   USNIP, LXVII (1941), 218-224.
       The last in his series was the carrier.

2765   _____.   --Lexington. "   USNIP, LII (1926),
       171-178.
       The last in his series was the carrier.

2766   _____.   --Peacock. "   USNIP, LXIII (1937),
       1581-1586.
       The last in his series was AM-46.

2767   _____.   --Porpoise. "   USNIP, LXVI (1940),
       647-649.
       The last in his series was SS-172.

2768   _____.   --Ranger. "   USNIP, LV (1929),
       209-214.
       The last in his series was the carrier.

2769   _____.   Ship Names of the United States Navy:
       Their Meaning and Origin.   New York: Moffat,
       Yard, 1921.   261p.

2770   "Negotiations, not Battleships. "   Christian Century,
       LV (November 16, 1938), 1392-1393.

2771   Neilson, Francis.   The Makers of War.   Appleton,
       Wisc. : Nelson, 1950.   240p.

2772   Nelson, Dennis D.   "The Integration of the Negro into
       the United States Navy. "   Unpublished M. A. Thesis,
       Howard University, 1947.

2773   _____.   The Integration of the Negro into the U. S.
       Navy.   New York: Farrar, Straus, and Young,
       1951.   238p.

2774   Nelson, Frank E.   "Handling Vessels in Restricted
       Waters. "   USNIP, LIV (1928), 446-456.

2775   Nelson, Frederick J.   "And Now--Naval ROTC Students
       Become Ensigns of the Line. "   USNIP, LXVII
       (1941), 539-544.

2776 _____. "The Beaufort Wind Scale. " USNIP, LX
          (1934), 1546-1548.

2777 _____. "Guam, Our Western Outpost. " USNIP,
          LXVI (1940), 83-88.

2778 _____. "The History of Aerology in the Navy. "
          USNIP, LX (1934), 522-528.

2779 _____. "Lighter-than-Aircraft and Line Squalls. "
          USNIP, LX (1934), 369-372.

2780 _____. "More Education for the Naval Officer. "
          USNIP, LVII (1931), 1364-1366.

2781 _____. "The Neutrality Zone of the Americas. "
          USNIP, LXVI (1940), 1241-1244.

2782 _____. "Notes on an Asiatic Cruise. " USNIP,
          LXII (1936), 390-400.

2783 _____. "Thumb Rule for Altimeter Corrections. "
          USNIP, LIX (1933), 1573-1580.

2784 _____. "Upper Air Soundings by Aerograph. "
          USNIP, LXI (1935), 1140-1144.

2785 _____. "Why Guam Alone is American. " USNIP,
          LXII (1936), 1131-1135.

2786 Nelson, Roger E. "We Should Have Shipboard Shoot-
          ing Galleries. " USNIP, LXV (1939), 1258-1263.

2787 Nelson, Wallace M. "Antiaircraft Protection for Our
          Naval Bases. " Marine Corps Gazette, XXII (De-
          cember 1938), 17-18, 40-43.

2788 Nelson, William. "Airships, or Not?" USNIP, LIX
          (1933), 1327-1328.

2789 _____. "The Autogiro as a Military Craft. "
          USNIP, LVII (1931), 1092-1094.

2790 _____. "Duralumin Welding. " USNIP, LIII (1927),
          360-364.

2791 _____. "The Heat Treatment of Duralumin. "

USNIP, LIII (1927), 483-488.

2792 _____. "Salvage of the U. S. S. DeLong, No. 129. "
USNIP, XLVIII (1922), 1345-1363.

2793 Neuchterlein, Donald E. Iceland, Reluctant Ally.
Ithaca, N. Y. : Cornell University Press, 1961.

2794 Neumann, William L. America Encounters Japan
From Perry to MacArthur. Goucher College Series.
Baltimore: Johns Hopkins University Press, 1963.
353p. Rpr. 1969.

2795 _____. "Franklin Delano Roosevelt, a Disciple of
Admiral Mahan. " USNIP, LXXVII (1952), 712-719.

2796 _____. "Franklin D. Roosevelt and Japan, 1913-
1933. " Pacific Historical Review, XXII (May 1953),
143-153.

2797 _____. "How American Policy Toward Japan Con-
tributed to War in the Pacific. " In: Harry E.
Barnes, ed. Perpetual War for Perpetual Peace.
Caldwell, Idaho: Caxton Printers, 1953. p. 231-269.

2798 "Neutral Problem Spotlighted by City of Flint's Seizure. " Newsweek, XIV (November 6, 1939), 13-
15.

2799 "The Neutrality Act. " Washington Information Service
of the National Peace Conference, II (April 3,
1939), 1-3.

2800 No Entry

2801 Nevada, U. S. S. U. S. S. Nevada, BB-36, 1916-1946.
San Francisco: James H. Barry, 1946. 195p.
In reality a World War II cruise book; however,
by including a considerable amount of pre-war data
and photos, this compilation must be considered a
good bit more.

2802 Neville, L. E. "The Hall Shipboard Fighter: Wasp-
Powered XFH-1. " Aviation, XXVII (November 30,
1929), 1067-1072.

2803 Nevins, Allan. "Bigger Navies for All. " Current

History, XLII (September 1935), 624-625.

2804 _____. "Japan Denounces the [Washington] Naval
Treaty. " Current History, XLI (February 1935),
581-582.

2805 _____. "London Naval Talks: Preliminary Bilateral
Conversations. " Current History, XLI (December
1934), 327-329.

2806 _____. "The Naval Conference. " Current History,
XLIII (February 1936), 507-509.

2807 _____. "The Naval Conference Fails. " Current
History, XLIII (March 1936), 614-616.

2808 "New American Warships. " Engineer, CXXXI (March
4, 1921), Supplement, 227-230.

2809 "The New and Dominant Factor in the Limitation of
Naval Armaments. " Current Opinion, LXXII (January 1922), 85-87.

2810 "The New Battleship Indiana. " SciAmer, CXXIII (December 11, 1920), 587.
BB-50, scrapped under the terms of the Washington Treaty.

2811 "The New Cruiser Minneapolis Commissioned. "
Marine Review, LXIV (July 1934), 24+.
The heavy cruiser CA-36 was launched the year
before.

2812 "New Design for Freighter and Aircraft Carrier Frees
Warships from Convoy Duty. " Steel, CIX (September 1, 1941), 76.

2813 "New Fleets for Old: The London Naval Conference
Plan for Limiting the Size of Warships. " Literary
Digest, CXXI (February 8, 1936), 13.

2814 "New Hope for Naval Reduction. " Literary Digest,
XCV (December 3, 1927), 10-11.

2815 "The New Menace to Sea Power. " Literary Digest,
LXX (August 6, 1921), 16-17.
The airplane.

2816 "A New Menace to Sea Power: Bombing and Ordnance
      Tests, June-July 1921. " USNIP, LXVII (1921),
      1451-1461, 1826, 1828-1829.

2817 "The New Navy Airship Macon. " SciAmer, CXLVII
      (October 1932), 238-240.

2818 "The New Navy Recruiting Formula: 1,000 Line-Ads
      Plus Popeye. " Newsweek, XVIII (July 28, 1941),
      46-47.

2819 "New Pearl Harbor Facts: Full Story, How the U. S.
      Got Jap Secrets. " Chicago Tribune Special Supple-
      ment, (December 7, 1966), 1-3, 5, 10-12.
      Operation "Magic. "

2820 "A New Race in Navy Building. " Literary Digest,
      CXVI (August 19, 1933), 12.

2821 "New Rescue Chamber Laughs at the Sea. " Popular
      Mechanics, LVI (September 1931), 366-368.

2822 "New Scout Cruisers of Immense Engine Power. "
      Marine Engineering, XXVI (February 1921), 121-
      123.

2823 "New Strength for the Navy. " Literary Digest, CXXV
      (February 13, 1938), 3-5.

2824 "The New S-Type Submarines Embody War Experience."
      Popular Mechanics, XXXVI (August 1921), 244-245.

2825 "New U. S. Warships to Cost $70,000,000 Each. "
      Popular Mechanics, LXIX (April 1938), 508-511.

2826 "New Uses for Old Battleships. " SciAmer, CXXIV
      (March 26, 1921), 249.
      Aircraft bombing targets.

2827 New York.   Citizen's Committee for Navy Day.   Navy
      Day in the State of New York, 27 October 1937.
      New York, 1937.   24p.

2828 New York.   (City) Metropolitan Museum of Art.   Our
      Navy; Its Contribution to America from Colonial
      Days to World Leadership.   A Special Exhibition
      Arranged in Collaboration with the Department of

the Navy. New York, October 24 through December 5, 1948. New York: 1948. 10p.

2829   "New York Plays Host to the Fleet." Newsweek, III
       (June 9, 1934), 7.

2830   New York Shipbuilding Corporation. 50 Years New
       York Shipbuilding Corporation, Camden, N. J.
       Camden, N. J. , 1949. 78p.

2831   New York Times. New York Times Index. New York,
       1919-1941.

2832   "New Zealand Hails Our Fleet." Literary Digest,
       LXXXIV (January 3, 1925), 19.
           When it passed during the great Pacific cruise
       of 1925.

2833   Newman, Q. B. Marine Electric Power. New York:
       Simons-Boardman, 1937. 160p.
           An elementary explanation of electricity and
       electrical equipment used on shipboard.

2834   Newport News Shipbuilding and Dry Dock Co. "At the
       Gateway of the Sea": The Story of a Great Ship-
       building Plant at Hampton Roads. Newport News,
       Va. , 1921. 72p.

2835   _____ . Fifty Years of Shipbuilding: A Brief History
       of the Newport News Shipbuilding and Dry Dock
       Company, and the Part This Organization Has Played
       Over Half a Century in Building Up the United States
       Merchant Marine and United States Navy. Newport
       News, Va. , 1940. 23p.

2836   _____ . For National Defense. Newport News, Va. ,
       1941. 44p.

2837   _____ . General Arrangement Plans of Typical Ves-
       sels Built by the Newport News Shipbuilding and
       Dry Dock Company, 1890-1939. 3 vols. Newport
       News, Va. , 1939.

2838   Newsom, Joel. "Results vs. Training." USNIP, LXV
       (1939), 20-24.

2839   Newton, R. N. Practical Construction of Warships.

New York: Longmans, Green, 1941. 318p.

2840   Newton, W. B.   "Various Units Used by the United
       States Navy for Ship Propulsion." Marine Engin-
       eering, XL (June 1935), 229-230.

2841   Niblack, Albert P.   "Athletics, Beneficial and Other-
       wise." USNIP, XLIX (1923), 1609-1622.

2842   _____.   "Forms of Government in Relation to Their
       Efficiency for War" and "The Office of Naval In-
       telligence." Unpublished Lectures, Files of the
       U. S. Army Military History Research Collection,
       1919.
             The first of these two essays was printed in
       USNIP, XLVI (1920), 1399-1430.

2843   _____.   "New Naval Fronts of the World Powers."
       Current History, XXIII (November 1925), 234-237.

2844   _____.   "Safety of Life at Sea and Lifesaving."
       USNIP, LIII (1927), 1018-1020.

2845   Nichols, Egbert R. , ed.   "A Larger Navy in the Pa-
       cific: Debate." In: his Intercollegiate Debates.
       New York: Noble and Noble, 1938.   p. 187-205.

2846   Nicholson, C. A.   "Shipboard Catapults." Aero Digest,
       XXXVI (February 1940), 58, 61-62.

2847   Niles, Palmer A.   The Navy, Coast Guard, and Mer-
       chant Marine. Boston: Bellman, 1941.   24p.
       Enlistment opportunities in each.

2848   Nimitz, Chester W.   "The Naval Reserve Officers'
       Training Corps." USNIP, LIV (1928), 441-445.

2849   _____. , jt. ed.   See   Potter, Elmer B. , no. 3101.

2850   "Nine Arm Badges Rates Marine Corps' Enlisted Men."
       Popular Science, CXXXVIII (March 1941), 55.

2851   "The 1934 Building Program." Marine News, XXI
       (October 1934), 65.

2852   "1917-1937." Leatherneck, XL (November 1957), 16-31.
       Marine Corps history between the World Wars.

2853 Nixon, Edgar B. Franklin D. Roosevelt and Foreign
      Affairs. 3 vols. Cambridge, Mass.: Harvard
      University Press, 1969.

2854 "No Trip to England: Mosquito Boats." Business
      Week, (June 29, 1940), 17.

2855 Nobody Can Attack Us: The Super-Navy Will be for
      War Abroad. Washington: National Council for the
      Prevention of War, 1938. 2p.

2856 Noel-Baker, Philip J. Disarmament. London: Hogarth,
      1926. 366p. Rpr. 1970.

2857 Noerden, Maynard M. "Our New Service Rifle. "
      USNIP, LXV (1939), 865-867.

2858 Noggle, Burton. Teapot Dome: Oil and Politics in the
      1920s. Baton Rouge: Louisiana State University
      Press, 1962. 234p.
         Our concern is mainly with the origin and upkeep
      of the precious naval oil reserves.

2859 Nomura, Kichisaburo. "Japan's Demand for Naval
      Equality. " Foreign Affairs, XIII (January 1935),
      196-203.

2860 Norfleet, Joseph P. "Have Airships a Military Value?"
      USNIP, LVI (1930), 708-710.

2861 _____. "One Rigid Airship has the Military Value
      of Two Battlecruisers. " U. S. Air Services, IV
      (August 1920), 15-17.
         A noted balloonist, the author served on Admiral
      Sims' staff during World War I.

2862 _____. "Shall We Abandon the Battleship?" Avia-
      tion, X (January 24, 1921), 526.

2863 Norris, George. "Why a Great Peace Advocate Favors
      a Strong Navy. " U. S. News, VI (March 28, 1938),
      6.

2864 "North Atlantic Ice Patrol: How the Coast Guard Cut-
      ters Broadcast the Position of Icebergs to Ship-
      ping. " SciAmer, CXXVI (June 1922), 370-371.

2865 "North Carolina, America's New and Mighty Battle-
         ship. " Illustrated London News, CXCVIII (May 10,
         1941), 611.

2866 Norton, Harold F. Lectures in Naval Architectures
         and Marine Engineering. Newport News, Va.:
         Newport News Shipbuilding & Dry Dock Co., 1928.
         78p.

2867 Norton, Henry K. "The Perils of Parity. " Outlook,
         CLIV (January 29, 1930), 172-173.

2868 _____. "Preface to Parity. " Outlook, CLIV (Jan-
         uary 22, 1930), 130-132.

2869 _____. "Such Stuff as Wars are Made of. " Cen-
         tury, CXV (January 1928), 288-295.
         Naval rivalry.

2870 "Norway Frees [City of] Flint. " Scholastic, XXXV
         (November 13, 1939), 6.

2871 "Novel Checking Device Used in Launching U. S. Air-
         plane Carrier Lexington. " Marine Engineering,
         XXX (November 1925), 604-605.

2872 "Now Another Naval Tragedy: The Sinking of the S-51."
         Literary Digest, LXXXVII (October 10, 1925), 7- 9.

2873 Nugent, Rolf. Guns, Planes, and Your Pocketbook.
         Public Affairs Pamphlet, no. 59. New York: Public
         Affairs Committee, 1941. 31p.

2874 Nye, Edgar U. "Bill Nye Sees the Navy. " USNIP,
         XLI (1935), 489-492.

2875 Nye, Willis L. "The Genealogy of the Curtiss Spar-
         rowhawk Dirigible Fighters. " American Aviation
         Historical Society Journal, III (April-June 1958),
         70-99.

2876 Ober, Warren V., jt. editor. See Burtness, Paul S.,
         no. 573.

2877 "Objectives of U. S. Foreign Policy: The British Navy
         as America's First Line of Defense. " U. S. News,
         VII (February 13, 1939), 3.

2878 O'Brien, T.J. "The Navy's Part in Modern Aero-
     logical Development. " USNIP, LXI (1935), 385-
     399.

2879 O'Connor, Raymond G. Perilous Equilibrium: The
     United States and the London Naval Conference of
     1930. Lawrence: University of Kansas Press,
     1962. 188p. Rpr. 1969.

2880 _____. "The United States and the London Naval
     Conference of 1930. " Unpublished PhD Disserta-
     tion, Stanford University, 1957.

2881 _____. "Yardstick and Naval Disarmament in the
     1920s. " Mississippi Valley Historical Review,
     XLV (December 1958), 441-463.

2882 O'Connor, Richard. Pacific Destiny: An Informal His-
     tory of the U.S. in the Far East, 1776-1968. Bos-
     ton: Little, Brown, 1969. 505p.
     Contains several chapters relative to our period.

2883 O'Donnell, James. "How Men Act in a Sunken Sub-
     marine. " Literary Digest, XC (September 18,
     1926), 50-52.
     The S-51.

2884 "Odyssey of the PN-9 no. 1. " Literary Digest,
     LXXXVI (September 26, 1925), 14-15.
     Her flight to Hawaii.

2885 "Official Whitewash: Navy Aircraft Purchases. " Na-
     tion, CXXXVIII (April 18, 1934), 431.

2886 Offner, Arnold A. American Appeasement: United
     States Foreign Policy and Germany, 1933-1938.
     Cambridge, Mass. : Harvard University Press, 1969.

2887 _____, ed. America and the Origins of World War
     II, 1933-1941. New Perspectives in History. Bos-
     ton: Houghton, Mifflin, 1971. 229p.

2888 Offutt, Milton. The Protection of Citizens Aboard by
     the Armed Forces of the United States. Johns
     Hopkins Studies, Series 48, no. 4. Baltimore:
     Johns Hopkins University Press, 1928. 170p.

2889 Ogilvie, Gordon F.   "Remember the Rochester."
      USNIP, XCVII (1971), 68-71.
      CA-2 in the 1930s.

2890 Oglesby, Joseph E.   "First Landing at the [South]
      Pole." USNIP, LXXXIII (1957), 1188-1195.

2891 Ohmae, Toshikazu and Roger Pineau.   "Japanese Naval
      Aviation." USNIP, XCVIII (1972), 68-78.
      Prior to and including World War II.

2892 Okumiya, Masatake.   "How the Panay was Sunk."
      USNIP, LXXIX (1953), 587-596; LXXX (1954), 572-
      575.

2893 Olch, Isaiah.   "Hurricane Security." USNIP, LXI
      (1935), 28-30.

2894 _____. "Pan Americanism and Naval Policy."
      USNIP, LXVII (1941), 1527-1532.

2895 _____. "A Resume of National Interests in the
      Caribbean." USNIP, LXVI (1940), 165-176.

2896 _____. "St. Thomas." USNIP, LIX (1933), 1734-
      1738.

2897 "Old Battleships Made New by World Powers: Draw-
      ings." Popular Mechanics, LXVII (May 1937), 659.

2898 Oldendorf, Jesse B.   "The Control of Neutral Trade
      by Belligerents." Unpublished General Staff Mem-
      orandum, Files of the U. S. Army Military History
      Research Collection, 1930.
            The Navy commander would win fame as the last
      victorious commander in a battleship action, off
      Leyte in October 1944.

2899 Oliver, Edward.   "The Openwald Incident." USNIP,
      LXXXII (1956), 379-384.
            The November 1941 meeting off Brazil of the
      U. S. cruiser Omaha and a German merchantman
      wearing an American flag.

2900 Oliver, Frederick L.   "Adjustment of the Type III
      Azimuth Circle." USNIP, LV (1929), 794-798.

2901 _____. "The Danger of Unpreparedness. " USNIP,
LXXI (1945), 763-775.

2902 _____. "Standing Rigging of Wire. " Yachting,
LXVII (February 1940), 55-57.

2903 _____. "Tool Supervision in the Navy: The U. S.
Naval Gun Factory. " Iron Age, CXLVIII (October
16, 1941), 25-28.

2904 _____. "Two Code Messages. " USNIP, LXIV
(1938), 16-19.

2905 Oliver, J. B. "Japan's Role in the Origin of the London Naval Treaty of 1930: A Study in Diplomatic
History. " Unpublished PhD Dissertation, Duke University, 1954.

2906 Olson, Harry C. "43 Years of Motor Transport. "
Marine Corps Gazette, XXXVI (December 1952),
54-61.
      Beginning in 1909 and continuing through our
period.

2907 Opdycke, Leonard. Naval Visits to Bar Harbor. Bar
Harbor, Me. : Times Publishing Company, 1952.
31p.
      A pamphlet describing all U. S. visits during the
years 1876-1951.

2908 Ordtolf, Paul. "Forty-four Hours on the Sea Bottom."
Living Age, CCCXXXIV (February 15, 1928), 310-
313.
      Submarines.

2909 Osbourne, Alan, ed. Modern Marine Engineer's
Manual. 2 vols. New York: Cornell Maritime
Press, 1941-1942.

2910 Oswald, Boyd G. Life and Humor in Our Navy. Boston, Mass. : Ball Publishing Company. 1919. 63p.

2911 Ott, Lester. Aircraft Spotter. New York: Harcourt,
1941. 64p.
      Silhouette drawings, photographs, and brief de-
scriptive text on the identification of Allied and
Axis warplanes in the air.

2912 Oulahan, Richard V.   "Cruisers Withdrawn from
      Service. " USNIP, LV (1929), 987-991.
      Reprinted from the New York Times of Septem-
      ber 16, 1929.

2913 "Our Battleship Fleet is not Junk. " SciAmer, CXXI
      (July 1924), 12.

2914 "Our Big-Navy Plan Torpedoed. " Literary Digest,
      LXI (June 14, 1919), 15.

2915 "Our Duty, a Navy Second to None. " Newsweek, XI
      (February 7, 1938), 11.

2916 "Our First Big Plane Carrier. " Literary Digest,
      LXXXV (April 18, 1925), 11.
      U. S. S. Lexington.

2917 "Our First Rigid Airship, the Shenandoah. " SciAmer,
      CXXX (February 1924), 82-83.

2918 "Our Great Sham Battle in the Pacific. " Literary
      Digest, LXXXIV (March 14, 1925), 16.
      During the great cruise of 1925.

2919 "Our Great ZR-1 in the Making. " SciAmer, CXXVIII
      (April 1923), 235.
      U. S. S. Shenandoah.

2920 "Our Latest Battleship. " SciAmer, CXXX (May 1924),
      320.
      The dreadnought Colorado.

2921 "Our Latest Dreadnought, the Idaho. " SciAmer, CXX
      (May 3, 1919), 169.

2922 "Our Marines in Nicaragua. " Nation, CXXI (August
      26, 1925), 243-244.

2923 "Our Marines Return to Nicaragua. " Literary Digest,
      XC (September 18, 1926), 13-14.

2924 "Our Naval Aircraft Carriers. " Airway Age, IX
      (September 1928), 60-61.

2925 "Our Naval and Army Waste. " Nation, CXXII (March
      3, 1926), 221.

2926   "Our Naval Building Program is no Menace." Current
       Opinion, LXX (March 1921), 399-401.

2927   "Our Naval Policy." Nation, CX (April 10, 1920), 453.

2928   "Our Navy and the Japanese Bogy." SciAmer, CXXIII
       (November 27, 1920), 540.

2929   "Our Navy Grows: Sketches of Types of Warships."
       New York Times Magazine. (September 28, 1941),
       16-17.

2930   "Our New 'Big-Navy' Policy: The Fleet Grows."
       U. S. News, (February 12, 1934), 7+.

2931   "Our New Sky Battleship, the Akron." Literary Digest,
       CX (August 22, 1931), 8.

2932   "Our Peaceable Pacific Fleet." Literary Digest, LXII
       (August 9, 1919), 13-14.

2933   "Our Second Large Airship, Built as the ZR-3, Now
       the Los Angeles." American Machinist, LXII
       (January 29, 1925), 192-193.

2934   "Over-Age Heroes: The Destroyers Transferred to
       Britain in September 1940." New York Times Mag-
       azine, (October 18, 1942), 39.

2935   Overstreet, Luther M. "Always on Guard: The Navy,
       in Peace." Outlook, CXXXII (October 18, 1922),
       290-293.

2936   _____. "The Danger of Disarming America, from
       a Naval Officer's Viewpoint." USNIP, L (1924),
       1492-1498.

2937   _____. "The Merchant Marine, Its Value in Peace
       and War." USNIP, LIII (1927), 1094-1096.

2938   _____. "Naval Strategy as Affected by Aircraft and
       Battleships." Outlook, CXXXIII (January 17, 1923),
       130-133.

2939   _____. "The Navy Strives for Peace." USNIP,
       LII (1926), 2060-2067.
       Reprinted from the April 29, 1926 issue of the
       Congregationalist.

2940 Owen, Russell. South of the Sun. New York: John
      Day, 1934. 288p.
      The Byrd expedition of 1928.

2941 Oyos, Lynwood E. "The Navy and the United States
      Far Eastern Policy, 1930-1939." Unpublished PhD
      Dissertation, University of Nebraska, 1958.

2942 "The PN-9, no. 1, on the West Coast-Hawaiian Flight."
      Aviation, XIX (September 14-21, 1925), 315-317,
      350-352.

2943 "Pacifists Responsible for Navy Unpreparedness."
      Marine News, XXII (September 1935), 37-39.

2944 "Packard Marine Engines Drive the Navy's Mosquito
      Fleet." Machinery, XLVII (April 1941), 168-171.
      For further data on these PT boat motors, see
      the article by A. H. Allen cited above.

2945 "Packard Powers the Mosquito Fleet." Automotive In-
      dustries, LXXXIV (February 15, 1941), 168-171.

2946 Padelford, Norman J. "An Atlantic Naval Policy for
      the United States." USNIP, LXVI (1940), 1297-
      1308.

2947 _____. The Panama Canal in Peace and War. New
      York: Macmillan, 1942. 327p.
      From the beginning to issue date, with consid-
      erable data on the Mahan theory of racing a fleet
      from one side to the other.

2948 Padfield, Peter. The Battleship Era. New York:
      David McKay, 1972. 321p.

2949 Pagano, Dom A. Bluejackets. Boston: Meador, 1932.
      138p.
      The story of the Special Service Squadron of the
      Navy and the landings at Nicaragua.

2950 Page, Robert M. The Origin of Radar. Garden City,
      N. Y. : Anchor Books, 1962. 196p.

2951 "Paging Icebergs with the Coast Patrol." Literary
      Digest, XCIII (May 7, 1927), 67-71.

2952 Pagon, W. Watters, jt. author. See Blakemore,
      Thomas L, no. 392.

2953 Paige, H. R. "Comment on La Flor Engagement. "
      Marine Corps Gazette, XVII (May 1932), 58.

2954 Painter, K. M. "Spotting Smugglers from the Air. "
      Popular Mechanics, LIII (May 1930), 715-716.
      Coast Guard activities.

2955 Paist, Paul H. "Monitors--Ships that Changed War."
      USNIP, LXXXVII (1961), 76-89.
      A pictorial from the Civil War to the 1930s.

2956 Palmer, Frederick. "Our Navy as a Billion-Dollar
      Corporation. " World's Work, LIV (June 1927),
      157-169.

2957 Palmer, Henry R. , Jr. The Seaplanes. New York:
      Arco, 1965. 52p.
      From the end of World War I to the end of
      World War II.

2958 Palmer, Wayne F. "Deaf and Dumb Ships: Weakness
      of Naval Communications. " New Outlook, CLXII
      (November 1933), 36-39.

2959 _____. "The Fleet of the Future. " New Outlook,
      CLXIV (September 1934), 48-52.

2960 _____. "Men of the Navy. " New Outlook, CLXIII
      (January 1934), 34-39.

2961 _____. "The Navy Looks Over the Next One. "
      New Outlook, CLXII (October 1933), 26-29.
      One-war.

2962 _____. "Submarine Mining, Orphan Child of the
      Service. " USNIP, LX (1934), 1582-1592.

2963 _____. "World Powers Afloat, Steaming East. "
      New Outlook, CLXIV (July 1934), 36-40.

2964 _____ and Hanson W. Baldwin. Men & Ships of
      Steel. New York: W. Morrow, 1935. 160p.

2965 "Panama Alert: Men, Ships, and Guns Rushed to

Strengthen Canal Defense. " Newsweek, XVI
(March 17, 1941), 36-37.

2966 "Panay Backwash. " Literary Digest, CXXV (January
      1, 1938), 11.

2967 "The Panay Bombed and Sunk. " Literary Digest,
      CXXIV (December 25, 1937), 10-11.

2968 "Panay Incident Closed?" Literary Digest, CXXV
      (January 8, 1938), 7-8.

2969 "Panay Pandemonium. " Time, XXX (December 27,
      1937), 7-8.

2970 "Panay Repercussions. " Time, XXXI (January 3,
      1938), 7-8.

2971 "A Paper Navy's no Security. " National Republic,
      XXI (April 1934), 10.

2972 Parker, Ralph C. "An Analysis of the Air Menace. "
      USNIP, LVIII (1932), 1349-1350.

2973 _____. "Evaluating a Series of Bearings. " USNIP,
      LX (1934), 79.

2974 _____. "Leadership. " USNIP, XLVII (1921), 323-
      330.

2975 _____. "Make It Yourself. " USNIP, LVI (1930),
      1012-1018.

2976 _____. "A Method of Calibrating Ranger Finders
      at Sea. " USNIP, LVI (1930), 137-141.

2977 _____. "Some Special Uses of Smoke Screens. "
      USNIP, LXVI (1940), 953-961.

2978 Parker, Thomas C. "Interdepartmental Instruction
      Aboard Ship. " USNIP, LXV (1939), 1110-1112.

2979 Parker, Thomas D. "Limitation, Pure and Applied."
      USNIP, LVII (1931), 1677-1684.
      Resulting from the Washington Treaty, 1922.

2980 Parker, William D. , author. See U. S. Marine Corps,
      no. 4740.

2981   Parkes, Oscar.   "A Forecast of World Navies. "   Sci-
       Amer, CLIII (November 1935), 246-250.

2982   _____.   "The Future of Navies. "   SciAmer, CLX
       (June-July 1939), 351-354, 10-14.

2983   Parkinson, Roger.   Blood, Toil, Tears and Sweat: The
       War History from Dunkirk to Alamein. Based on
       the War Cabinet Papers of 1940 to 1942.   New
       York: McKay, 1973. 539p.
          The work of Winston Churchill's war cabinet
       during the period, with considerable data on British
       attempts to get America into the war.

2984   Parrott, Marc.   Hazard: Marines on Mission.   Garden
       City, N. Y. : Doubleday, 1962. 237p.

2985   Partridge, Eric, ed.   A Dictionary of Forces' Slang,
       1939-1945.   London: Secker and Warburg, 1948. 212p.
          The editor wrote the section on air force slang
       while Wilfred Granville contributed the one on naval
       slang.

2986   "The Past Year in Naval Aeronautics. "   Aviation, XII
       (March 20, 1922), 336-338.

2987   Patch, Buel W.   "American Naval and Air Bases. "
       Editorial Research Reports 1939, II (February 16,
       1939), 109-128.

2988   _____.   "American Naval Policy. "   Editorial Re-
       search Reports, 1935, II (November 19, 1935),
       399-416.

2989   Pater, Alan F.   United States Battleships: The History
       of America's Greatest Fighting Fleet.   Beverly
       Hills, Calif: Monitor Book Company. 1968.

2990   Patrick, Kenneth W.   "Midshipman Cruises. "   USNIP,
       LXI (1935), 1545-1551.

2991   Patton, Willoughby.   "Bermuda as a Naval Base. "
       Travel, LXXIII (October 1939), 35-37.

2992   Pattullo, George.   "One Man's War. "   Saturday Even-
       ing Post, CC (July 16, August 13, 1927), 3-5, 8-9,
       A Marine in Nicaragua.

2993 Pawlowski, Gareth L. Flat-Tops and Fledglings: A
      History of American Aircraft Carriers. New York:
      Castle Books, 1971. 530p.
      A large illustrated volume beginning with the
      Langley.

2994 Paxson, F. L. "The Naval Air Station at Alameda,
      1916-1940: A Case Study in the Aptitude of De-
      mocracy for Defense. " Pacific Historical Review,
      XIII (September 1944), 235-250.

2995 "The Pay of Enlisted Personnel in the United States
      Army and Navy. " Monthly Labor Review, LI
      (July 1940), 1-4.

2996 "Peace and a Strong Navy: The United States Cannot
      Work for World Peace with a Middle-Sized Navy. "
      Review of Reviews, XCI (February 1935), 16-20.

2997 Pearl, Jack. Admiral "Bull" Halsey. Derby, Conn.:
      Monarch Books, 1962. 139p.

2998 Peck, Franklin W. "Suggestions for Training a Volun-
      teer Naval Reserve. " USNIP, LXV (1939), 503-
      507.

2999 Peck, Frederick T. "History of the Naval Gun Fac-
      tory in Washington, D. C. " Unpublished PhD Dis-
      sertation, Georgetown University, 1950.

3000 Peck, J. L. H. "Helldivers, Techniques of Dive-Bomb-
      ing Conceived for United States Naval Use. " Sci-
      Amer, CLXIII (October 1940), 186-188.

3001 Peck, Scott E. "The Navigation of Rigid Airships. "
      USNIP, LIX (1933), 1150-1153.

3002 Peck, Taylor. Round-Shot to Rockets. Annapolis:
      U. S. Naval Institute, 1949. 267p.
      A history of the Washington Navy Yard and Naval
      Gun Factory.

3003 "A Peek Under the Navy Lid: Censorship Lifted. "
      Newsweek, XVIII (September 29, 1941), 52.

3004 Pell, Herbert C. "Why a Navy?" North American
      Review, CCXXXIII (May 1932), 425-431.

3005 Pence, Harry L. "Material Procurement Planning. "
      USNIP, LVII (1931), 1653-1660.

3006 Pennoyer, F. W. "Navy Air Maintenance. " Society
      of Automotive Engineers Journal, XXXIX (November
      1936), Supplement, 15-16.

3007 Pennoyer, Ralph G. "Rigid Airships in the United
      States Navy. " USNIP, XLVIII (1922), 517-529.

3008 Pennsylvania. Department cf Public Instruction, Divi-
      sion of Industrial Education. Shipfitting Practice.
      Bulletin 345. Harrisburg, 1941. 120p.

3009 "Pensacola: The U. S. Navy Trains the World's Best
      Pilots. " Life, IX (August 26, 1940), 55-63.

3010 Pensacola, U. S. S. U. S. S. Pensacola, CA-24, 1929-
      1946. San Francisco: Phillips & Van Orden, 1946.
      108p.
             In reality a World War II cruise book; however,
      by including a considerable amount of pre-war data
      and photos, this compilation must be considered a
      good bit more.

3011 Pepper, Robert H. "Antiaircraft Notes. " Marine
      Corps Gazette, XX (August 1936), 28-31.
             Responsibilities for defense of advanced bases
      or landing fields.

3012 Percival, Franklin G. "Building Tomorrow's Navy. "
      Popular Mechanics, LXXVI (September 1941), 34-
      37.

3013 _____. "The Cruiser Problem. " USNIP, LVI
      (1930), 387-402.

3014 _____. "Cruiser Quotas of the 1935 Conference. "
      USNIP, LVII (1931), 373-376.

3015 _____. "Cruiser Types. " USNIP, LIII (1927),
      278-288, 798-800.

3016 _____. "Elements Contributing to Aerial Superi-
      ority. " USNIP, LVII (1931), 437-447.

3017 _____. "Future Cruisers. " USNIP, LXVII (1941),
      163-171.

The American Navy, 1918-1941

3018 _____. "The Future Fleet." USNIP, LXVII (1941),
1075-1087.

3019 _____. "Future Naval War." USNIP, LXVI (1940),
1699-1712.

3020 _____. "Peace Time Artificiality." USNIP, LX
(1934), 1665-1677.

3021 _____. "The Small Cruiser." USNIP, LXI (1935),
641-653.

3022 _____. "The Speed of Battleships." USNIP, LV
(1929), 273-283.

3023 _____. "What This War Means to the U. S. Navy."
USNIP, LXVII (1941), 1701-1708.

3024 "The Peril of Renewed Naval Rivalry." Literary Digest, LXXXIII (December 27, 1924), 5-7.

3025 Perimutter, Edward. "Coast Guard Fliers: The Coast
Patrol." New York Times Magazine, (June 22,
1941), 26.

3026 Perkins, Dexter. The New Age of Franklin Roosevelt,
1932-1945. Chicago History of American Civilization. Chicago: University of Chicago Press, 1957.

3027 Perkins, Earle B. "Plankton and Invertebrates of the
Antarctic." Scientific Monthly, XLIII (December
1936), 568-574.
As examined by a member of the 1933-1935 Byrd
Expedition.

3028 Perry, Emil B. "All is Lost but Honor." USNIP,
LXIV (1938), 1107-1110.

3029 _____. "Notes from Submarine Divisions, Asiatic."
USNIP, LV (1929), 1031-1038.

3030 _____. "Pyrometry Applied to Submarine Diesel
Engines." USNIP, LVII (1931), 210-214.

3031 _____. "Some Hows and Whys of Electric Meter
Calibration." USNIP, LV (1929), 118-120.

Perry   255

3032   No Entry

3033   No Entry

3034   _____. "Some Whys and Wherefores of Power. "
       USNIP, LII (1926), 2253-2274.
       Relates to naval engineering.

3035   _____. "Three Texas Mules and the Navy. " USNIP,
       LXXXIV (1958), 66-69.
       On the author's experiences with the Federal
       government, especially the Navy Department, while
       building a Navy shipyard at Orange, Texas, in
       1940.

3036   _____. "The U. S. S. Edsall on Relief. " USNIP,
       LXV (1939), 1128-1140.

3037   _____. "Unruly Rules of the Road. " USNIP, LX
       (1934), 641-646.

3038   Perry, Glen. Watchmen of the Sea. New York:
       Scribners, 1938. 229p.
       The Coast Guard in action with such examples
       as the running hot war with rum-runners and the
       spectacular rescues off the burning Morrow Castle.

3039   Perry, Hamilton D. The Panay Incident: Prelude to
       Pearl Harbor. New York: Macmillan, 1969. 295p.

3040   Perry, Lyman S. "Three Veterans of the United
       States Navy. " USNIP, LVII (1931), 632-638.
       The battleships Florida, Utah, and Wyoming.

3041   Peterson, Mendel L. "The Navy Cross. " Numis-
       matist, LXV (December 1952), 1170-1174.

3042   Pfaff, Roy. "Sea Duty and the Yangtze. " USNIP,
       LIX (1933), 1612-1616.

3043   Pflugk, H. A. F. "Torpedo Boats. " USNIP, LXVII
       (1941), 1115-1120.

3044   Phayre, Ignatius. "The Big Navy of the United States."
       Quarterly Review, CCLII (January 1929), 147-169.
       A British view.

3045   . "Great Wall or Big Stick? Naval Problems
and Policy of America. " Fortune, CXXVIII (December 1927), 817-828.

3046 Phelps, Edith M. , ed. "The Anglo-American Alliance. " In: University Debaters Annual. New
York: H. W. Wilson, Co. , 1939. p. 65-109.

3047   . "Japan and Naval Parity. " In: University
Debaters Annual. New York: H. W. Wilson, 1934-
1936. p. 409-450.

3048   . "Japanese Aggression in the Far East,
Should the U. S. Oppose It?" In: University Debaters Annual. New York: H. W. Wilson Company,
1941. p. 185-242.

3049   . "Should the Nations of the Western Hemisphere Form a Defensive Alliance?" In: University Debaters Annual. New York: H. W. Wilson
Company, 1939. p. 263-313.

3050 Phelps, William W. "Keeping the United States Neutral. " USNIP, LX (1934), 1353-1354.

3051 Pierce, Edwin H. "On Some Old Bugle-Calls of the
U. S. Navy. " Musical Quarterly, XVIII (January
1932), 134-139.

3052 Pierce, Francis E. "Infantry-Air Communication. "
Marine Corps Gazette, XIII (December 1928), 266-
270.
As practiced during the banana wars in Latin
America.

3053 Pierce, Philip N. and Frank O. Hough. The Compact
History of the United States Marine Corps. New
York: Hawthorn, 1960. 326p.
Contains considerable data relative to our period.

3054 Piggott, F. T. "The Greatest Navy in the World. "
19th Century, LXXXIX (March 1921), 511-520.
Writing in a British magazine, the author con-
tends that the British fleet has been surpassed by
the American.

3055 Pihl, Paul E. "Happy Landing!" USNIP, LVII (1931),

1018-1038.

3056   Pineau, Roger. "The U. S. S. Noa and the Fall of
        Naking. " USNIP, LXXXI (1955), 1221-1228.
        The city went under to the Japanese.

3057   Pineau, jt. author. See Ohmae, Toshikazu, no. 2891.

3058   "Pioneer Engineering in Deep-Water Salvage--Raising
        the Submarine S-51. " Engineering News, XCVII
        (August 5, 1926), 210-213.

3059   Piper, J. F. Marine Electrical Installation. New York:
        Cornell Maritime Press, 1941. 380p.

3060   Pitkin, Walter B. Must We Fight Japan? New York:
        Century, 1921. 586p.

3061   "The Plan of the United States to Lease Six Obsolete
        Warships to Brazil. " Commercial and Financial
        Chronicle, CXLV (August 21-28, 1937), 1196, 1352.

3062   Platt, Jonas H. "The Marines Have Landed: Why?"
        Independent, CXVI (January 9, 1926), 36-37.
        The article concerns Haiti.

3063   "Plebe Summer Infantry [at the Naval Academy]. "
        USNIP, LXI (1935), 1529-1531.

3064   Plummer, Edward C. "Merchant Ships and the Navy."
        North American Review, CCXXIV (November 1927),
        505-515.

3065   Pocock, Arthur. Red Flannels and Green Ice. New
        York: Random House, 1949. 272p.
        A Coast Guard Officer's reminiscences of the
        early World War II Greenland Patrol.

3066   Pogue, Forrest C. George C. Marshall. 3 vols.
        New York: Viking Press, 1961-1973.
        Considers his relations with the navy as well
        as his own army.

3067   "The Policy and Status of the United States Navy, with
        an Analysis of the Vinson Bill. " Congressional
        Digest, XVII (March 1938), 69-70, 74.

3068   Pollen, Arthur J. H.   Disarmament in Its Relation to
       the Naval Policy and the Naval Building Program
       of the U. S.   New York: American Association for
       International Conciliation, 1921.

3069   Polley, Clad E. , ed.   The U. S. S. Augusta Under Fire:
       The Sino-Japanese Incident, 1937-1938.   Shanghai,
       China: Press of the North China Daily News, 1938.
       136p.

3070   Pollock, Edwin T.   "American Samoa: How the United
       States Came into Possession of Part of the Samoan
       or Navigators' Islands, with a Short Account of the
       Entire Group, Including Swain's Island. "   USNIP,
       LIII (1927), 1029-1036.
           For the events of 1889, see also the citations in
       Vol. IV of this series.

3071   Polmar, Norman, et al.   Aircraft Carriers: A Graphic
       History of Carrier Aviation and Its Influence on
       World Events.   Garden City, N. Y. : Doubleday,
       1969.   788p.

3072   Pomeroy, Earl S.   "The Problem of American Over-
       seas Bases: Some Reflections on Naval History. "
       USNIP, LXXIII (1947), 688-700.

3073   Pomeroy, L. K.   "The Navy and National Policy. "
       USNIP, LXXXVI (1960), 90-97.
           Since the earliest days.

3074   Pond, Horace B.   "The Philippine Dilemma. "   Asia,
       XXXVI (August 1936), 511-513.

3075   Pond, John K.   "Naval Training. "   USNIP, XLVIII
       (1922), 1-13.

3076   Poolman, Kenneth.   The Illustrious.   London: Kimber,
       1955.   246p.
           The noted British carrier repaired at Newport
       News in 1941.

3077   Poor, Charles L.   "The Naval Reserve, Its Organiza-
       tion, Administration, and Training in Time of
       Peace. "   USNIP, XLVI (1920), 39-53.

3078   Pope, Jennie B. , jt. author. See Albion, Robert G. , no.64

3079   Popov, Dusko. "Pearl Harbor: Did J. Edgar Hoover
       Blunder?" True, LIV (October 1973), 47, 107-114.
       How British secret agent learned of Japanese
       plans and attempted to warn the FBI.   An excerpt
       from the author's Code Name: Tricycle (New York:
       Grosset & Dunlap, 1973).

3080   Popper, David H.   "America's Defense Policies. "
       Foreign Policy Reports, XV (1940), 34-48.

3081   _____.   "America's Naval Preparedness. " Foreign
       Policy Reports, XVII (1941), 14-24.

3082   _____.   "The End of Naval Disarmament. " Foreign
       Policy Reports, XI (1936), 202-212.

3083   _____.   "Policies and Problems of the U. S. Navy."
       Foreign Policy Reports, XVII (1941), 38-48.

3084   Porter, Catherine L.   Crisis in the Philippines. New
       York: Published for the American Council of the
       Institute of Pacific Relations by A. A. Knopf, 1942.
       156p.
             A summary of defense plans, etc. , through De-
       cember 1941.

3085   Porter, Russell.   "Seven Danger Spots Still Disturb
       the World and Peace by Co-operation. " USNIP,
       LI (1925), 2023-2029.
             Reprinted from the August 9 and 23, 1925 issues
       of the New York Times.

3086   "Portfolio of Aircraft Carriers. " USNIP, LXXVI
       (1951), 874-879.
             Includes 8 plates. Mostly those employed in
       World War II and before.
             Contains sketches and paintings by Thomas C.
       Skinner.

3087   "A Portfolio of U. S. Military Airplanes, and a Lay-
       man's Handbook of Types, Their Tactical Uses,
       and Their Characteristics. " Fortune, XXIII (March
       1941), 70-74.

3088   Posner, William H.   "American Marines in Haiti,
       1915-1922. " The Americas, XX (January 1964),
       231-266.

3089 "Post-Treaty Standing of the World's Navies. " Sci-
      Amer, CXXX (May 1924), 320-321.

3090 Potect, Fred H. "Joining the United States Navy. "
      USNIP, LVI (1930), 619-622.

3091 Potter, David. "The Annual Naval Appropriation Bill:
      How It Becomes a Law. " USNIP, LVIII (1932),
      1723-1728.

3092 _____. "The Naval Finance and Supply School. "
      USNIP, LXII (1936), 1138-1140.

3093 No Entry

3094 _____. "Our Newest Navy: How Its Cost is Being
      Determined. " USNIP, XLV (1919), 201-222.

3095 _____. "Reckless Readings of a Naval Officer. "
      USNIP, XLV (1919), 61-70.

3096 _____. "The Training of a Government Official. "
      USNIP, L (1924), 1982-1988.
      A July 13, 1923 address before students at the
      University of Minnesota.

3097 Potter, Elmer B. "Chester William Nimitz, 1885-
      1966. " USNIP, XCII (1966), 30-55.

3098 _____. The Naval Academy Illustrated History of
      the United States Navy. New York: Crowell, 1971.
      299p.

3099 _____ ed. Sea Power: a Naval History. Associate
      Editor: Chester W. Nimitz. Englewood Cliffs,
      N. J. : Prentice-Hall, 1960. 932p.
      The basic modern text.

3100 _____ ed. The United States and World Sea Power.
      Englewood Cliffs, N. J. : Prentice-Hall, 1955. 963p.
      Superseded by Sea Power: A Naval History.

3101 _____ and Chester W. Nimitz, eds. The Great Sea
      War: The Story of Naval Action in World War II.
      Englewood Cliffs, N. J. : Prentice-Hall, 1960. 468p.
      Adapted from their Sea Power: A Naval History
      cited above, with some data relative to this work.

3102 Potter, Frank H. The Naval Reserve. New York:
      H. Holt, 1919. 167p.

3103 Potter, John D. Yamamoto: The Man Who Menaced
      America. New York: Viking, 1965. 332p.
      As C. -in-C. of the Imperial Japanese Navy,
      Isoroku Yamamoto oversaw the planning for war
      with America.

3104 Poulter, Thomas C. "The Scientific Work of the
      Second Byrd Antarctic Expedition. " Scientific
      Monthly, XLIX (July 1939), 5-20.
      That undertaken in the years 1933-1935.

3105 Powell, Frederick W. , jt. author. See Smith, Dar-
      rell H. , no. 3700.

3106 Powell, Hickman. "The Coast Guard Mobilizes a
      Small Boat Navy. " Popular Science, CXXXIX
      (September 1941), 76-79.

3107 _____ . What the Citizen Should Know About the
      Coast Guard. New York: W. W. Norton, 1941.
      194p.
      Similar to the other "What the Citizen" books
      cited throughout this volume.

3108 "The Power of an Airplane Carrier to Equal the Energy
      of a City. " Popular Mechanics, XLIII (June 1925),
      887.
      A forecast concerning U. S. S. Lexington.

3109 Powers, Melville W. "U. S. S. Omaha Salvage Opera-
      tions. " USNIP, LXV (1939), 1311-1324.

3110 "The Powers Start Mad Race as Treaties Expire with
      the Old Year. " Newsweek, IX (January 9, 1937),
      14-15.

3111 Pownall, Charles A. "Airphobia of 1925. " USNIP,
      LII (1925), 459-463.

3112 _____ . "Better Engines for Navy Planes. " Sci-
      Amer, CXLV (December 1931), 376-378.

3113 Prak, W. "Problems of the Pacific: Causes of War."
      USNIP, LXI (1935), 917-927.

3114 Pratt, Fletcher. "The Basis of Our Naval Tradition."
      USNIP, LXIII (1937), 1107-1114.

3115 _____. "The Battleship Comes Back. " American
      Mercury, XLI (June 1937), 169-174.

3116 _____. _____. North American Review,
      CCXLVIII (September 1939), 127-139.

3117 _____. "Columbia, the Gem of the Ocean. " Satur-
      day Evening Post, CCXII (October 7, 1939), 8-9.

3118 _____. "Commerce Destruction, Past and Future."
      USNIP, LX (1934), 1513-1518.

3119 _____. "The Destroyer Grows Up. " USNIP, LXI
      (1935), 683-691.

3120 _____. "The Disarmament Hoax. " American Mer-
      cury, XLII (October 1937), 173-180.

3121 _____. "The Future of Blockade. " USNIP, LIX
      (1933), 868-872.

3122 _____. "Hold the Pacific: Reply with a Rejoinder."
      New Republic, CV (November 24, 1941), 703.
      This reply is in response to the article by W.H.
      Hale cited above.

3123 _____. "The Intermediate Warship. " USNIP, LXV
      (1939), 1147-1152.

3124 _____. "A Naval Game and a Formula. " USNIP,
      LVIII (1932), 1758-1762.

3125 _____. The Navy: A History, The Story of a Service in
      Action. Garden City, N.Y.: Garden City Publish-
      ing, 1941. 496p.
      Very colorful.

3126 _____. "A Plea for Ciphers. " USNIP, LIX (1933),
      692-696.

3127 _____. "Portrait of the Naval Academy. " American
      Mercury, XLI (July 1937), 321-328.
      The reply by D.W. Farnham is cited above.

3128 _____ . Sea Power and Today's War. New York:
Harrison-Hilton, 1939. 237p.
Pages 181-202 discusses the American navy and
its preparedness.

3129 _____ . "Some Naval Eccentricities. " USNIP, LVII
(1931), 1192-1196.

3130 _____ . "To Have and to Hold: Defense of the Panama Canal Against Air Attack. " Saturday Evening
Post, CXII (June 8, 1940), 18-19+.

3131 _____ . "The U-boats are Coming. " Saturday
Evening Post, CCXIV (December 6, 1941), 29+.

3132 _____ . "United States Naval Strategy. " Fortune,
XXIII (June 1941), 72-81.

3133 _____ ed. "Ships, Men, and Bases. " Saturday
Evening Post, CCXIII (April 5, 1941), 16-17, 35-
41.

3134 _____ and Hartley E. Howe. The Compact History
of the United States Navy. Rev. ed. New York:
Hawthorn, 1967. 350p.

3135 Pratt, Laurence. "The Anglo-American Naval Conversations on the Far East of January 1938. " International Affairs, XLVII (1971), 745-763.

3136 Pratt, William V. "Airships Might Come in Handy
These Days. " Newsweek, XVII (May 19, 1941),
30.

3137 _____ . "America's Aces in the Far Eastern
Game. " Newsweek, XV (January 29, 1940), 29.

3138 _____ . "America's Problem in Sea Power. " Newsweek, XVII (January 13, 1941), 27.

3139 _____ . "The Aspects of Higher Command. " Unpublished Lecture, Files of the U. S. Army Military
History Research Collection, 1929.

3140 _____ . "The Broad Aspect of Our Pacific Problem. " USNIP, LIII (1927), 1-12.

3141 _____ . "Cooperation of Army and Navy, Limitation of Armaments. " Unpublished Lecture, Files of the U. S. Army Military History Research Collection, 1930.

3142 _____ . "Disarmament and the National Defense. " USNIP, LX (1929), 751-764.

3143 _____ . Freedom of the Seas. Round Table Pamphlets, no. 183. Chicago: University of Chicago Press, 1941. 29p.

3144 _____ . "How the U. S. Must Face New Problems in Sea Power. " Newsweek, XV (May 27, 1940), 24.

3145 _____ . "The Language the Navy Understands. " Newsweek, XVIII (September 22, 1941), 26.

3146 _____ . "Leadership. " USNIP, LX (1934), 1049-1060.

3147 _____ . "The Local Defense of the Canal Zone. " Unpublished Lecture, Files of the U. S. Army Military History Research Collection, 1933.

3148 _____ . "Meaning of the Attack on the Kearney. " Newsweek, XVIII (October 27, 1941), 25. Torpedoed by a German U-boat.

3149 _____ . "Naval Command and Administration. " Unpublished Lecture, Files of the U. S. Army Military History Research Collection, 1927.

3150 _____ . "The Naval Job Facing the U. S. in the Pacific. " Newsweek, XVIII (November 3, 1941), 24.

3151 _____ . "Naval Policy and Its Relation to World Politics. " USNIP, XLIX (1923), 1073-1084. A February 27, 1923 speech before the Council on Foreign Relations.

3152 _____ . "Naval Policy and the Naval Treaty. " North American Review, CCXV (May 1922), 590-599.

3153 _____ . "The Naval Side of the Atlantic Conference."

Newsweek, XVIII (August 25, 1941), 24.

3154 _____. "The Naval War College: An Outline of the
Past and Description of the Present. " USNIP,
LIII (1927), 937-947.

3155 _____. "The Navy is National Insurance. " American Bankers Association Journal, XXV (March
1933), 28-29, 48.

3156 _____. "Preparation of the Fleet for Battle: The
Exercise of High Command. " Unpublished Lecture,
War Planning Course 15, Files of the U.S. Army
Military History Research Collection, 1927.

3157 _____. "Protection Against the Submarine. " Newsweek, XVII (June 16, 1941), 28.

3158 _____. "Setting for the 1935 Naval Conference. "
Foreign Affairs, XII (July 1934), 541-552.
For the Japanese rejoinder, see the article by
Masanori Ito cited above.

3159 _____. "Some Aspects of Our Air Policy. " USNIP,
LII (1926), 444-458, 1171-1178.

3160 _____. "Some Thoughts on the Reuben James Sinking. " Newsweek, XVIII (November 10, 1941), 30.

3161 _____. "The Three Phases of a Naval Career. "
Unpublished Lecture, Files of the U.S. Army Military History Research Collection, 1929.

3162 _____. "The Tide is Turning Against the U-boat. "
Newsweek, XVIII (November 17, 1941), 28.
Our retired admiral-commentator is here a bit
over optimistic. Admiral Donitz had not yet begun
to fight.

3163 _____. "Warfare in the Atlantic. " Foreign Affairs,
XIX (July 1941), 729-736.

3164 _____. "Why the Navy is Tired of Strikes. " Newsweek, XVIII (December 1, 1941), 28.
It would not have to worry much longer!

3164a _____. "Why the U.S. Plans to Arm It's Ships. "

Newsweek, XVIII (October 20, 1941), 26.

3165 Prendergast, Maurice. "Sonar and Asdic: Anti-Submarine Sisters. " USNIP, LXXIV (1948), 1009-1011.

3166 "Present Naval Bases of the Three Powers in the Pacific. " Asia, XXXVI (December 1936), 760. Features a map.

3167 "The President and the Navy. " Nation, CXXXIII (November 11, 1931), 503.

3168 "President, Congress, and the Navy. " Nation, CXXXIII (October 14, 1931), 378.

3169 "President Endorses Plan to Build 32 Additional War Vessels at a Cost of $238,000,000 Within Three Years--Sec. Swanson Says the Expenditure Will be Made from the Public Work Fund with 85 per cent of the Money to be Spent on Labor. " Commerical and Financial Chronicle, CXXXVII (July 8, 1933), 245.

3170 "President Hoover and the [London] Naval Conference." World Today, LV (January 1930), 108-111.

3171 "The President Is Authorized to Increase the Navy: World Rumblings Kindled. " Newsweek, III (March 17, 1934), 8.

3172 "President Pushes Big Navy Construction Program. " Scholastic, XXXII (February 5, 1938), 15.

3173 "President Roosevelt Bars Submarines of Belligerents From Using United States Ports and Territorial Waters. " Commercial and Financial Chronicle, CXLIX (October 21, 1939), 2446.

3174 "The President's Naval Victory in Congress. " Literary Digest, XCII (January 22, 1927), 8-9.

3175 "Press Disgust at the [London] Naval Pow-Wow. " Literary Digest, CIV (March 8, 1930), 12.

3176 Presseisen, Ernst L. Germany and Japan: A Study in Totalitarian Diplomacy, 1933-1941. International Scholars Forum. The Hague: Nijhoff, 1958. 368p. Rpr. 1970.

3177   Price, Charles. "Yachtsmen in the Navy." New York
       Times Magazine, (March 9, 1941), 25.

3178   Price, Willard. "Mistress of the Yellow Sea." Fort-
       nightly, CXLVIII (November 1937), 525-533.
       The Japanese navy.

3179   Prickett, William F. "The Old Corps." Marine Corps
       Gazette, XL (July 1956), 36-40.
       That of the 1930s.

3180   Pride, A. M. "Big Boats in Navy Service." Aero
       Digest, XXXVI (August 1940), 30-32+.
       Refers to flying boats such as the PBY.

3181   Pringle, J. R. P. "Naval Strategy and Combat." Un-
       published Lecture, War Planning Division Course
       15.   Files of the U. S. Army Military History Re-
       search Collection, 1928.
       The admiral was then President of the U. S.
       Naval War College.

3182   "Private Kemp Reports on Our War in Santo Domingo."
       Literary Digest, LX (February 22, 1919), 105-108.

3183   "Probe Continued." Time, XXXI (February 21, 1938),
       18-19.
       By Congress into the need for naval prepared-
       ness.

3184   "The Problem of Cruiser and Destroyer Limitation."
       Engineering, CXXIX (January 24, 1930), 111-113.

3185   "The Problem of the Submarine." Engineer, CXL
       (November 27, 1925), 583-584.

3186   "Problems in Cruiser Design." Engineer, CXXXVIII
       (October 31, 1924), 497-498.

3187   Proctor, Andre M. "Diesels for Battleships?" Sci-
       Amer, CLIV (January 1936), 18-20.
       Installed aboard German "Pocket Battleships, "
       but not in the American navy.

3188   _____. "Protection of the Modern Battleship."
       USNIP, LXII (1936), 187-188.

3189 "Production in the First Year of Defense--Navy. "
      Factory Management, XCIX (August 1941), 70-71.

3190 "Professional Fighters. " Time, XXXVI (November 11,
      1940), 21-24.
      The same article, abridged, appeared in the
      Reader's Digest, XXXVIII (January 1941), 103-105,
      under the title "The Marines Have the Situation in
      Hand. "

3191 "Professionals to London: U. S. Delegates to the 1935
      Naval Limitation Conference. " Time, XXVI (De-
      cember 9, 1935), 17-19.

3192 "Progress of the United States Government Expedition
      to the Antarctic. " Geographic Review, XXX (April
      1940), 325-327.
      The 1939 Byrd Expedition.

3193 "The Protest of the American Republics to the Bellig-
      erent Countries, December 23, 1939, with the
      Text of Replies. " Bulletin of the Pan-American
      Union, LXXIV (May 1940), 403-408.

3194 Puleston, William D. The Armed Forces of the
      Pacific: A Comparison of the Military and Naval
      Power of the United States and Japan. New Haven:
      Yale University Press, 1941. 274p.

3195 _____. "Comparative Study of Operations and Train-
      ing as a Staff Function in Our Army and Navy. "
      Unpublished General Staff Memorandum, Files of
      the U. S. Army Military History Research Collec-
      tion, 1924.

3196 _____. "Cultured Naval Officers. " SciAmer,
      CXLII (May 1930), 362-364.

3197 _____. "Eight-inch Gun Cruiser. " SciAmer,
      CXLIII (August 1930), 120-122.

3198 _____. "Midshipmen at Landlubber Colleges: Six
      Institutions Co-operate with the Navy in Preparing
      Naval Reserve Officers. " SciAmer, CXLII (June
      1930), 444-447.

3199 _____. "Modernizing the U. S. S. Mississippi. "

SciAmer, CL (June 1934), 298-300.

3200 _____. "The Probable Future Trend of Joint Oper-
ations. " Unpublished Lecture, Conduct of War
Course 24, Files of the U. S. Army Military History
Research Collection, 1930.

3201 _____. "A Reexamination of Mahan's Concept of
Seapower. " USNIP, LXVI (1940), 1229-1236.

3202 _____. "A Strategic Survey of the Western Atlantic
and Caribbean from the Viewpoint of the United
States. " Unpublished Lecture, War Plans Course
8, Files of the U. S. Army Military History Research Collection, 1930.

3203 _____. "Strategy with a One-Ocean Navy. " Atlantic
Monthly, CLXVI (1940), 707-711.

3204 _____. "The United States Fleet of Today. " Unpublished Lecture, Analytical Course 6, Files of
the U. S. Army Military History Research Collection 1932.

3204a Pulsifer, Pitman, comp. Navy Yearbook. 3 vols.
Washington: Government Printing Office, 1919-
1921.
The final three volumes of a series on naval
appropriations, strength, and shipbuilding dating
back to 1883.

3205 "The Purpose of the Cruisers. " New Republic, LVII
(January 30, 1929), 285-286.

3206 Pusey, Merlo J. Charles Evans Hughes. 2 vols.
New York: Macmillan, 1961.
Data on his role in the events of the 1922 Washington Naval Conference are found in Chpts. 44-46
of Volume II.

3207 "Putt-Putts Holed: Navy Contracts for Small, Speedy,
Motor Torpedo Boats and Submarine Chasers. "
Time, XXXIV (December 18, 1939), 13.

3208 Pye, Norman. "The United States as a Caribbean
Power: The Geographical Background of the Naval
and Air Bases Leased from Britain. " Scottish Ge-

ographical Magazine, LVII (June 1941), 73-78.

3209 Pye, William S. "The Importance of Maritime
Power. " Marine News, XXIII (October 1936), 22-
24.

3210 _____. "Joint Army and Navy Operations. " USNIP,
L (1924), 1963-1976; LI (1925), 1-14, 233-245,
386-399, 589-599, 975-1000.

3211 _____. "The Office of Naval Operations. " Unpublished Lecture, War Plans Course 7, Files of the
U. S. Army Military History Research Collection,
1936.
The author was a Navy rear admiral.

3212 _____. "The Strength of Gibraltar: Has Aviation
Affected the Strength of Gibraltar, Hawaii, and the
Canal Zone?" USNIP, LIII (1927), 1160-1165.

3213 _____. "War Plans from a Navy Point of View. "
Unpublished Lecture, War Planning Division Course
11, Files of the U. S. Army Military History Research Collection, 1924.

3214 "The Question of Battleships vs. Airplanes: How It Is
Viewed by the General Board of the Navy and by
Admirals Fullam and Moffett. " Aviation, XIV
(June 11, 1923), 634-638.

3215 "The Question of Submarine Warfare. " Review of Reviews, LXV (March 1922), 328-329.

3216 Quigley, Harold S. "The Drift in the Pacific. " Atlantic Monthly, CLXVI (September 1940), 333-338.

3217 _____ and G. H. Blakeslee. "Navies, Naval Bases,
and Air Routes. " In: their The Far East: An International Survey. Boston: World Peace Foundation, 1938. p. 237-254.

3218 Quinlan, Robert J. "The United States Fleet: Diplomacy, Strategy, and the Allocation of Ships, 1940-
1941. " In: Harold Stein, ed. American Civil-Military Decisions: A Book of Case Studies. Birming-
ham: University of Alabama Press, 1963. p. 153-
201.

Rabl   271

3219 Rabl, Samuel S.   Practical Principles of Naval Archi-
        tecture.   New York: Cornell Maritime Press,
        1941.   181p.

3220 Raby, James J.   "Naval Aviation Training. "   USNIP,
        LI (1925), 1646-1651.

3221 "Racing Destroyer Fires Stream of Torpedoes: Draw-
        ings. "   Popular Mechanics, LXXI (March 1939),
        398-399.

3221a Radom, Matthew.   "The Americanization of the U. S.
        Navy. "   USNIP, LXIII (1937), 231-234.

3221b _____.   "Promotion of Officers in the British Japa-
        nese, French, and German Navies. "   USNIP, LXIII
        (1937), 1293-1301.
        Useful for comparison with the American Navy.

3222 Raeder, Erich.   My Life.   Translated by Henry W.
        Drexel.   Annapolis: U. S. Naval Institute, 1960.
        430p.
        Autobiography of the top German admiral of
        World War II.   Contains some data of interest to
        this work.

3223 _____.   "The Navy, Hitler, and the Nazi Party. "
        USNIP, LXXXVI (1960), 43-46.

3224 Raftery, Thomas J.   "Aerology and Chemical War-
        fare. "   USNIP, LIX (1933), 559-560.

3225 Ragland, Reginald W.   A History of the Naval Petro-
        leum Reserves and of the Development of the Pre-
        sent National Policy Respecting Them.   Los
        Angeles, 1944.

3226 Ragusin, Anthony R.   "Fighting the Treachery of the
        High Seas. "   Travel, LXVIII (March 1937), 36-39.
        The work of the Coast Guard.

3227 Ramsey, DeWitt C.   "Aviation Training for Midship-
        men and Line Officers. "   USNIP, LVII (1931), 18-
        24.

3228 _____.   "The Course of Training for Student Naval
        Aviators. "   USNIP, LIII (1927), 303-307.

272   The American Navy, 1918-1941

3229 _____. "The Development of Aviation in the Fleet."
    USNIP, XLIX (1923), 1395-1417.

3230 Ramsey, Logan C. "Aerial Attacks on Fleets at
    Anchor." USNIP, LXIII (1937), 1126-1132.
    Quite prophetic!

3231 _____. "The Aircraft Bomb and the Naval Gun."
    USNIP, LIX (1933), 1289-1295.

3232 _____. "Aircraft and Naval Engagement." USNIP,
    LVI (1930), 679-687.

3233 _____. "Air Power is Sea Power." USNIP, LXVII
    (1941), 921-926.
    Interestingly enough, this article was written
    before Pearl Harbor!

3234 _____. "The Influence of Aircraft on the Exercise
    of Sea Command." USNIP, LXIV (1938), 1401-
    1407.

3235 _____. "A Neglected Phase of Naval Aviation."
    USNIP, LVII (1931), 1052-1055.

3236 _____. "The Torpedo Planes Advantage of the
    Naval Bomber." Aviation, XXXI (April 1932), 179.

3237 Randall, Jack, as told to Meigs O. Frost. I'm Alone.
    Indianapolis: Bobbs-Merrill, 1930. 317p.
    The author, a Canadian rum smuggler, had his
    boat shot out from under him by Coast Guard Cut-
    ters in March 1929. The name of his craft was
    the I'm Alone.

3238 "Ranger: Fourth Carrier Ship Will Mother 140 Navy
    Planes." Newsweek, I (March 4, 1933), 31.

3239 "The Ranger 12-cylinder 450 hp Inverted Engine."
    Aero Digest, XXXVI (June 1940), 72-73+.
    For further details, see the article by J. P.
    AuWerter cited above.

3240 Rankin, Robert H. "The DN-1, the Navy's First
    Dirigible." USNIP, LXXXIII (1957), 1144-1145.

3241 _____. "Goodbye to the Gas Bags." USNIP,

LXXXVII (1961), 91-108.
The use of dirigibles in the American Navy.

3242 _____. "A History of Selective Service." USNIP,
LXXVII (1951), 1073-1081.

3243 _____. "The Navy's Tin Bubble." USNIP, XCI
(1965), 170-172.
The airship ZMC-2 employed during the 1930s.

3244 _____. "The Pulitzer Races, 1920-1925." USNIP,
LXXXV (1959), 67-71.
Contains discussion of some navy planes entered
therein.

3245 _____. Small Arms of the Sea Services: A History
of the Firearms and Edged Weapons of the U.S.
Navy, Marine Corps, and Coast Guard from the
Revolution to the Present. New Milford, Conn.:
N. Flayderman, 1972. 227p.

3246 _____. "The Story of Coast Guard Aviation."
USNIP, LXXXV (1959), 87-90.

3247 _____. Uniforms of the Sea Services: A Pictorial
History. Annapolis: U.S. Naval Institute, 1963.
324p.

3248 _____ and H.R. Kaplan. Immortal Bear: The
Stoutest Polar Ship. New York: Putnam's, 1970.
160p.

3249 Rankin, William H. The Man Who Rode the Thunder.
Englewood Cliffs, N.J.: Prentice-Hall, 1960. 208p.
An autobiography of Marine service since 1940.

3249a Ransom, Harry H. "The Battleship Meets the Airplane." Military Affairs, XXIII (Spring 1959), 21-
27.
On the bombing tests conducted by the navy on
old capital ships after the First World War.

3250 Ransom, Mudge A. "The First Around the World
Flight." USNIP, LXIV (1938), 1589-1592.

3251 _____. "The Little Gray Ships." USNIP, LXII
(1936), 1281-1286.

Minelayers and Minesweepers.

3252 _____. Sea of the Bear: Journal of a Voyage to
       Alaska and the Arctic, 1921. Annapolis: U. S.
       Naval Institute, 1964. 119p.

3253 Rapaport, Stella F. The Bear: Ship of Many Lives.
       New York: Dodd, Mead, 1962. 146p.

3254 Rappaport, Armin. The Navy League of the United
       States. Detroit: Wayne State University Press,
       1962. 271p.

3255 Rattan, S. "The Four-Power Treaty of 1921 and
       American National Interest." Unpublished PhD
       Dissertation, American University, 1967.

3256 Rauch, Basil. Roosevelt: from Munich to Pearl Har-
       bor, a Study in the Creation of a Foreign Policy.
       New York: Creative Age Press, 1950. 527p. Rpr.
       1967.

3257 Rauch, George. "The Present State of Our Naval De-
       fenses." In: Julia E. Johnson, ed. Naval Arma-
       ments and a Foreign Policy. Vol. XII of The
       Reference Shelf. New York: H. W. Wilson, 1938.
       p. 176-180.

3258 Rawlinson, W. F. "The Reception of Wireless Signals
       in Naval Ships." Institute of Electrical Engineers
       Journal, LXXV (September 1934), 293-311.

3258a Ray, Thomas W. "The Bureaus Go On Forever."
       USNIP, XCIV (1968), 50-63.
       Naval administration.

3259 Read, C. "More Light on the London Naval Treaty of
       1930." American Philosophical Society of Pro-
       ceedings, XCIII (1949), 290-308.

3260 Read, William A. "Anti-Submarine Measures Old and
       New." USNIP, LXVII (1941), 638-640.

3261 "A Real Entente Cordiale: The American Submarine
       Flotilla in Ecuadorian Waters." Bulletin of the
       Pan American Union, LIII (September 1921), 277-
       281.

3262 Reams, Benton. The Grumman F3F Series. Aircraft
      Profiles, no. 92. Leatherhead, Surrey, England:
      Profile Publications, n. d.

3263 "Recalling the Marines. " Outlook, CLVII (February
      25, 1931), 288-289.
      From Nicaragua.

3264 "Recommendations of the Naval Board: Summary of
      Report. " Current History, XLIX (February 1939),
      53-54.

3265 "Record Building Program is Now Launched for the
      Nation's New Navy: With a Fighting Fleet Second
      to None the Goal in View, Bids are Opened for
      Construction of 21 Vessels of Various Classes. "
      U. S. News, (July 22-29, 1933), 15.

3266 "Red Cross Nursing and the Navy. " American Journal
      of Nursing, XL (September 1940), 981-984.

3266a Redman, Rod. "The F9C-2 Sparrowhawk. " Air Clas-
      sics, IX (April 1973), 14-17, 78.

3267 Reed, Byron L. "The Contributions of the Coast Guard
      to the Development of Alaska. " USNIP, LV (1929),
      406.

3268 _____. "Starting a Ship's Library in the Coast
      Guard. " USNIP, L (1924), 436-438.

3269 Reed, James. "Navy Yard Administration as a Prob-
      lem in Industrial Engineering. " USNIP, XLVI
      (1920), 509-528.

3270 Reed, Kendall S. "The Wreck of the Tacoma (PG-
      32). " USNIP, XCVII (1971), 74-76.
      She ran aground on a reef off the harbor of
      Vera Cruz, Mexico, in January 1924.

3271 Reed, William A. "Sea Power and Air Power in
      1940. " USNIP, LXVII (1941), 478-480.

3272 Reeves, John W. "Engineering Forms for Destroy-
      ers. " USNIP, LIV (1928), 265-267.

3273 Reeves, Joseph M. "Aviation in the Fleet. " USNIP,

LV (1929), 867-870.

3274 "Re-Gunning a Battleship's Turrets. " SciAmer, CXXI
      (August 16, 1919), 161.

3275 Reichmann, William D. "The Supremacy of the Battle-
      ship. " SciAmer, CXXII (May 22, 1920), 569.

3276 Reid, George C. "The Control of the Flow of Traffic
      in the United States from Source to Shipboard. "
      Unpublished General Staff Memorandum, Files of
      the U. S. Army Military History Research Collec-
      tion, 1924.

3277 _____. "Is Proper Provision Made for Cooperation
      of Army and Navy Air Forces in Coastal Warfare?"
      Unpublished General Staff Memorandum, Files of
      the U. S. Army Military History Research Collec-
      tion, 1924.
              This memorandum by a Marine Corps colonel,
      like all memos cited herein, was used in connec-
      tion with the educational aims of the Army War
      College in the years between the wars.

3278 _____. "The Organization of Negro Combat Units."
      Unpublished General Staff Memorandum, Files of
      the U. S. Army Military History Research Collec-
      tion, 1924.
              One of the few pre-World War II studies written
      from a Marine Corps background.

3279 Reilly, Henry J. "Our Crumbling National Defense. "
      Century, CXIII (March 1927), 513-522.

3280 _____. "The Truth About the Navy. " Outlook,
      CLIX (November 25, 1931), 395-397+.

3281 Reisinger, Harold G. "Coast Guard Ambulance
      Flights. " USNIP, LXII (1936), 57-64.

3282 _____. "The Flying Lifeboat of the Coast Guard."
      USNIP, LIX (1933), 81-88.

3283 _____. "The Flying Reserve of the Leathernecks."
      USNIP, LIX (1933), 1466-1472.

3284 _____. "The High Quality of Our Reserve. " USNIP,

LX (1934), 1526-1528.

3285 _____. "La Palabra Del Grinto: Leadership of the Nicaraguan National Guard. " USNIP, LXI (1935), 215-221.

3286 _____. "The Naval Aviator in Reserve. " USNIP, LX (1934), 381-388.

3287 "Remember the Panay. " Time, XXXIV (October 2, 1939), 25.

3288 Rentz, George S. "Naval Aviators Relieve Flood Victims. " USNIP, LV (1929), 690-692.

3289 "Repairing the Shenandoah. " SciAmer, CXXXI (July 1924), 20.

3290 "Replacement of the Shenandoah. " In: U.S. Congress. House. Naval Affairs Committee. Hearings on Sundry Legislation Affecting the Naval Establishment, 1925-1926. 69th Cong. , 1st sess. 1925-1926. p. 539-1176.

3291 "Report of the Navy General Board. " Aviation, X (February 14, 1921), 198-199.
Concerning the naval air service and its relation to the rest of the fleet.

3292 "Reports on Scientific Results of the United States Antarctic Service Expedition, 1939-1941: A Symposium. " American Philosophical Society Proceedings, LXXXIX (1945), 1-398.
The Byrd Expedition.

3293 "Reports on the Scientific Results of the Byrd Expedition: Abstracts. " Science, XCIV (December 12, 1941), 548-560.

3294 "Rescue Fails, Byrd Continues Lonely Vigil. " Newsweek, IV (August 4, 1934), 20.

3295 "Rescuing the Admiral. " Commonweal, XX (August 24, 1934), 398.
Refers to Byrd's "stay" in Antarctica.

3296 Reuse, Harry J. "Improved Maneuvering and Mooring Board. " USNIP, XLV (1919), 1009-1026.

3297 Reynolds, Clark G. The Fast Carriers: The Forging
      of an Air Navy. New York: McGraw-Hill, 1968.
      498p.
      Contains some data relative to our period.

3298 Reynolds, John L. "Recreation for the Navy. " Rec-
      reation, XXXIV (February 1941), 663-664.

3299 Rhodes, Peter C. "Bolstering Far East Defenses. "
      USNIP, LXVI (1940), 1506-1509.
      Reprinted from the July 30, 1940 issue of Japan
      Advertiser.

3300 Rice, Homer M. "Navy Point, World's Smallest Base."
      USNIP, LXI (1935), 1795-1796.

3301 Richards, Carmen, ed. "Louis H. Roddis. " In: his
      Minnesota Writers. Minneapolis: Denison, 1961.
      p. 272-275.

3302 Richards, David K. K. "The Beginnings of Pearl Har-
      bor, July 1909 to December 7, 1941. " USNIP,
      LXX (1944), 536-545.

3303 Richards, George. "Flying Paymasters. " USNIP, LV
      (1929), 685.

3304 _____. "The Monroe Doctrine: Its Application To-
      day. " USNIP, LVIII (1932), 1405-1431.

3305 _____. "Naval and Military Decorations. " USNIP,
      LVII (1931), 575-583.

3306 Richards, Norman. Giants in the Sky. Chicago:
      Childrens Press, 1967. 143p.
      A pictorial of airships, including those operated
      by the U. S. Navy.

3307 Richardson, C. W. E. "Aircraft Carriers: Comparative
      Strengths of the Rival Navies. " Illustrated London
      News, CXCIX (November 22, 1941), 645.

3308 Richardson, Clifford G. "Teaching Landing Operations
      with Models. " USNIP, LX (1934), 796-800.

3309   Richardson, Gill M.   "A Method of Search for the
       [Airship] Akron. "   USNIP, LX (1934), 470-472.

3310   Richardson, Holden C.   "Airplane and Seaplane En-
       gineering. "   Society of Automotive Engineers Trans-
       actions, XIV (1919), 333-372.

3311   _____. _____. Aviation, VII (August 1, 1919),
       36-38.

3312   _____. "Some Lessons of the Transatlantic Flight."
       Aviation, IX (July 1, 1919), 445-446.
              These articles refer to the flight and engineer-
       ing of the NC's.

3313   Richardson, Leslie E.   "Striking for Wings. "   USNIP,
       LVII (1931), 1242-1244.
              On becoming a naval pilot.

3314   Richardson, William A.   Manual of Athletic Require-
       ments, United States Naval Academy.   2nd ed. ,
       rev. and enl.   Annapolis: U. S. Naval Institute,
       1922.   573p.

3315   Richenor, F. A.   "Rear Admiral Moffett's Views on
       the Need for Flying-Deck Cruisers. "   Aero Digest,
       XX (February 1932), 28+.

3316   _____. "Retain Admiral Moffett. "   Aero Digest,
       XXII (February 1933), 15+.

3317   Richmond, Herbert.   "The Case Against Big Battle-
       ships. "   19th Century, CXVI (August 1934), 186-
       193.

3318   _____. Economy and Naval Security.   London:
       Benn, 1931.   227p.

3319   _____. "The Leased Bases. "   Fortnightly, CLIV
       (October 1940), 385-389.

3320   _____. "Geneva and the Navies. "   19th Century,
       CXII (September 1932), 279-288.

3321   _____. "Immediate Problems of Naval Reduction."
       Foreign Affairs, IX (April 1931), 371-388.

3322 _____ . "Mahan and Sea Power Today." Spectator,
CLXV (September 27, 1940), 313.

3323 _____ . "Naval Conference, Prestige or Common
Sense?" Fortnightly, CXLIV (December 1935),
661-669.

3324 _____ . "Naval Disarmament." 19th Century, CXVI
(December 1934), 640-650.

3325 _____ . "Naval Problems of 1935." Foreign Affairs, XIII (October 1934), 45-58.

3326 _____ . "Naval Rearmament?" 19th Century, CXIX
(January 1936), 38-46.

3327 _____ . The Naval Role in Modern Warfare. Oxford Pamphlets on World Affairs, no. 26. New
York: Oxford University Press, 1940. 32p.

3328 _____ . Naval Training. Oxford, Eng.: Oxford
University Press, 1933. 141p.

3329 _____ . The Navy. London: William Hodge, 1937.
128p.
     The three citations immediately above, while
British in origin, contain some ideas useful to and
employed by the American navy of our period.

3330 _____ . "Security Depends on Sea Power." Fortnightly, CXLVI (August 1936), 129-139.

3331 _____ . Sea Power in the Modern World. New
York: Reynal & Hitchcock, 1934. 323p. Rpr. 1973.
     Considered heretical in its time, the author's
work opposed the concept of fleet concentration
stressed by Mahan, giant battleships, and spon-
sored joint commands among ground, sea, and air
forces.

3332 Rickover, Hyman G. Alternating Current in the U.S.
Navy. New York: Society of the Naval Architects
and Marine Engineers, 1941. 15p.

3333 _____ . "International Law and the Submarine."
USNIP, LXI (1935), 1213-1237.

3334   Riddiford, A. B. , Jr.   "Airplane Carrier: The U. S. S.
       Lexington. " Sibley Journal, XLII (June 1928), 196-
       197+.

3335   Riddle, Truman P.   "Enlisted Men's Families. "
       USNIP, LXVI (1939), 83-88.

3336   _____ .   "Recreational Camps for Enlisted Men. "
       USNIP, LXIII (1937), 1765-1768.

3337   Ridgely, Randolph, Jr.   "Watchmen of Our Coast
       Line. " SciAmer, CXLVIII (April 1933), 216-218.
       The Coast Guard.

3338   Riesenberg, Felix.   "The Naval Reserve. " USNIP, L
       (1924), 654-655.
       Taken from the February 16, 1924 issue of
       Nautical Gazette.

3339   _____ .   Sea War: The Story of the U. S. Merchant
       Marine in World War II.   New York: Rinehart,
       1956.   320p.
       Contains some data relative to the last year or
       two of our compilation.

3340   _____ .   "Semper Paratus. "   In: his Yankee Skippers
       to the Rescue: A Record of Gallant Rescues on the
       North Atlantic by American Seamen.   New York:
       Dodd, Mead, 1940.   p. 186-208.
       The work of the Coast Guard.

3341   Rigg, E. H.   "Launching the Airplane Carrier Saratoga."
       Marine Engineering, XXX (July 1925), 391-395.

3342   Riggs, Arthur S.   "What The Country Gets for Its
       Navy Dollar. "   Review of Reviews, XCIV (Decem-
       ber 1936), 32-35.

3343   "Rights and Duties of Neutral States in Naval and
       Aerial War: Draft Convention, with Comments,
       Prepared by the Research in International Law of
       the Harvard Law School. " American Journal of
       International Law, XXXIII (July 1939), Supplement,
       167-817.

3344   Rindahl, Gilbert F.   "A History of the U. S. S. North
       Dakota. "   North Dakota History, XXXII (1965), 107-

116.
Commissioned in 1910, BB-29 was decommissioned in 1923 and sold out in 1931.

3345   Rippy, James F.   The Caribbean Danger Zone.   New
York: Putnam, 1940.   296p.

3346   "Risks Men Face in Submarines. "   Popular Mechanics,
XLIX (March 1928), 353-355.

3347   Roane, Charles P.   "The Carrier Story: A Saga of Sea
Power. "   Bureau of Ships Journal, I (August 1952),
2-8.
A general history.

3348   Roberts, Walter A.   "The New Naval Bases in the
Caribbean. "   Travel, LXXVI (February 1941), 12-
15.
Those obtained from Great Britain in the trade
for 50 World War I four stacker destroyers.

3349   Robertson, A. H.   "The United States Navy and the
Problem of International Peace. "   Institute for International Relations Proceedings, IV (1929), 18-29.

3350   Robertson, H. T.   "Motor Torpedo Boats. "   USNIP,
LXVI (1940), 1289-1290.

3351   Robinson, Douglas H.   "The Airplane-Carrying Airship: The First Experiment. "   American Aviation
Historical Society Journal, IV (Winter 1959), 265-
268.

3352   _____.   Giants in the Sky: A History of the Rigid
Airship.   Seattle: University of Washington Press,
1973.   376p.

3353   _____.   "The Zeppelin Bomber: High Policy Guided
by Wishful Thinking. "   The Airpower Historian, VII
(July 1961), 130-147.

3354   Robinson, John K.   "Our Navy as a Great Industrial
Asset. "   Iron Age, CIX (June 29, 1922), 1833-1834.

3355   _____.   "The Part of Engineering in Command. "
USNIP, XLIX (1923), 203-220.

3356 _____. "The Wise Man Knows His Tools." USNIP, LI (1925), 1882-1896.

3357 Robinson, O. P. "Expanding Uncle Sam's Underseas Fleet: The Electric Boat Company." Machinery, XLVIII (November 1941), 138-145.

3358 Robinson, S. M. "The United States Battleship New Mexico." Marine Engineering, XXIV (May 1919), 322-334.

3359 Robinson, Theodore D. "Gentlemen, the Navy!" USNIP, LI (1925), 1817-1824.

3360 _____. "The Second Element in Sea Power." USNIP, LII (1926), 1919-1926.

3361 Robinson, Walton L. "America's Heavy Cruisers." SciAmer, CLVI (March 1937), 158-160.

3362 _____. "The Battleship Returns." SciAmer, CLVI (April 1937), 217-219.

3363 _____. "Naval Indispensables." In: William H. Fetridge, ed. The Navy Reader. Indianapolis: Bobbs-Merrill, 1943. p. 62-69. Rpr. 1971.
A rundown on pre-war U. S. cruisers, their classes and statistics.

3364 _____. "Status of the Carrier." SciAmer, CLVII (September 1937), 146-158.

3365 _____. "The Submarine in the Next War." SciAmer, CLVII (July 1937), 22-24.

3366 Robison, Samuel S. A History of Naval Tactics from 1530-1930: The Evolution of Tactical Maxims. Annapolis: U. S. Naval Institute, 1942. 956p.

3367 _____. Robison's Manual of Radio Telegraphy and Telephony for the Use of Naval Electricians. Annapolis: U. S. Naval Institute, 1919. 307p.

3368 Rochester, Harry A. "A Bachelor Looks at the Navy Pay Bills." USNIP, LI (1925), 1455-1458.

3369 _____. "The Navy's Support of Foreign Policy."

USNIP, LVII (1931), 1491-1500.
Refers to the London Naval Treaty.

3370   . "Some Strategical Aspects of Radio. "
USNIP, LIII (1927), 853-857.

3371   . "The Water Rises. " USNIP, LXIII (1937),
215-219.

3372 Rock, George H.   "Better Ships for Less Money. "
USNIP, LIII (1927), 599-605.

3373   . "Costs in Navy Yards. " USNIP, L (1924),
424-435.

3374   . "The Design and Construction of Warships."
USNIP, LVII (1931), 967-970.
Reprinted from the April 1931 issue of Ship-
builder and Marine Engine Builder.

3375   . "The Design of Airplane Carriers: Obser-
vations on the Structure of New Craft With Notes
on the Saratoga and Lexington. " Airway Age, X
(March 1929), 298-301.

3376   . "Planning and Estimating Navy Yards. "
USNIP, XLIX (1923), 969-981.

3377   . "The Ten Thousand Ton Cruisers. " Engineering, CXXX (December 19, 1930), 769-770.

3378   . The 10,000 Ton Treaty Cruisers, with Particular Reference to the Salt Lake City and Pensacola. New York: Society of Naval Architects and
Marine Engineers, 1930. 11p.

3379 Rodd, Herbert C.   "Across the Ocean in the NC-4. "
Wireless Age, VI (August-September 1919), 13-17,
25-28; VII (October 1919), 13-19.

3380 Roddis, Louis H.   "The Bureau of Medicine and Surgery: A Brief History. " USNIP, LXXV (1949),
457-467.

3381   . "The United States Navy and Polar Exploration. " USNIP, LXVIII (1942) 1369-1378.

3382 Rodman, Hugh. "The Sacred Calabash. " USNIP, LIII
      (1927), 867-872.

3383 _____. _____. Journal of the Polynesian Society,
      XXXVII (March 1928), 75-87.

3384 _____. Yarns of a Kentucky Admiral. Indianapolis:
      Bobbs-Merrill, 1928. 320p.

3385 Rodgers, John. "The Spoils of War. " USNIP, LII
      (1926), 2020-2028.
      Refers to the leavings of World War I, particu-
      larly aircraft.

3386 Rodgers, William L. "American Naval Policy and the
      Tri-power Conference at Geneva, 1927. " USNIP,
      LIV (1928), 572-578.

3387 _____. "The Navy as an Aid in Carrying Out Diplo-
      matic Policies. " USNIP, LV (1929), 99-104.

3388 Roe, Thomas G. , author. See U. S. Marine Corps. ,
      no. 4725.

3389 Rogers, Donald I. "Our Ships at Sea: 1941. " In: his
      Since You Went Away. New Rochelle, N. Y. :
      Arlington House, 1973. p. 52-61.
      The undeclared naval war with Germany in the
      Atlantic.

3390 Rogers, G. Sherburne. "Helium, the New Balloon
      Gas. " National Geographic, XXXV (May 1919),
      441-456.

3391 Rogers, Robert E. "The General Mess of a De-
      stroyer. " USNIP. LIV (1928), 360.

3392 _____. "A Shorter and Simpler Aquino Process. "
      USNIP, LIV (1928), 22-25.

3393 Rogers, Royden H. "The World's Experimental Ship
      Model Basins. " USNIP, LXV (1939), 1708-1718.

3394 Rogers, Walter S. "International Electrical Communi-
      cations. " USNIP, LII (1926), 1044-1051.

3395 Roloff, O. S. "One Hundred and Eighty Years of Naval

Recruiting. " USNIP, LXXII (1956), 1300-1308.

3396   Rooks, Albert H. "Character and Success. " USNIP,
       LV (1929), 38-43.

3397   _____. "Entrance Requirements of the U. S. Naval
       Academy. " USNIP, LXI (1935), 1468-1481.

3398   _____. "On the Prevention of War. " USNIP, LIV
       (1928), 257-264.

3399   Roop, Wendell P. "The Naval Policy of the United
       States in the Pacific Area. " USNIP, XLIX (1923),
       409-426.

3400   Roos, S. E. , et al. "Some Geographical Results of the
       Second Byrd Antarctic Expedition, 1933-1935. "
       Geographic Review, XXVII (October 1937), 574-614.

3401   Roosevelt, Elliott. As He Saw It. New York: Duell,
       Sloan and Pearce, 1946. 270p.
           Some data on the President's trips abroad aboard
       American naval vessels, including the voyage which
       resulted in the Atlantic Charter.

3402   Roosevelt, Franklin D. The Call to Battle Stations,
       1941. Vol. X of The Public Papers and Addresses
       of Franklin D. Roosevelt. New York: Random
       House, 1942. Rpr. 1969.
           These Public Papers are part of a 13 volume
       set edited by Samuel I. Rosenman.

3403   _____. "Our Defense is not Limited to One Ocean-
       One Coast: President Roosevelt's Message to
       Congress, Jan. 28, Asking for Expansion of the
       Navy and Strengthening of the Army. " U. S. News,
       VI (January 31, 1938), 5.

3404   _____. "The President Defends His Big Navy Pro-
       gram. " Journal of Commerce, (October 27, 1938),
       20.

3405   _____. "President Roosevelt Discusses National
       Defense Policy: Testimony Before the House Naval
       Affairs Committee. " Commercial and Financial
       Chronicle, CXLVI (February 19, 1938), 1168-1169.

3406 _____ . Roosevelt's Foreign Policy, 1933-1941:
Franklin D. Roosevelt's Unedited Speeches and
Messages. New York: W. Funk, 1942. 634p.

3406a _____ . "Sinking of the Robin Moor: Message to
Congress, June 20, 1941." Vital Speeches, VII
(July 1, 1941), 546+.

3406b _____ . "The Shooting Has Started: Navy Day
Address, October 27, 1941." Vital Speeches, VIII
(November 15, 1941), 66-68.

3407 _____ . War--and Aid to Democracies, 1940. Vol.
IX of The Public Papers and Addresses of Franklin
D. Roosevelt. New York: Random House, 1940.
Rpr. 1969.

3408 _____ . War--and Neutrality, 1939. Vol. VIII of
The Public Papers and Addresses of Franklin D.
Roosevelt. New York: Random House, 1939. Rpr.
1969.

3409 _____ . "Why Naval Aviation Won." U.S. Air
Services, I (July 1919), 7-9.
The flight of the NC's.

3410 Roosevelt, Henry L. "The American Navy." Vital
Speeches, I (November 19, 1934), 117-119.

3411 _____ . "Providing a Navy Adequate for Defense
Under the Limitations of the Treaty." U.S. News,
II (September 23, 1933), 9.
The treaty was, of course, the Washington Treaty,
1922, and London Treaty, 1930.

3412 _____ . "The United States Navy and Its Functions."
USNIP, LXII (1936), 1383-1390.
A February 19, 1936 speech before the Metro-
politan Club of Washington, D.C.

3413 _____ . "What is an Adequate Navy?" Vital
Speeches, II (December 16, 1935), 179-182.

3414 _____ . _____ . In: Julia E. Johnson, ed. Peace
and Rearmament. Vol. XI of The Reference Shelf.
New York: H.W. Wilson, 1938. p. 166-168.

3415   _____. "Why the New Naval Building Program is
        Necessary. " SciAmer, CL (April 1934), 186-188+.

3416   Roosevelt, Nicholas. "Japan's Challenge to American
        Policy. " Asia, XXXV (February 1935), 76-81.

3417   _____. The Restless Pacific. New York: C. Scrib-
        ner's, 1928. 291p.
        A study of Far Eastern questions.

3418   Roosevelt, Theodore, Jr. "Maintenance of the Treaty
        Navy. " USNIP, XLIX (1923), 739-746.

3419   _____. "What Navy Reduction Means to You. "
        Ladies' Home Journal, XXXIX (May 1922), 6.

3420   "Roosevelt and Churchill Meet at Sea and Draft a Long-
        Term Program for the Post-Nazi World. " Life,
        XI (August 25, 1941), 26-29.
        The Atlantic Charter.

3421   Ropp, Theodore. War in the Modern World. Durham,
        N. C. : Duke University Press, 1959. 400p.
        A rev. ed. was published by Macmillan in 1966.

3422   Roscoe, Theodore. On the Seas and in the Skies: A
        History of the U. S. Navy's Air Power. New York:
        Hawthorne, 1970. 690p.

3423   Roseberry, C. R. The Challenging Skies: The Colorful
        Story of Aviation's Most Exciting Years, 1919-1939.
        Garden City, N. Y. : Doubleday, 1966. 533p.
        Some considerable mention of the development of
        naval aviation, with other data relative to our
        period.

3424   Rosendahl, Charles E. "Airship Costs and Casual-
        ties. " U. S. Air Services, XXI (January 1936),
        21-26.

3425   _____. "Airship Personnel. " USNIP, LV (1929),
        305-310.

3426   _____. "Commander Rosendahl Pleads for U. S.
        Airships. " Science News Letter, XXXIII (May 7,
        1938), 301.

3427 _____. "Experiences of the ZR-3 in Crossing the Atlantic Ocean and of the Shenandoah in Making the Trip Across the American Continent. " Society of Automotive Engineers Journal, XV (December 1924), 484-486.

3428 _____. "The Loss of the Akron. " USNIP, LX (1934), 921-933.

3429 _____. "Moffett Field. " USNIP, LXXXIII (1957), 1347-1348.

3430 _____. "The Mooring and Ground Handling of a Rigid Airship. " American Society of Mechanical Engineers Transactions, LV (1933), AER 55-6, 45-52.

3431 _____. "Mooring Masts and Landing Trucks for Airships. " Society of Automotive Engineers Journal, XXV (July 1929), 34-38.

3432 _____. "Reflections on the Airship Situation. " USNIP, LIII (1927), 745-758.

3433 _____. "Report on the Loss of the U. S. Airship Shenandoah. " Engineer, CXLII (October 8, 1926), 399-400.

3434 _____. "U. S. S. Los Angeles. " USNIP, LVII (1931), 751-756.

3435 _____. Up Ship! New York: Dodd, Mead, 1931. 311p.
       Experiences with the Shenandoah and Los Angeles.

3436 _____. What About the Airship? New York: Charles Scribner's, 1938. 437p.
       Contains data on his command of the Akron.

3437 _____. "What Really Happened to the Akron." Liberty Magazine, X (December 16, 1933), 4-8.

3438 Roskill, Stephen W. Naval Policy Between the Wars. London: Collins, 1968--.
       An ongoing series the first volume of which is entitled The Period of Anglo-American Antagonism, 1919-1929.

3439 _____ . The Strategy of Sea Power: Its Development
and Application, Based on the Lees-Knowles Lectures Delivered in the University of Cambridge,
1961. London: Collins, 1964. 287p.

3440 _____ . The War At Sea. History of the Second
World War: United Kingdom Military Series. 3
vols. London: H. M. Stationery Office, 1954.

3441 _____ . White Ensign: The British Navy at War,
1939-1945. Annapolis: U. S. Naval Institute, 1960.
480p.
      These two citations contain some data relative to
the last year or so of this compilation.

3442 Roskolenko, Harry, ed. "The Antarctic: Admiral
Richard E. Byrd. " In: his Solo: The Great Adventures Alone. Chicago: Playboy Press, 1973. p. 93-
109.

3443 Ross, Frank, Jr. Historic Plane Models: Their
Stories and How to Make Them. New York: Loth-
rop, Lee & Shepard, 1973. 188p.
      Aircraft from our period include the NC-4 and
Admiral Byrd's The Floyd Bennett.

3444 Rossell, Henry E. The Battle Cruiser. New York:
Society of Naval Architects and Marine Engineers,
1934. 9p.

3445 _____ . "Battlecruiser: Extracts. " Marine Engineering, XL (January 1935), 10-14.

3446 _____ . "The Case of the Battleship. " Marine
Engineering, XLII (June-July 1937), 246-250, 326-
330.

3447 _____ . "The Colleges, the Technical School, and
the Naval Academy. " USNIP, LVI (1930), 123-131.

3448 _____ . "The Development of the Modern Cruiser."
SciAmer, CL (January 1934), 18-20.

3449 _____ . "Ship Scrapping: Extracts. " Marine Engineering, XXIX (December 1924), 733-735.

3450 Rothers, L. "Electricity as the Motive Power for

Ships. " USNIP, L (1924), 1004-1008.

3451 Rougeron, C. "Protection Against Bombs and High
      Angle Shell Fire. " USNIP, LVIII (1932), 229-237.

3452 Rowe, Leo S. "The Havana Meeting of the Ministers
      of Foreign Affairs of the American Republics, with
      the Text of Resolutions. " Bulletin of the Pan
      American Union, LXXIV (September 1940), 609-625.

3453 Rowe, Lionel L. "The U. S. S. Gannet Visits Attu,
      Aleutian Islands, May 28, 1932. " USNIP, LXIV
      (1938), 831-836.
          The Bird-class minesweeper AM-41.

3454 Rowell, Chester H. "Has America a Naval Policy?"
      Amerasia, I (March 1937), 5-8.

3455 Rowell, Ross E. "The Air Service in Minor Warfare."
      USNIP, LV (1929), 871-877.
          Describes the first use of dive-bombing in
      Nicaragua.

3456 _____ . "Aircraft in Bush Warfare. " Marine Corps
      Gazette, XIV (September 1929), 180-203.
          A detailed treatise on Marine aviation in Nica-
      ragua.

3457 _____ . "Annual Report cf Aircraft Squadrons,
      Second Brigade, U. S. Marine Corps, July 1, 1927,
      to June 20, 1928. " Marine Corps Gazette, XIII
      (December 1928), 248-265.
          The use of this group in Nicaragua.

3458 _____ . "Experiences with the Air Service in Minor
      Warfare. " Unpublished Lecture, G-3 Course 27,
      Files of the U. S. Army Military History Research
      Collection, 1929.
          Prepared by a Marine major based on his ex-
      periences in Nicaragua.

3459 Rucker, Colby G. "Excess Weight in Submarines. "
      USNIP, LXII (1936), 1755-1758.

3460 _____ . "Leadership Can't be Taught. " USNIP,
      LXIII (1937), 1235-1238.

3461 Ruge, Friedrich. Der Seekrieg, the German Navy's
      Story. Annapolis: U. S. Naval Institute, 1957.
      440p.

3462 _____. Sea Warfare, 1939-1945: A German View.
      London: Cassell, 1957. 337p.
      The above two editions of the same work contain
      some information relative to the last years of this
      compilation.

3463 Ruoff, Frederick A. "The Story of a Dream. " Marine
      Corps Gazette, XXXIV (February 1950), 14-21.
      The Marine Corps Institute, 1919-1950.

3464 Rush, Charles W.   The Complete Book of Submarines.
      Cleveland: World, 1958. 159p.

3465 Russell, Bruce. No Clear and Present Danger: A
      Skeptical View of the United States Entry into World
      War II. New York: Harper & Row, 1972.

3466 Russell, Charles F. "Suggestions for Improving Navy
      Morale. " USNIP, XLVII (1921), 169-176.

3467 Russell, Herbert. "America's Naval Policy: A British
      View. " USNIP, LI (1925), 1267-1270.

3468 _____. "Concerning Guns. " USNIP, LIV (1928),
      419-421.
      Reprinted from the February 15, 1928 issue of
      Naval and Military Record.

3469 _____. "A Curious Plea for Big American Building
      Program. " USNIP, L (1924), 1319-1324.

3470 _____. "The Freedom of the Seas. " USNIP, LVII
      (1931), 125-127.

3471 _____. "Future Naval Tactics. " USNIP, LVI
      (1930), 352-354.

3472 _____. "Gun Power and Battle Tactics. " USNIP,
      LIV (1928), 1104-1106.

3473 _____. "Jutland and Modern Tactics. " USNIP, L
      (1924), 1930-1932.

3474 _____ . "Limitations of Modern Sea War. " USNIP,
LI (1925), 1546-1548.

3475 _____ . "The Line of Disarmament, and Disarmament Difficulties. " USNIP, LII (1926), 362-367.

3476 _____ . "The Mobility of the Capital Ship. " USNIP,
LXIV (1938), 120-122.

3477 _____ . "Naval Bases. " USNIP, LII (1926), 367-
370.

3478 _____ . "The Pacific Zone: British View of the
United States Naval Policy. " USNIP, LI (1925),
1480-1488.

3479 _____ . "Peace Without Security: A British View. "
USNIP, LI (1925), 814-817.

3480 _____ . "Sea Power, a Factor for Peace. " USNIP,
LXIV (1938), 1819-1822.

3481 _____ . "Sea Power, the Challenging Form of War."
USNIP, LXIV (1938), 772-774.

3482 _____ . "Sea Power Without Bases. " USNIP, LXIV
(1938), 1197-1199.

3483 _____ . "The Security of Armaments. " USNIP,
LVI (1930), 458-460.

3484 _____ . "The Shadow of the Rising Sun. " USNIP,
LI (1925), 1514-1516.
Refers to naval advances by Japan.

3485 _____ . "The Ship of Heresy. " USNIP, LII (1926),
1255-1258.

3486 _____ . "Smaller Fighting Ships: The Reaction from
Colossal Displacement. " USNIP, LI (1925), 2349-
2362.

3487 _____ . "Submarine Warfare. " USNIP, LV (1929),
159-161.

3488 _____ . "Torpedo Warfare. " USNIP, LVII (1931),
268-270.

3489   _____ . "The Washington Experiment. " <u>USNIP</u>, LI
            (1925), 675-678.
            Refers to the Washington Naval Treaty.

3490   _____ . "What Happens in the Absence of Sea
            Power. " <u>USNIP</u>, LXIV (1938), 137-140.

3491   _____ . "What the Fighting Seaman Has to Face. "
            <u>USNIP</u>, LXV (1939), 1800-1801.

3492   _____ . "Will the Capital Ship Pass?" <u>USNIP</u>, LI
            (1925), 1548-1551.

3493   Russell, John H.   "The Birth of the FMF. " <u>USNIP</u>,
            LXXII (1946), 49-51.

3494   _____ . "The Fleet Marine Force. " <u>USNIP</u>, LXII
            (1936), 1408-1410.

3495   Russell, William H.   "Amphibious Doctrines of A. T.
            Mahan. " <u>Marine Corps Gazette</u>, XL (February
            1956), 34-42.
            How these have been interpreted since 1885.

3496   _____ . "Diplomatic Relations Between the United
            States and Nicaragua, 1920-1933. " Unpublished
            PhD Dissertation, University of Chicago, 1953.

3497   Ryan, Paul B.   "How Young We Were. " <u>USNIP</u>, XCIV
            (1968), 26-36.
            U. S. naval over optimism toward any thought of
            a sea war with Japan in the years before Pearl
            Harbor.

3498   "SOS from the Navy. " <u>Current Opinion,</u> LXXV (June
            1924), 753-756.

3499   Saerchinger, Cesar.   "Defending our Interests in the
            Pacific. " <u>Bulletin of the Story Behind the Head-
            lines,</u> II (February 28, 1939), 1-13.
            A publication printed by Columbia University
            Press.

3500   "Safety Belt: Americas' Zone Annoys the Powers But
            They'll Have to Accept It. " <u>Newsweek,</u> XIV (Octo-
            ber 16, 1939), 27.

3501   "Safety Zone: The Declaration of Panama. " Scholas-
       tic, XXXV (October 16, 1939), 9.

3502   "Sale, Navy, Sale, by a Naval Officer's Wife. " Out-
       look, CLIII (December 18, 1929), 612-613.

3503   Salt Lake City, U. S. S.   The Story of the U. S. S. Salt
       Lake City, 1929 to 1946.   Long Beach, Calif. :
       Green's, 1946.   72p.
            In reality the World War II cruise book of CA-
       25; however, by including a considerable amount of
       pre-war data and photos, this compilation must be
       considered a good bit more.

3504   "Salt Water Maintenance: The Navy's Great Overhaul
       Base at San Diego. " Aviation, XXXIX (December
       1940), 38-41.

3505   "The Salvage of the U. S. Submarine Squalus. " Engi-
       neer, CLXVIII (December 15-22, 1939), 584-586,
       606-608.

3506   Samuels, Leo M.   "Airplane Hydrography. " USNIP,
       LV (1929), 509-510.

3507   Sanborn, Frederic R.   Design for War: A Study of
       Secret Power Politics, 1937-1941.   New York: De-
       vin-Adair, 1951.   607p.

3508   Sanford, H. B. , jt. author.   See Westervelt, George
       C. , no. 4284.

3509   "San Francisco, New Orleans, U. S. Cruisers Launched.
       Marine Review, LXIII (May 1933), 17.

3510   Sargeant, Thomas A.   "America, Britain, and the Nine
       Power Treaty. " Unpublished PhD Dissertation,
       Fletcher School of Law and Diplomacy, 1969.

3511   Saulsbury, William.   "American Naval Efficiency. "
       Current History, XVI (April 1922), 32-33.

3512   Saunders, H. E.   "Flight of Admiral Byrd to the South
       Pole and the Exploration of Marie Byrd Land. "
       American Philosophical Society Proceedings, LXXXII
       (1940), 801-820.

3513 Savage, Carlton. The Policy of the United States
      Toward Maritime Commerce in War. 2 vols.
      Washington: U. S. Government Printing Office, 1934-
      1936. Rpr. 1969.

3514 Scammell, J. M. "The Army-Navy Fusion Mistake."
      USNIP, L (1924), 999-1002.

3515 _____. "A Combined Staff." USNIP, XLVII (1921),
      1553-1558.

3516 _____. "Early Indoctrination of New Recruits. "
      USNIP, XLIX (1923), 1447-1450.

3517 _____. "Higher Naval Education. " USNIP, XLVIII
      (1922), 753-759.

3518 _____. "The Industrial College of the Armed
      Forces: Twenty Years of Army-Navy Co-operation."
      USNIP, LXXIII (1947), 295-301.
      Covers the years 1927-1947.

3519 _____. "Military Genius and the Naval War Col-
      lege. " USNIP, L (1924), 61-67.

3520 _____. "The Nation in Arms and National Doc-
      trine. " USNIP, LI (1925), 1684-1695.

3521 _____. "Perseus and Sphinx; or, Science and War."
      USNIP, LIII (1927), 179-183.

3522 Scarborough, James B. Some Problems on the Lift
      and Rolling Movement of Airplane Wings. U. S.
      National Advisory Committee for Aeronautics Re-
      port, no. 200. Washington: Government Printing
      Office, 1925. 16p.
      Based on a 1923 Johns Hopkins University thesis.

3523 "Schedule of Wages for Civil Employees Under the
      Naval Establishment. " Monthly Labor Review, LVII
      (October 1923), 838-840.

3524 _____. Monthly Labor Review, LVIII (February
      1924), 315-318.

3525 Schilling, Warner R. "Weapons Doctrine and Arms
      Control: A Case from the Good Old Days. " Journal

of Conflict Resolution, VII (1963), 192-214.
What happened to the U. S. recommendation made
at Versailles for the outlawing of submarines and
blockades.

3526 Schlesinger, Arthur M. , Jr. The Age of Roosevelt.
3 vols. Boston: Houghton, Mifflin, 1959-1960.
Some useful data on our years.

3527 Schmidt, Carl S. "The Navy: Its Contact with Congress. " USNIP, LIX (1933), 239-245.

3528 Schmidt, H. "Aircraft Engine Relations to the Needs
of Naval Aviation. " Society of Automotive Engineers Journal, XVIII (May 1926), 509-513.

3529 Schmidt, Hans R. , Jr. The United States Occupation
of Haiti, 1915-1934. New Brunswick, N. J. :
Rutgers University Press, 1971. 303p.

3530 _____. "The United States Occupation of Haiti,
1915-1934. " Unpublished PhD Dissertation, Rutgers
University, 1968.

3531 Schmitt, Bernadotte E. "The United States on the
Verge of World War II. " In: his The Fashion and
Future of History. Cleveland: Press of Western
Reserve University, 1960. p. 165-182.
Reprinting of an address given on April 29, 1941.

3532 Schoeffel, Malcom F. "The Objective of Aerial Warfare. " USNIP, LXIV (1938), 163-174.

3533 _____. "Tactics of Large Aircraft Forces. " USNIP,
LIX (1933), 376-383.

3534 Schofield, Frank H. "The Heart of the Navy. " USNIP,
LIV (1928), 634-639.

3535 _____. "Incidents and Present Day Aspects of Naval
Strategy. " USNIP, XLIX (1923), 777-800.

3536 _____. "Naval Strategy. " USNIP, L (1924), 1408-
1421.

3537 _____. "Some Effects of the Washington Conference
in American Naval Strategy: The Present Status of

U. S. Naval Shops and Bases. " Unpublished Lecture, G-2 Course 3, Files of the U. S. Army Military History Research Collection, 1923.
The author was a Navy rear admiral.

3538   . "The U. S. Naval Reserve Force: What It
Is, What It Ought to Be. " USNIP, L (1924), 1453-
1472.

3539 "School for Deep Sea Divers at the Washington Navy
Yard. " Popular Mechanics, LXXV (March 1941),
386-388.

3540 Schornstheimer, Graser. "America's Present Naval
Organization. " Current History, XIX (October
1923), 131-134.

3541   . "Our Navy Unready for War. " Current
History, XVII (January 1923), 624-631.

3542   . "The Renewal of Naval Competition. " Current History, XVII (November 1922), 239-248.

3543 Schornstheimer, Gregory. "The Airplane Bomb vs.
the Battleship. " Current History, XIV (September
1921), 923-927.

3544 Schroeder, Paul W. The Axis Alliance and Japanese-
American Relations, 1941. Ithaca, N. Y.: Cornell
University Press, 1958. 246p.

3545 Schubert, Paul. Come on, Texas. New York: J. Cape
& H. Smith, 1930. 244p.
Texas ship biography.

3546 Schultheis, F. D. A Primer of the Pacific Area.
Seattle: University of Washington, 1941. 73p.
A mimeographed guide written in brief form with
encyclopedic arrangement.

3547 Schultz, Leonard P. Fishes of the Phoenix and Samoan
Islands Collected in 1939 During the Expedition of
the U. S. S. Bushnell. United States National Museum Bulletin, no. 180. Washington: U. S. Government Printing Office, 1943. 316p.

3548 Schumacker, Theodor L. "Protection Against Underwater Attack. " <u>USNIP</u>, XLIX (1923), 1261-1274.

3549 _____, jt. author. <u>See</u> Manning, George C. , no.
2417.

3550 Schuon, Karl, ed. <u>The Leathernecks: An Informal</u>
<u>History of the United States Marine Corps. Articles</u>
<u>Selected from Leatherneck, a Periodical.</u> New
York: Watts, 1969. 277p.

3551 _____. <u>U. S. Marine Corps Biographical Dictionary.</u>
New York: Watts, 1963. 278p.

3552 _____. <u>U. S. Navy Biographical Dictionary.</u> New
York: Watts, 1965. 277p.

3553 Schuyler, Garret L. "Bombing Radius as Affected by
Wind. " <u>USNIP</u>, LI (1925), 2242-2243.

3554 _____. "The Distribution of Shots in Long Range
Salvos. " <u>USNIP</u>, LV (1929), 24-26.

3555 _____. "Empirical Representations of Experimental
Data Involving Several Variables. " <u>USNIP</u>, LVIII
(1932), 88-90.

3556 _____. "An Introduction to the Use of Nomograms
or Alignment Charts. " <u>USNIP</u>, XLVII (1921), 547-
557.

3557 _____. "A Note on Off-Shore Positions as Deter-
mined by Sextant Altitudes of Distant Mountain
Peaks. " <u>USNIP</u>, XLVIII (1922), 259-261.

3558 _____. "Pattern Sizes in Formation Bombing. "
<u>USNIP</u>, LVI (1930), 1126-1128.

3559 _____. "The Size and Spacing of Units in Certain
Large Scale High Explosive Depots. " <u>USNIP</u>, LVI
(1930), 31-32.

3560 _____. "Some Sound Phenomena Connected with
Gunfire. " <u>USNIP</u>, XLVII (1921), 345-350.

3561 Schwartz, Andrew J. <u>America and the Russo-Finnish</u>
<u>War.</u> Washington: Public Affairs Press, 1960.
103p.

3562 "Science in the Navy." SciAmer, CXLIX (November 1933), 228.

3563 Scott, F. P. "Aviation Training in Peace and War."
      USNIP, LVII (1931), 1273-1276.
      Reprinted from the July 1, 1936 issue of Aeroplane.

3564 Scott, Hoyt S. "The Naval Communications Reserve."
      USNIP, LXVI (1940), 369-371.

3565 Scott, Sampson. "Three Functions and Three Needs of
      the Naval Reserve." USNIP, L (1924), 1646-1657.

3566 Scroggs, William O., jt. author. See Shepardson,
      Whitney H., no. 3615.

3567 "Sea Going Good Samaritans: The Bering Sea Patrol."
      Popular Mechanics, LIX (January 1933), 33-37.

3568 "Sea Going Soldiers." Popular Mechanics, LXXV
      (February 1941), 216-219.
      U. S. Marines.

3569 "Sea Law: Which Should Come First, Conference or
      Cruisers?" Outlook, CLI (February 13, 1929), 250.

3570 "Sea Phone Aids Rescue of Submarine Crews, Water
      Parachutes Lifts Survivors to the Surface." Popular Mechanics, LXII (August 1934), 254-255.

3571 Sea Power, [Editors of.] "Fiske's Folly: Torpedo
      Planes." In: William H. Fetridge, ed. The Navy
      Reader. Indianapolis: Bobbs-Merrill, 1943. p.137-
      141. Rpr. 1971.
          Prepared for a 1942 issue of Sea Power, this
      brief article discusses the life and career of Rear
      Admiral Bradley A. Fiske, who figured prominently
      in Vol. IV of this series, his various inventions,
      including his torpedo-plane idea. It is finished with
      a discussion of naval torpedo planes in service by
      1942.

3572 "Sea Power: An Anglo-American Front." Literary Digest, CXVII (June 30, 1934), 16.

3573 "Sea Power and Pacific Destiny: The London Naval

Conference. " Literary Digest, CXXI (January 18, 1936), 15.

3574 "Sea Power and Parity Around the Table: The Delegates Prepare for the London Conference, December 6. " Literary Digest, CXX (November 23, 1935), 13-14.

3575 "Sea Power, Bulwark of Peace. " Literary Digest, CXX (October 26, 1935), 24+.

3576 "Sea Race. " Collier's, XCIX (January 16, 1937), 66. Naval rearmament.

3577 "A Seagoing Air Fleet Now a Permanent Part of the United States Navy. " Popular Mechanics, XXXIV (September 1920), 354-355.

3578 Seamans, A. B. "Armed Merchantmen a Factor in Naval Warfare. " Current History, XXX (July 1929), 593-602.

3579 Seamell, J. M. "Higher Naval Education. " USNIP, XLVIII (1922), 753-759.

3580 "Seamen of the Deep: Training for Sub Duty Speeded." Newsweek, XVIII (October 6, 1941), 30-31.

3580a "The Seaplane That Sailed to Glory. " Air Classics, II (May 1966), 14-18.
        The flight of the PN-9's cross country and on to Hawaii in 1925.

3581 "The Second Meeting of Ministers of Foreign Affairs of the American Republics: Text of Secretary Hull's Address, July 22, and Text of the Final Act and Convention Signed July 30, 1940. " International Conciliation, CCCLXII (September 1940), 263-317.

3582 "Second to None. " Time, XXXI (February 7, 1938), 9-10.
        The navy to be built.

3583 "Secret Diplomacy at London. " New Republic, LXI (February 5, 1930), 287-288.

3584 Seiwell, Harry R. "Anchoring Ships on the High Sea."

USNIP, LXVI (1940), 1733-1740.

3585 Seifert, E. M. "The Evolution of the Torpedo. "
       Ordnance, XXXIX (March-April 1955), 720-724.

3586 Sekin, Gumpel. "Japan's Case for Sea Power. " Cur-
       rent History, XLI (November 1934), 129-135.

3587 Seligman, J. L. "Joint Army and Navy Procurement."
       USNIP, LXI (1935), 33-35.

3588 _____. "Pensacola, Alma Mater of Naval Aero-
       nautics. " USNIP, LXIV (1938), 344-345.

3589 Sellers, David F. "Foreword: The Naval Academy. "
       USNIP, LXI (1935), 1357.

3590 _____. "The United States Naval Academy: Its Be-
       longs to the Fleet. " USNIP, LXII (1936), 1427-
       1432.

3591 "Semper Fidelis. " Saturday Evening Post, CCV (Feb-
       ruary 18, 1933), 20.
       Concerns the U. S. Marine Corps.

3592 Seth, Ronald S. Secret Servants: A History of Japa-
       nese Espionage. New York: Farrar, 1957. 278p.
       Considerable data on their attempts on American
       naval secrets during the 1930s.

3593 Settle, Thomas G. W. "Airships Engines. " USNIP,
       LVI (1930), 745-747.

3594 _____. "The Mission of Naval Airships. " USNIP,
       LVIII (1932), 1621-1626.

3595 _____. "Some Recent Aspects of Rigid Airships."
       Mechanical Engineering, LIII (August 1931), 567-574.

3596 _____. "Why no Blimps?" USNIP, LXV (1939),
       238-240.

3597 Sexton, H. C. "Launching the Submarine Dolphin [SS-
       169]. " Marine Engineering, XXXVII (September
       1932), 395-396.
       At the Portsmouth Navy Yard, March 6, 1932.

3598 Shafter, Richard A. Destroyers in Action. Cambridge,
      Md.: Cornell Maritime Press, 1945. 256p.
      Much data on our period.

3599 "Shall the United States Withdraw from the Far Pa-
      cific?" Christian Science Monitor Magazine, (Jan-
      uary 6, 1937), 1-2+.
      A debate between William C. Rivers and Com-
      modore Dudley W. Knox.

3600 "Shall We go on a Naval Building Spree?" Christian
      Century, XLIX (May 18, 1932), 628-629.

3601 Shamburger, Page and Joe Christy. The Curtis Hawks.
      Kalamazoo, Mich.: Wolverine Press, 1973.
      Contains data on the Navy Sparrowhawks which
      were launched from the dirigible Macon.

3602 Shappee, Nathan D. "Fort Dallas and the Naval Depot
      on Key Biscayne, 1836-1926." Tequesta, XXI
      (1961), 20-24.

3603 Sharp, Alexander. "Postgraduate Instruction." USNIP,
      L (1924), 48-60.

3604 Sharp, Archie B. "The Navy vs. 'News'." USNIP,
      LX (1934), 529-531.

3605 Sharp, Walter D. "An Ideal Navy Supply Depot."
      USNIP, XLVIII (1922), 251-258.

3606 Shaw, Albert. "War Scares and a Big Navy." Review
      of Reviews, LXXXIX (March 1934), 40-43.

3607 Shaw, Roger. "The London Naval Conference of 1930:
      A Study in Naval and Political Relations Among the
      Western Powers." Unpublished PhD Dissertation,
      Fordham University, 1946.

3608 Shaw, S. Adele. "5:5:3 in Terms of Newport News."
      Survey, XLVII (December 31, 1921), 494-498.
      With reference to the large amount of naval ship-
      building done there and the potentials for unemploy-
      ment.

3609 "Shenandoah Court Findings." Aviation, XX (January
      11, 1926), 44-46.

3610   "The Shenandoah Disaster. " Engineer, CXLII (September 10, 1026), 279-280.

3611   "Shenandoah Disaster Holds Technical Lessons for Aircraft Builders. " Automotive Industries, LIII (September 10, 1925), 404-405.

3612   "The Shenandoah Investigation. " Aviation, XIX (October 5, 1925), 437+.

3613   "Shenandoah Verdict. " Literary Digest, LXXXVIII (January 16, 1926), 11-12.

3614   "The Shenandoah Weathers a Storm. " Aviation, XVI (January 28, 1924), 90-91.

3615   Shepardson, Whitney H. and William O. Scroggs. The United States in World Affairs: An Account of American Foreign Relations. 10 vols. New York: Published for the Council on Foreign Relations by Harper, 1931-1942.
        Documents are included in the appendices of each volume.

3616   Shepherd, William G. "Big Catch on Rum Row. " Collier's, LXXV (June 6, 1925), 13-14.
        The Coast Guard vs. the booze smugglers.

3617   _____. "Catching up With Japan. " Collier's XCII (October 21, 1933), 12-13+.
        With regard to naval building.

3618   _____. "The Rum-Runner's New Enemy. " Collier's, LXXV (May 23, 1925), 5-6.
        The Coast Guard.

3619   Shepherd, William R. "Uncle Sam, Imperialist: A Survey of Our Encroachments in the Caribbean, 1898-1927. " New Republic, XLIX (January 26, 1927), 266-269.

3620   Sheridan, Thomas W. "Swell Damage. " USNIP, LXVI (1940), 177-180.

3621   Sherman, Forest P. "Air Tactics and Strategy. " USNIP, LII (1926), 855-865.

3622 _____. "Air Warfare." USNIP, LII (1926), 62-71.

3623 _____. "Fighters." USNIP, LVI (1930), 831-833.

3624 _____. "Main Battery Elevations and Fighting Aircraft." USNIP, LI (1925), 600-603.

3625 _____. "Naval Aircraft in International Law."
USNIP, LI (1925), 2259-2264.

3626 _____. "Some Aspects of Carrier and Cruiser Design." USNIP, LVI (1930), 997-1002.

3627 Sherman, Frederick C. "A Proposed System for Stim-
ulating Interest in Operating Engineering." USNIP,
XLVI (1920), 1437-1442.

3628 Sherrod, Robert. "Marine Corps Aviation: The Early
Days." Marine Corps Gazette, XXXVI (June 1952),
52-61.
From 1919 to 1941.

3629 Sherwood, Robert E. "The Phoney War." In: Donald
Sheehan, ed. The Making of American History.
3rd ed. 2 vols.; New York: Holt, Rinehart and
Winston, 1963. II, 452-475.
From 1939 on.

3630 _____. Roosevelt and Hopkins, an Intimate History.
Rev. ed. New York: Harper, 1950. 1002p.

3631 Shields, Henry S. "A Historical Survey of the United
States Naval Attaches in Russia, 1904-1941." Unpublished Paper, Individual Personnel File, Operational Archives, U. S. Navy Department, Naval History Division, 1970. 83p.
An M.A. thesis.

3632 Shigemitsu, Mamoru. Japan and Her Destiny. New
York: E. P. Dutton, 1958.
A former Japanese stateman's view of the road
to Pearl Harbor.

3633 Shillman, J. H. "The Evolution of the Navy Ration."
USNIP, LX (1934), 1678-1681.

3634 "Ship Seizure: City of Flint's Capture Complicates

U. S. Neutrality. " Newsweek, XIV (October 30, 1939), 15.

3635 "Shipbuilding Increases 150 per cent: Naval Vessels Completed and Under Construction in 1940. " Marine Engineering, XLVI (January 1941), 48-50.

3636 Shipbuilding Terms, Especially Prepared for Shipbuilding Workers. New York: American Technical Society, 1942. 64p.

3637 "Ships or Planes or Naval Pacts: A Symposium of Opinion. " Christian Science Monitor Magazine, (March 9, 1938), 2+.

3638 "Ships Under Construction in Various Yards of the United States Navy: Tables. " Marine Engineering, XXVI (May 1921), 418-419.

3639 Shirer, William L. The Rise and Fall of the Third Reich: A History of Nazi Germany. New York: Simon and Schuster, 1960. 1245p.
      Contains some information relative to this compilation.

3640 Shoemaker, W. R. "To Build a Naval Reserve from the Merchant Marine. " Marine Engineering, LVI (October 1926), 25+.

3641 "The Shooting War: Nazi Submarines Strike Again off Iceland. " Life, XI (November 10, 1941), 35-39.
      The sinking of the U. S. destroyer Reuben James.

3642 "Shooting Without War. " New Republic, CV (September 15, 1941), 327-328.
      America's undeclared war on the U-boat.

3643 "Short- or Long-Range Navy?" Literary Digest, LXXXIV (January 24, 1925), 9-10.

3644 Shotwell, James T. "England and America: A Reply to F. H. Simonds. " Saturday Review of Literature, V (March 9, 1929), 758.

3645 _____. "The Problems of Disarmament. " Annals of the American Academy, CXXVI (July 1926), 51-55.

3646 _____ . "Sea Power and the Pacific. " Current History, XLI (March 1935), 660-666.

3647 "Should the Submarine be Outlawed?" Literary Digest, LXXXVII (November 28, 1925), 5-7.

3648 "Should the U. S. Navy be Built up to Treaty Strength?" Congressional Digest, XIII (April 1934), 120-121.
A debate with Admiral William H. Standley in the affirmative and Congressman Ross A. Collins opposed.

3649 Shugg, Charles. "Reverse Launching: An Unusual Method of Hauling Out a Submarine from the Water." Marine Engineering, XXXIII (june 1928), 321-325.

3650 Sidebotham, Hugh. "A High Seas Fleet. " New Republic, XXI (December 17, 1919), 71-72.
The reply by D. Figgis is cited above.

3651 Silver, Steven M. and Thomas H. Etzold. "Tactical Implications of the Washington Naval Conference. " USNIP, XCIX (1973), 109-111.

3652 Simmons, J. S. , jt. author. See Hawley, P. R. , no. 1623.

3653 Simonds, Frank H. "American Ships and British Opinion. " Review of Reviews, LXXVII (February 1928), 175-182.

3654 _____ . "Disarmament Conference. " Review of Reviews, LXXVI (August 1927), 163-166.
At Geneva, Switzerland.

3655 _____ . "England and America: A Reply. " Saturday Review of Literature, V (February 23, 1929), 714.
The offending article by Walter Lippmann is cited above.

3656 _____ . "Naval Disaster at Geneva. " Review of Reviews, LXXVI (September 1927), 270-278.
Growing out of the Geneva Conference.

3657 _____ . "Naval Discussion at Geneva: The Reduction of Armaments. " Review of Reviews, LXXIX (June 1929), 43-45.

3658 _____. "The Naval Issue. " Review of Reviews,
        LXXX (July 1929), 46-47.

3659 _____. "Postponing Our Cruisers. " Review of Re-
        views, LXXX (September 1929), 74-76.

3660 _____. "The Question of Naval Parity. " Review
        of Reviews, LXXX (August 1929), 60-62.

3661 _____. "What is a Naval Parity?" Review of Re-
        views, LXXVIII (November 1928), 502-504.

3662 _____. "What is Happening in London?" Review of
        Reviews, LXXXI (March 1930), 77-81.

3663 _____. "What was Wrong at the London [Naval]
        Conference?" Review of Reviews, LXXXI (May
        1930), 40-45.

3664 _____. "Why Navies Won't be Reduced. " Review
        of Reviews, LXXXI (April 1930), 65-66.

3665 Simons, Rodger L. "Ice Breakers. " USNIP, LXI
        (1935), 49-53.

3666 Simrell, V. E.   "The Senate Debate on the Cruiser
        Bill. " Quarterly Journal of Speech, XV (April
        1929), 280-282.

3667 Sims, William S.   "Accidents in the Navy: Safety First
        or Efficiency First?" Atlantic Monthly, CXXXVII
        (January 1926), 108-112.

3668 _____. "Admiral Sims on Aviation. " Aviation, XI
        (December 5, 1921), 659.

3669 _____. "Annapolis, Our Amateur Naval College and
        Some Suggestions for Its Improvement. " World's
        Work, LIII (April 1927), 664-669.

3670 _____. "The Battleship and the Airplane. " World's
        Work, XLII (May 1921), 25-28.

3671 _____. "Changing Methods in Submarine Warfare."
        Current History, XVIII (September 1923), 911-918.

3672 _____. "Fleet Gridiron: What the Naval War College

at Newport Really Does. " World's Work XLVI
(September 1923), 505-509.

3673 _____. "Military Conservation. " Aviation, XII
(April 24, 1922), 478-480.

3674 _____. "Naval Morale After War. " USNIP, XLVIII
(1922), 1461-1471.

3675 _____. "The Practical Naval Officer. " USNIP,
XLVII (1921), 525-546.

3676 _____. "Promotion in the Navy. " Atlantic Monthly,
CLVI (September 1935), 354-358.

3677 _____. "Status of the American Navy: Reply to
Wester-Wemyss. " Current History, XVI (May
1922), 184-194.
The original Wester-Wemyss article is cited below. For a reply to it and this one, see the
article by Admiral Fiske cited above.

3678 _____. "The United States Naval War College. "
USNIP, XLVII (1921), 705-721.
A May 1920 talk.

3679 _____. _____. USNIP, XLV (1919), 1485-1493.
An address before the class of 1919.

3680 _____. "The Value of Rigid Dirigibles for Naval
Operations. " Air Power, IV (April 1919), 451-
452.

3681 _____. "What's the Matter with the Navy?"
World's Work, LI (January 1926), 263-268.

3682 "Singapore and Alaska: The Question of Naval Bases. "
Living Age, CCCXVIII (September 22, 1922), 543-
546.

3683 "The Sinking of a Gunboat Changes the Aspect of the
China War. " Newsweek, X (December 27, 1937),
7-11.
The Panay.

3684 "The Sinking of the Panay. " Christian Century, LIV
(December 22, 1937), 1582-1583.

3685 "The Sinking of the Squalus. " Commonweal, XXX
       (June 9, 1939), 170-171.

3686 Sitterson, J. Carlyle. "Aircraft Production Policies
       Under the National Defense Advisory Commission
       and Office of Production Management: May 1940-
       December 1941. " Admin. Hist. Appen. War. Admin.
       Operational Archives, U. S. Navy Department, Naval
       History Division, 1946. 168p.

3687 "6, 500, 000 Cubic-Foot Rigid Airships for the U. S.
       Navy. " Engineering, CXXIII (April 29, 1927), 503.

3688 "$16, 458, 835 Asked for Naval Air Stations. " Aviation,
       XV (October 8, 1923), 441-442.

3689 "The Size of Leading Navies as of January 1, 1938. "
       Congressional Digest, XVII (March 1938), 70.

3690 Skerrett, Robert G. "Mechanically Marvelous Steel
       Fish. " Compressed Air Magazine, XLV (July
       1940), 6183-6189.
       Torpedoes.

3691 _____. "A Modern Submarine. " Compressed Air
       Magazine, XLV (April 1940), 123-128.

3692 _____. "Up From Forty Fathoms: Rescuing the
       Men from the Submarine Squalus. " Compressed Air
       Magazine, XLIV (November 1939), 6003-6009.

3693 Skiera, Joseph A. Aircraft Carriers in Peace and
       War. New York: Watts, 1965. 296p.
       Since U. S. S. Langley.

3694 Slayton, Charles C. "Notes on Handling Destroyers. "
       USNIP, XLV (1919), 1201-1219.

3695 _____. "Oceanography and the Navy. " USNIP, LX
       (1934), 33-43.

3696 "Sleeve Marks Tell Who's Who Among Navy Enlisted
       Men. " Popular Science, CXXXVIII (February 1941),
       87.

3697 Smart, Larry R. "Evolution of the Torpedo Boat. "
       Military Affairs, XXIII (Summer 1959), 97-101.

3698 Smiley, Samuel A. "Naval Warfare in Miniature. "
      USNIP, LXI (1936), 54-59.

3699 Smith, Charles. "Lend-Lease Aid to Great Britain in
      1941-1945. " Southern Quarterly, X (1972), 195-
      208.
         Our concern here is only 1941.

3700 Smith, Darrell H. and Frederick W. Powell. The
      Coast Guard: Its History Activities and Organiza-
      tion. Service Monographs of the United States
      Government, no. 51. Washington: Brookings Insti-
      tution, 1929. 265p. Rpr. 1970.

3701 Smith, Donald F. "Thrills of the Flying Sailors: Life
      on Our Aircraft Carriers. " Popular Science,
      CXXXVII (July 1940), 46-48+.

3702 Smith, Edgar C. A Short History of Naval and Marine
      Engineering. Cambridge, Eng.: At the University
      Press, 1938. 376p.

3703 Smith, Edward H. "Expedition of the U. S. Coast Guard
      Cutter Marion to the Region of Davis Strait in
      1928. " Science, New Series LXVIII (November 16,
      1928), 469-470.

3704 _____. "The North Atlantic Ice Menace and the
      Work of Protection Conducted by the U. S. Coast
      Guard. " USNIP, LV (1929), 393-400.

3705 Smith, Frederick H. "What is the Present Arrange-
      ment and What is Its Effectiveness for Cooperation
      Between Local Army and Navy Commands in All
      Matters Affecting Joint Operations, Local Policy
      Plans, and the Use of Local Installations?" Un-
      published General Staff Memorandum, Files of the
      U. S. Army Military History Research Collection,
      1924.
         The author was an Army major attached to the
      Coast Artillery.

3706 Smith, Gaddis. American Diplomacy During the Second
      World War, 1941-1945. New York: Wiley, 1965.
      194p.
         Our concern here is only 1941.

3707 Smith, Holland M. "The Development of Amphibious
      Tactics in the U. S. Navy. " Marine Corps Gazette,
      XXX (June-December 1946), 13-18, 27-30, 26-28,
      43-47, 41-46, 33-38, 42-50; XXXI (January-March
      1947), 45-52, 31-38, 30-38.

3708 Smith, John P. "Cooperation Between Army and Navy
      Air Services. " Unpublished General Staff Memo-
      randum, Files of the U. S. Army Military History
      Research Collection, 1925.
          The author was an Army major attached to the
      Coast Artillery.

3709 Smith, Lawrence. "Horsepower of the Mind: The
      United States Battleship Colorado--Engineering
      Efficiency. " Power, LXVI (October 25, 1927),
      616-621.

3710 Smith, Myron J. , Jr. "American Battleship Librar-
      ies. " Library Occurrent, XXIV (November 1973),
      335-338.

3711 _____. "The Second Indiana, BB-50. " Indiana His-
      tory Bulletin, L (January 1973), 8-12.
          Designed during World War I, she was scrapped
      in 1923 under the terms of the Washington Treaty
      when 34. 7 per cent completed.

3712 Smith, Oscar. "Back to Normalcy with Amalgama-
      tion. " USNIP, XLIX (1923), 2030-2034.

3713 _____. "The Fetish of Formulas. " USNIP, L
      (1924), 1841-1846.

3714 _____. "Naval Service Schools. " USNIP, LII
      (1926), 691-701.
          Based on the idea developed by the army.

3715 Smith, P. DeW. Modern Marine Electricity. New York:
      Cornell Maritime Press, 1941. 279p.

3716 Smith, Ralph H. "The Mosquito Stings. " USNIP,
      LXVI (1940), 1693-1698.
          Concerns PT boats.

3717 Smith, Reuben R. "Engineering Economy on Auxiliary
      Vessels. " USNIP, LI (1925), 2101-2109.

3718 _____ . "Engineering Economy on Battleships. "
      USNIP, L (1924), 18-30.

3719 _____ . "The Airships Akron and Macon, Flying
      Aircraft Carriers of the United States Navy. " Un-
      published PhD Dissertation, University of Chicago,
      1965.

3720 _____ . _____ . Annapolis: U. S. Naval Institute,
      1965.   228p.

3721 _____ . First Across: The U. S. Navy's Transat-
      lantic Flight of 1919.   Annapolis: U. S. Naval Insti-
      tute, 1972.   300p.

3722 _____ . "An Inventory of U. S. Navy Airships with
      Miscellaneous Characteristics, Performance, and
      Contract Data, 1916-1961. " Unpublished Paper,
      Individual Personnel File, Operational Archives,
      U. S. Navy Department, Naval History Division, n.d.
      138p.
           In addition to the many tables, chronological
      narratives are provided for each of the rigid air-
      ships, e. g. , Shenandoah.

3723 _____ . "The ZRCV: Fascinating Might-Have-Been
      of Aeronautics. " Aerospace Historian, XII (De-
      cember 1965), 115-121.
           Concerns the airships Akron and Macon.

3724 Smith, Robert F.   "American Foreign Relations, 1920-
      1942. " In: Barton J. Bernstein, ed. Towards a
      New Past: Dissenting Essays in American History.

3725 Smith, Roger C.   "Aircraft versus Battleships. "
      North American Review, CCXVI (October 1922),
      470-475.
           Bombing tests.

3726 Smith, Roy C.   "The Protection of American Nationals
      in China. " USNIP, LVI (1930), 1097-1104.
           The gunboat patrols.

3726a Smith, Roy C. , 3rd.   "The First Hundred Years Are
      .... " USNIP, XCIX (1973), 50-77.
           A history of the U. S. Naval Institute with in-
      teresting data for our period.

3726b Smith, W. B. Harriotte, jt. author. <u>See</u> Somerville,
       Keith F. , no. 3732.

3726c Smith-Hutton, Henry H.   "Naval Limitations. " <u>USNIP</u>,
       LXIII (1937), 463-476.

3726d "Snags in the Way of Naval Disarmament. " <u>Literary</u>
       <u>Digest</u>, XCIV (July 2, 1927), 5-7.

3726e Snedeker, James.   "The Ensign's Budget. " <u>USNIP</u>,
       LIV (1928), 1080-1082.

3726f Snell, Edwin M. , jt. author. <u>See</u> Matloff, Maurice,
       no. 2448.

3726g Snell, John L.   <u>Illusion and Necessity: The Diplomacy</u>
       <u>of Global War, 1939-1945.</u> Boston: Houghton,
       Mifflin, 1963.   229p.
          Our concern here is only 1939-1941.

3726h "The Snow Cruiser, a Mobile Base for Antarctica. "
       <u>SciAmer</u>, CLXII (January 1940), 25.
          A vehicle employed by Byrd and his followers.

3726i Snyder, Henry R.   "If I Were to do My Service Over
       Again. " <u>USNIP</u>, LI (1925), 59-67.

3726j _____ .   "The Naval Reserve: Looking In and Look-
       ing Out. " <u>USNIP</u>, L (1924), 1296-1303.

3727 Sobel, Robert. <u>The Origins of Interventionism: The</u>
       <u>United States and the Russo-Finnish War.</u>   New
       York: Bookman Associates, 1961.   204p.
          The U. S. Navy played only a "sword-rattling"
       part in this tragedy.

3728 Society of Naval Architects and Marine Engineers.
       <u>Historical Transactions,</u> 1893-1943.   New York;
       1945.   544p.

3729 _____ .   <u>The Training of Shipyard Personnel.</u>   New
       York, 1941.   42p.

3730 Solberg, Thorwald A.   "Rewinding a Main Drive Motor
       on a Dreadnought. " <u>USNIP</u>, XLVIII (1922), 1529-
       1538.
          Experiments aboard U. S. S. <u>Tennessee</u>.

3731 "Some Reactions to U. S. Naval Construction Plans. "
      China Weekly Review, XLVI (October 21, 1933),
      303-304.
          Particularly Japan's.

3732 Somerville, Keith F. and W. B. Harriotte Smith. Ships
      of the United States Navy and Their Sponsors,
      1924-1950. Annapolis: U. S. Naval Institute, 1952.
          Part of a series dating back to 1913.

3733 Sondern, Frederick, Jr. "The Navy, the Silent
      Service: A Review of Modern Fighting Craft and
      Weapons Used by Our First Line of Defense. "
      Current History, LII (April 1941), 10-13+.

3734 _____. "The Latest in Naval Weapons. " Reader's
      Digest, XXXVIII (May 1941), 95-99.
          An abridgement of the Current History piece
      cited above.

3735 Soule, Charles C. Naval Terms and Definitions. 2nd
      ed., rev. New York: D. Van Nostrand, 1923.
      124p.

3736 South American Handbook. Chicago: Rand McNally,
      1924-1941.

3737 Spanner, E. F. About Airships. London; 1929. 206p.

3738 _____. This Airship Business. London, 1927.
      423p.

3739 Spaulding, Mark M. "Early Salvage Work on the
      U. S. S. S-51, from a Reporter's Diary. " USNIP,
      LXII (1936), 329-336.

3740 Spear, Charles. "Our New Sea Fighters, Greatest and
      Most Remarkable of Warships. " Illustrated World,
      XXXV (March 1921), 75-76.
          Post-World War I U. S. battleships.

3741 Spear, L. Y. "Battleships or Submarines?" Foreign
      Affairs, VI (October 1927), 106-115.
          The author's bet is on the latter.

3742 _____. "The Submarine of Today. " Marine Engi-
      neering XXXIII (January 13, 1928), 28-30.

3743   Spears, William O.   "Naval Co-operation with Our
       Merchant Marine. "   USNIP, LXI (1935), 957-964.

3744   Spencer, G. K.   "The American Navy Uses More Sheet
       Steel. "   Iron Age, CXXI (January 19, 1928), 198-
       200.

3745   _____ .   "Behind the Big Guns of the Navy. "   Popu-
       lar Mechanics, XLIII (March 1925), 428-431.

3746   _____ .   "Breaking the World's Big Gun Record. "
       Popular Mechanics, XLIX (January 1928), 66-71.

3747   _____ .   "Financing the Pacific Cruise of the Fleet."
       Banker's Magazine, CX (June 1925), 981-984.

3748   _____ .   "Photography is Popular in the U. S. Navy. "
       Photo-Era, LX (June 1928), 339-342.

3749   _____ .   "Sheet Metal in the U. S. Navy. "   Sheet Metal
       Worker, XIX (May 18, 1928), 311-312.

3750   _____ .   "What is the Trend in Naval Design?"
       Marine Engineering, XXXIV (April 1929), 183-184.

3751   Spencer, Ivor D.   "U. S. Naval Air Bases from 1914-
       1939. "   USNIP, LXXV (1949), 1242-1255.

3752   Spender, Herbert F.   "Naval Conference. "   Fortnightly,
       CXXVIII (August 1927), 180-189.
       That held at Geneva.

3753   _____ .   "Riddle of the Cruisers. "   Fortnightly,
       CXXVIII (September 1927), 317-325.
       Dickering at the Geneva Naval Conference.

3754   Spotford, W.   "Naval Limitation and Shipping. "   Marine
       Engineering, XXXII (September 1927), 507-509.

3755   Sprout, Harold H.   America's Problem of National De-
       fense.   Princeton, N. J. : School of Public and In-
       ternational Affairs, 1939.   22p.

3756   _____ .   "Neutrality for the United States--Yester-
       day, Today, and Tomorrow. "   Unpublished Lecture,
       Conduct of War Course 11, Files of the U. S. Army
       Military History Research Collection, 1938.

3757   _____ .   "Some Aspects of the Neutrality Problem. "
Unpublished Lecture, Conduct of War Course 12,
Files of the U. S. Army Military History Research
Collection, 1937.
The author was the noted Princeton University
professor who, together with his wife Margaret, had
written the then definitive post-Mahan works on Sea
Power.

3758   _____ and Margaret.   Toward a New Order of Sea
Power: American Naval Policy and the World Scene,
1918-1922.   Princeton, N. J. : Princeton University
Press, 1940.   332p.   Rpr. 1971.

3759   "Squadrons Right!: How Warships Maneuver in Battle. "
Popular Science, CXXXVII (December 1940), 90-93.

3760   Stafford, Edward P.   The Far and the Deep: A Half
Century of Submarine History.   New York: G. P.
Putnam's, 1967.   384p.

3761   Standley, William H.   "The Functions of the Office,
Chief of Naval Operations. "   Unpublished Lecture,
G-3 Course 2, Files of the U. S. Army Military
History Research Collection, 1930.

3762   _____ .   "Naval War Planning. "   Unpublished Lecture,
War Planning Division Course 2, Files of the U. S.
Army Military History Research Collection, 1925.
The author served as Chief of Naval Operations
from 1933 to 1937.

3763   Stanworth, Charles S.   "The Battleship. "   USNIP, LVI
(1930), 36-37.

3764   Stapler, John T. G.   "The Naval War College. "   USNIP,
LVIII (1932), 1157-1163.

3765   _____ .   "Statistics on Our Naval Personnel. "   Sci-
Amer, CXXXIII (November 1925), 347-348.

3766   _____ .   "A Tactical Awakening. "   USNIP, XLVII
(1921), 849-855.

3767   "States That Build a Cruiser. "   SciAmer, CLIII (November 1935), 256-257.

3768 <u>Statesman's Year-Book.</u> New York: St. Martin's
         Press, 1919-1942.

3769 "Statistical Data on Combatant Vessels: Capital Ships,
         Aircraft Carriers, Cruisers, Destroyers, and Sub-
         marines in the Navies of the United States, British
         Empire, Japan, France, and Italy. " <u>USNIP</u>, LVI
         (1930), 924.
         Correct to June 1, 1930.

3770 "Statistical Data on Combatant Vessels: Summary of
         Vessels on April 1, 1933. " <u>USNIP</u>, LIX (1933),
         916-936.

3771 "Status of the Treaties and Conventions Signed at the
         International Conferences of American States and
         at Other Pan American Conferences: Revised to
         January 1, 1940. " <u>Bulletin of the Pan American
         Union,</u> LXXIV (March 1940), 168-171.

3772 _____: Revised to July 1, 1940. " <u>Bulletin of the
         Pan American Union,</u> LXXIV (August 1940), 572-
         575.

3773 . _____: Revised to January 1, 1941. " <u>Bulletin of
         the Pan American Union,</u> LXXV (February 1941),
         132-135.

3774 Steirman, Hy and Glenn D. Kittler. <u>Triumph: The In-
         credible Saga of the First Transatlantic Flight.</u>
         New York: Harper, 1961. 199p.
         The story of the NC's.

3775 Stephen, E. P. "The Race to Pearl Harbor: The
         Failure of the Second London Conference and the
         Coming of World War II. " Unpublished PhD Dis-
         sertation, Harvard University, 1971.

3776 Stephens, Emory W. "Aerology and the Hawaiian
         Flight. " <u>USNIP</u>, LXI (1935), 209-213.

3777 Stephenson, Charles S. "The Relationship of the Health
         of Civilians to the Efficiency of the Navy, with
         Special Reference to the Venereal Disease Prob-
         lem. " <u>American Journal of Public Health,</u> XXX
         (November 1940), 1291-1296.

3778   . "Social Hygiene and National Defense from
the Viewpoint of the Navy." Journal of Social Hygiene, XXVI (December 1940), 402-414.

3779 Stephenson, Floyd A. "Heavy Mobile Artillery in Base
Defense." Marine Corps Gazette, XIX (November
1934), 53-55.

3780 "Stereoscopic Range Finding." USNIP, LXVI (1940),
269-271.

3781 Stetson, Conn, et al. Guarding the United States and
Its Outposts. United States Army in World War II
--The Western Hemisphere. Washington: Office of
the Chief of Military History, U. S. Army, 1964.
593p.
The occupation of Iceland is covered on p. 459-
531.

3782 Stettinius, Edward R., Jr. Lend-Lease, Weapon for
Victory. New York: Macmillan, 1944.
Its origins and operations.

3783 Stevens, Leslie C. "Behind the Flying Lines." USNIP,
LVI (1930), 720-726.

3784   . "Wasp Nests of Our Navy." World's Work,
LIX (February 1930), 76-80.
U. S. Carriers.

3785 Stevens, William O. "The Naval Officer and the
Civilian." USNIP, XLVII (1921), 1725-1739.

3786   . "Our Yes-Man Navy." Forum, C (November 1938), 211-215.

3787   . "Scrapping Mahan." Yale Review, New
Series XII (April 1923), 528-542.
The apparent result of the Washington Naval
Treaty.

3788   . "What Has Happened to Sea Power?"
Forum, CIII (February 1940), 49-53.

3789   and Allan Westcott. History of Seapower.
Garden City, N. Y.: Doubleday, Doran, 1938. 426p.

3790 _____ and Carroll S. Alden. Composition for Naval Officers. Baltimore: Lord Baltimore Press, 1919. 230p.

3791 Stewart, George V. "Design for War: to Prepare for Peace. " USNIP, LXVI (1940), 941-944.

3792 _____. "Naming Ships of the Navy. " USNIP, LXIV (1938), 1693-1695.

3793 Stiles, William C. "Alternative War Plans. " General Staff Memorandum, Files of the U. S. Army Military History Research Collection, 1928.
The author was a Navy commander.

3794 _____. "The Art of Ship Control. " USNIP, XLIX (1923), 587-600.

3795 _____. "Naval Organization. " Unpublished Lecture, G-3 Course 5, Files of the U. S. Army Military History Research Collection, 1928.

3796 _____. "Somes Uses and Misuses of the Mooring Board. " USNIP, XLVIII (1922), 1087-1105.

3797 _____. "The Strategy of the Pacific from the Viewpoint of the United States. " Unpublished Lecture, War Plans Course 11, Files of the U. S. Army Military History Research Collection, 1930.

3798 Stimson, Henry L. American Policy in Nicaragua. New York: Arno, 1970. 129p.
A reprinting of the 1927 first edition in which the State Department justified its action in landing the Marines.

3799 _____. "Analysis of the Limitation Agreement. " Current History, XXXII (May 1930), 358-360.
Adopted at the London Conference of 1930.

3800 _____. "Defend Our Seas with Our Navy: Freedom Cannot be Saved Without Sacrafice. " Vital Speeches, VII (May 15, 1941), 450-453.

3801 _____. "Statement to the Congressional Joint Committee on the Investigation of the Pearl Harbor Attack, March 21, 1946. " U. S. News & World

Report, XX (March 29, 1946), 63-74.
Excerpts were also published in Newsweek,
XXVII (April 1, 1946), 21; and Time, XLVII (April
1, 1946), 20-21.
Concerning activities in the days before the
hatchet fell.

3802 _____ and McGeorge Bundy. On Active Service in
Peace and War. New York: Harper, 1948. 698p.
Rpr. 1971.
Memoirs of Roosevelt's War Secretary and
Hoover's Secretary of State.

3803 Stimson, Thomas E., Jr. "Uncle Sam's Schools for
Sailors." Popular Mechanics, LXXV (February
1941), 177-184.

3804 _____. "X-boats War on Smugglers." Popular
Mechanics, LVIII (August 1932), 242-247.
The work of the Coast Guard in the Rum War.

3805 "Stimson's Report on London." New Republic, LXII
(April 23, 1930), 257-259.
Highly critical thereof.

3806 Stirling, Yates. "America and the War." Forum, CII
(November 1939), 216-221.
Also features comments by Senator Borah.

3807 _____. "Bureaucracy Rules the Navy: The Absence
of a General Staff Seriously Imperils the Value of
Our Naval Forces." Current History, LI (March
1940), 30-32.

3808 _____. How to be a Naval Officer. New York:
Robert M. McBride, 1940. 194p.

3809 _____. "Naval Preparedness in the Pacific Area."
USNIP, LX (1934), 601-608.

3810 _____. "The Place of Aviation in the Organization
of War." USNIP, LII (1926), 1100-1110.

3811 _____. Sea Duty: The Memoirs of a Fighting
Admiral. New York: G. P. Putnam, 1939. 809p.

3812 _____. "Sea Power: The Foundation of Successful

World Trade. " USNIP, LXI (1935), 767-780.

3813 _____ . "Some Fundamentals of Sea Power. "
USNIP, LI (1925), 889-918.

3814 _____ . "U. S. Security in the Pacific. " Far
Eastern Review, XXXI (1935), 124, 139.

3815 _____ . "What America Must do to Maintain Naval
Parity with Great Britain. " China Weekly Review,
LXXX (May 22, 1937), 451.

3816 Stitt, Edward R. "Activities of the Medical Corps,
U. S. Navy. " USNIP, LIV (1928), 887-890.

3817 _____ . "The Medical Department of the Navy. "
USNIP, LII (1926), 1951-1965.

3818 Stockbridge, F. P. "Our Navy and a League of Nations. " World's Work, XXXVII (February 1919),
425-437.

3819 Stockton, Charles H. A Manual of International Law
for the Use of Naval Officers. 2nd rev. ed.
Annapolis: U. S. Naval Institute, 1921. 356p.

3820 Stone, Ellery W. "Communications for Byrd Antarctic
Expedition II. " USNIP, LXII (1936), 212-216.

3821 _____ . "Moral Preparedness. " USNIP, XLVI
(1920), 365-374.

3822 _____ . "The Poulsen Arc. " USNIP, XLVI (1920),
1049-1073.

3823 Stone, Howard W. "Field Exercises of the 10th Regiment at Camp Meade, Maryland. " Marine Corps
Gazette, X (December 1925), 157-160.

3824 Stone, Isidor F. Business as Usual: The First Year
of Defense. New York: Modern Age Books, 1941.
275p.
    A study of the lack of preparedness prior to
June 1941 by the Washington editor of Nation.

3825 Stone, Raymond. "Disposition to be Made of Neutral
Vessels and Their Cargoes Which May in Time of

War be Seized and Sent to an Advanced Base. "
USNIP, XLVI (1920), 565-575.

3826   Stone, William T.   "The London Naval Conference:
Outstanding Problems. " Woman's Journal, New
Series XV (January 1930), 22-23.

3827   _____. Memorandum: International Ramifications
of the U. S. Naval Program. Washington: National
Council for the Prevention of War, 1934. 4p.

3828   _____. "Naval Bases and American Policy in Asia."
Amerasia, I (1938), 175-178.

3829   _____. "The Navy and Its Strategic Problems: Demands in the Atlantic and the Pacific. " Amerasia,
IV (May 1940), 111-115.

3830   _____. "The Navy as an Instrument of Diplomacy."
In: Julia E. Johnson, ed. Peace and Rearmament.
Vol. XI of The Reference Shelf. New York: H. W.
Wilson, 1938. p. 62-69.

3831   _____. _____. Amerasia, II (1939), 63-67.

3832   _____. "Preparedness for What?" New Republic,
LXXVI (September 6, 1933), 91-93.

3833   _____. "Wanted: Boldness at London. " New Republic, LXII (March 12, 1930), 273-280.

3834   _____. "What Happened in London: The Naval Parley's Failures and Achievements. " Woman's
Journal, New Series XV (May 1930), 8-9.

3835   _____ and Ryllis A. Goslin. Billions for Defense.
Headline Books, no. 9. New York: Foreign Policy
Association, 1937. 46p.

3836   "Stop the Cruiser Bill!" Nation, CXXVII (December
26, 1928), 703.

3837   Strabolgi, Joseph M.   "The Battleship's Doom. " Current History, XLIV (August 1936), 45-49.

3838   _____. "Japan and the Pacific. " 19th Century,
CXVII (March 1935), 306-318.

The reply by Malcolm D. Kennedy is cited above.

3838a Strain, L. H.   "Aircraft vs. Submarines. "   Flying, X
       (July 1921), 202-206+.

3839   "The Strategic Geography of the Caribbean Sea. "
       Time, XXXVI (July 29, 1940), 32a-32d.

3840   Strett, C. K.   "Haiti: Intervention in Operation. "
       Foreign Affairs, VI (July 1928), 615-632.

3841   Strong, Ronald T.   "A Beginner's Outline of Strategy
       and Tactics. "   USNIP, LXVII (1941), 619-637.

3842   _____.   "Pressures Against Peace. "   USNIP, LXII
       (1936), 625-645.

3843   "Strong Arms. "   Time, XXXIII (February 20, 1939),
       12-14.

3844   "A Strong Navy. "   SciAmer, CXXIV (March 12, 1921),
       202.

3845   "Struggle of the London Naval Parley. "   Literary Di-
       gest, CXVIII (November 24, 1934), 15.

3846   Stryker, Perrin.   Arms and the Aftermath.   Boston:
       Houghton, Mifflin, 1942.   157p.
       A brief study of U. S. preparedness.

3847   Studley, Barrett.   "Bombing Planes or Battleships?"
       North American Review, CCXXVII (June 1929),
       727-736.

3848   _____.   "Flight Training of Student Naval Aviators."
       USNIP, LIII (1927), 764-776, 1318-1320; LIV
       (1928), 140.
       Professional discussion of the citation included.

3849   _____.   Learning to Fly for the Navy.   New York:
       Macmillan, 1931.   257p.

3850   Stump, F. B.   "Servicing Our Flying Fleet. "   Aviation,
       XXXVIII (July 1939), 28-31.

3851   Sturdee, David.   "Strategical and Tactical Considera-

tions Governing Warship Design. " Engineering,
CXVII (April 11, 1924), 475-476.

3852 Sturdevant, Edward W.   "Discipline in the Naval
      Service. " USNIP, L (1924), 1989-1997.

3853 Sturgis, Samuel D.   "The Naval Danger at Panama. "
      USNIP, XLIX (1923), 1026-1027.
           Reprinted from the April 14, 1923 issue of the
      Literary Digest.

3854 "Submarine Hunters: Navy Plans Call for a Flotilla of
      48 Blimps to Patrol the Coasts. " Newsweek, XVII
      (January 13, 1941), 35-36.

3855 "Submarine Lung Saves Two from the Ocean's Depth. "
      Popular Mechanics, LI (June 1929), 987.

3856 "Submarine Safety Advances: S-29 is now a Floating
      Laboratory. " SciAmer. CXLII (March 1930), 209.

3857 "Submarine Safety and Salvage Devices. " USNIP, LIV
      (1928), 321-326.
           Reprinted from the February 1928 issue of
      Mechanical Engineer, vol. 50, pp. 125-132.

3858 "[Submarine] Safety Under the Sea. " Review of Re-
      views, LXXIX (April 1929), 128-129.

3859 "Submarines and Submarine Air Conditioning. "
      American Society of Heating and Ventilating Engi-
      neers Journal, XXV (1919), 249-264.

3860 "Submarines, 1893-1958, Including Submarine Rescue
      Vessels and Submarine Tenders. " In: U. S. Navy
      Department.   Naval History Division Dictionary of
      American Naval Fighting Ships.   Washington: U. S.
      Government Printing Office, 1959--. I, 227-268.

3861 "Submarines to the Scrap Heap?" Independent, CXV
      (November 28, 1925), 602-603.

3862 "Suicide Submarines in the Making: Naval Torpedoes."
      Steel, CVII (December 30, 1940), 38-39.

3863 Sullivan, Mark.   The Great Adventure at Washington:
      The Story of the Conference.   Garden City, N. Y.:

                Doubleday, Page, 1922.   200p.

3864   Summerall, Charles P.   "Morale and Leadership."
           USNIP, LVI (1930), 767-769.

3865   "The Super Navy is not for Defense!"   Christian Cen-
           tury, LV (May 4, 1938), 550-551.

3866   Sutphen, Harold J.   "The Anglo-American Destroyer-
           Bases Agreement, September, 1940." Unpublished
           PhD Dissertation, Fletcher School of Law and
           Diplomacy, 1967.

3867   Swanborough, Gordon and Peter M. Bowers.   United
           States Navy Aircraft Since 1911.   New York: Funk
           & Wagnalls, 1968.   518p.

3868   Swanson, Chandler W.   "The Navy Gave Me Wings."
           USNIP, LXVI (1940), 1890-1891.

3869   Swanson, Claude A.   "Our Navy Today."   In: Julia E.
           Johnson, ed.   Peace and Rearmament.   Vol. XI of
           The Reference Shelf.   New York: H. W. Wilson,
           1938.   p. 117-120.

3870   _____. _____.   USNIP, LXII (1936), 1379-1382.

3871   _____.   "Secretary of the Navy Swanson Advocates
           a United States Fleet 'Second to none'--Report to
           President Roosevelt Urges Construction to Full
           Treaty Strength--Opposed to Consolidation of the
           Air Service."   Commercial and Financial Chronicle,
           CXXXIX (December 8, 1934), 3571.

3872   _____.   "Secretary Swanson Urges Navy 'Second to
           None'--Report to President Says 'Impaired Navy' an
           Invitation to War--Asks Building up to Treaty
           Levels."   Commercial and Financial Chronicle,
           CXXXVII (December 9, 1933), 4111.

3873   _____.   "Strengthening the First Line of Defense, a
           Navy Second to None: Other Nations Building Faster
           than the U. S."   U. S. News, (December 11, 1933),
           9-10.

3874   Swanson, Harlan J.   "The Panay Incident: Prelude to
           Pearl Harbor. USNIP, XCIII (1967), 26-37.

3875 Swartz, Raymond H. "Navy Men in the Olympic
      Games. " USNIP, LXXXVI (1960), 56-67. 1912-
      1956.

3876 "Sweltering in a Submarine Under the Pacific. " Lit-
      erary Digest, LXXXI (May 24, 1924), 48.

3877 Swezy, Kenneth M. "Boys Build Battleships in Navy-
      Yard Apprentice Schools. " Popular Science, CXXX
      (March 1937), 56-57+.

3878 _____. "How Our Navy Trains Its Divers. " Popu-
      lar Science, CXXXVI (March 1940), 98-101.

3879 _____. "Picked Men Trained to Lead Our Police
      of the Sea: The Coast Guard Academy, New London,
      Conn. " Popular Science, CXXII (January 1933),
      38-39+.

3880 Sykes, Maurice. "Ready at the Drop of the Hat. "
      Commercial and Financial Chronicle, CXXIII (June
      6, 1934), 487-488.

3881 Sykes, Wayne. "Electric Propelling Machinery for
      U. S. S. Tennessee. " American Institute of Elec-
      trical Engineering Journal, XXXIX (January 1920),
      52-54.

3882 Symington, Peter. "A Battleship in Action. " Scrib-
      ner's Monthly, LXXVIII (October 1925), 367-371.

3883 Tables of Comparative Naval Data for Powers Signing
      the Washington Treaty Limiting Naval Armaments.
      Annapolis: U. S. Naval Institute, 1926. 7p.

3884 Talbot, Melvin F. "After 1936: The Problem of the
      Naval Treaties. " USNIP, LX (1934), 745-753.

3885 _____. "The Battleship: Her Evolution and Present
      Place in the Scheme of Naval Warfare. " USNIP,
      LXIV (1938), 645-653.

3886 _____. "Beyond the Naval Treaties. " USNIP, LXI
      (1935), 465-474.

3887 _____. "Building Our London Naval Treaty Navy. "
      Review of Reviews, LXXXII (December 1930), 5-54.

3888   . "East Through a Port Hole. " North
        American Review, CCXXIX (June 1930), 674-682.
        Navy life.

3889   . "The Future of Sea Power. " 19th Century,
        CVII (February 1930), 179-188.

3890   . "The Interrelationship of Foreign and Naval
        Policies in American History. " USNIP, LXVI
        (1940), 650-660.

3891   . "Navies and National Policy. " Yale Review,
        XXVII (December 1937), 333-347.

3892   . "The Navy America Needs. " Current His-
        tory, XXXVIII (April 1933), 1-8.

3893   . "Our Armor of Self Containment. " USNIP,
        LXIII (1937), 1381-1390.

3894   . "Our Navy Under the London Treaty. "
        Atlantic Monthly, CXLVI (September 1930), 410-419.

3895   . "A Younger Officer Views the Navy. "
        Scribner's Monthly, LXXXII (October 1927), 439-
        443.

3896   Talbot-Booth, Eric C.   All the World's Fighting Fleets.
        New York: D. Appleton-Century, 1937.   694p.

3897   , ed.   Naval Calendar: An Authentic Handbook
        of the Navies of Every Nation.   New York: Apple-
        ton, 1939.   272p.

3898   "Tallent, Robert W.   1937-1947. "   Leatherneck, XL
        (November 1957), 34-40.

3899   Tanner, W. E. , jt. author.   See Hughes, James J. ,
        no. 1771.

3900   Tansill, Charles C.   Back Door to War: The Roosevelt
        Foreign Policy, 1933-1941.   Chicago: Henry Reg-
        nery, 1952.   690p.
            "With regard to Japan, 'the question is how we
        should maneuver them into the Position of firing the
        first shot without allowing too much danger to our-
        selves' ... Secretary Hull answered that question

by submitting an ultimatum that he knew Japan
could not accept. The Japanese attack on Pearl
Harbor fulfilled the fondest hopes of the Roosevelt
Cabinet. "--Preface.

3901 _____. "Japanese-American Relations, 1921-1941:
The Pacific Back Road to War. " In: Harry E.
Barnes, ed. Perpetual War for Perpetual Peace.
Caldwell, Idaho: Caxton Printers. 1953. p. 269-315.

3902 _____. "The United States and the Road to War in
Europe. " Ibid. , p. 79-187.

3903 Tarbell, Ida M. Peacemakers--Blessed and Otherwise.
New York: Macmillan, 1922. 227p.
The Washington Naval Conference.

3904 Tarbuck, Raymond D. "The Nicaraguan Policy of the
United States. " USNIP, LVI (1930), 113-120.
Written by an American naval lieutenant.

3905 Tarr, Curtis W. "The [Navy] General Board Staff
Proposal of 1941. " Military Affairs, XXXI (Summer 1967), 85-90.

3906 _____. "Unification of America's Armed Forces:
A Century and a Half of Conflict, 1798-1947. " Unpublished PhD Dissertation, Stanford University,
1962.

3907 Tate, E. Mowbray. "U. S. Gunboats on the Yangtze:
History and Political Aspects, 1842-1922. " Unpub-
lished Paper, Individual Personnel File, Operational
Archives, U. S. Navy Department, Naval History
Division, 1965. 14p.
Events following the reorganization of the
Yangtze Patrol in 1920, including the Panay Inci-
dent of 1937, are briefly mentioned.

3908 _____. _____. In: Studies on Asia. Lincoln:
University of Nebraska Press, 1966. p. 121-131.

3909 Tate, Merze. The United States and Armaments.
Cambridge, Mass. : Harvard University Press,
1948. 312p. Rpr. 1969.
Some discussion of the Washington and London
naval conferences.

3910 Taussig, Joseph K. "The Answer to 135,000 Men--
      "A Just Man Armed Keepeth His House in Order'."
      USNIP, XLIX (1923), 1642-1654.

3911 _____. "A Balanced Fleet for the United States
      Navy." USNIP, LI (1925), 1107-1132.

3912 _____. "The Case for the Big Capital Ship."
      USNIP, LXVI (1940: 929-940.

3913 _____. "A Destroyer Leader for the United States
      Fleet." USNIP, LII (1926), 1111-1128, 1179, 1783-
      1791.
           The author gained fame in World War I.

3914 _____. "Is Enactment of the Britten Bill Desir-
      able?" USNIP, LIII (1927), 1256-1262.

3914a _____. "The Joint Army and Navy Problem in the
      Pacific." Unpublished Lecture, Command Course
      74, Files of the U.S. Army Military History Re-
      search Collection, 1925.

3915 _____. "Length of Service Retirement vs. Age in
      Grade Retirement." USNIP, LI (1925), 919-933.

3916 _____. "The Old Navy." USNIP, XLVII (1921), 1-6.

3917 _____. "An Organization of the Navy Department."
      USNIP, LXVI (1940), 52-57.

3918 _____. "An Organization of the United States Fleet."
      USNIP, LXV (1939), 639-652.

3919 _____. "Some Reflections on Our Commissioned
      Personnel Situation." USNIP, LXV (1939), 204-216.

3920 _____. "A Study of Our Navy Personnel Situation."
      USNIP, XLVII (1921), 1153-1200.

3921 _____. "A Study of Our Promotion and Graded Re-
      tirment Laws." USNIP, L (1924), 523-560.

3922 Tawresey, Alfred P. "Inspections." USNIP, LV
      (1929), 105-112.

3923 _____. "The Line Task: Command." USNIP, LV

(1929), 296-302.

3924 _____. "Some Aspects of Radio Telephone Broad-
casting. " USNIP, L (1924), 893-902.

3925 _____. "Training Naval Officers. " USNIP, LII
(1926), 1746-1757.

3926 _____., jt. author. See Hogg, William S. , no.
1700.

3927 _____., jt. author. See Moore, John W. , no.2592.

3928 Tawresey, John G. "The Portsmouth, New Hampshire,
Navy Yard. " In: Society of Naval Architects and
Marine Engineers. Historical Transactions, 1893-
1943. New York, 1945. p. 28-31.

3929 Taylor, Alan J. P. The Origins of the Second World
War. London: Hamilton, 1961. 296p.
The American edition was published by Atheneum
in 1962 while an expanded version of 357p. was
published by the Harmondsworth, Eng., firm of
Hamilton in 1964.

3930 Taylor, Albert H. The First Twenty-five Years of the
Naval Research Laboratory. Washington: Navy De-
partment, 1948. 75p.
Covers the years 1923-1945.

3931 Taylor, Albert P. "The American Navy in Hawaii. "
USNIP, LIII (1927), 907-924.

3932 Taylor, Conant. "The Effect of Current on Target
Approaches. " USNIP, LIV (1928), 467.
Features a large diagram.

3933 Taylor, David W. "The Design of Warships as Affected by the World War. " Journal of the Franklin
Institute, CXC (August 1920), 157-185.

3934 _____. "Some Reflections Upon Commissioned
Naval Personnel Problems. " USNIP, L (1924),
1771-1785.

3935 _____. The Speed and Power of Ships: A Manual
of Marine Propulsion. Rev. ed. Washington: Press

of Ransdell, 1933.   366p.

3936   Taylor, F.   "A Dollar for Every Drive." Popular
       Mechanics, XLV (February 1926), 218-223.
       Submarining.

3937   Taylor, George E.   "America's Pacific Policy: The
       Role and the Record."   Pacific Affairs, XIV (De-
       cember 1941), 430-447.

3938   Taylor, James H.   "A Legal Problem on Board Ship."
       USNIP, L (1924), 713-722.
       And what to do about it.

3939   _____.   "The Psychological Factor in Promotion by
       Selection."   USNIP, LIII (1927), 436-439.

3940   Taylor, James S.   "The Commanding Officer, Recruit-
       ing Officer, and Medical Officer vs. Desertion."
       USNIP, XLVII (1921), 39-60.

3941   _____.   "The Crime of the Colleges."   USNIP, XLV
       (1919), 2559-2565.

3942   Taylor, M. M.   "Landing Troops from Ships."   Unpub-
       lished Lecture, Miscellaneous Course 9, Files of
       the U. S. Army Military History Research Collec-
       tion, 1926.
       The author was a Navy admiral.

3943   Taylor, Robert L.   "Hanger No. 1: Recruitment at the
       Headquarters of the Naval Reserve of the New York
       District."   New Yorker, XVI (July 27, 1940), 34-37.

3944   Taylor, Theodore.   "A Matter of Judgment."   USNIP,
       LXXXVI (1960), 70-75.
       The German seizure of the City of Flint.

3945   Taylor, Walter L.   "The Philippine Question."   USNIP,
       LXVII (1941), 1223-1233.

3946   _____.   "Policy and the Naval Officer."   USNIP,
       LXV (1939), 1393-1404.

3947   Teale, Edwin.   "Does the Latest Disaster Spell the
       Doom of the Dirigible?"   Popular Science, CXXVI
       (May 1935), 26-27+.

Refers to the loss of the airship <u>Akron.</u>

3948 "Technical Aspects of the Loss of the U. S. S. Shenandoah. " <u>Journal of the American Society of Naval
Engineers,</u> XXXVIII (August 1926), 487-694.

3949 "Telephoning Men Trapped in Sunken Subs. " <u>Popular
Mechanics,</u> LIII (May 1930), 792.

3950 "The <u>Tennessee,</u> Our Latest Battleship. " <u>SciAmer,</u>
CXXIII (November 13, 1920), 501.

3951 "The Ten-year Naval Holiday. " <u>SciAmer,</u> CXXVI
(February 1922), 95-96.

3952 "Testimony of the Major General Commandant Before
the Senate Committee on Foreign Relations. "
<u>Marine Corps Gazette,</u> XIII (March 1928), 46-66.
With regard to Marine operations in Nicaragua.

3953 "Testing the Canal as America's Life-Line: A Most
Secret War Game Develops Hawaiian-Panama Defense. " <u>Literary Digest,</u> CXXI (May 9, 1936), 36.

3954 "Text of Five Power Naval Treaty Agreed on at Armament Conference. " <u>Commercial and Financial
Chronicle,</u> CXIV (February 4, 1922), 476-479.

3955 "Text of Five Power Submarine and Poison Gas Treaty
Approved at Armament Conference. " <u>Commerical
and Financial Chronicle,</u> CXIV (February 4, 1922),
479-480.

3956 "Text of Proposals by the United States for the Limitation of Naval Armaments. " <u>Commercial and
Financial Chronicle,</u> CXIII (November 19, 1921),
2147-2148.

3957 "Text of Treaties in Regard to Limitation of Armaments. " <u>USNIP,</u> XLVIII (1922), 476-490.
The Washington Treaty.

3958 Thacker, Joel D.   "Highlights of United States Marine
Corps Activities in the District of Columbia. "
<u>Columbia Historical Society Record,</u> LI-LII (1955),
78-86.

3959   _____ . "Marine Corps Aviation on Aircraft Car-
            riers Prior to World War II." Unpublished Paper,
            USMC File, Operational Archives, U. S. Navy De-
            partment, Naval History Division, n. d. 4p.

3960   Thebaud, L. H., comp. Naval Leadership, With Some
            Hints to Junior Officers and Others: A Compilation
            by and for the Navy. Annapolis: U. S. Naval Insti-
            tute, 1925. 209p.

3961   Theiss, Lewis E. On Board a U. S. Submarine. Bos-
            ton: W. A. Wilde, 1940. 308p.

3962   Theobald, Robert A. "Admiral Theobald Replies to the
            Kittredge Article." U. S. News and World Report,
            XXXVIII (January 28, 1955), 117-118.
            The Kittredge article is cited above.

3963   _____ . The Final Secret of Pearl Harbor: The
            Washington Contribution to the Japanese Attack.
            Forewords by Husband E. Kimmel and William F.
            Halsey. New York: Devin-Adair, 1954. 202p.
            Quite controversial!

3964   _____ . "Final Secrets of Pearl Harbor." U. S.
            News and World Report, XXXVI (April 2-7, 28,
            1954), 21-23, 48-93, 30-32, 48-50.

3965   "The Thirteenth Battalion." Leatherneck, XXIII (Aug-
            ust 1940), 18-20.

3966   "Thirty-Seven [Naval] Ships About to be Built: Edi-
            torial." New Republic, LXXV (June 28, 1933), 165.

3967   Thom, John C. "Rebuilding the Navy's Enlisted Per-
            sonnel and Reestablishing Its Morale and Spirit."
            USNIP, XLVI (1920), 1627-1636.

3968   Thomas, Charles W. Ice is Where You Find It. Indi-
            anapolis: Bobbs-Merrill, 1951. 378p.
            Another Coast Guard Officer's memoirs of the
            World War II Greenland Patrol.

3969   Thomas, David Y. "A Pacific Policy for the Pacific:
            An Open Letter to President Roosevelt and Secre-
            tary Hull." South Atlantic Quarterly, XXXVI (1937),
            121-136.

Condemns provocative naval policies in the
Pacific.

3970 Thomas, Donald I. "The Four-Stackers." USNIP,
LXXVI (1950), 752-757; LXXVII (1951), 86-87.
The World War II service of old World War I
destroyers; including those transferred to Great
Britain.

3971 Thomas, Lowell and Lowell Thomas, Jr. Famous
First Flights That Changed History. Garden City,
N. Y.: Doubleday, 1968. 340p.
Two chapters apply to our period, both concern-
ing Admiral Byrd: Chpt, VIII, "The Race to the
North Pole, " and Chpt. XII, "Byrd, Balchen, June,
and McKinley Fly Over the South Pole. "

3972 Thomas, Peter. "Self-Catapulting Autogiros for the
Protection of Cargo Vessels. " Aero Digest, XXXIX
(July 1941), 69-70+.

3973 Thomason, John W. , Jr. "Mail Day. " Scribner's
Monthly, LXXIX (April 1926), 421-426.
For Marines.

3974 _____. "The Marine Brigade. " USNIP. LIV (1928),
963-968.

3975 _____. "Marines See the Revolution. " Scribner's
Magazine, LXXXII (July 1927), 3-13.
Nicaragua.

3976 _____. "With the Special Service Squadron. "
Marine Corps Gazette, XII (June 1927), 76-81.
A contemporary look at the Caribbean and the
banana wars.

3977 Thompson, John D. "Feeding the Crew of a Battleship. " SciAmer, CXLIII (December 1930), 443-445.

3978 _____. "Housekeeping Aboard a Battleship. " Sci-
Amer, CXLIII (October 1930), 258-260.

3979 No Entry.

3980 Thompson, L. "Guam: Study in Military Government,
Lessons to be Learned from Forty Years of Amer-

ican Naval Rule. " Far Eastern Survey, XIII
(August 9, 1944), 149-154.

3981 Thompson, Terry B.   "The Navy--A Leader in Educa-
      tion. " USNIP, LVIII (1932), 555-556.

3982 Thomson, Charles A.   "Omnipotent Marines. " World
      Tomorrow, XIII (September 1930), 380-381.
      With reference to Nicaragua.

3983 Thone, Frank E. A.   "Listening in on War: Microphones
      Find Both Submarines and Planes. " Science News
      Letter, XXXVI (October 14, 1939), 246-247.

3984 Thorndike, Joseph J. , Jr.   "King of the Atlantic:
      America's Triple-Threat Admiral, Ernest J. King."
      Life, XI (November 24, 1941), 92-96.

3985 _____.   "King of the Fleet. " Reader's Digest, XL
      (March 1942), 53-56.
      A condensation of the article cited above.

3986 Thornton, J. M.   Warships, 1860-1970.   New York:
      Arco, 1973.   128p.
      A collection of 420 drawings with accompanying
      descriptive text tracing the development and de-
      ployment of modern warships of various classes.

3987 Thornycroft, J. E.   "Torpedo Boats. " Institute of
      Mechanical Engineering Proceedings, CXXXVI (1937),
      177-192.

3988 Thorpe, George C.   "Dominican Service. " Marine
      Corps Gazette, IV (December 1919), 315-326.

3989 "Thoughts on the Recurrence of Another Navy Day. "
      Christian Century, LIV (November 10, 1937), 1381.

3990 Thum, E. E.   "The Pitting of 18-8 in Navy Use. "
      Metal Progress, XXVII (February 1935), 37-39.

3991 Thurber, Henry R.   "Collarin' Cape Cod: Experiences
      on board a U. S. Navy Destroyer. " National Geo-
      graphic, XLVIII (October 1925), 427-472.

3992 _____.   "Some Notes on Destroyer Handling Along-
      side. " USNIP, LI (1925), 1202-1216.

3993 _____. "With the Wasps of the Sea." Popular
       Mechanics, XLVI (July 1926), 39-43.
       Destroyer maneuvers.

3994 Thursfield, Henry G. "The Atlantic." National Re-
       view, CXVIII (April 1941), 409-416.

3995 _____. "Battleships." National Review, CXV (No-
       vember 1940), 531-542.

3996 _____. "Modern Trends in Warship Design."
       Engineer, CLXI (April 3, 1936), 375-376.

3997 _____. "The Naval Conference, 1935-36." 19th
       Century, CXIX (June 1936), 734-747.

3998 _____. "Sea and Air." National Review, CXVII
       (September 1941), 285-293.

3999 Tieman, H. D. "That Big Navy." SciAmer, CXXI
       (July 5, 1919), 19.

4000 Tiffany, Frank K. "The Naval Communication Reserve
       Program." USNIP, LXV (1939), 534-538.

4001 Tilden, Arnold. "Why That Bigger Navy?" World
       Tomorrow, XVI (October 12, 1933), 562-563.

4002 Tilley, Benjamin F. "Handling 117 Decommissioned
       Destroyers." USNIP, XLIX (1923), 1105-1111.

4003 Tiltman, H. Hessell, jt. author. See Etherton, Percy
       T., no. 1173.

4004 Tily, James C. The Uniforms of the United States
       Navy. New York: Yoseloff, 1964. 338p.

4005 Times of London. Index to the Times. London, 1919-
       1941.
       Useful for locating in the newspaper the British
       view of such events as the Washington Conference.

4006 Tinker, Clifford A. "The American Occupation of
       Haiti and Santo Domingo." Review of Reviews,
       LXVI (July 1922), 46-60.

4007 _____. "Battleships on the Pacific: Capital War-

craft Essential for any U. S. Naval Campaign in the
Orient. " USNIP, LII (1926), 1454-1460.

4008 _____. "Jinx or Jeopardy: Causes of Naval Accidents. " Atlantic Monthly, CXXXIX (January 1927),
128-137.

4009 _____. "The Navy the Right Arm of the State Department. " Current History, XXV (October 1926),
53-59.

4010 _____. "Riding the Clouds in an Air Pullman: The
Los Angeles. " Popular Mechanics, XLVIII (July
1927), 100-104.

4011 _____. "What Price Pacifism?" USNIP, LII (1926),
2458-2469.

4012 _____. "The Whys and Wherefores of Airships. "
USNIP, XLVIII (1922), 691-702.

4013 Tisdale, Mahlon S. "Communications Afloat. " USNIP,
XLVIII (1922), 35-47.

4014 _____. "Intelligence Tests at the U. S. Naval
Academy. " USNIP, LI (1925), 202-214.

4015 _____. "Lo! The Poor Janitor. " USNIP, LIX
(1933), 167-174.

4016 _____. "The Naval Academy of Today and Its Mission. " USNIP, XLIX (1923), 453-463.

4017 _____. "Speeding Up Communications. " USNIP,
XLVII (1921), 1413-1415.

4018 "To Solve the Battlecruiser Problem. " SciAmer, CXX
(March 22, 1919), 280.

4019 "To Unite the Navy in the Pacific. " Literary Digest,
LXIX (April 2, 1921), 16-17.

4020 Todd, Forde A. "The Boatswain's Mate Passes the
Word. " USNIP, LXIVI (1937), 1458-1460.
A brief study in naval terms and phrases.

4021 _____. "The Factor of Safety in Navigation. "

USNIP, XLVII (1921), 1221-1232.

4022 _____. "Growth of Naval Officers." USNIP, LVIII
(1932), 1325-1332.

4023 _____. "The Present Vital Need of a Navy Personnel Policy." USNIP, XLV (1919), 377-382.

4024 _____. "Working During Working Hours." USNIP,
LIX (1933), 666-668.

4025 Todd, M. "How Commander Byrd Forecasts the Coming Age of the Air: An Interview." Literary Digest,
XCVII (April 7, 1928), 66-69.

4026 Togo, Shigenori. The Cause of Japan. Translated and
Edited by Togo Fumihiko and Ben B. Blakeney.
New York: Simon and Schuster, 1956. 372p.
A former Japanese statesman's view of the road
to Pearl Harbor.

4027 _____. "Why Japan Attacked Pearl Harbor." U.S.
News and World Report, XLI (August 31, 1956),
122-151.
An excerpt from 4026.

4028 Toland, John. "Death of a Dirigible." American
Heritage, X (February 1959), 18-24, 90-93.
The downing of the Shenandoah.

4029 _____. The Rising Sun. 2 vols. New York: Random House, 1970. Rpr. 1971.
U. S. -Japanese relations and war from the latter
viewpoint. Such incidents as the sinking of the
Panay are explored.

4030 _____. Ships in the Sky: The Story of the Great
Dirigibles. New York: Henry Holt, 1957. 352p.
Rpr. 1972.
Chronicles all the large Navy airships. The title
of the Dover reprint is The Great Dirigibles: Their
Triumphs & Disasters.

4031 Tolischus, Otto D. Tokyo Record. New York: Reynal
& Hitchcock, 1943. 462p.
A chronological report on political, economic,
diplomatic, military and naval events in Japan from

January 24-December 7, 1941. The author was on
the scene as Tokyo correspondent of the New York
Times.

4032 Tolley, Kemp. "The Cruise of the Lanikai." USNIP,
      XCIX (1973), 76-79.

4033 _____. Cruise of the Lanikai. Annapolis: U.S.
      Naval Institute, 1973. 356p.

4034 _____. "The Strange Assignment of the Lanikai."
      USNIP, LXXXVIII (1962), 70-83.
      The author's small schooner was to be placed in
      front of a Japanese task force (position unknown).
      Her sinking would then provide America with an
      excuse for entering (officially) World War II.

4035 _____. "The Strange Mission of the Lanikai."
      American Heritage, XXIV (October 1973), 56-61,
      93-95.

4036 _____. "Yangpat--Shanghai to Chungking." USNIP,
      LXXXIX (1963), 80-94.
      U.S. gunboats on the Yangtze, particularly dur-
      ing the years 1937-1941.

4037 _____. Yangtze Patrol: The U.S. Navy in China.
      Annapolis: U.S. Naval Institute, 1971. 320p.
      The best operational study of the patrol seen by
      this compiler.

4038 Toner, Raymond J. "Flood." USNIP, LXIV (1938),
      1162-1166.

4039 _____. "The Great Lakes Training Squadron."
      USNIP, LXIII (1937), 538-542.

4040 _____. "Impressions of Duty with the CCC."
      USNIP, LXII (1936), 670-676.

4041 Toney, Albert L. "The New Series of Army and Navy
      Commemorative Stamps." USNIP, LXIII (1937),
      557-558.
      Illustrated.

4042 "Tooling Tells the Tale in Making Torpedo Parts."
      Steel, CVIII (January 27, 1941), 42-43.

It would be more than tooling that came under
examination when American torpedoes proved less
than reliable early in the Big War.

4043 Toombs, Alfred. "The Navy Wants 4, 000 Radio Oper-
      ators. " Radio News, XXIV (November 1940), 8-9.

4044 Toon, Frank L. "To the Pole by Zep. " U. S. Coast
      Guard Magazine, IV (July 1931), 3.
          Rear Admiral Edward H. Smith and the Eckener
      flight.

4045 Topping, A. D. "The Etymology of Blimp. " American
      Aviation Historical Society Journal, VIII (Winter
      1963), 253-255.

4046 "Torpedo Attack by Airplane. " SciAmer, CXXX (June
      1924), 389.

4047 "Torpedo Boats and Destroyers, 1887-1958. " In: U.S.
      Navy Department. Naval History Division. Dic-
      tionary of American Naval Fighting Ships. Wash-
      ington: U. S. Government Printing Office, 1959--.
      I, 273-349.

4048 "Torpedoed Boats: Power Boat Association Fires on
      the Navy's Contract for British-Type Mosquito
      Craft. " Business Week, (January 13, 1940), 16.

4049 Towers, John H. "The Navy Expands Its Aircraft and
      Base Facilities. " Aviation, XXXIX (August 1940),
      38-39+.

4050 _____. "Operations of Naval Aircraft. " Society of
      Automotive Engineers Transactions, XIV (1919),
      373-385.

4051 _____. "The Great Hop. " Everybody's Magazine,
      XLI (November 1919), 9-15, 74-76.
          Relates to the flight of the NC's.

4052 _____. "Pilots and Mechanics for the Navy. "
      Aviation, XL (June 1941), 40-41+.

4052a "Track of the Cat. " Air Classics, V (October 1968),
      62+.
          Evolution of the PBY Flying Boat during our period.

4053 "Tragic Loss of the Submarine S-51. " SciAmer,
      CXXXIII (December 1925), 373.

4054 Train, C. R.   "Libraries in the Navy. " ALA Bulletin,
      XVI (1922), 129-131.

4055 "Training High School Boys for the Navy Proposed as
      a Permanent Method of Navy Recruiting. " Christian
      Century, LIV (August 11, 1937), 988.

4056 "Training Sailors to Shoot. " Popular Mechanics, XLIII
      (June 1925), 979-981.
           Naval target practice.

4057 Treadwell, Laurence P.   "From Cavite to Portsmouth:
      A Narrative of a Cruise of the U. S. S. Wilmington
      During the Summer of 1922. " USNIP, L (1924),
      1082-1093.

4058 Trefousse, Hans L.   Germany and American Neutrality,
      1939-1941.   New York: Bookman Associates, 1951.
      247p.   Rpr. 1969.

4059 _____, ed.   What Happened to Pearl Harbor? Docu-
      ments Pertaining to the Japanese Attack of Decem-
      ber 7, 1941 and Its Background.   New York: Twayne,
      1958.   324p.

4060 "Trend of Design in Aircraft Carriers: Drawings. "
      SciAmer, CLVIII (February 1938), 68.

4061 Trevelyan, George M.   Admiral Sir Herbert Richmond,
      1871-1946.   London, 1948.   15p.

4062 "The Trial Run of the Navy's Highest-Powered Cruis-
      er. " Marine Engineering, XXVIII (February 1923),
      109-110.

4063 "Tribute to Those Who Did not Die in Vain. " U. S.
      Coast Guard Magazine, VI (August 1933), 3.
           Coast Guard sailors killed enforcing Prohibition.

4064 Tripp, Gary E.   "A Manufacturer on Preparedness. "
      USNIP, LI (1925), 831-833.

4065 Troublous Pacific. " Literary Digest, LXXXV (May
      30, 1925), 17.

Stirred up by the great cruise of the American fleet in 1925.

4066 True, Arnold E. "Aerology and the Navy." USNIP, LVIII (1932), 1116-1118.

4067 Trueblood, Howard J. "The Havana Conference of 1940." Foreign Policy Reports, XVI (September 15, 1940), 158-164.

4068 "Trumpet Blast to Halt Ruinous Naval Rivalry." Literary Digest, XCII (February 26, 1927), 5-7.

4069 Tucker, Gilbert N. The Naval Service of Canada: Its Official History. 2 vols. Ottawa: King's Printer, 1952.
With data on its cooperation with the American navy relative to our period.

4070 Tuleja, Thaddeus V. Statesmen and Admirals: The Quest for a Far Eastern Naval Policy. New York: W. W. Norton, 1963. 256p.
In the years between the two world wars.

4071 _____. "United States Naval Policy in the Pacific, 1930-1941." Unpublished PhD Dissertation, Fordham University, 1961.

4072 Turnbladh, Edwin T., jt. author. See Condit, Kenneth W., no. 801.

4073 Turnbull, Archibald D. "Battleship or Airship?" Current History, XXII (April 1925), 10-18.

4074 _____. "Destroyers." St. Nicholas Magazine, XLIX (July 1922), 956-960.

4075 _____. "Economy and Naval Personnel." North American Review, CCXV (April 1922), 459-463.

4076 _____. "Our Deep-Sea Defenders." St. Nicholas Magazine, LIV (October 1927), 945.

4077 _____. "Our Navy Divers." St. Nicholas Magazine, LV (June 1928), 638-639.

4078 _____. "Our Navy in the Air. St. Nicholas Magazine, LI (July 1924), 899-906.

4079 _____ . "Shaking-down with the Cruisers. " St.
Nicholas Magazine, LI (October 1924), 1264-1270.

4080 _____ . "Seven Years of [Josephus] Daniels. "
North American Review, CCXII (November 1920),
606-617.

4081 _____ . "Stuff that Byrds are Made of. " St. Nicholas Magazine, LV (September 1928), 871-874.

4082 _____ . "The United States a Second-class Naval
Power. " Current History, XIX (August 1924), 969-
983.
       Mostly due, the author believes, to the signing
of the Washington Naval Treaty.

4083 _____ and Clifford L. Lord. History of United
States Naval Aviation. New Haven: Yale University
Press, 1949. 345p. Rpr. 1971.

4084 Turner, C. E. "A Capital Ship's Structural Defense:
Drawings. " SciAmer, CLIV (May 1936), 259.

4085 _____ . "Experiences in an American-Built Destroyer in the Atlantic. " Illustrated London News,
CXCVIII (March 15, 1941), 345, 348-349.
       One of the four-stackers exchanged with 49 others
for British air bases--narrative.

4086 _____ . "Sketches on board a U. S. -Built Destroyer
Now Serving with the Royal Navy. " Illustrated
London News, CXCVIII (March 15, 1941), 346-347.

4087 Tuthill, John T. He's in the Navy Now. New York:
McBride, 1941. 256p.
       "Exactly what happens to an applicant from the
moment he applies to the time he is accepted and
what he experiences when he is assigned to a receiving station, battleship, submarine, PT boat, or
when he is assigned to shore duty. "--p. 9.

4088 "Twilight of the Battleship. " Literary Digest, CIV
(February 1, 1930), 9-10.

4089 "Twister Wrecks the Shenandoah. " Aviation, XIX

(September 14, 1925), 310-314.
A discussion by Cmdr. Charles Rosendahl
appeared in the same publication for November 2,
1925, p. 635.

4090   "Two Airplanes Successfully Launched from a Dirig-
       ible. " SciAmer, CXXXVI (February 1927), 112.

4091   Tyson, David O.   "The Story of the Battleship Arizona
       [BB-39]. " Arizona History, XXIX (September
       1953), 34-39.
       A memorial now covers her wreckage at Pearl
       Harbor; however, this ship's history covers her
       entire career 1916-1941.

4092   "Ugly Duckling: The Torpedo-Torn Kearny Shows Up
       Her Critics. " Newsweek, XVIII (November 10,
       1941), 22.

4093   "Uncle Sam's Big New Submarine, the V-4, Mine-Lay-
       ing Submarine. " Literary Digest, XCV (November
       26, 1927), 12.
       SS-166, U. S. S. Argonaut, was indeed a giant!

4094   "Uncle Sam's Latest Treaty Cruiser in Action: An
       Artist's Drawing of the Cruiser Northampton. "
       Popular Mechanics, LIV (October 1930), 604-605.
       CA-26 would not survive World War II.

4095   "Uncle Sam's 9-Acre Wonder Hanger on Wheels: Hanger
       Built at Akron for the ZRS-4. " Literary Digest,
       CIX (January 4, 1930), 50-51.

4096   "Uncle Sam's Spidery Flying Fort, ZRS-4, or the
       Akron. " Literary Digest, CIX (June 13, 1931), 28-
       29.

4097   "The United States Aircraft Carrier Langley. " Avia-
       tion, IX (December 27, 1920), 478-479.

4098   "The United States Aircraft Carrier Lexington. " Engi-
       neering, CXX (October 9, 1925), 452-453.

4099   "The U. S. Aircraft Carriers, Saratoga and Lexington,
       Have Huge Steam-Electric Power Plants. "
       Mechanical Engineer, L (April 1928), 280-284.

4100 "U. S. Airplane Carrier <u>Lexington</u> to be Launched October 3. " <u>Marine Engineering</u>, XXX (October 1925), 558.

4101 "The United States Antarctic Expedition. " <u>Science</u>, New Series XC (October 20, 1939), 366.

4102 "United States Antarctic Expedition, 1939-1941: Abstract of Symposium. " <u>Nature</u>, CXLIX (March 21, 1942), 319-321.
       The Byrd Expedition.

4103 "United States Antarctic Service. " <u>Geographic Journal</u>, XCV (June 1940), 476-477; XCVI (September 1940) 224.

4104 "The United States Battleship <u>Colorado</u>. " <u>Engineer</u>, CXXXVII (January 25-February 1, 1924), 90-92, 96, 120.
       BB-45, launched in 1921 and scrapped in 1959.

4105 "The U. S. -British Destroyer-Naval Base Deal and Far Eastern Repercussions. " <u>China Weekly Review</u>, XCIV (September 14, 1940), 42-44.

4106 "U. S. Defense: Appendix, Sea Power and the U. S. " <u>Fortune</u>, XXII (September 1940), 136-140.

4107 "A U. S. Destroyer in Clash With a U-boat. " <u>China Weekly Review</u>, XCVIII (September 13, 1941), 57.
       U-652 vs. the four-stacker U. S. S. <u>Greer</u>.

4108 "U. S. Fleet to be Second to None. " <u>Popular Mechanics</u>, LXI (May 1934), 657-672.

4109 "The United States Fleet Visits Panama. " <u>Pan American Magazine</u>, XLI (March 1929), 300-306.

4110 "United States Inaugurates Huge Naval Program. " <u>China Weekly Review</u>, LXV (August 12, 1933), 434-435.

4111 "United States Invokes Escalator Clause in 1936 London Naval Treaty--Will Build Battleship Larger than 25, 000 Tons--Britain and France Ready to Take Similar Step. " <u>Commercial and Financial Chronicle</u>, CXLVI (April 2, 1938), 2141.

4112 "U. S. -Japanese Naval Expansion Rivalry Disturbs the
      Japanese Mind. " China Weekly Review, LXVI
      (September 23, 1933), 146-147.

4113 "The United States Light Cruiser Omaha. ' SciAmer,
      CXXIV (January 15, 1921), 49.

4114 "The United States Naval Air Service, 1922-1923. "
      Aviation, XVI (January 14, 1924), 34-37.

4115 "U. S. Naval Aircraft Construction, 1920. " Aviation,
      X (January 3, 1921), 10-11.

4116 "The United States Naval Aviation Program, 1923. "
      Aviation, XII (March 27, 1922), 364-365.

4117 "U. S. Naval Bases Recently Acquired from Great
      Britain and Other U. S. Naval Bases. " National
      Geographic Magazine, LXXIX (January 1941), 41.
      A map.

4118 "U. S. Naval Expansion and the Question of Mediating
      the Sino-Japanese War. " China Weekly Review,
      XC (November 18, 1939), 423-426.

4119 "U. S. Naval Games. " Scholastic, XXXVI (April 15,
      1940), 4.

4120 U. S. Naval Institute. Naval Leadership, with Some
      Hints to Junior Officers and Others: A Compilation
      by and for the Navy. 2nd ed. Annapolis, 1925.
      209p.

4121 _____. The Navy and Its Relation to the Nation: A
      Collection of Articles and Statistical Data. Annap-
      olis, 1930. 78p.

4122 "The United States Navy: A Plain Statement. " Atlantic
      Monthly, CXXXIV (August 1924), 242-251.

4123 "U. S. Navy Airplanes, 1911-1969. " In: U. S. Navy
      Deparment. Naval History Division. Dictionary of
      American Naval Fighting Ships. Washington: U. S.
      Government Printing Office. 1959--. V, 526-628.

4124 "The U. S. Navy Airship ZR-1. " Aviation, XII (August
      28, 1922), 254-256.
      The Shenandoah.

4125 "U. S. Navy Class 'C' Dirigible. " Aerial Age Weekly,
      IX (August 1919), 1095-1908.

4126 "U. S. Navy Dirigible Shenandoah Destroyed by Storm. "
      Engineering News, XCV (September 10, 1925), 415,
      437-441.

4127 "The U. S. Navy Finds Trouble: The Greer and Kearny
      Cases. " Time, XXXVIII (October 27, 1941), 28-
      29.

4128 "The United States Navy Gets the World's Mightiest
      Ship: U. S. S. North Carolina. " Life, X (April 21,
      1941), 38-39.

4129 "The United States Navy Reorganized into Three
      Fleets. " Commercial and Financial Chronicle,
      CLII (January 11, 1941), 206.

4130 "The United States Navy Through 150 Years, 1798-
      1948. " USNIP, LXXIV (1948), 882-891.

4131 "The United States Navy Today: Policy, Organization,
      Activities, Glossary of Terms: A Symposium. "
      Congressional Digest, IV (January 1925), 119-123.

4132 "U. S. Navy Yards Repair Bombed British Warships. "
      Life, XI (October 20, 1941), 42-43.

4133 "The United States Now the Great Naval Power. "
      World's Work, XLI (February 1921), 326-327.

4134 "United States Refuses British Suggestion to Delay
      Cruiser Construction: The Navy Now Building Four
      Ships of the Type to Which the British Objected. "
      Commercial and Financial Chronicle, CXXXVII
      (September 30, 1933), 237+.

4135 "The United States Rigid Airship Akron. " Engineering,
      CXXXII (August 21, 1931), 215-218, 230.

4136 "U. S. Strategic Pacific Sites, Which Envelop Japan at
      All Points. " Illustrated London News, CXCVIII
      (March 1, 1941), 275.

4137 "U. S. to Proceed with Guam and Other Air-Naval
      Bases in the Pacific. " China Weekly Review, XCII

(March 30, 1940), 144-146.

4138 "U. S. Warships on the Auction Block. " Popular
      Mechanics, XLI (January 1924), 24-25.

4139 "U. S. A. and Japan: Two Navies in a Chart Silhouette."
      Illustrated London News, CXCIX (October 25, 1941),
      532.

4140 "The U. S. A. and Naval Disarmament. " Contemporary
      Review, CXIX (March 1921), 398-400.

4141 "U. S. A. Help in the U-boat War: The Catalina Flying
      Boat. " Illustrated London News, CXCVIII (April
      19, 1941), 516.

4142 "The U. S. A. in European Waters: The American Occu-
      pation of Iceland. " Illustrated London News, CXCIX
      (July 26, 1941), 103.

4143 "U. S. S. Colorado. " Marine Engineering, XXVIII
      (October 1923), 605-608+.

4144 "U. S. S. Flusser Launched. " Marine Engineering, XL
      (November 1935), 425-426.

4145 "U. S. S. Ranger Performance. " Marine Engineering,
      XXXIX (September 1934), 337-338.

4146 U. S. S. Shenandoah. West Roxbury, Mass.: W. W. I.
      Aero Publishers, n. d.
      The airship.

4147 "The U. S. S. West Virginia Goes into Commission This
      Month. " Marine Engineering, XXVIII (December
      1923), 783.
      BB-48, launched in 1921, would survive Pearl
      Harbor.

4148 "U. S. S. Wright: Our First Balloon-and-Airplane Car-
      rier. " SciAmer, CXXVI (April 1922) 267.

4149 Upham, Frank B. "Leadership of Men. " USNIP,
      XLVII (1921), 487-496.

4150 _____. "The Philosophy of Loyalty. " USNIP, LVII
      (1931), 1157-1162.

Address delivered at the opening of the Naval
post-graduate school at Annapolis, June 29, 1931.

4151 Upshur, Williap P. "The United States Marine Corps
      Reserve. " USNIP, LXV (1939), 437-493.

4152 Upson, Ralph H. "Metalclad Rigid Airship Develop-
      ment. " Society of Automotive Engineers Journal,
      XVIII (February 1926), 94-96, 117-131; XIX (Octo-
      ber 1926), 391-398.

4153 _____. "Past Adventures and Future Prospects of
      Metalclad Airships. " Society of Automotive Engi-
      neers Journal, XXVI (May 1930), 567-575.

4154 Urquidi, Donald, jt. author. See Burns, Richard D.,
      no. 567.

4155 Usborne, Cecil V. "Modern Aspects of Naval Stra-
      tegy. " 19th Century, CXXVI (July 1939), 14-28.

4156 "The Uses of the Navy. " SciAmer, CXXI (December
      13, 1919), 574.

4157 Utley, Harold H. "Special Boats for Landing Opera-
      tions. " USNIP, LVII (1931), 520-524.

4158 Vaeth, J. Gordon. "Blimps for Defense: Sea Patrol."
      Current History, LII (February 13, 1941), 24-26.

4159 _____. "Daughter of the Stars. " USNIP, XCIX
      (1973), 61-67.
      ZR-1, the airship Shenandoah.

4160 Vagts, Alfred. Landing Operations: Strategy, Psychol-
      ogy, Tactics, Politics, from Antiquity to 1945.
      Harrisburg, Pa.: Military Service Publishing Com-
      pany, 1946. 831p.

4161 _____, jt. author. See Beard, Charles A. , no. 311.

4162 Van Auken, Wilbur R. Notes on a Half Century of
      United States Naval Ordnance, 1880-1930. Wash-
      ington, 1939. 56p.

4163 Van Blarcom, Frederick. "Speed Versus Armor. "
      SciAmer, CXXII (January 24, 1920), 89.
      Battlecruisers.

4164   Van Boskerok, F. S.   "The United States Coast Guard:
       Its Military Necessities. " USNIP, XLV (1919).
       623-636.

4165   Vandercook, John W.   "America's New Front Line of
       Defense. " Liberty Magazine, XVII (October 19,
       1940), 45-47.
       The Western Hemisphere.

4166   Van Gelder, Paul H.   "What Our Warships Cost: A
       Rejoinder. " Nation, CXLIX (October 21, 1939),
       451.
       The offending article was written by D. W.
       Mitchell and is cited above.

4167   Vangeli, M. G.   "Building a Fleet. " Iron Age, CXXXIX
       (May 20, 1937), 30-31+.

4168   Van Hook, J. Q.   "Genesis of the War in the Pacific
       Area. " Southwestern Social Science Quarterly,
       XXIII (March 1943), 381-398.
       The road to Pearl Harbor.

4169   Van Keuren, A. H.   "Why Battleships are Necessary in
       All Major Naval Fleets. " Marine Review, LIX
       (October 1929), 17-19.

4170   Van Meter, William J. , Jr.   "Thoughts on Leaving the
       Naval Service. " USNIP, LIX (1933), 1323-1326.

4171   Van Swearingen, E. E.   "The Vulnerability of Airships
       to Airplane Attacks. " USNIP, LXII (1936), 1244-
       1246.

4172   Van Wyen, Adrain O.   "Chronology of Lighter-Than-
       Air-History in the U. S. Navy, 1915-1962. " Un-
       published Paper, Individual Personnel File, Opera-
       tional Archives, U. S. Navy Department, Naval His-
       tory Division, 1962. 18p.

4173   _____.   "Notes on the Origin of Torpedo Attack in
       the United States Navy. " Unpublished Paper, Indi-
       vidual Personnel File, U. S. Navy Department,
       Naval History Division, 1948.   6p.
       The first assignment of carrier-based torpedo
       units was made in 1927.

4174 Varg, Paul. "Alternatives in the Far East." World
     Affairs, XXVI (1955), 247-254.
     At and before the time of Pearl Harbor.

4175 "The Vast U. S. Navy Program is Put Under the Con-
     gressional Microscope." Newsweek, XV (January
     22, 1940), 11-14.

4176 Veatch, Roy. "Can Battleships Be Abolished Now?"
     New Republic, LXI (February 12, 1930), 329-330.

4177 Verrill, Hyatt. "The Greatest of All Smugglers." In:
     his Smugglers and Smuggling. New York: Duffield,
     1924. p. 197-211.
     Describes the smuggling of liquor into America
     during Prohibition and the efforts of the Coast Guard
     to prevent it.

4178 "Very Cold Facts: Highlights of Reports to the Ameri-
     can Philosophical Society." Time, XXXVIII (De-
     cember 1, 1941), 41.
     Related to the 1939-1941 Byrd Expedition.

4179 Vickery, Howard L. "Naval Yardstick." Foreign
     Affairs, VIII (October 1929), 142-144.

4180 Villard, Oswald G. "Issues and Men." Nation, CXLVI
     (January 8, 1938), 56.
     The U. S. naval building program.

4181 _____. "The President and a Big Navy." Nation,
     CXXXVI (April 19, 1933), 435.

4182 _____. "What Good are Battleships?" Nation, CL
     (January 20, 1940), 76.

4183 Vinney, John, jt. comp. See Kendall, Park, no. 1950.

4184 Vinson, Carl. "Argument in Favor of Improving the
     Aviation Facilities on the Island of Guam." Con-
     gressional Digest, XVIII (March 1939), 86-87.

4185 _____. "Provisions of the Vinson Navy Bill." Con-
     gressional Digest, XIII (April 1934), 119.

4186 Vinson, Fred M. "Navy Needs." USNIP, LVIII (1932),
     580.

Extract from a speech by the congressman.

4187 Vinson, John C.   The Parchment Peace: The United
States Senate and the Washington Conference, 1921-
1922.   Athens: University of Georgia Press, 1955.
259p.

4188 The Vinson Act and a Treaty Navy.   Washington: Navy
League of the United States, 1934.   2p.

4189 "The Vinson Bill Authorizes a Limit Navy. "   Christian
Century, LI (April 4, 1934), 445.

4190 Vogel, Bertram.   "Diplomatic Prelude to Pearl Harbor. "   USNIP, LXXV (1949), 414-421.

4191 Von Karman, T.   "Wind Vortex Wrecked the Airship
Akron. "   SciAmer, CXLIX (September 1933), 125.

4192 Vosseller, Aurelius B.   "Bombers Plus Battleships:
Both Are Needed for Co-ordinated Effort. "   Sci-
Amer, CLXIII (October 1940), 183-185.

4193 _____.   "The Patrol Plane and the Future. " USNIP,
LXVI (1940), 1577-1586.

4194 Votaw, Homcer C.   "Midway--the North Pacific's Tiny
Pet. "   USNIP, LXVI (1940), 1601-1607.
An historical treatment.

4195 "Vought Corsair Naval Airplane. "   Aviation, XXII
(May 2, 1927), 934+.

4196 "The Vought V-100 Corsair. "   Aero Digest, XXVI
(March 1935), 40-41.

4197 "The, Voyage of the [Coast Guard Cutter] Marion. "
Science, Supplement, New Series LXVIII (July 20,
1928), 12-14.

4198 Vroom, Guysbert B.   "Strategic Value of the Aircraft
Carrier. "   USNIP, LI (1925), 78-82.

4199 Wade, Franklin A.   "The U.S. Government Expedition
to the Antarctic. "   Scientific Monthly, XLIX (October 1939), 382-387.
Captained by Admiral Byrd.

4200   Waesche, Russell R.   "Armaments and Gunnery in the
       Coast Guard. "   USNIP, LV (1929), 381-384.

4201   "Wages in the Mechanical Service of the Navy Depart-
       ment, 1941. "   Monthly Labor Review, LII (Feb-
       ruary 1941), 445-451.

4202   "Wages of Civil Employees in the Field Service of the
       Navy Department and Marine Corps, 1932. "
       Monthly Labor Review, XXXIV (May 1932), 1146-
       1149.

4203   "Wages of Civil Employees in the Field Service of the
       Navy Department and Marine Corps, 1936. "
       Monthly Labor Review, XLIII (July 1936), 151-154.

4204   "Wages of Civil Employees Under the Naval Establish-
       ment. "   Monthly Labor Review, XX (February
       1925), 311-314.

4205   _____ . _____ .   XXII (February 1926), 361-364.

4206   _____ . _____ .   XXIV (April 1927), 733-736.

4207   _____ . _____ .   XXVI (March 1928), 603-605.

4208   "Wages of Civil Employees Under the United States
       Naval Establishment, 1929. "   Monthly Labor Re-
       view, XXVIII (February 1929), 298-301.

4209   Wainwright, John D.   "What Strategic Changes in the
       Pacific Would be Caused by the Independence of the
       Philippine Islands?"   Unpublished Staff Memoran-
       dum, Files of the U. S. Army Military History Re-
       search Collection, 1933.
       The author was a Navy rear admiral.

4210   Wakeman, S. W.   "The Launching of the Airplane Car-
       rier U. S. S. Lexington. "   Engineering, CXXII (De-
       cember 10-17, 1926), 737-741, 770-772.

4211   Walker, Fred.   Destination Unknown: Running Away
       from Danger.   Philadelphia: Lippincott, 1935. 273p.
       Memoirs of a soldier of fortune who fought with
       Sandino's Nicaraguan bandits against the American
       marines.

4212   Walker, John B.   "Annapolis, the Famous College
        Where Our Future Admirals Receive Their First
        Training." SciAmer, CXXXIV (June 1926), 392-
        394.

4213   _____. "Giant Floating Aircraft Bases: Saratoga
        and Lexington." SciAmer, CXXXV (August 1926),
        104-105.

4214   _____. "Last Word on the 5-5-3 Ratio." SciAmer,
        CXXXII (May 1925), 306-307.
            For the reply by Commodore Knox, see the
        citation above.

4215   _____. "The Naval Strength of the United States,
        Great Britain, and Japan: How the Age of Ships
        will Affect Relative Fighting Efficiency by 1924."
        SciAmer, CXXV (November 1921), 11-13.

4216   _____. "The New Battlecruiser Constellation."
        SciAmer, CXXIV (January 29, 1921), 91.
            Cancelled in 1923 under terms of the Washington
        Treaty and scrapped before completion.

4217   _____. "Post-War Navies: How the War Fleets of
        the United States and Great Britain Were Brought
        Down to a Peacetime Basis." SciAmer, CXXXVII
        (December 1927), 526-528.

4218   _____. "The Reconstructed Battleship Texas."
        SciAmer, CXXXVI (April 1927), 252.

4219   _____. "The Return of the American Fleet." Sci-
        Amer, CXX (January 11, 1919), 32-33.
            From European waters after World War I.

4220   _____. "Scrapping the Battleships." SciAmer,
        CXXVI (March 1922), 185-188.
            Under the terms of the Washington Treaty.

4221   _____. "Some Naval Theories Exploded: A Re-
        joinder." SciAmer, CXXXIII (September 1925),
        178-179.
            A reply to Commodore Knox's reply to the
        author's original article.

4222   _____. "Tragedy of the Shenandoah." SciAmer,

CXXXIII (November 1925), 301.

4223 _____. War in the Air: Fighting Planes and Pilots
in Action. New York: Random House, 1941. 74p.

4224 Walker, Robert J. "Fleet Repair Facilities Ashore."
USNIP, LXI (1935), 1120-1124.

4225 Waller, George M., ed. Pearl Harbor: Roosevelt and
the Coming of the War. Problems in American
Civilization. Boston: D. C. Heath, 1953. 112p.
Rpr. 1965.

4226 Wallin, Homer N. "Permissible Building Programs
Under the London Naval Treaty." USNIP, LVI
(1930), 1074-1079.

4227 Walls, Mary, jt. author. See McPherson, Guy, no.
2383.

4228 Walsh, David I. "The Naval Expansion Program." In:
Julia E. Johnson, ed. Peace and Rearmament.
Vol. XI of The Reference Shelf. New York: H. W.
Wilson, 1938. p. 120-122.
A speech by the Massachusetts senator reprinted
from the April 19, 1938 issue of the Congressional
Record.

4229 _____. "Speech in the Senate, January 10, 1940,
on the Harrison Budget Resolution and the Naval
Expansion Proposal." Congressional Digest, XIX
(February 1940), 57-60.

4230 Walsh, Richard J. "On the Tail of the Grand Banks:
The [Coast Guard] Ice Patrol." Collier's, LXXV
(April 11, 1925), 26.

4231 Wambaugh, Stephen. "American and World Disarmament." Independent, CXII (June 21, 1924), 334-336.

4232 "Wanted: Honest Naval Negotiations." Christian Century, LI (October 31, 1934), 1367-1369.

4233 "War Fleets of the Nations." Engineering, CXIX
(April 17, 1925), 467-468.

4234 "War in the Wind." Newsweek, XXVII (February 11,

           1946), 25-26.
           The days before Pearl Harbor.

4235   Ward, Robert E.   "The Inside Story of the Pearl Har-
           bor Plan. "   USNIP, LXXVII (1951), 1271-1283.

4236   Wardrop, G. D.   "Future Defensive Navy: What Rela-
           tion Should Aeronautics Have to the Modern Effi-
           cient Navy?"   Flying X (February 1921), 6-12.

4237   Ware, Bruce R. "Winning the Engineering White E. "
           USNIP, XLV (1919), 593-621.

4238   Warner, Edward P.   "An Air Policy for the United
           States. "   USNIP, LI (1925), 722-736.

4239   _____.   "The Design and Supply of Naval Aircraft."
           Mechanical Engineer, L (August 1928), 611-614.

4240   _____.   "Naval Aviation Activities. "   Society of
           Automotive Engineers Journal, XXI (September
           1927), 310.

4241   _____.   "Naval Aviation and Its Common Interest
           with Our Commerce. "   USNIP, LIII (1927), 1052-
           1055.

4242   Warner, Oliver.   "The United States Fleet. "   In: his
           Great Battle Fleets.   London: Hamlyn, 1973.
           p. 212-238.
           Some data on our period.

4243   Warren, L. P.   "The Battleship Still Supreme. "
           World's Work, XLI (April 1921), 556-559.

4244   "Warship as a Peace Laboratory. "   Literary Digest,
           LXXVIII (September 15, 1923), 15.
           The dreadnought Colorado.

4245   "Warship Design and Torpedo Attacks. "   Engineering,
           CXI (May 20, 1921), 619-620.

4246   "Warships Tested in Miniature Ocean. "   Popular Sci-
           ence, CXXXII (January 1938), 36-37.

4247   Washington, Bowden.   "What is the Matter with Our
           Navy's Radio?" USNIP, XLVII (1931), 21-27.

4248 "Washington Conference Battleships. " SciAmer,
      CXXVIII (May 1923), 304.

4249 "The Washington Treaties, 1922. " USNIP, LII (1926),
      1057-1076.

4250 "Watch by the S-51. " Literary Digest, LXXXVII (Octo-
      ber 17, 1925), 58-62.
          Attempts to save the men inside the stricken
      submarine.

4251 Waterman, Hawley. "The Motor Convoy. " Leather-
      neck, XXIII (September 1940), 7.

4252 Waters, Harold. Smugglers of Spirits: Prohibition and
      the Coast Guard Patrol. New York: Hastings
      House, 1971. 220p.

4253 _____ and Aubrey Wisberg. Patrol Boat 999. New
      York: Chilton, 1959. 256p.
          Efforts of a 75-foot Coast Guard cutter to pre-
      vent liquor smuggling into Florida during the Pro-
      hibition Era.

4254 Watson, Ernest. "The Birth of the Flat-top. " USNIP,
      LXXXII (1956), 474-481.

4255 Watson, John. "The Gas-Bag Fleet: The Navy Counts
      on Blimps for Patrol and Convoy Work. " Popular
      Science, CXXXIX (July 1941), 82-87.

4256 Watson, Mark S. Chief-of-Staff: Prewar Plans and
      Preparations. U. S. Army in World War II: The
      War Department. Washington: Historical Division,
      U. S. Army, 1950. 551p.
          Contains data concerning military co-operation
      with the navy and vice versa.

4257 Watts, Marion B. "Service Wife. " American Mer-
      cury, XXV (February 1932), 160-166.

4258 Watts, Peter. "Naval Design and the Washington Con-
      ference. " Engineering, CXIV (July 21, 1922), 88.

4259 "We Should Hasten Battle-cruiser Construction. " Sci-
      Amer, CXX (June 28, 1919), 680.

4260 Wead, Frank W. "Airplane Racing and Record Chas-
      ing. " USNIP, LIII (1927), 782-786.

4261 _____ . Gales, Ice, and Men: A Biography of the
      Steam Barkentine Bear. New York: Dodd, Mead,
      1937. 272p.

4262 _____ . "Naval Aviation To-day. " USNIP, L (1924),
      561-574.

4263 _____ . "The Navy and Naval Aviation. " USNIP,
      LII (1926), 880-899.

4264 Weaver, G. C. "Developments in the Construction of
      Submarines: The United States Submarine Cacha-
      lot. " Marine Engineering, XXXVIII (February
      1933), 44-47.

4265 Webb, Hanor A. "How Byrd Broadcasts. " St. Nicho-
      las Magazine, LXI (February 1934) 216-217.

4266 Webb, L. D. "Airplane Carrier Operations. " Society
      of Automotive Engineers Journal, XXVIII (May
      1931), 593-594.

4267 _____ . "Plane Operations on Carriers. " Society
      of Automotive Engineers Journal, XXVI (January
      1930), 10-11.

4268 Webster, William. "The Cruiser. " USNIP, LII
      (1926), 607-620.

4269 Weems, Philip V. H. "Decommissioning Destroyers
      at Philadelphia. " USNIP, XLIX (1923), 449-452.

4270 _____ . "The Peace Time Navy and Merchant
      Marine. " USNIP, XLVIII (1922), 1731-1747.

4271 Weigley, Russell F. The American Way of War: A
      History of United States Military Strategy and
      Policy. The Wars of the United States Series.
      New York: Macmillan, 1973. 584p.
          Two chapters relate to our period: Chpt. XI,
      "A Strategy of Air Power: Billy Mitchell, " and
      Chpt. XII, "A Strategy for Pacific Ocean War:
      Naval Strategists of the 1920s and 1930s. "

4272 Welch, Philip P. "Uniform Jig for Jersey." USNIP,
      LXII (1936), 1169-1170.

4273 Welles, Sumner. "Far Eastern Policy Before Pearl
      Harbor." In: his Seven Decisions That Shaped
      History. New York: Harper, 1950. Chpt. III.

4274 _____. Naboth's Vineyard: The Dominican Republic,
      1844-1924. 2 vols. New York: Payson and Clarke,
      1928. Rpr. 1973.
           Material of interest to users of this compilation
      appears in Vol. II.

4275 Welliver, Judson C. "The Naval Fight for Peace."
      Review of Reviews, LXXV (May 1927), 483-493.
           Over the tables of the disarmament conferences.

4276 Wertenbaker, Thomas J. Norfolk: Historic Southern
      Port. Duke University Studies. Durham, N. C. :
      Duke University Press, 1931. 378p.

4277 West, James H. "A Short History of the New York
      Navy Yard." Unpublished Paper, Subject File 1911-
      1927, ZPN-3, Box 820, National Archives, 1942.
      190p.
           Prepared under the direction of its commandant,
      Rear Admiral C. H. Woodward, this history traces
      the development of the yard as a privately-owned
      enterprise through 1941.

4278 West, Richards. "The Superintendents of the Naval
      Academy." USNIP, LXXI (1945), 801-809; LXXII
      (1946), 59-67.
           Brief biographies with lists of duties and ac-
      complishments.

4279 Westcott, Allan F., ed. American Sea Power Since
      1775. Rev. ed. Philadelphia: Lippincott, 1952.
      609p.

4280 _____., jt. author. See Stevens, William O., no.
      3789.

4281 Westervelt, George C. "The Design and Construction
      of NC Flying Boats." USNIP, XLV (1919), 1529-
      1581.

4282 _____. "The Flight of the NC Boats." World's
Work, XXXVIII (August 1919), 424-438.

4283 _____. "The Future of Naval Aeronautics." Society of Automotive Engineers Journal, VI (May
1920), 292-293.

4284 _____ and H. B. Sanford. "The Possibilities of a
Trans-Pacific Flight." USNIP, XLVI (1920), 675-
712.

4285 _____., et al. The Triumph of the N. C. 's.
Garden City, N. Y.: Doubleday, 1920. 308p.
    Cmdr. Westervelt was in charge of the design
and building of the N. C. flying boats. Cmdr.
Holden C. Richardson's contribution concerns his
design and testing of the N. C. hulls while Cmdr.
Albert C. Read's story tells of his command of the
N. C. 4 in her 1919 Atlantic crossing.

4286 Wester-Wemyss. "Washington and After." 19th Century, XCI (March 1922), 405-416.
    The American Navy in poor shape. For the
reply, see the articles by Admiral Sims and Admiral Fiske cited above.

4287 Weybright, Victor. "The Long Shadow of John Paul
Jones." Survey Graphic, XXXVII (April 1938),
222-223+.
    Concerns naval preparedness.

4288 Weyerbacher, Ralph D. "Cooperation of Air Forces in
Coast Defense." USNIP, LVI (1930), 692-694.

4289 _____. "Proposed Functions of the Naval Aircraft
Factory." USNIP, LII (1926), 2428-2436.

4290 Wharton, Wallace S. "The Navy--A National Investment." USNIP, L (1924), 1833-1842.

4291 _____. "The Old Oregon Gets A New Home."
USNIP, LXIV (1938), 1628-1632.

4292 _____. "Our Chinese Navy." USNIP, LI (1925),
68-77.
    U. S. naval operations on China's inland rivers.

4293 "What About Our Naval Standing?" Review of Reviews,
      LXXXIV (December 1931), 31.

4294 "What Are the New Cruisers For?" New Republic,
      LIII (January 11, 1928), 204-206.

4295 "What Happened to the Shenandoah?" Popular Mechan-
      ics, XLIV (November 1925), 711-717.

4296 "What Is the Navy For?" New Republic, XCIV (Feb-
      ruary 16, 1938), 32.

4297 "What It Takes to Build a Battleship." Popular Sci-
      ence, CXXXIX (October 1941), 94.

4298 "What the Failure of the [Geneva] Naval Conference
      Means." Literary Digest, XCIV (August 20, 1927),
      8-9.

4299 "What the 5-5-3 Victory Means." Literary Digest,
      LXXI (December 31, 1921), 9-11.

4300 "What Wrecked the Akron?" Literary Digest, CXV
      (May 6, 1933), 21.

4301 "What's the Super-Navy For?" New Republic, XCIV
      (April 6, 1938), 260.

4302 Wheeler, Gerald E.   "Japan's Influence on American
      Naval Policies, 1921-1931." Unpublished PhD Dis-
      sertation, University of California at Berkeley,
      1955.

4303 _____. "Origins of the Naval Reserve Officers
      Training Corps." Military Affairs, XX (Fall 1956),
      170-174.
          Begun at St. John's College in 1924.

4304 _____. Prelude to Pearl Harbor: The U.S. Navy
      and the Far East, 1921-1931. Columbia: Univer-
      sity of Missouri Press, 1963.   212p.

4305 _____. "The United States Navy and the Japanese
      'Enemy': 1919-1931." Military Affairs, XXI (Sum-
      mer 1957), 61-74.

4306 _____. "The United States Navy and War in the

Pacific. " World Affairs Quarterly, XXX (1959), 199-225.
U. S. naval policy for the Pacific, 1918-1941.

4307 _____. "William Veazie Pratt, U. S. Navy: A Silhouette of an Admiral. " Naval War College Review, XXII (May 1969), 36-61.

4308 Wheeler, William B. "Anglo-American Pact Against Rum Smuggling. " Current History, XX (April 1924), 98-100.

4309 _____. "The Romance of Rum Row. " Forum, LXXIII (January 1925), 99-102.

4310 "When the Next Submarine Sinks. " Review of Reviews, LXXX (September 1929), 146-148.
Safety devices to be employed in rescue work.

4311 "Where the Money Goes: Naval Aviation Costs About $35,000,000 a Year. " Aviation, XVI (May 12, 1924), 509-510.
A mere fraction of today's cost!

4312 "Where the Money Goes to Provide and Maintain Our Navy. " Current Opinion, LXXI (November 1921), 664-666.

4313 Whitaker, Joseph. Almanack. London, 1919-1941.

4314 White, Lillian C. Pioneer and Patriot: George Cook Sweet, Commander U. S. Navy, 1877-1953. Delray Beach, Fla.: Southern Publishing Company, 1965.
A pioneer in naval aviation.

4315 White, Richard D. "Hauling 'em off Before Dinner. " USNIP, XLVI (1920), 1079-1087.
Naval salvage operations.

4316 _____. "Leadership. " USNIP, XLVII (1921), 655-668.

4317 White, Theodore. "Uncle Sam's Fire Canoe: The Coast Guard Cutter Bear. " Outlook, CXLVI (June 15, 1927), 217-218.

4318 "The White Squadron Sails Again. " Popular Mechanics,

LVI (August 1931), 195-197.

4319   Whitehill, W. M., jt. author. See King, Ernest J.,
       no. 1975.

4320   Whiteley, Albert S. "Get the Big Navy Men Together."
       New Republic, LXIII (May 21, 1930), 20-21.

4321   Whiting, John D. "Knights of the Wave: A Story of
       Rescue at Sea." Mentor, XIII (July 1925), 1-17.
       The work of the Coast Guard.

4322   Whiting, Kenneth. "Aviation Facilities on Naval Car-
       riers." Civil Engineering, I (June 1931), 834-835.

4323   Whiting, W. R. G. "The Strength of Submarine Vessels."
       Engineering, CXI (May 27, 1921), 662-664.

4324   Whitman, R. "The Port of New York: Interests of the
       U. S. Navy." Civil Engineer, X (June 1940), 333-
       336.

4325   Whitton, John B. "The International Naval Situation."
       Current History, XXXIV (June 1931), 421-422.

4326   "Who Is to Blame for Our Submarine Disasters?"
       Literary Digest, XCVI (January 7, 1928), 5-7.

4327   Who's Who in America. Chicago: A. N. Marquis,
       1919-1942.
       Includes naval officers.

4328   "Why Build Up Our Navy Now?" SciAmer, CXLVII
       (July 1932), 26-28.

4329   "Why Is a Navy?: The London Naval Conference."
       Christian Century, LII (December 18, 1935), 1614-
       1615.

4330   "Why Mr. Roosevelt Wants a Super-Navy." Christian
       Century, LV (February 23, 1938), 230-231.

4331   "Why More Battleships?" New Republic, LXXIX (July
       4, 1934), 194-195.

4332   "Why Naval Experts Say There Will Never be Another
       American Submarine Tragedy." Popular Mechanics,

LII (March 1930), 428-429.
Overly optimistic!

4333 "Why the Navy Recommends the Completion of ZR-1."
Automotive Industries, XLVI (June 22, 1922), 1388.
The Shenandoah.

4334 "Why the President Seeks a Bigger Navy. " U.S. News,
VI (January 3, 1938), 2.

4335 "Why the Shenandoah Failed. " Aviation, XIX (September 21, 1925), 346-349.

4336 "Why This Naval Program?" Outlook, CXLVIII (February 29, 1928), 334-335.

4337 Whyte, Alexander F. "America, Britain, and the Far
East. " Contemporary Review, CLII (November
1937), 513-520.

4338 Wickersham, George W. "America's Naval Challenge."
Current History, XXX (April 1929), 31-37.

4339 Wicks, Zeno W. "Helium and Its Relation to Airships."
Aero Digest, III (December 1923), 404-405.

4340 _____. "Six Years with the Navy in Helium Production. " Journal of the American Society of Naval
Engineers, XXXVII (November 1925), 698-718.

4341 Wieand, Harold T. "The History of the Development
of the United States Naval Reserve, 1889-1941. "
Unpublished PhD Dissertation, University of Pitts-
burgh, 1953.

4342 Wiedersheim, William A. , 3rd. "Factors in the
Growth of the Reichmarine, 1919-1939. " USNIP,
LXXIV (1948), 316-325.

4343 _____. "Officer Personnel Selection in the German
Navy, 1925-1945. " USNIP, LXXIII (1947), 445-449.

4344 Wilbur, Curtis D. "Aeronautics With the Navy. "
Aviation, XX (June 7, 1926), 868-871.

4345 _____. "A Balanced Navy. " Saturday Evening Post,
CXCVII (April 18, 1925), 10-11.

4346   _____. "Naval Developments Since 1921." Con-
             gressional Digest, VIII (January 1929), 1-3.

4347   _____. "Naval Inventions." Overland Monthly, New
             Series LXXXII (October 1924), 443-445.

4348   _____. "New Cruisers for the United States Navy,
             with the Text of the Cruiser Bill." Current His-
             tory, XXIX (March 1929), 918-921.

4349   _____. "The Secretary of the Navy Reports on
             Aviation." Aviation, XXI (December 27, 1926),
             1074-1075.

4350   _____. "Secretary Wilbur Reports on Naval Aero-
             nautics." Aviation, XIX (December 25, 1925), 872.

4351   _____. "Secretary Wilbur's Report to the House on
             the Condition of the United States Navy." Com-
             mercial and Financial Chronicle, CXVIII (May 31,
             1924), 2656-2659.

4352   _____. "Training for the Navy is Training for Oc-
             cupations in Civil Life." School Life, X (March
             1925), 121-124.

4353   _____. "The United States Navy." SciAmer,
             CXXXV (November 1926), 325.

4354   _____. "The United States Navy: A Trade School
             of Extraordinary Scope." School Life, X (May
             1925), 164-167.

4355   _____. "The United States Needs More Ships to
             Keep Up the Navy." Commercial and Financial
             Chronicle, CXXV (August 6, 1927), 731-733.

4356   Wilbur, Theodore. "The First Flight Across the
             Atlantic." Naval Aviation News, (May 1969), 7-36.

4357   _____. "Paint and Pluck--And the NC-4." USNIP,
             XCV (1969), 146-149.

4358   "Wild Night on the Shenandoah." SciAmer, CXXX
             (March 1924), 158+.

4359   Wilds, Thomas. "How Japan Fortified the Mandated

Islands. " <u>USNIP</u>, LXXXI (1955), 400-407.

4360 Wiley, Henry A. <u>An Admiral From Texas</u>. Garden
City, N. Y. : Doubleday, 1934. 322p.
The author's autobiography from his Naval Aca-
demy graduation in 1888 through his service as
Commander-in-Chief of the U. S. Fleet in 1927-
1929.

4361 Wiley, Herbert V. "A Celestial Cruise. " <u>USNIP</u>, LI
(1925), 604-609.
Aboard the airship <u>Los Angeles</u>.

4362 _____. "PVT Prime Takes a Hop. " <u>USNIP</u>, LV
(1929), 33-37.
Problems of an airship in changing atmospheric
conditions.

4363 _____. "The Value of Naval Airships. " <u>USNIP</u>,
LX (1934), 665-671.
Important.

4364 Wilhelm, D. "Is the Capital Ship Doomed by Aircraft?" <u>Illustrated World</u>, XXXV (July 1921), 788-
792.

4365 Wilkinson, Ford L. , Jr. "The United States Navy
Post-graduate School, 1909-1948. " <u>Scientific
Monthly</u>, LXVI (March 1948), 183-194.

4366 Wilkinson, Paul H. <u>Aircraft Engines of the World</u>.
New York, 1941. 256p.

4367 Willebrandt Mabel W. "Routing Rum Row. " In: her
<u>The Inside of Prohibition</u>. Indianapolis: Bobbs
Merrill, 1929. p. 220-230.
Discusses the work of the Coast Guard.

4368 Williams, Benjamin H. "Sea Power and Prosperity. "
<u>Current History</u>, XXXI (February 1930), 890-895.

4369 _____. <u>The United States and Disarmament</u>. New
York: McGraw, Hill, 1931. 361p. Rpr. 1973.

4370 _____. "What is the Navy League?" <u>Nation</u>,
CXXXIII (November 25, 1931), 569-570.

4371 Williams, Charles D.   "The Navy's Stake in Reserve
      Aviation. "   USNIP, LXV (1939), 665-668.

4372 Williams, Dion.   "Captain Richard Bell Buchanan, U.S.
      Marine Corps. "   Marine Corps Gazette, XII (June
      1927), 73-75.
      Active in Nicaragua.

4373 _____.   "Co-ordination in Army and Navy Training."
      USNIP, XLVIII (1922), 593-620.

4374 _____.   "The Marines March Past. "   Marine Corps
      Gazette, XVI (November 1931), 5-23.

4375 _____.   "The Nicaraguan Situation. "   Marine Corps
      Gazette, XV (November 1930), 19-22, 53-57.

4376 Williams, Henry.   "Notes on Administration of Indus-
      trial Work in Navy Yards. "   USNIP, LI (1925),
      1391-1397.

4377 _____.   "A Record in Destroyer Construction. "
      USNIP, XLVI (1920), 531-438.

4378 Williams, John.   "More American Air Bases. "   Asia,
      XXXVII (June 1937), 409-413.

4379 Williams, John E.   "The Essentials of the Radio Com-
      pass. "   USNIP, XLVIII (1922), 203-215.

4380 Williams, M. R.   "Chicago, 10, 000 Ton Cruiser. "
      Marine Engineering, XXXV (August 1930), 422-425.

4381 Williams, R. H.   "Marine Parachute Training. "   USNIP,
      LXVII (1941), 999-1000.

4382 Willingham, Solomon D.   "Modern Submarine versus a
      Major Warship. "   USNIP, LXVII (1941), 513-520.

4383 Willis, Thurston A.   "The Martin Plan. "   Leatherneck,
      XXIII (December 1940), 14-17.

4384 Willmore, T. L.   "Medicine and Engineering in Sub-
      marines, 1919-1948. "   Mechanical Engineering,
      LXXI (July 1949), 583-586.

4385 Willoughby, Malcolm F.   Rum War at Sea.   Washington:

U. S. Government Printing Office, 1964.   183p.

4386 Willson, Russell. "Aids to Accuracy in Battleship
      Manoeuvres. " USNIP, XLVIII (1922), 1369-1387.

4387 _____. "A Direct Reading Course and Speed Indi-
      cator. " USNIP, XLIX (1923), 1655-1660.

4388 _____. "Direct Reading Manoeuvering Diagrams. "
      USNIP, LI (1925), 2276-2285.

4389 _____. "Our Tactical Readiness for War. " USNIP,
      XLIX (1923), 553-570.

4390 Wilson, Eugene E. "Air-Cooled Engines in Naval Air-
      craft. " Society of Automotive Engineers Journal,
      XIX (September 1926), 221-227.

4391 _____. "Air Tactics and Aircraft Design. " USNIP,
      LXI (1935), 1767-1771.

4392 _____. "Air Transport and Security. " USNIP, LX
      (1934), 177-182.

4393 _____. "Aircraft Engine Progress. " USNIP, LI
      (1925), 657-663.

4394 _____. "The Evolution of an Aircraft Engine. "
      USNIP, LII (1926), 72-82.

4395 _____. "The Gift of Foresight. " USNIP, LXXXIX
      (1963), 46-53.
      Defends the naval opponents of General William
      Mitchell.

4396 _____. "The Influence of Flying Boat Development
      on Sea Power. " USNIP, LXIII (1937), 1433-1436.

4397 _____. "Management and Command. " USNIP, LIX
      (1933), 1103-1106.

4398 _____. "Naval Air Tactics and Aircraft Design. "
      Society of Automotive Engineers Journal, XXIII
      (October 1928), 353-358.

4399 _____. "Navy Types of Heavier-Than-Air Craft. "
      USNIP, L (1924), 2029-2040.

4400 _____. "The Navy's First Carrier Task Force. "
USNIP, LXXVI (1950), 158-169.

4401 _____. Slipstream: The Autobiography of an Air
Craftsman. 2nd ed. New York: Science Press,
1965. 366p.

4402 Wilson, G. G. "Submarine and Place of Safety. "
American Journal of International Law, XXXV (July
1941), 496-497.

4403 Wilson, Henry B. "Schedule of the Bombing Tests. "
Aviation, XI (July 4, 1921), 8-12.

4404 Wilson, L. P. R. , trans. See Bush, Harold, no. 574.

4405 Wiltz, John E. From Isolation to War, 1931-1941.
New York: Crowell, 1968. 152p.

4406 Winans, Leonard G. Our Navy's Striking Power: Close-
ups and Its Latest Equipment. New York: Grosset
and Dunlap, 1941.

4407 Windrow, Martin C. , ed. Aircraft in Profile. 8 vols.
Garden City, N. Y. : Doubleday, 1969-1970.
Contains data on early naval aircraft.

4408 Wines, J. P. "Naval Reserve Aviation. " Aviation,
XXIV (June 4, 1928), 1594-1598+.

4409 _____. "New Training Course for Naval Reserve
Aviators. " Aviation, XXVI (May 4, 1929), 1498-
1500.

4410 "Wing Talk: The Luckiest Guys in the Navy are Those
Who Man the Big, Long-Range Patrol Bombers. "
Collier's, CVII (June 7, 1941), 6.

4411 "Wing Talk: The Navy Martin XPB2M-1 Long Range
Patrol Bomber. " Collier's, CVIII (November 15,
1941), 6.

4412 Winslow, John C. "Mr. Roosevelt's 'Little' Navy. "
Current History, XLVIII (May 1938), 18-20.

4413 _____. "School for Admirals. " Christian Science
Monitor Magazine, (August 17, 1940), 6-7.

The Naval War College.

4414 Winston, Robert A. Aircraft Carrier. New York:
      Harper, 1942. 88p.
      A history of carriers to World War II.

4415 _____. Dive Bomber: Learning to Fly the Navy's
      Fighting Planes. New York: Holiday House, 1939.
      191p.

4416 _____. "Wheels Over Water: Landing on the Deck
      of an Aircraft Carrier in a Storm. " Reader's Di-
      gest, XXXV (July 1939), 129-131.

4417 Wisberg, Aubrey, jt. author. See Waters, Harold,
      no. 4241.

4418 Wise, James E. , Jr. "Ford Island. " USNIP, XC
      (1964), 77-91.
      The Hawaiian naval air base before, during, and
      after Pearl Harbor.

4419 "With the Mosquito Fleet. " Popular Mechanics, LXXV
      (April 1941), 487-490.

4420 "With the Navy in Peace Times. " Popular Mechanics,
      XLII (September 1924), 377-388.

4421 "With Uncle Sam's Devil Dogs. " Popular Mechanics,
      L (July 1928), 67-73.
      The Marines.

4422 Wohlstetter, Roberta. Pearl Harbor: Warning and De-
      cision. Stanford, Calif. : Stanford University Press,
      1962. 426p.

4423 _____. "What Really Happened at Pearl Harobr. "
      U. S. News & World Report, LXI (December 12,
      1966), 46-47.
      Very useful for events leading up to the attack.

4424 Wood, Chester C. "The Flow of Strategic Intelligence."
      USNIP, LIX (1933), 1296-1304.

4425 _____. "A Game for All Hands. " USNIP, LVIII
      (1932), 340-342.
      Tactics.

4426 Wood, John C. "Sandino Strikes Again. " Leather-
      neck, XXII (February 1939), 8-12, 55-57.
      Reprinted from the Nicaragua Monograph, this
      piece concerns Marine activities in Nicaragua in
      April 1931.

4427 Wood, Ralph F. "Sanity in Aviation. " USNIP, LI
      (1925), 1133-1142.

4428 _____. "Saratoga and Squadrons. " USNIP, LVII
      (1931), 234-238.

4429 _____. "A Wrinkle in Tactics. " USNIP, XLV
      (1919), 1739-1741.

4430 Woodhouse, Henry. "The Torpedo Plane, the New
      Weapon Which Promises to Revolutionize Naval
      Tactics. " USNIP, XLV (1919), 743-752.

4431 _____. "U. S. Naval Aeronautic Policies, 1904-
      1942. " USNIP, LXVIII (1942), 161-175.

4432 Woodside, Elmer L. "The Naval Ordnance Plant. "
      USNIP, LVII (1931), 223-227.

4433 Woodward, Clark H. "Naval Strength. " Academy of
      Political Science Proceedings, XIX (January 1941),
      130-141.

4434 _____. "The Navy and the Merchant Marine. "
      National Republic, XXII (February 1935), 6-7+.

4435 _____. "The Navy's Mission: Only in Preparedness
      is There Protection. " Vital Speeches, V (May 1,
      1939), 438-441.

4436 _____. "Relations Between the Navy and the Foreign
      Service. " American Journal of International Law,
      XXXIII (April 1939), 283-291.

4437 _____. "The Status of Our Navy: We Will Be
      Ready in Two Oceans. " Vital Speeches, VII (De-
      cember 1, 1940), 111-114.

4438 "The Worker is Worthy ... Section 3B of the Vinson
      Bill. " SciAmer, CLIII (November 1935), 237.

4439 World Almanac and Book of Facts. New York: World
       Telegram, 1919-1941.

4440 The World Book Encyclopedia Yearbook. Chicago:
       Field Enterprises Educational Corp., 1922-1942.

4441 "World Naval Construction." Current History, LIII
       (June 1941), 38.

4442 "World Naval Strength and the Geneva Problem." In-
       dependent, CXIX (July 9, 1927), 29.

4443 "The World Navy Race is On." Scholastic, XXXII
       (February 26, 1938), 15.

4444 "World Sea Power: The Plane Challenges the Reign of
       Ships." Life, VIII (April 29, 1940), 75-85.
       Illustrated.

4445 "The World's Largest Naval Vessel, U.S.S. Lexing-
       ton." St. Nicholas Magazine, LIV (October 1927),
       995-996.

4446 Wotherspoon, Alexander S. "War Colleges and Recre-
       ational Reading Courses for Officers." USNIP, LIV
       (1928), 770-772.

4447 "The Wreck of the Shenandoah." Engineering, CXX
       (September 18, 1925), 359-360.

4448 Wright, James L. "The Rebirth of the United States
       Navy: President Roosevelt and Sec. Swanson Stand
       Staunchly Behind the Program to Build up Sea
       Forces Second to None." Literary Digest, CXVI
       (July 15, 1933), 3-4+.

4449 Wright, James N. "San Diego, the Largest Marine
       Base." Leatherneck, XXIV (September 1941), 10-
       15.

4450 Wright, Quincy. "The Washington Conference."
       American Political Science Review, XVI (May 1922),
       285-297.

4451 Wygant, Benyaurd B. "[Naval] Problem of Tomor-
       row." Outlook, CXXXII (December 13, 1922), 670-
       671.

4452 _____. "The Naval Staff Afloat. " USNIP, LII
      (1926), 249-259.

4453 Wyllie, Robert E. Orders, Decorations and Insignia,
      Military and Civil, with the History and Romance
      of their Origin and a Full Description of Each.
      New York: Putnam, 1921. 269p.
      Includes navy and marine corps.

4454 Yanaga, Chitoshi. Japan Since Perry. Series in His-
      tory. New York: McGraw-Hill, 1949. 723p.

4455 Yarnell, Harry E. "Navy Regulations. " USNIP,
      XLVIII (1922), 577-591.
          An October 21, 1920 lecture delivered at the
      Destroyer Staff College, Charleston, S. C.

4456 _____. "The Peace Time Services and Costs of the
      Navy. " USNIP, L (1924), 1499-1508.
          An address at Huntington, W. Va. , before the
      West Virginia Manufacturers' Association, Novem-
      ber 1, 1923.

4457 _____. Will Land, Air, or Sea Power Win This
      War? Town Meeting Series, V. 7, no. 2. New
      York: Columbia University Press, 1941. 30p.

4458 Yates, Brock W. Destroyers and Destroyermen: The
      Story of Our "Tin Can" Navy. New York: Harper,
      1959. 207p.

4459 "You'll Never Get Rich!" Fortune, XVII (March 1938),
      66-68.
          As a naval officer.

4460 Young, George. "Anglo-American Command of the
      Seas. " Contemporary Review, CXXXIII (March
      1928), 294-302.

4461 _____. _____. Living Age, CCCXXXIV (April
      15, 1928), 680-686.

4462 _____. "Twilight in London. " Commonweal, XI
      (March 26, 1930), 579-580.
          The London Naval Conference.

4463 Young, Morgan. Imperial Japan, 1926-1938. London:

Allen & Unwin, 1938.

4464 Yust, Walter. Ten Eventful Years: A Record of Events of the Years Preceding, Including, and Following World War II, 1937 through 1946. 4 vols. Chicago: Enyclopedia Britannica, 1947.

4465 "ZR-1 Makes Successful 2200-mi. Flight." Aviation, XV (October 15, 1923), 490-491.
The Shenandoah.

4466 Zeus, M. D. "United States Naval Government and Administration of Guam." Unpublished PhD Dissertation, University of Iowa, 1950.

4467 Zeusler, Frank G. "Bergs." U. S. Coast Guard Magazine, VIII (March 1935), 14.
The ice patrol.

4468 _____. "Bogoslof Island." USNIP, LXVIII (1942), 494.

4469 _____. "Ice in the Bering Sea and Arctic Ocean." USNIP, LXVII (1941), 1102-1106.

4470 _____. "Standing Iceberg in the North Atlantic." National Geographic, L (July 1926), 1-31.

4471 Zimmerman, John L. The First Marine Brigade (Provisional), Iceland, 1941-1942. Philadelphia: Marine Corps Publicity Bureau, 1946. 18p.

4472 _____. "Force in Readiness." USNIP, LXXXIII (1957), 165-171.
The U. S. occupation of Iceland.

4473 Zogbaum, Rufus F. From Sail to Saratoga: A Naval Autobiography. Np, n. d. 466p.

II: SELECTED U.S. GOVERNMENT DOCUMENTS

What follows is not a comprehensive listing of all federal documents relating to the American sea services of the inter-war period. Rather, it is an attempt to list some of the more important or interesting items uncovered by the author in the process of compiling this volume. Because of the large increase of documents during this period, any attempt to list all of them here would be a very expensive operation, both in time and printing costs. For example, just those relating to the Byrd Expeditions are very numerous.

For all their imperfections, two useful tools already exist which should be consulted by those seeking further listings. These are:

U.S. Government Printing Office. Catalog of the Public Documents of the United States. Vols. 15-25. Washington, 1919-1940.
   Commonly known as The Documents Catalog.

_____. Monthly Catalog of U.S. Government Publications. Washington, 1919-1941.

Neither of the above lists the multitude of documents issued directly by the Navy Department, or other U.S. sea service agencies. Those seeking this type of material are urged to write or visit the respective branches whose operational archives or libraries contain much of this data. The U.S. National Archives also possess some of these items and should not be overlooked.

As in earlier volumes of the American Naval Bibliography, the documents listed below are arranged chronologically by date of issue and then alphabetically by author agency.

377

No Date

4474   Navy Department. Office of Procurement and Material.
       "History of Surplus Property Disposal [following]
       World War I. " Unpublished paper, Operational
       Archives, U. S. Navy Department, Naval History
       Division, n. d.   128p.

1916

4475   National Advisory Committee for Aeronautics. Annual
       Report.   44 vols.   Washington: U. S. Government
       Printing Office, 1916-1959.

1919

4476   Coast Guard.   United States Coast Guard 1919.   Wash-
       ington: Government Printing Office, 1919.   24p.

4477   Navy Department.   Annual Report of the Secretary of
       the Navy.   Washington: Government Printing Office,
       1919-1941.

4478   _____.   Interallied Radio Conference.   Washington:
       Government Printing Office, 1919.   14p.

4479   _____.   Bureau of Ships.   Ships' Data, U. S. Naval
       Vessels.   Washington: Government Printing Office,
       1919-1949.
           The volumes published after 1949 are still
       classified as many of our present ships yet date
       from that period.

1920

4480   Navy Department.   The Military Efficiency of the Navy.
       Washington: Government Printing Office, 1920. 8p.

4481   _____.   Naval Printing Plants.   Washington: Govern-
       ment Printing Office, 1920.   80p.

4482   _____.   Bureau of Navigation.   Instructions Govern-
       ing the Handling of Enlisted Personnel.   Washington:
       Government Printing Office, 1920.   200p.

4483   _____.   _____.   The Navy Speller: 3000 Words.
       Washington: Government Printing Office, 1920. 89p.

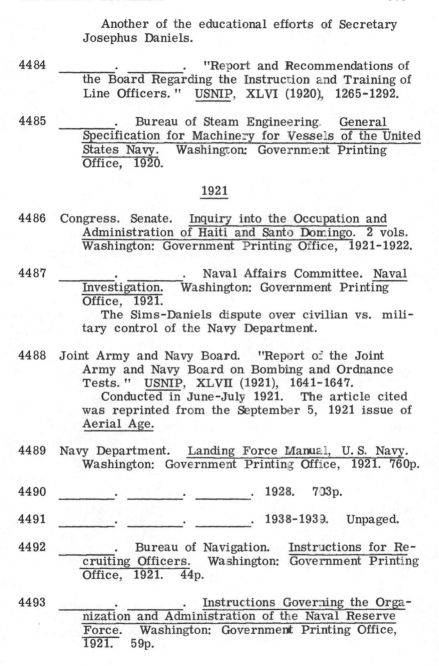

Another of the educational efforts of Secretary Josephus Daniels.

4484 _____. _____. "Report and Recommendations of the Board Regarding the Instruction and Training of Line Officers. " USNIP, XLVI (1920), 1265-1292.

4485 _____. Bureau of Steam Engineering. General Specification for Machinery for Vessels of the United States Navy. Washington: Government Printing Office, 1920.

1921

4486 Congress. Senate. Inquiry into the Occupation and Administration of Haiti and Santo Domingo. 2 vols. Washington: Government Printing Office, 1921-1922.

4487 _____. _____. Naval Affairs Committee. Naval Investigation. Washington: Government Printing Office, 1921.
The Sims-Daniels dispute over civilian vs. military control of the Navy Department.

4488 Joint Army and Navy Board. "Report of the Joint Army and Navy Board on Bombing and Ordnance Tests. " USNIP, XLVII (1921), 1641-1647.
Conducted in June-July 1921. The article cited was reprinted from the September 5, 1921 issue of Aerial Age.

4489 Navy Department. Landing Force Manual, U. S. Navy. Washington: Government Printing Office, 1921. 760p.

4490 _____. _____. _____. 1928. 703p.

4491 _____. _____. _____. 1938-1939. Unpaged.

4492 _____. Bureau of Navigation. Instructions for Recruiting Officers. Washington: Government Printing Office, 1921. 44p.

4493 _____. _____. Instructions Governing the Organization and Administration of the Naval Reserve Force. Washington: Government Printing Office, 1921. 59p.

4494 _____. _____. Keep Fit! Washington: Government Printing Office, 1921. 30p.
Physical fitness.

4495 _____. _____. Register of the Commissioned
and Warrant Officers of the United States Naval Reserve Force. 4 vols. Washington: U. S. Government Printing Office, 1921-1943.

1922

4496 Coast Guard. Brief Sketch of the Naval History of the
United States Coast Guard, with Citations of Various Statutes Defining Its Military Status from 1790-
1922. Washington: B. S. Adams, 1922. 16p.

4497 Navy Department. Material Features of Submarines in
the United States Navy. Washington: Government
Printing Office, 1922. 9p.
Lettered specifications.

4498 _____. Bureau of Aeronautics. Syllabus for Training Naval Aviation Observers. Washington: Government Printing Office, 1922. 28p.

4499 _____. _____. Syllabus for Training Naval Aviators and Naval Aviation Pilots. Washington:
Government Printing Office, 1922. 39p.

4500 _____. Bureau of Navigation. Ship and Gun Drills,
U. S. Navy. Washington: Government Printing
Office, 1922. 213p.

4501 _____. _____. _____. _____. 1927. 350p.

4502 President. American Naval Policy, as Outlined in
Messages of the Presidents of the United States
from 1790. Washington: Government Printing
Office, 1922. 30p.

1923

4503 Naval War College. International Law Documents:
Conference on the Limitation of Armament, with
Notes and Index, 1921. Washington: Government
Printing Office, 1923. 392p.

4504 Navy Department. Naval Courts and Boards. Wash-
      ington: Government Printing Office, 1923. Unpaged.

4505 _____. _____. _____. 1937. 532p.

4506 _____. Bureau of Aeronautics. Bureau of Aero-
      nautics Manual. Washington: Government Printing
      Office, 1923. 122p.

4507 _____. _____. _____. _____. 1927. 104p.

4508 _____. _____. _____. _____. 1940. 266p.

4509 _____. _____. Naval Aviation: The Eyes of the
      Fleet. Washington: Government Printing Office,
      1923. 13p.

4510 _____. _____. Syllabus for Training Naval Avi-
      ators and Naval Aviation Pilots--Airplane. Wash-
      ington: Government Printing Office, 1923. 30p.

4511 _____. Bureau of Navigation. Hints to Instructors
      of Recruits. Washington: Government Printing
      Office, 1923. 12p.

4512 _____. Bureau of Ordnance. Small Arms Firing
      Regulations, U. S. Navy. Washington: Government
      Printing Office, 1923. 102p.

4513 _____. _____. _____. 1931. 122p.

4514 _____. Commission on Navy Yards and Naval Sta-
      tions. "America's Outposts in the Pacific: Report
      of the Special Board Headed by Rear Admr. Hugh
      Rodman. " USNIP, XLIX (1923), 496-500.
         Reprinted from the January 20, 1923 issue of the
      Boston Transcript.

4515 _____. United States Fleet. Commander-in-Chief.
      "Annual Reports of the Commander-in-Chief, U. S.
      Fleet, 1923-1940. " Discontinued Commands File,
      Operational Archives, U. S. Navy Department, Naval
      History Division, 1923-1940. 1169p.

                         1924

4516 Navy Department. Naval Arctic Air Board. "Report

of Naval Arctic Air Board Calls for the Use of the
Shenandoah, Six Planes, Mooring Masts, and Two
Airship Tenders. " Aviation, XVI (January 21,
1924), 65-66.

1925

4517 Navy Department.   Bureau of Aeronautics.   Ground
School Course.   3 vols.   Washington: Government
Printing Office, 1925-1926.

4518 _____. Bureau of Navigation. Naval Reserve Regulations. Washington: Government Printing Office,
1925. 76p.

4519 _____. _____. _____. _____. 1929. 84p.

4520 _____. _____. _____. _____. 1931. 90p.

4521 _____. Office of Naval Intelligence. Information
Concerning the United States Navy and Other Navies:
Information and Tables Compiled to Answer Popular
Inquiry.   Washington: Government Printing Office,
1925.   257p.
"American Naval Chronology": p. 204-217.
"Bibliography of the History of the United States
Navy": p. 179-189.

4522 _____. Special Board. "Results of the Development of Aviation on the Development of the Navy. "
Aviation, XVIII (March 2, 1925), 238-240.

4523 _____. _____. _____. _____. Engineering,
CXIX (March 27, 1925), 390-391.

4524 President.   Aircraft Board.   The President's Aircraft
Board Hearings.   4 vols.   Washington: Government
Printing Office, 1925.

4525 _____. _____. "Report by a Special Board
Appointed to Determine the Results of the Develop-
ment of Aviation on the Development of the Navy. "
USNIP, LI (1925), 636-641.
Reprinted from the February 19, 1925 issue of
the Washington Star.

1926

4526 Coast Guard. United States Coast Guard. Washington:
      Government Printing Office, 1926. 15p.

4527 National Advisory Committee for Aeronautics. Nomen-
      clature for Aeronautics. Washington: Government
      Printing Office, 1926. 77p.

4528 _____. "Report of the National Advisory Committee
      for Aeronautics, 1925." USNIP, LII (1926), 579-
      589.

4529 Navy Department. Bureau of Aeronautics. "Findings
      of the Shenandoah Court-of-Inquiry, 1925." USNIP,
      LII (1926), 396-404.
          Reprinted from the January 2, 1926 issue of the
      New York Times.

4530 _____. _____. Syllabus for Training Naval Avi-
      ation Observers--Airship. Washington: Government
      Printing Office, 1926. 13p.

4531 _____. _____. Syllabus for Training Naval Avi-
      ators--Airship. Washington: Government Printing
      Office, 1926. 10p.

4532 _____. Naval Academy. Trident Society. The
      Book of Navy Songs, Collected and Edited by the
      Trident Society of the United States Naval Academy
      at Annapolis, Maryland. Garden City, N.Y.:
      Doubleday, Page, 1926. 200p.

1927

4533 Coast Guard. Functions, Duties, Organization, and
      Equipment of the United States Coast Guard. Wash-
      ington: Government Printing Office, 1927. 36p.
          A rather full look at the Coast Guard of that
      period.

4534 National Advisory Committee for Aeronautics. "The
      Present Status of Technical Development in Avia-
      tion: From the Annual Report, 1926." USNIP,
      LIII (1927), 223-227.

4535 Navy Department. Bureau of Navigation. Regulations

and Instructions for the Administration and Training
of the Naval Reserve Officer Training Corps.
Washington: Government Printing Office, 1927. 31p.

4536   _____ . _____ . _____ . _____ . 1932. 48p.

4537   _____ . _____ . _____ . _____ . 1935. 73p.

4538   _____ . _____ . _____ . _____ . 1940. 79p.

1928

4539   Congress. Senate. Foreign Relations Committee. The
Use of the United States Navy in Nicaragua. Washington: Government Printing Office, 1928.

4540   _____ . _____ . Naval Affairs Committee. Investigation of the Sinking of the Submarine S-4. Washington: Government Printing Office, 1928. 326p.

4541   Navy Department. Instructions Governing the Signalling
Between U. S. Merchant Vessels and U. S. Govern-
ment Vessels. Washington: Government Printing
Office, 1928. 16p.

4542   _____ . Bureau of Aeronautics. Rigid Airship
Manual. Washington: Government Printing Office,
1928. [299]p.

1929

4543   Navy Department. Board on Naval Airship Base.
Naval Airship Base Report. Washington: Government Printing Office, 1929. 58p.

4544   _____ . Bureau of Aeronautics. Naval Aviation
Engine Manual. Washington: Government Printing
Office, 1929. 122p.

4545   _____ . Bureau of Navigation. "Education in the
Navy: Report of a Board to Inquire into and Report
Upon the Curriculum of the General Line Course at
the Postgraduate School and the Courses at the
Naval War College. " USNIP, LV (1929), 746-750.

4546   _____ . Naval Academy. Department of Engineering
and Aeronautics. Marine and Naval Boilers.

Annapolis: U. S. Naval Institute, 1929. 194p.

4547 _____ . _____ . Naval Auxiliary Machinery.
Annapolis: U. S. Naval Institute, 1929. 165p.

1930

4548 Navy Department. Bureau of Medicine and Surgery.
Handbook of the Hospital Corps, U. S. Navy. Washington: Government Printing Office, 1930. 730p.

4549 _____ . Bureau of Navigation. Information Pamphlet for Officers Ordered to the Asiatic Squadron.
Washington: Government Printing Office, 1930. 8p.

4550 _____ . _____ . Interior Control Manual for the
Use of the Naval Reserve. Washington: Government
Printing Office, 1930. 47p.

4551 President. Limitation and Reduction of Naval Arma-
ment: Message from the President of the United
States Transmitting Treaty for the Limitation and
Reduction of Naval Armament, Signed at London on
April 22, 1930. Washington: Government Printing
Office, 1930. 33p.
The Senate Foreign Relations Committee, to
which President Hoover referred his message, had
it printed as Senate doc. 141, 71st Cong. , 2nd
sess.

1931

4552 Coast Guard. The Marion Expedition to Davis Strait
and Baffin Island Under the Direction of the United
States Coast Guard, 1928. 3 vols. Washington:
Government Printing Office, 1931-1937.

4553 Congress. House. Naval Affairs Committee. Hearings
on Sundry Legislation Affecting the Naval Establishment. 20 vols. Washington: Government Printing
Office, 1920-1940.

4554 Marine Corps. Marine Corps Manual, 1931. Washington: Government Printing Office, 1931. 939p.

4555 Navy Department. Anacostia Naval Air Station. Report on XF9C-1 Curtis Single Seater Fighter. Re-

port, no. 91. Washington, 1931. 69p.

4556 _____. Bureau of Navigation. Leadership: Military
Character. Washington: Government Printing Office,
1931. 120p.

4557 _____. Naval Academy. Department of Engineering
and Aeronautics. Internal-Combustion Engines:
Their Principles and Application to Automobile,
Aircraft, and Marine Purposes. Annapolis: U. S.
Naval Institute, 1931. 308p.

4558 _____. Office of Naval Intelligence. The United
States Navy in Peace Time: The Navy in Its Rela-
tion to the Industrial, Scientific, Economic, and
Political Development of the Nation. Washington:
Government Printing Office, 1931. 176p.

4559 State Department. Treaties and Other International
Acts of the United States of America. Edited by
Hunter Miller. v. 2-- Washington: Government
Printing Office, 1931--.
"Vol. I will not appear in final form until all
documents to which it refers have been published."
--Pref.

1932

4560 Navy Department. Anacostia Naval Air Station. Report on F9C-2 Curtis Airship and Carrier Fighter.
Report, ono. 122. Washington, 1932. 66p.

4561 _____. Bureau of Navigation. Information on Living Conditions in Honolulu and Pearl Harbor.
Washington: Government Printing Office, 1932. 6p.

4562 _____. _____. Reserve Officers' Manual, United
States Navy. Washington: Government Printing
Office, 1932. 720p.

4563 _____. Bureau of Supplies and Accounts. Naval
Expenditures. Washington: 1932--.

4564 _____. Naval Academy. Department of Electrical
Engineering and Physics. Laboratory Manual:
Physics. Menasha, Wisc.: Banta, 1932. 135p.

4565 _____ . Office of the Chief of Naval Operations.
"Annual Report of the Chief of Naval Operations,
1932-1941. " CNO File, Operational Archives, U.S.
Navy Department, Naval History Division, 1932-
1941. 343p.
Individual annual reports providing overall information and statistics.

4566 State Department. The United States and Nicaragua.
Washington: Government Printing Office, 1932.

1933

4567 Congress. Joint Committee. Hearings and Investigation of Dirigible Disasters. Senate doc. 75, 73rd
Cong. , 2nd sess. , 1933. 944p.

4568 _____ . _____ . _____ Report of Colonel
Henry Breckinridge. 73rd Cong. , 1st sess. , 1933.
177p.
Provides analytical summaries of testimony taken
during the Dirigible Disasters hearings cited above.

4569 Navy Department. Fourteenth Naval District. "A
Brief Study of Pearl Harbor in Its Relation to the
U. S. Navy. " Unpublished Paper, Shore Establishments File, Operational Archives, U. S. Navy Department, Naval History Division, 1933. 121p.

4570 _____ . Naval Academy. Department of Electrical
Engineering and Physics. Radio Manual for the Instruction of Midshipmen. Menasha, Wisc. : Banta,
1933. 152p.

4571 _____ . _____ . Department of Seamanship and
Navigation. Naval Aviation: A Textbook for Mid-
shipmen. Annapolis, 1933. 88p.
Based on various navy department publications,
the volume was prepared by the officers of VN
Squadron 8D5 stationed at the academy and by the
Seamanship and Navigation Department. --Preface.

1934

4572 Congress. House. H. R. 6604, an Act to Establish the
Composition of the Navy, with Respect to Categories of Vessels Limited by Treaties Signed at

Washington, Feb. 6, 1922, and at London, April 22,
1930, at Limits Prescribed by Those Treaties, to
Authorize the Construction of Certain Naval Vessels,
and for Other Purposes. Approved Mar. 27, 1934,
Public Law 135. Washington: Government Printing
Office, 1934. 3p.
    One of the most important pieces of legislation
inacted during the 1930s as far as the U. S. Navy
was concerned, this act was commonly known as
the Vinson-Trammell Naval Construction Bill.

4573   . Senate. Naval Affairs Committee. Construction of Certain Naval Vessels at the Limits Prescribed by the Treaties Signed at Washington and
London. Washington: Government Printing Office,
1934. 25p.

4574   .   .   .   : Hearings.
Washington: Government Printing Office, 1934. 16p.

4575 Marine Corps. Marine Corps Schools. Tentative
Manual of Landing Operations. Quantico, Va. , 1934.
    The doctrinal foundation for all future Marine
activity in this area.

4576 Navy Department. Acts and Resolutions Relating Chiefly
to the Navy, Navy Department, and Marine Corps
Passed by Congress. Washington: Government
Printing Office, 1934-1938.

4577   . Instructions Governing the Use of Naval
Communication Facilities at Washington, D. C. , by
Government Departments Other than the Navy De-
partment. Washington: U. S. Government Printing
Office, 1934. 4p.

4578   .   .   . 1938. 7p.

4579   . Uniform Regulations, United States Navy,
1922. Washington: Government Printing Office,
1934. 60p.
    Includes changes authorized to publication date.

4580   . Naval Academy. Department of Languages.
Naval Phraseology in French, Spanish, Italian and
German. Annapolis: U. S. Naval Institute, 1934.
19p.

4581 State Department. The Right to Protect Citizens in
Foreign Countries by Landing Forces. Washington:
Government Printing Office, 193⁴. 130p.

1935

4582 Coast Guard. Office of Assistant Commandant. Records
of Movements, Vessels of the United States Coast
Guard, 1790-December 31, 1933. 2 vols. ; Washington: Government Printing Office, [1935?].
Records for each individual vessel, even the
smallest, are included.

4583 Congress. Senate. Naval Affairs Committee. Longevity,
Public Works, Aviation Cadets, and Naval Line
Personnel: Hearings. Washington: Government
Printing Office, 1935. 27p.

4584 Marine Corps. A Text on the Employment of Marine
Corps Aviation. Quantico, Va. : Marine Corps
Schools, 1935. 84p.

1936

4585 Congress. Senate. Foreign Relations Committee.
London Naval Treaty, 1936, Hearings. Washington:
Government Printing Office, 1936. 64p.

4586 _____ . _____ . Naval Affairs Committee. To
Amend the Act Establishing the Composition of the
United States Navy: Hearings. Washington: Govern-
ment Printing Office, 1936. 35p.

4587 State Department. The London Naval Conference,
1935; Report of the Delegates of the United States
of America [and] Text of the London Naval Treaty
of 1936 and Other Documents. State Department
Publication, no. 896, Conference Series, no. 24.
Washington: Government Printing Office, 1936.
444p.

4588 _____ . Naval Mission: Agreement Between the
United States of America and Brazil, Signed May
27, 1936, Effective June 25, 1936. Department of
State Publications, no. 926. Washington: Government Printing Office, 1936. 11p.

1937

4589   Congress. Senate. The United States Navy: Informa-
        tion Relative to Organization, Personnel, Fleet and
        Shore Establishments of the U. S. Navy.   Senate
        doc. 35, 75th Cong. , 1st sess. , 1937.   69p.
        Also printed by the Government Printing Office.

4590   _____._____. Naval Affairs Committee. Con-
        struction of Certain Auxiliary Vessels for the Navy:
        Hearings. Washington: Government Printing Office,
        1937. 44p.

4591   _____._____._____. Construction of Certain
        Public Works: Hearings. Washington: U. S. Govern-
        ment Printing Office, 1937.   35p.

4592   Navy Department.   Bureau of Construction and Repair.
        History of the Construction Corps of the United
        States Navy.   Washington: Government Printing
        Office, 1937.   57p.

4593   _____._____. "Progress of Work on the Battle-
        ships North Carolina and Washington. " USNIP,
        LXIII (1937), 1475-1478.

4594   _____. Bureau of Ships. Instructions for the Oper-
        ation, Care, and Repair of Compressed Air Plants.
        Washington: Government Printing Office, 1937. 49p.

4595   _____._____. Instructions for the Operation,
        Care, and Repair of Main Propelling Machinery--
        Diesel Engines. Washington: Government Printing
        Office, 1937. 28p.

4596   _____._____. Instructions for the Operation,
        Care, and Repair of Main Propelling Machinery--
        Turbines. Washington: Government Printing Office,
        1937. 69p.

4597   Treasury Department.   Bureau of Internal Revenue.
        Excess Profits on Navy Contracts Subject to Vin-
        son-Trammell Act, Regulations Under Sec. 3 of Act
        of Mar. 27, 1934, as Originally Enacted and as
        Amended. Washington: Government Printing Office,
        1937. 11p.
        Reprinted from Treasury Decisions, Vol. 71,

this circular supersedes Treasury decision 4434,
C. B. , XIII-I, 540.

4598 Veteran's Administration. Laws and Executive Orders
Relating to Compensation, Pension, Emergency
Officer's Retirement, Insurance, and Medical, Hospital, and/or Domiciliary Care by Reason of Service
in the Military or Naval Forces of the U. S. Washington, 1937.

1938

4599 Congress. House. Naval Affairs Committee. Establish
the Composition of the United States Navy: Hearings. Washington: Government Printing Office,
1938. 2889p.

4600 _____ . _____ . _____ : Report and
Minority Views. House rpt. 1899, 75th Cong. ,
3rd sess. , 1938. 25, 16p.
The 25 page report was submitted by Congressman Vinson while the 16 page minority views were
signed by Congressmen Church, Cole, Brewster,
and Shannon.

4601 _____ . Senate. Naval Affairs Committee. Naval
Expansion Program: Hearings. Washington:
Government Printing Office, 1938. 489p.

4602 _____ . _____ . _____ : Report and
Personal Views. Senate rpt. 1611, 75th Cong. ,
3rd sess. , 1938. 52, 8p.
The 52 page report was submitted by Chairman
Walsh while the 8 page "personal views" was sub-
mitted by Senator Bone.

4603 Library of Congress. Legislative Reference Service.
Appropriations for the Army and Navy Made During
the 75th Congress, 3rd Session. Washington, 1938.
2p.

4604 _____ . Appropriations for the Army and Navy of
the United States for the Fiscal Years 1900 to 1938,
Inclusive. Washington, 1938. 2p.
Both reports were compiled by Margaret Blachly.

4605 Navy Department. Bureau of Aeronautics. Naval

Aviation Insignia.   Washington: Government Printing Office, 1938.   28p.

4606 _____ . _____ . The Progress of Naval Aviation.
Washington, 1938.   17p.

4607 _____ . Bureau of Construction and Repair.   Submarine Safety, Respiration, and Rescue Devices.
Washington: Government Printing Office, 1938. 137p.

4608 _____ . Bureau of Navigation.   United States Naval
Academy, a Sketch Containing the History, Entrance
Requirements, Curriculum, Athletics, After Grad-
uation Service and Other Factual Information.
Washington: Government Printing Office, 1938. 71p.
Prepared at the request of Senator David I.
Walsh, Chairman of the Senate Naval Affairs Com-
mittee.

4609 _____ . Bureau of Ships.   Lubrication, and In-
structions for the Operation, Care, and Repair of
Lubrication Systems.   Washington: Government
Printing Office, 1938.   28p.

1939

4610 Congress. Senate.   Naval Affairs Committee. Auxiliary
Vessels for the Navy: Hearings.   Washington:
Government Printing Office, 1939.   9p.

4611 _____ . _____ . _____ . Construction of Certain
Public Works: Hearings.   Washington: Government
Printing Office, 1939.   212p.

4612 _____ . _____ . _____ . Profits of Certain
Contractors with the United States: Hearings.
Washington: Government Printing Office, 1939. 4p.

4613 Library of Congress.   Legislative Reference Service.
Appropriations for U. S. War and Navy Departments
for the Fiscal Years 1933 to 1940, Inclusive.
Washington, 1939.   1p.

4614 _____ . _____ . Expenditures of the U. S. War
and Navy Departments, by Years, 1933-1938, Inclusive.   Washington, 1939.   2p.
Both reports were compiled by Margaret Blachly.

4615 Navy Department. Board on Submarine, Destroyer, Mine and Naval Air Bases. Report on the Need of Additional Bases to Defend the Coasts of the United States. Washington: Government Printing Office, 1939. 39p.

4616 _____. Bureau of Ships. Instructions for the Operation, Care, and Repair of Main Propelling Machinery--Reciprocating Steam Engines. Washington: Government Printing Office, 1939. 50p.

1940

4617 Coast Guard. Activities of the United States Coast Guard. Washington: Government Printing Office, 1940. 8p.

4618 _____. Operation of the Coast Guard in Time of War. Washington, 1940. 15p.

4619 _____. Regulations Governing Appointment to Cadetships in the United States Coast Guard. Rev. ed. Washington, 1940. 26p.

4620 _____. The United States Coast Guard Academy: The Coast Guard as a Career. Washington, 1940. 24p.

4621 Congress. Senate. Naval Affairs Committee. Expediting Naval Shipbuilding and for Other Purposes. Senate rpt. 1863, 76th Cong., 3rd sess., 1940. 15p.

4622 Marine Corps. Marine Corps Aviation, General, 1940. Washington: Government Printing Office, 1940. 70p. Pre-World War II thinking on the use of this aerial weapon.

4623 _____. Marine Corps Manual. Washington, 1940. 1099p.

4624 Maritime Commission. New Ships for the Merchant Marine. Washington, 1940. 23p.

4625 Navy Department. Neutrality Instructions, U.S. Navy. Washington: Government Printing Office, 1940. 130p.

4626 _____. Atlantic Squadron. "Annual Report of the
Commander, Atlantic Squadron, FY 1940. " Dis-
continued Commands File, Operational Archives,
U. S. Navy Department, Naval History Division,
1940. 34p.
Organization and operations.

4627 _____. Board on Regular and Reserve Aviation
Personnel of the Navy and Marine Corps. Report.
Washington: Government Printing Office, 1940. 41p.

4628 _____. Bureau of Navigation. Instructions for Use
in Preparation for the Rating of Bugler, U. S. Navy.
Washington, 1940. 47p.

4629 _____. _____. The Naval Reserve of the United
States Navy. Washington: Government Printing
Office, 1940. 73p.
Chester W. Nimitz was Chief of the Bureau at
the time this pamphlet was issued.

4630 _____. Bureau of Ships. Instructions for the
Operation and Maintenance of Propellers. Washington: Government Printing Office, 1940. 173p.

4631 _____. _____. Instructions for the Operation
and Maintenance of Pumps. Washington: Government Printing Office, 1940. 118p.

4632 _____. Bureau of Supplies and Accounts. The
Cook Book of the United States Navy. Washington:
Government Printing Office, 1940. 164p.

4633 _____. Naval Academy. Department of Marine
Engineering. Energy Analysis of Naval Machinery.
Annapolis: U. S. Naval Institute, 1940. 522p.

4634 Selective Service System. Soldiers' and Sailors' Civil
Relief Act of 1940: National Service Life Insurance
Act of 1940. Washington, 1940. 34p.

1941

4635 Congress. Laws Relating to National Defense Enacted
During the Seventy-Sixth Congress. Washington:
Government Printing Office, 1941. 231p.
Contains the texts of laws, arranged chronolog-

ically, which were approved between April 3, 1939
and October 14, 1940.

4636 _____. Senate. Strikes in Defense Industries.
Senate doc. 52, 77th Cong., 1st sess., 1941. 299p.

4637 _____. _____. The United States Navy: Informa-
tion Relative to Organization, Personnel, Fleet,
and Shore Establishments of the United States Navy.
Senate doc. 58, 77th Cong., 1st sess., 1941. 84p.
Various ships and planes and a statement of
U. S. naval policy.

4638 Navy Department. Nomenclature of Naval Vessels.
Washington: Government Printing Office, 1941. 52p.

4639 _____. Tentative Instructions for the Navy of the
United States Governing Maritime and Aerial Warfare. Washington: Government Printing Office,
1941. 184p.

4640 _____. Atlantic Fleet. "Annual Report, F[iscal]
Y[ear] 1941." Fleets File, Operational Archives,
U. S. Navy Department, Naval History Division,
1941. 12p.
Contains information on administration, material
readiness, repairs and overhaul, advanced bases,
and logistics. All FY's, as most users know, begin in July, e. g., FY 1941= July 1940-June 1941.

4641 _____. Bureau of Aeronautics. Aircraft Navigation
Manual, U. S. Navy. Washington: Government
Printing Office, 1941. 253p.

4642 _____. Bureau of Medicine and Surgery. Medical
Compend: For Commanding Officers of Naval
Vessels to Which no Member of the Medical De-
partment of the United States Navy is Attached.
Washington: Government Printing Office, 1941.
122p.
A general first aid manual.

4643 _____. Bureau of Naval Personnel. "Annual Re-
port of the Chief of the Bureau of Naval Personnel
for the Fiscal Year 1941." Shore Establishment
File, Operational Archives, U. S. Navy Department,
Naval History Division, 1941. 88p.
Submitted in September 1941.

4644 _____. _____. Uniforms and Insignia of Foreign
Navies. Washington: Government Printing Office,
1941. 28p.
Detailed data on the subject for Britain, Russia,
France, Japan, Italy, and Germany.

4645 _____. _____. Uniforms, Decorations, Medals
and Badges of the United States Navy: Taken from
the Naval Uniform Regulations, 1941. Washington:
Government Printing Office, 1941. 94p.

4646 _____. Bureau of Ships. Instructions for the Operation and Maintenance of Boilers. Washington:
Government Printing Office, 1941. 134p.

4647 _____. _____. Instructions for Operation and
Maintenance of Measuring Instruments. Washington: Government Printing Office, 1941. 52p.

4648 _____. _____. Instructions for the Operation and
Maintenance of Power Boat Machinery--Gasoline
Engines. Washington: Government Printing Office,
1941. 31p.

4649 _____. _____. Instructions for the Operation,
Care and Repair of Generating Sets, Motors, and
Motor Control Panels--Direct Current Apparatus.
Washington: Government Printing Office, 1941. 27p.

4650 _____. _____. Instructions for the Operation,
Care, and Repair of Main Propelling Machinery--
Electric Propulsion Installations. Washington:
Government Printing Office, 1941. 21p.

4651 _____. _____. Instructions Relative to Piping,
Fittings, and Packing. Washington: Government
Printing Office, 1941. 50p.

4652 _____. _____. Tables of Engineering Data.
Washington: Government Printing Office, 1941. 35p.

4653 _____. Hydrographic Office. Aircraft Navigation
Manual, U. S. Navy. Publication 216. Washington:
Government Printing Office, 1941. 258p.

4654 _____. Pacific Fleet. "Annual Report of the Commander-in-Chief, U. S. Pacific Fleet, FY 1941. "

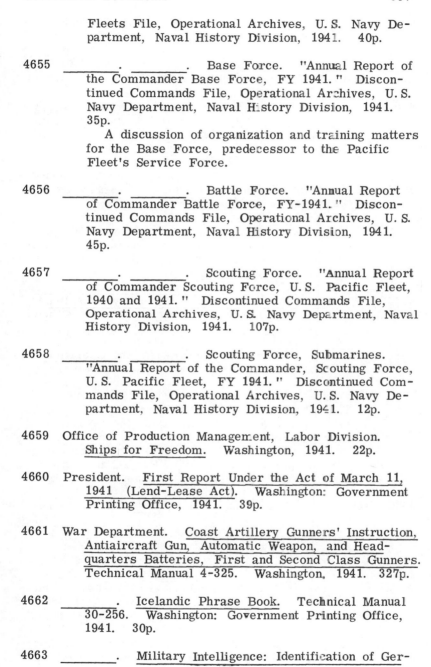

Fleets File, Operational Archives, U. S. Navy Department, Naval History Division, 1941. 40p.

4655   _____. _____. Base Force. "Annual Report of the Commander Base Force, FY 1941." Discontinued Commands File, Operational Archives, U. S. Navy Department, Naval History Division, 1941. 35p.
A discussion of organization and training matters for the Base Force, predecessor to the Pacific Fleet's Service Force.

4656   _____. _____. Battle Force. "Annual Report of Commander Battle Force, FY-1941." Discontinued Commands File, Operational Archives, U. S. Navy Department, Naval History Division, 1941. 45p.

4657   _____. _____. Scouting Force. "Annual Report of Commander Scouting Force, U. S. Pacific Fleet, 1940 and 1941." Discontinued Commands File, Operational Archives, U. S. Navy Department, Naval History Division, 1941. 107p.

4658   _____. _____. Scouting Force, Submarines. "Annual Report of the Commander, Scouting Force, U. S. Pacific Fleet, FY 1941." Discontinued Commands File, Operational Archives, U. S. Navy Department, Naval History Division, 1941. 12p.

4659   Office of Production Management, Labor Division. Ships for Freedom. Washington, 1941. 22p.

4660   President. First Report Under the Act of March 11, 1941 (Lend-Lease Act). Washington: Government Printing Office, 1941. 39p.

4661   War Department. Coast Artillery Gunners' Instruction, Antiaircraft Gun, Automatic Weapon, and Headquarters Batteries, First and Second Class Gunners. Technical Manual 4-325. Washington, 1941. 327p.

4662   _____. Icelandic Phrase Book. Technical Manual 30-256. Washington: Government Printing Office, 1941. 30p.

4663   _____. Military Intelligence: Identification of Ger-

man Naval Ships.   Basic Field Manual 30-55.
Washington, 1941.   78p.

4664 _____. Military Intelligence: Identification of Italian
Aircraft. Basic Field Manual 30-39.   Washington,

4665 _____. Military Intelligence: Identification of Japanese Naval Vessels. Basic Field Manual 30-58.
Washington, 1941.   182p.

1942

4666 Coast Guard.   Operations Division.   Research and
Statistical Section. Bering Sea Patrol. Washington 1942.   80p.
A discussion of the legal foundations and operations from a seal protection patrol in 1912 through
its more complex defense role with the coming of
World War II.

4667 _____. _____. _____. The Taking of Italian,
German, and Danish Merchant Vessels in Ports of
the United States in Protective Custody by the
United States Coast Guard. Washington, 1942. 52p.
A discussion of the legal justification and events
surrounding this event of March 30, 1941.

4668 Navy Department.   Task Force 24.   "The History of
Task Force 24. " Unpublished paper, Task Forces
File, Operational Archives, U. S. Navy Department,
Naval History Division, 1942.   150p.
Describes in detail the administrative organiza-
tion and planning of the U. S. Escorts protecting
convoys (TF-24) in the North Atlantic during 1941.

4669 State Department. Papers Relating to the Foreign Re-
lations of the United States, 1919: The Paris Peace
Conference. 2 vols. Washington: Government
Printing Office, 1942.

4670 _____. Peace and War: United States Foreign
Policy, 1931-1941. Washington: Government Printing Office, 1942.   144p.
"An introduction to a collection of documents
concerning the foreign relations of the United States
during the years 1931-1941, especially the policies
and acts of the United States toward promoting con-

ditions of peace and world order and toward meeting the world-wide dangers resulting from Japanese,
German, and Italian aggression. "--Introduction.

4671　　　　. The War Chronology, March 1938 to December 1941. Washington, 1942. 12p.
Reprinted from the December 27, 1941 issue of
the Department of State Bulletin.

4672 War Department. Bureau of Public Relations. The
Background of Our War, from Lectures Prepared
by the Orientation Course, War Department, Bureau
of Public Relations. New York: Farrar & Rinehart, 1942. 279p.
Why America is "fighting in this war," written
in pure military sentences. Good maps illustrate
this version of the road to Pearl Harbor.

1943

4673 Coast Guard. Deeds of Valor from the Annals of the
United States Coast Guard. Washington: Government Printing Office, 1943. 30p.

4674 Navy Department. Naval History Division. Ships'
History Section. Ships Histories. Washington,
1943--.
Contains nearly 2000 mimeographed U.S. Navy
vessel histories, many of which have yet to appear
in The Dictionary of American Naval Fighting Ships.

4675 Office of Lend-Lease Administration. All for One,
One for All: The Story of Lend-Lease. Washington: Government Printing Office, 1943. 15p.

4676　　　　. Report to the 78th Congress on the Lend-
Lease Operations, from the Passage of the Act.,
March 11, 1941 to December 31, 1942. Washing-
ton: Government Printing Office, 1943. 91p.

4677 State Department. Papers Relating to the Foreign Relations of the United States-Japan: 1931-1941.
2 vols. Washington: Government Printing Office,
1943.

1944

4678 Navy Department. The History of the Naval Petroleum
      Reserves. Washington: Government Printing Office,
      1944. 58p.

4679 _____. Principal Officials and Officers, Navy De-
      partment and United States Fleet, Sept. 1, 1939-
      May 24, 1944. Administrative Reference Service
      Report, no. 7. Washington, 1944. 9p.

4680 _____. Bureau of Naval Personnel, Officer Train-
      ing Section. "History of Navy Chemical Warfare
      Training After World War I." Unpublished paper,
      Operational Archives, U. S. Navy Department, Naval
      History Division, 1944. 11p.
      Faced the major problem of a lack of students
      due to the extended operating schedule of fleet units.

4681 _____. Office of Naval Intelligence. United States
      Naval Activity in Connection with the Armistice of
      1918 and the Peace Conference of 1919. Washing-
      ton, 1944. 56p.

4682 _____. Office of the Chief of Naval Operations,
      Director of Flight. "Administrative History of
      Naval Aviation." Unpublished paper, CNO File,
      Operational Archives, U. S. Navy Department, Naval
      History Division, 1944. 180p.
      Composed of several subordinate sectional sum-
      maries of operations, aerology, flight statistics,
      and medical liaison for the years 1921-1944, this
      history also includes a resume of significant events
      in naval aviation in the decade 1917-1927.

1945

4683 Navy Department. Centennial of the United States
      Naval Academy, 1845-1945: A Sketch Containing
      the History, the Growth, the Daily Routine, and
      the Activities of the United States Naval Academy.
      Washington: Government Printing Office, 1945. 27p.
      Prepared at the request of Senator David I.
      Walsh, Chairman of the Senate Naval Affairs Com-
      mittee, and also published as Senate doc. 91, 79th
      Cong., 1st sess.

4684   _____. Bureau of Ships. Ships Laid Down Since
        the Washington Treaty by Authorizing Acts. Nav-
        Ships 282, Finance Division Report. Washington,
        1945.

4685   _____. _____. Vessels Lost, Transferred, Re-
        turned, Sold, Scrapped, or Otherwise Disposed of
        Since 1 January 1940. NavShips 1851, Rpt. no. 104.
        Washington, 1945.

4686   _____. First Naval District. "First Naval Dis-
        trict History--Aviation. " Unpublished paper, Oper-
        ational Archives, U. S. Navy Department, Naval
        History Division, [1945?]. 220p.
        A comprehensive account covering the late 1930s
        and early 1940s.

4687   _____. _____. "History of Harbor Entrance Con-
        trol Post, Boston. " Unpublished paper, Operational
        Archives, U. S. Navy Department, Naval History
        Division, 1945. 70p.
        During the period August 4, 1941-June 27, 1945.

4688   _____. Third Naval District. "Historical Narrative
        of District Intelligence Office, 3ND. " Unpublished
        paper, Operational Archives, U. S. Navy Department,
        Naval History Division, 1945. 195p.
        Covering the period September 8, 1939 to
        August 14, 1945.

4689   _____. _____. "Historical Narrative of District
        Security Office, Third Naval District. " Unpublished
        paper, Operational Archives, U. S. Navy Depart-
        ment, Naval History Division, 1945. 35p.
        Covering the period October 13, 1941 to August
        14, 1945.

4690   _____. _____. "Historical Narrative of the Dis-
        trict Communications Office, 3ND. " Unpublished
        paper, Operational Archives, U. S. Navy Depart-
        ment, Naval History Division, 1945. 100p.
        During the period September 8, 1939 to August
        14, 1945.

4691   _____. _____. "Historical Narrative of the Dis-
        trict Material Office (October 13, 1939-April 30,
        1942) and Field Production Division, Navy Yard,

New York (May 1, 1942-December 31, 1945). Un-
published paper, Naval Districts File, Operational
Archives, U. S. Navy Department, Naval History
Division, 1945. 381p.

4692 _____. _____. "History of the Office of the In-
spector of Naval Material, Buffalo, New York,
September 1939-July 1945. " Unpublished paper,
Shore Establishment File, Operational Archives,
U. S. Navy Department, Naval History Division,
1945. 50p.

4693 _____. Fifth Naval District. Office of the Director
of Distribution. "History of the Office of Director
of Distribution, Fifth Naval District, N. O. B. " Unpublished paper, Operational Archives, U. S. Navy
Department, Naval History Division, 1945. 65p.
       Stresses the influx of personnel during the period
from 1939 to 1945.

4694 _____. Twelfth Naval District. "History of District Intelligence Office, Twelfth Naval District. "
Unpublished Paper, Naval Districts File, Operational Archives, U. S. Navy Department, Naval History Division, 1946. 81p.
       Covering the years 1921-1945, this report spot-
lights the types of intelligence efforts on the West
Coast during our period.

4695 _____. Iceland Naval Operating Base. "Administrative History of the Naval Operating Base, Iceland. " Unpublished paper, Shore Establishment
File, Operational Archives, U. S. Navy Department,
Naval History Division, 1945. 41p.

4696 _____. Naval Operating Facility, Natal, Brazil.
"Administrative History of Naval Operating Facility,
Natal, Brazil. " Unpublished paper, Operational
Archives, U. S. Navy Department, Naval History
Division, [1945?]. 45p.
       Covers the period October 14, 1941-mid-1945.

4697 _____. Norfolk Navy Yard. "History: Norfolk Navy
Yard, September 1939 to September 1945. " Unpublished paper, Shore Establishment File, Operational Archives, U. S. Navy Department, Naval History Division, 1945. 406p.

4698 _____. Pearl Harbor Navy Yard. "History of the Pearl Harbor Navy Yard." 4 vols. Shore Establishment File, Operational Archives, U. S. Navy Department, Naval History Division, 1945.
A 1195 page narrative history prior to the December 7, 1941 attack built around hundreds of attached documents.

4699 _____. White Oak Naval Ordnance Laboratory. "The History of the Naval Ordnance Laboratory, 1918-1945." Unpublished paper, Shore Establishment File, Operational Archives, U. S. Navy Department, Naval History Division, [1945?]. 570p.

1946

4700 Congress. Joint Select Committee. Hearings on the Pearl Harbor Attack. 39 vols. Washington: Government Printing Office, 1946. Rpr. 1972.
An important source out of which much speculation and criticism has grown.

4701 _____. _____. _____. Report. Washington: Government Printing Office, 1946. 604p.
Senate doc. 244, 79th Cong., 2nd sess., 1946.
Includes preceding events as well as the actual Japanese strike.

4702 Navy Department. Bureau of Ships. Contracts Awarded Private Shipyards for Construction of Naval Vessels Since 1 January 1934. NavShips 1851, Rpt. no. 92. Washington, 1946.

4703 _____. European Naval Forces. "Office of the United States Naval Attache, American Embassy, London England, 1939-1946." Unpublished Paper, Shore Establishment File, Operational Archives, U. S. Navy Department, Naval History Division, 1946. 90p.

4704 _____. Inspector of Machinery, Cleveland, Ohio. "Wartime History (1939-1945)--Office of the Inspector of Machinery, USN, Cleveland, Ohio." Shore Establishment File, Operational Archives, U. S. Navy Department, Naval History Division, 1946. 15p.
Concerns the production and inspection of diesel

engines for the navy at the Cleveland Diesel Engine
Division of GM.

4705 _____. Supervisor of Shipbuilding, Chicago, Illinois.
"Wartime History of Supervisor of Shipbuilding,
USN, Chicago, Illinois. " Shore Establishment File,
Operational Archives, U. S. Navy Department, Naval
History Division, 1946. 33p.
A critical review of the principles, practices,
and procedures utilized by the Supervisor from the
establishment of that office in early 1941 through
the war.

4706 _____. Supervisor of Shipbuilding, Philadelphia,
Pennsylvania. "Wartime History: Supervisor of
Shipbuilding, USN, Philadelphia, Pennsylvania, from
Establishment November 1940 up to 1 September
1945. " Unpublished paper, Shore Establishment
File, Operational Archives, U. S. Navy Department,
Naval History Division, 1946. 15p.

1947

4707 Navy Department. Europe Naval Forces. "Adminis-
trative History, U. S. Naval Forces in Europe,
1940-1946. " Unpublished paper, Forces File,
Operational Archives, U. S. Navy Department, Naval
History Division, 1947. 611p.
Covers the activities of the Special Naval Ob-
server, London, the Commander of U. S. Naval
Forces in Europe, and the Commander, 12th Fleet.

4708 _____. Submarine Escape Committee. "Submarine
Escapes--Past and Present. " Unpublished Paper,
Operational Archives, U. S. Navy Department, 1947.
32p.
Provides accounts of escapes from sunken sub-
marines, many relative to our period.

1948

4709 Navy Department. Office of the Chief of Naval Operations. Aviation History Unit. "Inter-Service Cooperation in Aeronautics. " Unpublished Paper,
CNO File, Operational Archives, U. S. Navy Department, Naval History Division, 1948. 58p.
Historical treatment of Army-Navy cooperation

in various aviation projects throughou: our period.

4710 _____. Office of the Chief of Naval Operations.
Aviation History Unit. "The Progress of Naval
Aviation. " Unpublished Paper, CNO File, Operational Archives, U. S. Navy Department, Naval History Division, 1948. 33p.
Provides particular historical coverage of the
1930s.

1950

4711 Coast Guard. Public Information Division. Some Unusual Incidents in Coast Guard History. Washington, 1950. 120p.

4712 Navy Department. Medal of Honor, 1861-1949, the
Navy. Washington: Government Printing Office,
1950. 327p.
A list of recipients with biographical data.

1951

4713 Coast Guard. United States Coast Guard in Action
Since 1790. Washington: Government Printing
Office, 1951. 14p.
Prepared for a display at the Truxton-Decatur
Naval Museum honoring the Coast Guard.

1952

4714 Navy Department. Hydrographic Office. United States
Navy Hydrographic Office. Washington: Government
Printing Office, 1952. 46p.
A brief history.

1954

4715 Navy Department. Bureau of Ships. "The Boston
Naval Shipyard. " Bureau of Ships Journal, II
(January 1954), 13-18.

4716 _____. _____. "The New York Naval Shipyard:
A Record of Progressive Achievement in Shipbuild-
ing Since 1801. " Bureau of Ships Journal, II
(April 1954), 22-28.

4717 _____. _____. "The Philadelphia Naval Ship-
      yard." Bureau of Ships Journal, III (June 1954),
      8-13.

1955

4718 Navy Department. Naval History Division. United
      States Naval Chronology, World War II. Washing-
      ton: Government Printing Office, 1955. 214p.
          Contains some data on U. S. naval operations in
      the undeclared war against Germany in the Atlantic,
      1941.

1956

4719 Navy Department. Naval History Division. Fifty Years
      of Naval District Development, 1903-1953. Wash-
      ington, 1956. 117p.
          Not generally available as are other NHD studies,
      copies may be examined at various facilities within
      the naval establishment.

1957

4720 Navy Department. Office of the Chief of Naval Opera-
      tions. The Steam Catapult: Its History and Opera-
      tion. Washington, 1957. 64p.

1958

4721 Coast Guard. Public Information Division. Coast
      Guard History. Washington: Government Printing
      Office, 1958. 32p.

4722 Navy Department. Office of the Chief of Naval Opera-
      tions. Naval Aviation in Review. Washington,
      1958. 338p.

1959

4723 Navy Department. Naval History Division. The Dic-
      tionary of American Naval Fighting Ships. Wash-
      ington: Government Printing Office, 1959-
          Five volumes are complete with volume VI
      (R-S) scheduled for publication in 1974.

1961

4724   Navy Department.   Naval History Division.   Aviation
       in the United States Navy.   Washington, 1961. 31p.

1962

4725   Marine Corps.   Historical Branch.   A History of
       Marine Corps Roles and Missions, 1775-1962.   By
       Thomas G. Roe.   Marine Corps Historical Refer-
       ence Series, no. 30.   Washington, 1962.   36p.
          The duties assigned the USMC by statue or regu-
       lation.

4726   Navy Department.   Naval History Division.   Destroyers
       in the United States Navy.   Washington: Government
       Printing Office, 1962.   40p.
          A general history with much material on our
       period.

1963

4727   Marine Corps.   Historical Branch.   Marine Corps
       Lore.   Marine Corps Historical Reference Series,
       no. 22.   Washington, 1963.   18p.

4728   _____.   _____.   A Brief History of the United
       States Marine Corps.   By Norman W. Hicks.
       Marine Corps Historical Reference Series, no. 1.
       Rev. ed.   Washington, 1964.   54p.

1964

4729   State Department.   Documents on German Foreign
       Policy: June 23-December 11, 1941.   Series D.,
       Vol. XIII of Documents on German Foreign Policy,
       1918-1945.   Washington: Government Printing
       Office, 1964.
          The period of the undeclared naval war with
       America.

1965

4730   Marine Corps.   Historical Branch, G-3.   A Chronology
       of the United States Marine Corps.   4 vols.   Wash-
       ington, 1965-1970.
          The first two volumes, covering the years 1775-

1934 and 1935-1946, are of interest here.

1968

4731 Congress. Senate.   Committee on Labor and Public
      Welfare. Subcommittee on Veterans' Affairs. Medal
      of Honor Recipients--1863-1968. Washington:
      Government Printing Office, 1968. 1087p.
          Includes Navy and Marine Corps recipients from
      our period.

4732 Navy Department.   Cruiser-Destroyer Force, Atlantic
      Fleet.   A History of the Cruiser-Destroyer Force,
      U. S. Atlantic Fleet, 1902-1968.   Norfolk, Va. ,
      1968.   32p.

1969

4733 Navy Department.   Naval History Division.   Historic
      Ship Exhibits in the United States. Washington:
      Government Printing Office, 1969.   67p.

4734 _____ . _____ . Monitors of the U. S. Navy, 1861-
      1937.   Washington: Government Printing Office,
      1969.   48p.

4735 _____ . _____ . The Submarine in the United
      States Navy.   Washington: Government Printing
      Office, 1969.   26p.

4736 _____ . _____ . The United States Navy.   Wash-
      ington: Government Printing Office, 1969.   40p.
          A brief general history with some data on our
      period.

1970

4737 Marine Corps.   Historical Division.   United States
      Marine Corps Ranks and Grades, 1775-1969.   By
      Bernard C. Nalty.   Marine Corps Historical Refer-
      ence Pamphlet.   Rev. ed.   Washington, 1970. 62p.
          Survey of the growth of commissioned and en-
      listed ranks and grades with an annotated list of
      USMC Commandants showing the progressing changes
      in rank for that position.

4738   Navy Department.   Naval History Division.   The
       Battleship in the United States Navy.   Washington:
       Government Printing Office, 1970.   64p.
       Considerable data on cur period.

4739   _____ .   _____ . Riverine Warfare: The U.S.
       Navy's Operations on Inland Waters.   Rev. ed.
       Washington: Government Printing Office, 1970. 55p.

                              1971

4740   Marine Corps.   A Concise History of the United States
       Marine Corps, 1775-1969.   By William D. Parker.
       Washington: Government Printing Office, 1971.
       141p.

                              1972

4741   Navy Department.   Naval History Division.   Battle
       Streamers of the United States Navy.   Washington:
       Government Printing Office, 1972.   24p.

SUBJECT INDEX

All vessels, places and personnel referred to in this index are keyed to the entry numbers of references in the two parts of the bibliography. Certain general categories familiar to many have been inserted, e. g. , ordnance; strategy and tactics, naval; engineering and naval machinery. In addition, one will find index-keys to general works concerning the American and a few other navies, the U. S. Coast Guard and Marine Corps. As in Volume IV of this series, we have dropped the American national designation (U. S. S.) in favor of the hull-numbering system. Thus, for example, one can readily differentiate between the first battleship Indiana (BB-1), the second (BB-50), and the third (BB-58). A complete key to these hull-designations can be found in the first volume of the U. S. Naval History Division's Dictionary of American Naval Fighting Ships. The only national designations which will appear are those denoting important foreign vessels which have crept into the compilation, e. g. , H. M. S. Illustrious or K. M. Deutschland. Extensive cross-referencing will be found among many of the entries.